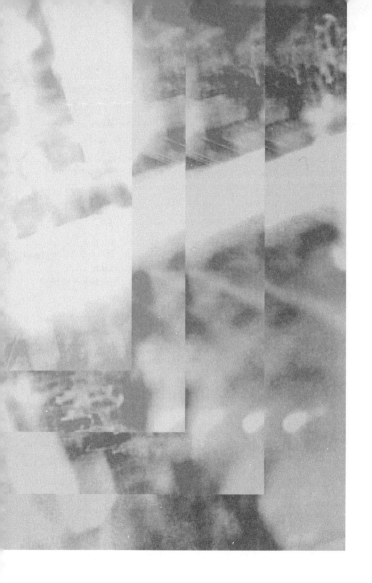

Configuring
CITRIX METAFRAME
for **WINDOWS 2000**
TERMINAL SERVICES

SYNGRESS®

KEY	SERIAL NUMBER
001	58PJUY7DSE
002	4RS36835HH
003	Q3NMCDE9V7
004	2C5C87BYMP
005	6AFLCA94DB
006	P636ALT7JA
007	MTPOKBB994
008	35DJKE3ZSV
009	G5EW2E9CFS
010	SM274PS25N

PUBLISHED BY
Syngress Publishing, Inc.
800 Hingham Street
Rockland, MA 02370

Configuring Citrix MetaFrame for Windows 2000 Terminal Services

Printed in the United States of America

1 2 3 4 5 6 7 8 9 0

ISBN: 1-928994-18-0

Copy edit by: Jennifer R. Coker
Technical edit by: Melissa Craft
Index by: Robert Saigh
Project Editor: Mark A. Listewnik

Proofreading by: Ben Chadwick
Page Layout and Art by: Shannon Tozier
Co-Publisher: Richard Kristof

Distributed by Publishers Group West

Acknowledgments

We would like to acknowledge the following people for their kindness and support in making this book possible.

Richard Kristof, Duncan Anderson, Jennifer Gould, Robert Woodruff, Kevin Murray, Dale Leatherwood, Rhonda Harmon, and Robert Sanregret of Global Knowledge, for their generous access to the IT industry's best courses, instructors and training facilities.

Ralph Troupe, Rhonda St. John, and the team at Callisma for their invaluable insight into the challenges of designing, deploying and supporting world-class enterprise networks.

Karen Cross, Lance Tilford, Meaghan Cunningham, Kim Wylie, Harry Kirchner, John Hays, Bill Richter, Kevin Votel, Brittin Clark, and Sarah MacLachlan of Publishers Group West for sharing their incredible marketing experience and expertise.

Mary Ging, Caroline Hird, Caroline Wheeler, Victoria Fuller, Jonathan Bunkell, Klaus Beran, and Simon Beale of Harcourt International for making certain that our vision remains worldwide in scope.

Annabel Dent, Anneka Baeten, Clare MacKenzie, and Laurie Giles of Harcourt Australia for all their help.

David Buckland, Wendi Wong, David Loh, Marie Chieng, Lucy Chong, Leslie Lim, Audrey Gan, and Joseph Chan of Transquest Publishers for the enthusiasm with which they receive our books.

Kwon Sung June at Acorn Publishing for his support.

Ethan Atkin at Cranbury International for his help in expanding the Syngress program.

Joe Pisco, Helen Moyer, and the great folks at InterCity Press for all their help.

Special thanks to the professionals at Osborne with whom we are proud to publish the best-selling Global Knowledge Certification Press series.

From Global Knowledge

At Global Knowledge we strive to support the multiplicity of learning styles required by our students to achieve success as technical professionals. As the world's largest IT training company, Global Knowledge is uniquely positioned to offer these books. The expertise gained each year from providing instructor-led training to hundreds of thousands of students worldwide has been captured in book form to enhance your learning experience. We hope that the quality of these books demonstrates our commitment to your lifelong learning success. Whether you choose to learn through the written word, computer based training, Web delivery, or instructor-led training, Global Knowledge is committed to providing you with the very best in each of these categories. For those of you who know Global Knowledge, or those of you who have just found us for the first time, our goal is to be your lifelong competency partner.

Thank your for the opportunity to serve you. We look forward to serving your needs again in the future.

Warmest regards,

Duncan Anderson
President and Chief Executive Officer, Global Knowledge

Contributors

Contributors

Paul Stansel (CCEA, MCSE, MCP+I, CNA, A+) works as a consultant specializing in remote access and Citrix technologies in Research Triangle Park, North Carolina, where he lives with his wife, Rachel. Paul started working with computers when his father got the family a TRS-80 and has never looked back. He enjoys good science-fiction, computer games, and the football season.

Travis Guinn (CCA, MCSE, CCSA, CCSE, A+) is from Jacksonville, Texas and is currently the Senior Systems Engineer with Data Transit International, a nationwide Citrix integrator based in Atlanta, Georgia. Travis served four years in the U.S. Navy in Advanced Electronics, then worked for a small computer store installing networks. Travis then started an ISP in Charleston, South Carolina, where he gained extensive experience in TCP/IP and large scale dial-in solutions from U.S. Robotics.

Travis has worked for Data Transit for three years on projects involving 3Com Total Control, Checkpoint Firewall-1, RSA SecurID, and AVT RightFax. Travis is now working on an ASP initiative for Data Transit.

Kris Kistler (CCA, MCSE, MCP+I, GSEC, CCNA, CNA, A+) is a Senior Network Engineer and Security Administrator for a large International Health Care Organization based in St. Louis, Missouri. He has been involved in computing for over 15 years and has experience with many different operating systems and various types of networking hardware. He currently specializes in Internet connectivity, security, and remote access ASP solutions. When not researching new projects, he enjoys spending time with his family.

Mick Gunter (CCA, MCSE, CCNA, A+) is the Senior Manager of Technical Services at Blue Rhino Corporation in Winston Salem, North Carolina. After serving as an Artillery Officer in the Marine Corps, Mick earned a Masters degree in Education from Wake Forest University before entering the IT field. When not working, Mick enjoys biking, playing golf, and spending time with his wife Tanya and son Bailey.

Melissa Craft (CCA, MCSE, CCNA, Network+, CNE-5, CNE-3, CNE-4, CNE-GW, MCNE, Citrix CCA) designs business computing solutions using technology and business process reengineering techniques to automate processes.

Currently, Melissa's title is Director of e-Business Offering Development for MicroAge Technology Services. MicroAge is a global systems integrator headquartered in Tempe, Arizona. MicroAge provides IT design, project management, and support for distributed computing systems. These technology solutions touch every part of a system's lifecycle—from network design, testing, and implementation to operational management and strategic planning.

Melissa holds a bachelor's degree from the University of Michigan, and is a member of the IEEE, the Society of Women Engineers, and American MENSA, Ltd. Melissa currently resides in Glendale, Arizona with her family, Dan, Justine and Taylor.

Douglas Laspe has over 25 years in the IT industry. His experience includes project management, process development and implementation, asset management, software quality assurance, and software configuration management. Doug's technical experience includes working with various types of programming languages from assembly code to fourth generation languages and robotics control code.

Doug has extensive experience in technical writing and professional editing. He has worked in large and small organizations, in ".com" companies, with government contractors, and in federal procurement. Doug and his wife, Carolyn have two children, Eric and Laura, who also share an interest in information technology.

Mary C. Zampino (CCA, MCSE) was born in Chicago and raised mostly in Tallahassee, Florida. Mary graduated from Florida State University with a B.S. degree in Information Science. Mary quickly went on to earn her MCSE and CCA certifications, in addition to authoring numerous technical documents. Mary enjoys spending time with her family, including two wonderful sisters. She also loves reading, writing, movies, and camping.

Chris Funderburg (CCEA, MCSE, MCP+I, CCNA) is an Associate Network Engineer for Greenwich Technology Partners where his duties include designing and implementing various network systems as well as troubleshooting and writing documentation.

Greenwich Technology Partners (GTP) is a leading network infrastructure consulting and engineering company. The company designs, builds, and manages complex networks that utilize advanced Internet protocol, electro/optical, and other sophisticated technologies. Founded in 1997, the company has employees in 19 locations in the U.S. and a location in London. Using its proprietary GTP NetValue™ methodology, GTP provides clients with the internetworking support necessary for e-business success.

Derrick Rountree (CCA, MSCE, MCT, CNE, ASE, CCNA, CCDA) has a degree in Electrical Engineering from Florida State University. Derrick has worked for Alltel Information Systems and Prudential Health Care and is currently working for a systems integrator in South Florida. Derrick has also done work for BOSON.COM testing software products. Derrick has contributed to other Syngress and Osborne/McGraw-Hill publications including the *Compaq ASE Study Guide* and the *CCA Citrix Certified Administrator for MetaFrame 1.8 Study Guide*. He would like to thank his mother, Claudine, and his wife, Michelle, for their help and support.

Jerrod Couser (CCA, MCSE+I, MCP+I, A+) currently manages the Technology Training Department of Review Technology Group (RTG). RTG specializes in training and consulting.

Dean A. Jones III (MCSE) has over six years experience managing national LAN/WAN administration services and has managed his company's migration to Windows 2000 and Citrix MetaFrame environments. He has been a test manager in the Unix, Windows, Solaris, DEC, DOS, and proprietary systems environments. Dean is currently the Lead System Administrator and Web Master for a major food producer headquartered in the Midwest.

Technical Editor

Melissa Craft (CCA, MCSE, CCNA, Network+, CNE-5, CNE-3, CNE-4, CNE-GW, MCNE, Citrix CCA) designs business computing solutions using technology and business process reengineering techniques to automate processes.

Currently, Melissa's title is Director of e-Business Offering Development for MicroAge Technology Services. MicroAge is a global systems integrator headquartered in Tempe, Arizona. MicroAge provides IT design, project management, and support for distributed computing systems. These technology solutions touch every part of a system's lifecycle—from network design, testing; and implementation to operational management and strategic planning.

Melissa holds a bachelor's degree from the University of Michigan, and is a member of the IEEE, the Society of Women Engineers; and American MENSA, Ltd. Melissa currently resides in Glendale, Arizona with her family, Dan, Justine, and Taylor. and her two Great Danes Marmaduke and Apollo and her Golden Retriever Pooka. Melissa can be contacted via e-mail at mmcraft@compuserve.com.

Technical Reviewer

Allen V. Keele (CCEA, CCI, MCT, MCSE, MCP+I, CCNA, CCDA, PSE) is Vice President of Certified Tech Trainers, Inc. They are an organization specializing in Citrix MetaFrame 1.8 and advanced Citrix server implementation, Cisco training courses on routing and switching (including CCNA and CCNP certification tracks), as well as Windows 2000 training. As an active and enthusiastic instructor, he personally provides training sessions throughout the United States and Europe.

Following two years of overseas academic pursuits at a German Gymnasium as a high school foreign exchange student, he attended school at the Universität Mannheim as an undergraduate. He is fluent in German and continues to enjoy contact with his original host family to this day. He also holds a Bachelor of Business Administration degree from the University of Georgia.

Contents

Chapter 13: Optimizing, Monitoring, and Troubleshooting Windows 2000 and Terminal Services

Introduction

A Brief History of Citrix

More than five years ago, Citrix had a product on the market that could do what no other product on the market could do. Citrix WinView allowed a single DOS or Windows 3.1 application to be simultaneously shared from a single computer to multiple computers over phone lines or network links. This meant that companies that had installed hundreds of computers with individual phone lines and remote control software could then reduce their remote services costs and administrative hassles.

Back then, a single WinView server could host an average of 14 remote dial-in users simultaneously. As a result, an application only needed to be installed one time as opposed to the administrator performing 13 separate installations. Users received a major benefit too, in the fast response that an application loaded and ran compared to other remote control software or remote node software packages. Citrix WinView worked wonders for many, until Microsoft released Windows 95.

Citrix Moves to 32-bit Applications with WinFrame

When Microsoft produced Windows 95, Citrix found that there was a problem that WinView couldn't solve. Windows 95 could *not* share out a 32-bit application because it was based on IBM's OS/2 using 16-bit Windows emulation.

As a result, Citrix went to work with Microsoft, licensed the Windows NT 3.5*x* operating system, and built Citrix WinFrame. The new WinFrame had the Windows 3.1 Graphical User Interface (GUI) because that's the GUI that Windows NT 3.5x also had. Even so, the new WinFrame product enabled the sharing of 32-bit applications, in addition to supporting high-end server hardware with Symmetrical Multiprocessors (SMP), so that fewer servers could support more users. Citrix built the WinFrame software with two components:

- MultiWin kernel

- Independent Computing Architecture (ICA) protocol

Actually, ICA stood for *Intelligent Console Architecture* back then. They changed it after Windows NT 4.0 came out and after they worked out an agreement with Microsoft. The new agreement gave Microsoft the license to MultiWin kernel, enabling Microsoft to introduce Windows NT 4.0 Terminal Server Edition many months after the release of Windows NT 4.0.

Citrix changed the ICA acronym to stand for *Independent Computing Architecture,* becaue ICA provided terminal sessions on any platform, whereas Microsoft's terminal sessions were limited to Microsoft 32-bit clients (or Windows 3.11 for Workgroups using 32-bit TCP/IP). At the time that Terminal Server Edition was released, Citrix released a new product called Citrix MetaFrame for Windows NT 4.0 Terminal Server Edition. MetaFrame enabled Terminal Server to share out sessions via ICA. A MetaFrame server could utilize the other products that Citrix creates—such as Application Load Balancing—that are not available for plain Terminal Server.

The difference between WinFrame and MetaFrame is this: WinFrame has a completely rewritten kernel from Windows NT 3.5x. When you install WinFrame, you are installing an entire operating system and do not need to have Windows NT 3.5x already installed. MetaFrame, on the other hand, is the ICA component combined with administrative interfaces to assist in managing the applications. It requires an under-lying Windows NT 4.0 (or now, Windows 2000) server operating system be installed, and it must have Terminal Services enabled.

So when all is said and done, Microsoft provides MultiWin and Citrix provides ICA plus more options.

Why Use a Thin-Client Application Server

One of the major benefits of using either plain old Terminal Services on Windows 2000 or the enhanced Citrix MetaFrame version is that you can conserve significant bandwidth that would otherwise have been consumed by *fat clients.* A fat client is typically a client/server application that spends time consuming bandwidth by loading up data into the client application from the server and adding chatty overhead traffic. Both Terminal Services and MetaFrame provide *thin clients*, which have minimal bandwidth requirements.

Fat clients take forever to connect and load up their data. It is so bad sometimes that someone from Citrix compared it to sucking peanut butter through a straw. (I think that is the most appropriate analogy I've ever heard considering how long some applications can take when they load over a 56 Kbps phone connection.)

One fat client is bad enough. When you compound the problem with hundreds of fat clients accessing the same application over links that range from phone lines to T3 leased lines, you have poor performance and dissatisfied users.

Current Shifts and Trends in the Industry

In recent years there has been a dramatic increase in corporate mergers, acquisitions, and migrations. These changes have created increasingly complex and far-reaching internetworks with a huge number of remote users and *virtual associates.* The new name for this type of company is the *virtual organization.* Becoming a virtual organization is not an easy thing to do. People tend to feel disconnected and turnover may increase. Communication and fast response is a key to the virtual organization's success. To help manage this for the virtual associates, companies are providing laptops, VPN service, online voice mail, teleconferencing, distance learning, browser-based desktops, and wireless devices. All of these items are facilitated by the Internet.

In addition to revolutionizing corporate communications, data processing, and applications deployment, the Internet has spawned a new business paradigm: e-business. E-business can be divided into two types of transactions:

- Business to Business (B2B) transactions are conducted between a business and its vendors.

- Business to Customer (B2C) transactions are conducted between a business and its customers.

Both virtual organizations and e-businesses require that applications be provided to end users through an Internet connection. Because there are so many different types of Internet connections, you may never know how fast someone can access your site. One thing you can be sure of—your Internet users will never experience the same speed of access or the reliability that you have when you are hooked directly into that network.

Speed, or rather performance, is the most important thing that you can provide to your Internet users. A customer will not tolerate a lagging download of an application that an employee onsite might tolerate. The customer is not paid to use your application and is, in fact, *paying* to receive a product or service from you. Indeed, if your Internet applications are not screaming along, your competition will begin to look like a better option. Vendors, too, will look to other partners if your application does not perform well.

But applications are not built on the Internet. They are built by a programming team in a software development firm, where every programmer has a 10MB or better connection to the server on which the application resides. It's a controlled environment, with controlled bandwidth and accessibility. It *must* be in order to maintain the proprietary software code. When the application is tested, it is ported to the Internet in a compiled format and executed from a remote site.

One of the benefits of using the ICA protocol from Citrix to provide applications is that almost all of the latest browsers support ICA natively. Your customers and vendors don't need to install anything in order to access an application that you publish on the Web with Citrix. Microsoft released its own Internet client in June, 2000 for publishing applications. I personally prefer the Citrix client for the Internet because it is simpler, has some client utilities, and is proven. You should check out Microsoft's version before making your own decision.

Wireless devices provide an even greater challenge. Some, like Palm Pilots, do not understand straight HyperText Markup Language (HTML), and rightly so. Can you imagine an entire Web page from Microsoft loading onto the three-inch screen of a Palm Pilot? You'd need a magnifying glass and some migraine medication to read through it. The point is, you don't want to supply an entire desktop to a wireless device, you want to limit it to a client application interface. Besides, wireless devices are somewhat unreliable and suffer from a high level of latency, which won't allow for an application to load quickly. In fact, for wireless devices to interact on your network, you'd want to use a thin client. That's where MetaFrame and Terminal Services come in. Citrix MetaFrame provides wireless device thin clients. Microsoft Terminal Services on Windows 2000 supports the Windows CE thin client.

Corporations have implemented thin clients for a variety of business reasons, including equipment cost reduction and centralized administration. Some expanded their services to end users. Plenty reduced their bandwidth consumption. Now, many are exploring e-business and wireless device usage in their virtual organizations without rewriting applications to native HTML.

The authors on this book describe all the ways that you can use both Microsoft Windows 2000 Terminal Services and Citrix MetaFrame in your environment. They cover:

- Designing the infrastructure

- Implementing the plan

- Troubleshooting the deployment

- Configuring servers and clients

- Deploying applications over the Internet

- Monitoring end users

- Securing applications and data

Most importantly, they tell you how to improve your applications' performance with thin clients so that users don't feel like their application is sucking peanut butter through a straw!

Chapter 1

Challenges of the Virtual Environment

Solutions in this chapter:

- What Defines a Mainframe?
- The Main Differences Between Remote Control and Remote Access
- The Thin-Client Revolution

1

Introduction

Businesses are teeing up to new challenges brought on by an increasingly virtual environment. Telecommuting has increased the number of remote access users who need to access applications with specific business configurations. The pervasive use of the Internet provides an easy, nearly universal, avenue of connectivity, although connections are sometimes slow. The use of hand-held computing has exploded, but questions remain as to what kind of applications can be used.

For a business facing these types of challenges, the hole in one can be found in thin-client technology. The leader in this technology is Citrix, whose main product is MetaFrame. MetaFrame runs over Microsoft's Windows 2000 with Terminal Services and provides fast, consistent access to business applications. With Citrix MetaFrame, the reach of business applications can be extended over an enterprise network and the public Internet.

What Defines a Mainframe?

Mainframe computers are considered to be a notch below supercomputers and a step above minicomputers in the hierarchy of processing. In many ways, mainframes are considerably more powerful than supercomputers because they can support more simultaneous programs. Supercomputers are considered faster, however, because they can execute a single process faster than a typical mainframe. Depending on how a company wants to market a system, the same machine that could serve as a mainframe for one company could be a minicomputer at another. Today, the largest mainframe manufacturers are Unisys and (surprise, surprise) IBM.

Mainframes work on the model of centralized computing. Although a mainframe may be no faster than a desktop computer in raw speed, mainframes use peripheral channels (individual PCs in their own right) to handle Input/Output (IO) processes. This frees up considerable processing power. Mainframes can have multiple ports into high-speed memory caches and separate machines to coordinate IO operations between the channels. The bus speed on a mainframe is typically much higher than a desktop, and mainframes generally employ hardware with considerable error-checking and correction capabilities. The mean time between failures for a mainframe computer is 20 years, much greater than that of PCs.

NOTE

Mean Time Between Failures (MTBF) is a phrase often used in the computing world. MTBF is the amount of time a system will run before suffering a critical failure of some kind that requires maintenance. Because each component in a PC can have a separate MTBF, the MTBF is calculated using the weakest component. Obviously, when buying a PC you want to look for the best MTBF numbers. Cheap parts often mean a lower MTBF.

All of these factors free up the CPU to do what it should be doing—pure calculation. With Symmetric Multiprocessing (SMP), today's mainframes are capable of handling thousands of remote terminals. Figure 1.1 shows a typical mainframe arrangement.

Benefits of the Mainframe Model

As you can see in Figure 1.1, the mainframe model supports not only desktop PCs, but also remote terminals. Traditionally called dumb terminals because they contained no independent processing capabilities, mainframe terminals today are actually considered "smart" because of their built-in screen display instruction sets. Terminals rely on the central mainframe for all processing requirements and are used only for input/output. The advantages to using terminals are considerable. First, terminals are relatively cheap when compared to a PC. Second, with only minimal components, terminals are very easy to maintain. In addition, terminals present the user with the same screen no matter when or where they log on, which cuts down on user confusion and application training costs.

The centralized architecture of a mainframe is another key benefit of this model. Once upon a time, mainframes were considered to be vast, complicated machines, which required dedicated programmers to run. Today's client/server networking models can be far more complex than any mainframe system. Deciding between different operating systems, protocols, network topography, and wiring schemes can give a network manager a serious headache. By comparison, mainframe computing is fairly straight-forward in its design and in many cases is far easier to implement. Five years ago, word was that mainframes were going the way of the dinosaur. Today, with over two trillion dollars of mainframe applications in place, that prediction seems to have been a bit hasty.

Figure 1.1 The mainframe computing environment.

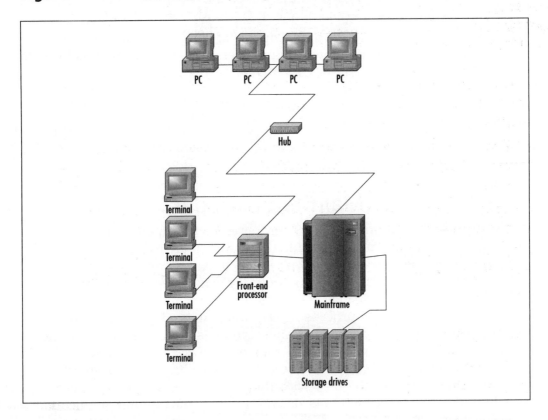

Centralized computing with mainframes is considered not only the past, but also possibly the future of network architecture. As organizations undergo more downsizing and shift towards a central, scalable solution for their employees, a mainframe environment looks more and more appealing. The initial price tag may put many companies off, but for those that can afford it, the total cost of ownership (TCO) could be considerably less than a distributed computing environment. The future of mainframes is still uncertain, but it looks like they will be around for quite some time.

History and Benefits of Distributed Computing

Distributed computing is a buzzword often heard when discussing today's client/server architecture. It is the most common network environment today, and continues to expand with the Internet. We'll look at distributed computing's origins in this section, and take a look at where it might be headed.

The Workstation

As we mentioned before, distributed computing was made possible when DEC developed the minicomputer. Capable of performing timesharing operations, the minicomputer allowed many users to use the same machine via remote terminals, but each had a separate virtual environment. Minicomputers were popular, but considerably slower than their mainframe counterparts. As a result, to scale a minicomputer, system administrators were forced to buy more and more of them. This trend in buying led to cheaper and cheaper computers, which in turn eventually made the personal computer a possibility people were willing to accept. Thus, the reality of the workstation was born.

Although originally conceived by Xerox Corporation's Palo Alto Research Center (PARC) in 1970, it would be some time before workstations became inexpensive and reliable enough to see mainstream use. PARC went on to design such common tools as the mouse, window-based computing, the first Ethernet system, and the first distributed-file-and-print servers. All of these inventions made workstations a reasonable alternative to time-sharing minicomputers. Since the main cost of a computer is the design and manufacturing process, the more units you build, the cheaper they are to sell. The idea of the local area network (Ethernet) coupled with PARC's Xerox Distributed File server (XDFS) meant that workstations were now capable of duplicating the tasks of terminals for a much lower price tag than the mainframe system. Unfortunately for Xerox, they ignored almost every invention developed by the PARC group and ended up letting Steve Jobs and Apple borrow the technology.

The most dominant player in distributed computing, however, is Microsoft. Using technology they borrowed (some may argue "stole") from Apple, Microsoft launched the Windows line of graphical user interface (GUI) products that turned the workstation into a much more valuable tool. Using most of the ideas PARC had developed (the mouse, Ethernet, distributed file sharing), Microsoft gave everyone from the home user to the network manager a platform that was easy to understand and could be rapidly and efficiently used by almost everyone. Apple may have been the first to give the world a point-and-click interface, but Microsoft was the company that led it into the 1990's. All of these features enabled Microsoft to develop a real distributed computing environment.

Enter Distributed Computing

Distributed computing has come a long way since that first local area network (LAN). Today, almost every organization employs some type of distributed computing. The most commonly used system is client/server architecture, where the client (workstation) requests information and services from a remote server. Servers can be high-speed desktops, microcomputers, minicomputers, or even mainframe machines. Typically connected by a LAN, the client/server model has become increasingly complex over the last few years. To support the client/server model a wide array of operating systems have been developed, which may or may not interact well with other systems. UNIX, Windows, Novell, and Banyan Vines are several of the operating systems that are able to communicate with each other, although not always efficiently.

However, the advantages to the client/server model can be considerable. Since each machine is capable of performing its own processing, applications for the client/server model tend to vary based on the original design. Some applications will use the server as little more than a file-sharing device. Others will actually run processes at both the client and server levels, dividing the work as is most time-effective. A true client/server application is designed to provide the same quality of service as a mainframe or minicomputer would provide. Client/server operations can be either two- or three-tiered, as described in the following sections.

Two-Tiered Computing

In two-tiered computing, an applications server (such as a database) performs the server-side portion of the processing, such as record searching or generation. A client software piece will be used to perform the access, editing, and manipulation processes. Figure 1.2 shows a typical two-tiered client/server solution. Most distributed networks today are two-tiered client/server models.

Three-Tiered Computing

Three-tiered computing is used in situations where the processing power required to execute an application will be insufficient on some or all existing workstations. In three-tiered computing, server-side processing duties are still performed by the database server. Many of the process duties that would normally be performed by the workstation are instead handled by an applications processing server, and the client is typically

Figure 1.2 Two-tiered computing solution.

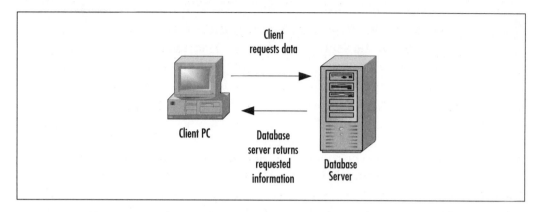

responsible only for screen updates, keystrokes, and other visual changes. This greatly reduces the load on client machines and can allow older machines to still utilize newer applications. Figure 1.3 shows a typical three-tiered client/server solution.

Figure 1.3 Three-tiered computing solution.

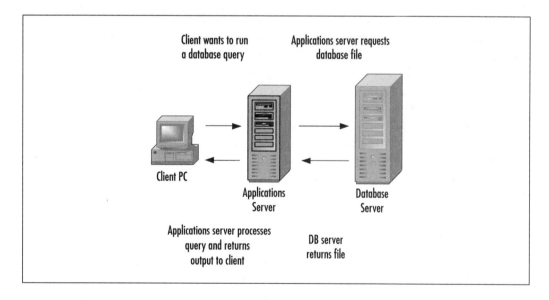

> **NOTE**
>
> Windows 2000 with Terminal Services and Citrix MetaFrame can be considered either two-tiered or three-tiered computing, depending on the network design. Although there are some differences between the methods used, both Terminal Services and MetaFrame use a client PC and an applications server.

Distributed Computing and the Internet

Recently, a new distributed-computing model has emerged: the Internet, which is one giant distributed-computing environment. Client PCs connect to servers that pass requests to the appropriate remote servers, which execute the commands given and return the output back to the client. The Internet was originally devised by the military to link its research and engineering sites across the United States with a centralized computer system. Called Advanced Research Projects Agency Network (ARPAnet), the system was put into place in 1971 and had 19 operational nodes. By 1977, a new network had connected radio packet networks, Satellite Networks (SATNET), and ARPAnet together to demonstrate the possibility of mobile computing. Called the Internet, the network was christened when a user sent a message from a van on the San Francisco Bay-shore Freeway over 94,000 miles via satellite, landline, and radio waves back to the University of Southern California campus.

In 1990, MCI created a gateway between separate networks to allow their MCIMail program to send e-mail messages to users on either system. Hailed as the first commercial use of the Internet, MCIMail was a precursor for the rapid expansion of Internet services that would explode across the United States. Now, a large portion of the world is able to surf the Internet, send e-mail to their friends, and participate in live chats with other users.

Another growing demand on the Internet is the need to use distributed computing to run applications remotely. Thin-client programs, which are capable of connecting to remote application servers across an Internet connection, are becoming more and more common for organizations that need to make resources available to users outside their local network. We'll talk about thin clients later in the chapter; for now it's enough to know that Citrix is the major supplier of thin-client technology and Web connectivity today.

Benefits of Distributed Computing

Distributed computing can be an excellent fit for many organizations. With the client/server model, the hardware requirements for the servers are far less than would be required for a mainframe. This translates into reduced initial cost. Since each workstation has its own processing power, it can work offline should the server portion be unavailable. And through the use of multiple servers, LANs, wide area networks (WANs), and other services such as the Internet, distributed computing systems can reach around the world. It is not uncommon these days for companies to have employees who access the corporate system from their laptops regardless of where they are located, even on airplanes.

Distributed computing also helps to ensure that there is no one central point of failure. If information is replicated across many servers, then one server out of the group going offline will not prevent access to that information. Careful management of data replication can guarantee that all but the most catastrophic of failures will not render the system inoperable. Redundant links provide fault-tolerant solutions for critical information systems. This is one of the key reasons that the military initially adopted the distributed computing platform.

Finally, distributed computing allows the use of older machines to perform more complex processes than what they might be capable of otherwise. With some distributed computing programs, clients as old as a 386 computer could access and use resources on your Windows 2000 servers as though they were local PCs with up-to-date hardware. That type of access can appear seamless to the end user. If developers only had to write software for one operating system platform, they could ignore having to test the program on all the other platforms available. All this adds up to cost savings for the consumer and potential time savings for a developer. Windows 2000 with Terminal Services and Citrix MetaFrame combine both the distributed computing qualities and the mainframe model as well.

Meeting the Business Requirements of Both Models

Organizations need to take a hard look at what their requirements will be before implementing either the mainframe or distributed computing model. A wrong decision early in the process can create a nightmare of management details. Mainframe computing is more expensive in the initial cost outlay. Distributed computing requires more maintenance over the long run. Mainframe computing centralizes all of the applications processing. Distributed computing does exactly what it says—it distributes it! The reason to choose one model over the other is a decision each organization has to make individually. With the addition of thin-client computing to the mix, a network administrator can be expected to pull all of his or her hair out before a system is implemented. Table 1.1 gives some general considerations to use when deciding between the different computing models.

Table 1.1 Considerations for Choosing a Computing Model

If you need...	Then consider using...
An environment with a variety of platforms available to the end user	Distributed computing. Each end user will have a workstation with its own processing capabilities and operating system. This gives users more control over their working environment.
A homogeneous environment where users are presented with a standard view	Mainframe computing. Dummy terminals allow administrators to present a controlled, standard environment for each user regardless of machine location.
Lower cost outlays in the early stages	Distributed computing. Individual PCs and computers will cost far less than a mainframe system. Keep in mind that future maintenance costs may outweigh that savings.
Easy and cost-efficient expansion	Mainframe computing. Once the mainframe system has been implemented, adding new terminals is a simple process compared with installing and configuring a new PC for each user.
Excellent availability of software packages for a variety of business applications	Distributed computing. The vast majority of applications being released are for desktop computing, and those software packages are often less expensive even at an enterprise level than similar mainframe packages.
An excellent Mean Time Between Failures (MTBF)	Mainframe computing. The typical mainframe incorporates more error-checking hardware than most PCs or servers do. This gives them a very good service record, which means less maintenance costs over the life of the equipment. In addition, the ability to predict hardware failures before they occur helps to keep mainframe systems from developing the same problems that smaller servers frequently have.

The Main Differences Between Remote Control and Remote Node

There are two types of remote computing in today's network environments and choosing which to deploy is a matter of determining what your needs really are. Remote node software is what is typically known as remote access. It is generally implemented with a client PC dialing in to connect to some type of remote access server. On the other side, remote control software gives a remote client PC control over a local PC's desktop. Users at either machine will see the same desktop. In this section we'll take a look at the two different methods of remote computing, and consider the benefits and drawbacks of each method.

Remote Control

Remote control software has been in use for several years. From smaller packages like PCAnywhere to larger, enterprise-wide packages like SMS, remote control software gives a user or administrator the ability to control a remote machine and thus the ability to perform a variety of functions. With remote control, keystrokes are transmitted from the remote machine to the local machine over whatever network connection has been established. The local machine in turn sends back screen updates to the remote PC. Processing and file transfer typically takes place at the local level, which helps reduce the bandwidth requirements for the remote PC. Figure 1.4 shows an example of a remote control session.

Figure 1.4 Remote control session.

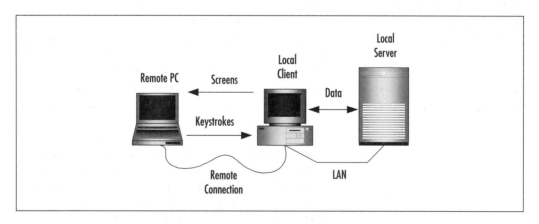

Benefits of Remote Control

Remote control software has become increasingly popular for enterprise management. With a centralized management tools package, support personnel are able to diagnose and troubleshoot problems on a remote machine. This can improve support response time and user satisfaction. In addition, centralized management tools give an administrator the ability to collect and manage information from a wide number of machines and to keep accurate logs of current configurations and installed software. This can be invaluable for keeping track of license usage and monitoring for violations of an organization's computing policies.

Remote control software can be used as a teaching tool. If an administrator was on the remote PC and connected to a user's local desktop, he or she could then use that connection to train the user in hands-on tasks through demonstration. Both the user and the administrator are seeing the same screens, which helps eliminate any confusion about what is being discussed. Since either person can take control of the session, the administrator can demonstrate a concept and then have the user perform the specific tasks with supervision.

Remote control software also can offer a more secure computing environment. In organizations that handle sensitive information, rules exist governing the proper use and storage of such information. Often, employee's personal computers are not allowed to contain regulated information, which could prevent remote workers from accessing their files unless they were on the organization's asset. With remote control computing, employees can dial in and control a company asset remotely. The administrator can prevent that user from downloading any restricted information to their home PC. This is invaluable both as a time saving system and as a way to stay within the legal boundaries required of the organization. Many organizations employ remote control solutions specifically for this purpose. With the growing emphasis on information security, good security policies can prevent possible future litigation. Both Windows 2000 with Terminal Services and Citrix MetaFrame offer solutions to this problem. We'll introduce them to you later in this chapter.

Downsides to Remote Control

Remote control software does have some limitations. Currently, most packages are limited in the screen resolution they can display. The maximum resolution for Terminal Services clients is 256 colors. Also, programs that heavily utilize graphics will bog down the session and greatly reduce any performance benefits that remote control otherwise provides. Citrix MetaFrame has recently released Feature Release 1, an add-on package for MetaFrame 1.8 that provides the capability to have clients use 24-bit color.

The Citrix client has the ability to scale the session graphics back if too much bandwidth is being used. The higher the graphical resolution required, the more bandwidth the application will attempt to consume and the more frequently the graphics will be updated. Because of this, high-end graphical packages such as a CAD application are not appropriate for a Terminal Services or MetaFrame environment. Windows Office applications such as Word and Excel are ideal for remote control sessions.

TIP

Feature Release 1 is available for holders of Citrix's Subscription Advantage. It provides both Service Pack 2 for MetaFrame 1.8 (available regardless of whether you have Subscription Advantage or not) and a whole set of new features, including multi-monitor support, higher color depth for client sessions, and SecureICA as a built-in feature. All of these features will also be available when Citrix releases MetaFrame 2.0.

Traditional remote control packages typically require more network ports than remote node for the same number of users. This is because the user must not only dial in and connect to a local machine, they must then use that local machine to the exclusion of other users. In many cases, this means actually using two separate machines to merely accomplish the tasks that one local machine could normally fill. Sounds a bit wasteful, right? Thankfully, Microsoft and Citrix have developed ways around those requirements.

Another potential danger of remote-control computing is that it is a possible point of failure for network security. If someone from outside the network could gain access to the local PC with the remote control software, they could perform any task as if they were local to that network. For this reason, many administrators prefer not to leave remote-controlled PCs constantly on, to carefully control the list of people that know they exist, and to carefully control the security mechanisms that are used to authenticate remote users.

A final drawback to remote control is that file transfers between the local and remote PC will obviously be limited to the connection speed of the network connection between the two machines. For most users, this will be a POTS (Plain Old Telephone System) connection with a maximum speed of around 56 Kbps. Although MetaFrame typically runs well on a 28.8 Kbps modem connection, high-speed connections such as ADSL or cable modems are excellent to use with both remote-controlled and remote-access sessions. These types of services are still only offered in select areas. As their coverage grows, expect to see more organizations using remote control computing packages such as Terminal Services and MetaFrame.

Remote Node

Remote node computing, also known as remote access computing, can be considered the traditional dial-in method. A remote PC, equipped with a modem or another type of network connector, makes a connection across a WAN to a local server. That remote PC is now considered a local node on the network, capable of accessing network resources like any local PC would (within the security limitations imposed by the remote access system). The local server is responsible for providing all network information, file transfers, and even some applications down to the remote node. The remote node is responsible for processing, executing, and updating the information with which it is working. It all has to be done over whatever connection speed the client is capable of achieving.

Due to these limitations, remote node computing can use a lot of bandwidth. Careful consideration needs to be used when planning a remote-node environment. As shown in Figure 1.5, there is little difference between a client on a local PC and a remote-node client. The server will handle requests from either machine in the same fashion. If the local client were to request 2MB worth of data, the server would send it over the LAN connection. If the remote PC requested the same data, it would have to be sent over the WAN connection. For a 2MB file on a 56 Kbps connection, it could be around 6 minutes just to pull that data down. After modifications, the remote PC would then have to push that file back up to the server. A remote node using a dial-up connection is treated like any other local user on the network.

Figure 1.5 Remote access computing.

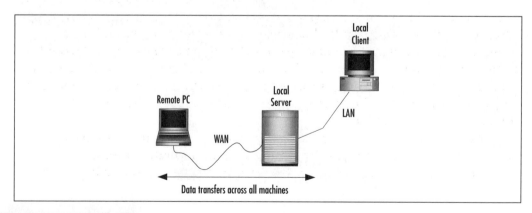

Why Use Remote Access?

With all of the problems inherent in the connection speed, why would companies consider remote access instead of remote control? For starters, remote access is relatively simple to configure. All that is required is a way for the remote computer to connect to a local server. Common solutions are direct dial (with NT RAS or an equivalent solution) and connecting though the Internet. The remote machine can join the network as long as some sort of connection can be established.

Another key benefit is that a variety of operating systems can utilize remote access to connect to central servers. This means organizations with differing platforms among their users can provide remote access services to all of them. The services available may differ from client to client, but all users will be able to access network resources at least at a very basic level.

Remote access computing is in some ways more secure than remote control computing. Since many systems can be direct dialed, there is little chance of anyone interrupting the signal between the remote PC and the local remote access server. For clients that connect through some other WAN connection such as the Internet (dial-up ISP, high-bandwidth connections, and so on) there are many packages that can provide secure communications between the remote client and the local servers. Securing these communications is essential for a good network security plan since at least some of the packets will contain user logon information.

Recently, a slew of new virtual private network (VPN) products have hit the shelves. These packages attempt to allow remote nodes to have secure communications with the centralized server, typically through a protocol such as Point-to-Point Tunneling Protocol (PPTP). With encryption strengths up to 128-bit, these software packages can encode packets so tightly that it is virtually impossible for them to be decrypted. Unfortunately, much of this technology is not available outside of North America due to U.S. export laws.

Remote access sessions also have no self-imposed graphics restrictions. If the client PC is set to display 24-bit True Color, then that is what it will attempt to show. This can be beneficial when trying to view detailed images. Unfortunately, this also means that large images coming from the remote access server can take a long time to display correctly. If executing a program that pulls a large number of graphics files from the remote network, performance will certainly be slowed, perhaps to the point of affecting system usability.

However, the biggest advantage of remote access computing over remote control computing is the hardware requirement. In remote access computing, a minimal number of local machines can typically handle a large number of user connections. This eliminates the need for each user to have a local machine that they can remote control. Users can work offline on their remote PC, and then connect to the local network to upload changes. This also centralizes the possible failure points, making it easier to diagnose and troubleshoot problems.

Drawbacks of Remote Node Computing

As mentioned earlier, speed is the key issue with remote node computing. Since users are moving a lot more data than with remote control computing, speed limitations can be crippling. High-speed Internet connections using cable modems and ADSL can alleviate some of the problems, but even then maximum speeds will typically be about 1/5 that of a LAN connection unless the user is willing to pay a large monthly fee (upwards of $1,000 a month for a personal T1 connection); with those types of connections, there is the added necessity of ensuring that secure communications are maintained or you risk leaving your network vulnerable to outside intrusion. For this reason, many organizations are unwilling to permit any type of remote access beyond direct-dial solutions.

Since remote access computing requires that the remote PC be capable of performing the application processing, the hardware requirements for the remote PCs could become more of a factor. This could mean more frequent replacement of PCs, or holding off on new software upgrades because the clients will not be able to run them. The remote PC is also much more vulnerable to virus attacks than it would be in a remote control situation. Another drawback with remote access computing is the issue of client licensing. If clients are allowed to individually install and maintain copies of the software on home PCs, tracking license compliance becomes difficult for IT management.

A final consideration for remote access computing is hardware platform compatibility. With no control over the individual's PC configuration, it is often necessary to strictly define the types of configurations that will be supported. This often limits client's use, since many will not be compliant with the standards defined. Installing a remote control server can alleviate many of these problems.

So How Do You Choose?

There are pros and cons to both access models. Both have certain key features that make them very desirable. Thankfully, Microsoft and Citrix have realized the benefits of both models and developed Terminal Services and MetaFrame, respectively. As a combination of remote access and remote control services, these two packages are capable of fulfilling the requirements of any organization's remote computing needs. Later in this chapter we'll explore the details of each program. Table 1.2 lists some of the reasons to consider either a remote control or remote access solution.

Table 1.2 Remote Control Versus Remote Access

Remote Control	Remote Access
Only passes screen updates and keystrokes back and forth between the remote PC and the local PC. This means that considerably less bandwidth is required.	Many users can connect to a single piece of hardware because processing and application execution is taking place on the remote PC.
Allows remote clients with older technology to access new applications by using the local client as an intermediary between itself and the local server.	Full availability of screen resolutions to support graphical applications. Since the remote PC is limited only by it's own capabilities, higher quality graphics can be displayed that would not be viewable on a remote control session.
Administrators can prevent sensitive data from being copied off an organization's assets.	Familiarity with the desktop, since it is always their own.

The Thin-Client Revolution

Microsoft and Citrix have been quick to see the limitations imposed by mainframe computing, distributed computing, remote control, and remote access—yet all of the models presented to this point have had features that could make them desirable to an organization. A mainframe has a central server that handles applications processing, distributed computing gives each user a customizable desktop and applications set, remote control computing lets older clients access newer software, and remote access computing lets multiple users connect to a single access point. So why not take the best of all worlds?

That's what Windows 2000 Terminal Services and MetaFrame do. By offering a combination of all of those benefits, the two packages allow remote users to connect to a server, open a virtual desktop, and perform remote control computing without the necessity of a local PC. The server handles all applications processing and sends only screen updates to the client. There is some variation in how the two services work, which we will discuss later in this chapter. One key point is that MetaFrame uses Windows 2000 Terminal Services as the underlying structure of its computing environment.

Key Concepts

Two important terms to learn for this section are *fat clients* and *thin clients*. The terms "thin" and "fat" refer to the bandwidth requirements that a client places on the network. A fat client is a machine or application that requires a large amount of bandwidth to function. Fat clients are typically run on self-contained machines that have everything from memory to a processor. Fat-client machines can run their own applications locally or pull them off a server in a client/server environment. Fat clients are easily customized and can be used independent of a network connection. Because fat-client machines execute processes locally, they free up the server solely to serve information. Most operating systems and the majority of computers today are fat-client machines.

The term thin client was originally used to indicate a specific type of software that provided applications and information to remote PCs at a reduced bandwidth level. Using the best parts of remote control computing, thin client programs send only screen updates and keyboard strokes back and forth between the client PC and the server providing the thin-client environment. Thin-client software is popular because it can alleviate bandwidth problems by compressing data into packets small enough to fit over even a moderately slow dial-up connection. Today, the term *thin client* can be used to reference either a software package or a machine that is designed specifically for use in a thin-client environment.

Thin-client machines possess only a few of the hardware components of their fat-client counterparts. They are akin to the old terminals of mainframe computing. Thin-client machines are considered "intelligent" terminals. This means that they often contain their own memory and display instructions, but get all their information from a server. There is no local operating system, no hard drive, and very little processing capability. The true differentiation between a thin-client machine and fat-client machine is that a fat client has a hard drive and a thin client doesn't.

So how does all this apply to Windows 2000 Terminal Services and Citrix MetaFrame? For starters, both are thin-client software packages. They each provide the user with a virtual desktop, a concept familiar to users of Windows and other similar graphical environments. Application processing is handled at the server level, allowing older PCs with operating systems such as DOS or even UNIX to execute applications seamlessly within a Windows 2000 desktop. Seamless execution means that the fact that the application's processing is taking place at the server level should be transparent to the end user. Terminal Services and MetaFrame both provide a multiuser environment to the Windows 2000 operating system and both utilize the same underlying infrastructure.

NOTE

Windows 2000 Terminal Services is commonly referred to as simply Terminal Services.

The Beginning of Terminal Services and MetaFrame

It is impossible to discuss the history of Windows NT Terminal Services without also discussing the history of Citrix. Ed Iacobucci was the head of the IBM/Microsoft joint effort to develop OS/2. As part of that development effort, Iacobucci conceived an idea whereby different types of computers on the network would be able to run OS/2 even though they were not designed to do so.

His idea marked the beginnings of MultiWin technology. MultiWin permits multiple users to simultaneously share the CPU, network cards, I/O ports, and other resources that the server has available. This technology is the basis for multiuser support.

Iacobucci left IBM in 1989 to form Citrix Systems when neither Microsoft nor IBM was interested in his MultiWin technology. Citrix developed the technology, known as MultiView, for the OS/2 platform. Unfortunately for them, the days of OS/2 were numbered. In 1991, sensing that his company was in trouble, Iacobucci turned to Microsoft to try to develop the same technology for the Windows NT platform.

Microsoft granted Citrix license to their NT source code and bought a six-percent stake in the company. The success of Citrix would only help Microsoft's market share grow at a time when they had a relatively small percentage of the market. The investment paid off. In 1995, Citrix shipped WinFrame and brought multiuser computing to Windows NT for the first time. However, the success not only of WinFrame but also of the NT platform in general would be a problem for Citrix. With sales of Windows NT at an enormously strong level, Microsoft decided they no longer needed the help of Citrix for thin-client computing. As a result, they notified Citrix of their intent to develop their own multiuser technology in February of 1997.

Citrix's stock took an immediate nose-dive when the announcement was made public. Shares fell 60 percent in a single day, and the future of the company was uncertain. After several months of intense negotiations between the two companies, a deal was struck. Microsoft's desire was to immediately become a player in the thin-client world, but developing their own architecture to do so would be time consuming. So Citrix agreed to license their MultiWin technology to Microsoft to incorporate into future versions of Windows. In return, Citrix had the right to continue the development of the WinFrame 1.*x* platform independent of Microsoft, and also to develop the MetaFrame expansions of Microsoft's new Terminal Services platform. These two products are based on Citrix's Independent Computing Architecture (ICA) protocol, which we will discuss later in this chapter.

Introduction of Terminal Services

By the middle of 1998, Microsoft had developed and released Windows NT Server 4.0, Terminal Services Edition. This was Microsoft's first attempt at a thin-client operating system, and it borrowed heavily from Citrix's earlier efforts. While NT 4.0 Terminal Services looks the same as a regular NT 4.0 server, they are substantially different. Service packs for one will not work for the other. Hot fixes have to be written separately as well. Even printer drivers sometimes need to be "Terminal Services aware," or certified to work with Terminal Services. Windows NT 4.0, Terminal Services Edition shipped as a completely independent platform with a rather hefty price tag.

Citrix soon followed with MetaFrame 1.0 for Windows NT 4.0, Terminal Services Edition, and later with MetaFrame 1.8. Both versions of MetaFrame had several advantages over Windows' Terminal Services. Microsoft borrowed some of those advantages when they developed Windows 2000 with Terminal Services. With this release, Terminal Services is incorporated directly into the Windows 2000 platform as a service rather than an entirely separate architecture. This simplifies maintenance by allowing Windows 2000 servers with Terminal Services to receive the same upgrades and hot fixes as any other Windows 2000 server, rather than waiting for a specific Terminal Services version. Any Windows 2000 server can install Terminal Services, though a separate license may be required depending on the role the server will play. We'll look at those roles under the Windows 2000 Terminal Services section.

Continuing with their agreement, Citrix has released MetaFrame 1.8 for Windows 2000 Servers. There are no upgrades from the MetaFrame for NT 4.0 Terminal Services addition, but it still provides functionality that Terminal Services alone cannot. In addition, Citrix's ICA protocol is considered to be faster than Microsoft's Remote Desktop Protocol (RDP). Citrix also provides some additional tools that can be added to MetaFrame to extend its functionality and administration abilities. We'll look at each product individually and explore their advantages and disadvantages.

Windows 2000 Terminal Services

Terminal Services provides Windows 2000 administrators with the ability to distribute a multiuser environment to fat- and thin-client machines. We've already discussed the advantages of managing a centralized computing system. Microsoft makes full use of those advantages in presenting Windows 2000 Terminal Services as a viable thin-client solution. Microsoft bases Terminal Services on the RDP protocol. RDP 5.0 is the version currently shipping with Windows 2000 and it is considerably improved over RDP 4.0 that shipped with NT 4.0 Terminal Services. We'll go into RDP in much more detail a little later in this chapter. For now, it's enough to know that RDP is the underlying technology for Terminal Services. Terminal Services, just like ICA, is the underlying technology used by Citrix.

What Exactly Is Terminal Services?

Terminal Services is a complete multiuser technology used in conjunction with Windows 2000 Server or Advanced Server to give users that connect to the Terminal Services-enabled server a traditional Windows 2000 desktop view. Typically users will use a client piece on their local PC that makes the connection to the remote Terminal Services. Figure 1.6 shows how this client presents the remote desktop on the local user's machine.

Figure 1.6 Terminal Services client view.

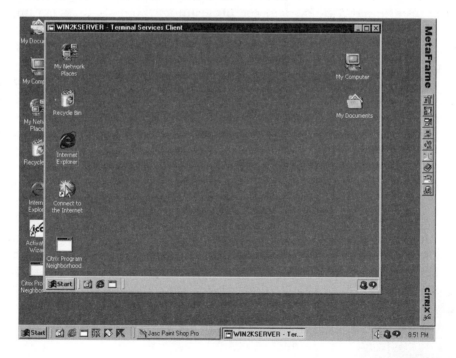

In the new lingo of Windows 2000, there are now application servers and standard servers capable of providing BackOffice application packages. BackOffice products are common server packages like Web servers, file and print services, and database tools. These packages require the client to download the information and execute the programs locally. Applications servers can provide remote applications support to users of packages like Office, Exchange, or even Netscape Communicator. A Windows 2000 server with Terminal Services is considered to be an applications server. The key difference between applications servers and standard servers lies in the fact that BackOffice programs are unable to provide multiple logins. This means that while many users can access the same resources, only one can be presented with a console login at a time.

This is where Terminal Services differs from BackOffice products. Since each user is in effect creating their own session with the server, they can each simultaneously execute applications that would normally be impossible to separate into so many sessions. With Terminal Services, many clients besides the console client may be logged into an application at any given time. Each of these clients is running a separate instance of the application, and the application processing takes place entirely on the Terminal Services server.

To enable this multiuser support, Microsoft made changes to the standard Win32 API calls so that they would be capable of allowing multiple interactive users. In a traditional Windows application, a single user would run the program at a time. Because programmers based their assumptions on this standard model, many applications make use of configuration files and attempt to modify the registry in a way that would make it impossible for multiuser support. Without these changes, applications would be incapable of providing more than a single instance with conflicts. Terminal Services deals with this problem by carefully monitoring registry changes and .INI file modifications and replicating them for each user who accesses an application. When an application is installed on a Terminal Services server, the machine must be placed in what is known as install mode. The normal mode of operation is execution mode. We will discuss install mode more later in the chapter.

In addition, Microsoft has modified the Process Manager for Terminal Services to change the way new tasks are handled in a multiuser environment. New processes are assigned the same priority as foreground tasks, which is quite different from a standard Windows NT/2000 server where foreground tasks always have a higher priority than new processes. Time slices on Terminal Services have also been shortened since most of the processing is being done in the foreground as a Windows 2000 Professional workstation would.

Install Mode

There are two methods of placing a Terminal Services server in install mode. When using Add/Remove programs on a server with Terminal Services available, the installer has the option to install the program for all users or just him or herself. If "all users" is selected, the machine will be placed in install mode for the duration of the install. The second method of placing a machine in install mode is to go to the command prompt and use the **change user/install** command. This command accomplishes the same thing as the Add/Remove programs option. This special mode carefully records the changes necessary for each user, and will configure all other users with the appropriate settings. Unlike Windows NT 4.0 Terminal Services Edition, you *must* use Add/Remove programs when running an install routine in Windows 2000 with Terminal Services. Be very careful that you always use the **change user/execute** command when you have finished the installation. Leaving the system in install mode can cause serious problems.

WARNING

Install mode should be used very carefully. When a machine is placed in install mode, portions of the registry that would not normally be accessible by users are now capable of being modified. It is strongly recommended that you ensure no users are currently logged on to the system when you use install mode.

System Requirements for Terminal Services

Windows 2000 Server has much higher system requirements than NT 4.0 Server. When planning the installation or upgrade of a Terminal Services, close consideration should be paid to the new hardware specifications. Table 1.3 lists the minimum and recommended hardware specs for Windows 2000 versus the recommended specs for Terminal Services with 100 users.

Table 1.3 Windows 2000 Hardware Specifications

Minimum Requirements	Recommended Specifications
Pentium 133 Processor	Quad PIII 450s or higher
128 megabytes (MB) of RAM	2 gigabytes (GB) of RAM
Minimum of 1GB of free space on the hard drive (potentially much more depending on the options selected)	Enough space to support the additional virtual memory requirements as well as the increased SAM size for each user. SAM records can be double that of non-Terminal Services records. Be aware that *any* SAM created with the Terminal Services version of User Manager for Domains will be larger than a standard Windows 2000 Server SAM.
VGA or higher monitor, standard keyboard, standard mouse	Same as standard Windows 2000 Server

Types of Terminal Services Installations

There are two types of Terminal Services installations with Windows 2000. We have already touched on the first, *applications server installations*. This is the server type that presents a multiuser environment and allows concurrent access to standard Windows applications. When a Windows 2000 server has Terminal Services installed as an applications server, it requires that a Client Access License (CAL) be available in the Terminal Services Licensing tool for each user who accesses the server. These CALs are in addition to the standard per-seat licensing. There must be a separate per-seat license for each user who could connect to the Terminal Services. Per-server licensing is not a valid option.

The second type of Terminal Services installation is the *remote administration* mode. With remote administration mode, remote users are still granted console access but no special licensing considerations are enforced. In addition, the changes to server tuning that are performed for an applications server are not performed. What remote administration mode allows for is the remote management of the Windows 2000 server from a central point in the organization. Any user with an RDP client can access the server, so careful consideration needs to be paid to the security procedures used on servers activated with remote administration Terminal Services.

Terminal Services Licensing

In addition to the standard CALs available for a Windows 2000 Server, there are four unique types of Terminal Services CALs available:

- **Terminal Services CAL** This is the standard CAL for every user except those described below. Each user must have a TS CAL to log in to the server.

- **Built-in CAL** A user who has an NT Workstation or 2000 Professional CAL does not require a new TS CAL to access the server.

- **Work-at-Home CAL** This license may only be purchased in con-junction with the standard TS CAL. It is a discounted CAL that lets organizations provide a user with the ability to log in to Terminal Services from work or from home. It combines the standard server CAL and the TS CAL into a single license.

- **Internet Connection License** Many companies make Terminal Services connections available via the Internet. This special CAL will allow a maximum of 200 anonymous users to concurrently connect to the Terminal Services server. These CALS are intended only for non-employees.

Once a Windows 2000 server is installed with Terminal Services as an applications server, you are given 90 days to activate a license server. The license server can exist on the Windows domain controller in a Windows 2000 domain, or any Windows 2000 server in an NT 4.0 domain. The license server tracks available client licenses and distributes them to client devices as they connect. No client can connect without a valid license. Receiving a digital certificate from the Microsoft Clearinghouse and apply-ing it to the license server activates the license server management. Once the license server is activated, client licenses can be installed. Table 1.4 shows how the license server handles a license request.

Table 1.4 Client Requesting a Terminal Services Connection

Client	Server
Establishes connection to a Windows 2000 Terminal Services	Sends request for client license
Returns cached license -or- Requests a new one from the server	Checks the cached license. If it is valid, the connection is completed. -or- If there is no cached license or it is invalid, the Terminal Services attempts to contact the license server to request a new client license.
Completes the connection -or- Waits for the server to return a new or valid license. If one is not available, the connection is not completed.	Server functions as normal -or- If no licenses are available of the licensing server cannot be reached, the connection is denied. If a valid license is returned, the connection is completed.

For Managers

Upgrading to Windows 2000 Terminal Services

Based on your current operating system, you have several options when upgrading an existing server to Windows 2000 Terminal Services. Standard NT 4.0 servers that are upgraded to applications servers will have to have all programs reinstalled to make them available to Terminal Services clients. For this reason, Microsoft recommends that you install Terminal Services in remote administration mode. If an upgrade to an applications server is required, it is recommended that the machine be wiped clean and the program reinstalled.

The second upgrade path is for NT 4.0 Terminal Services edition. These machines can be upgraded directly to Windows 2000 Terminal Services and all installed applications will continue to function normally. An NT 4.0 Terminal Services edition server that is upgraded to Windows 2000 Terminal Services will automatically be set as an applications server.

Continued

To install Terminal Services as a remote administration server, the machine will have to be wiped and reinstalled. See Terminal Services Tools for more information on where the new Terminal Services tools are located and what functions they perform.

Servers that are currently installed with Citrix MetaFrame 1.0 and 1.8 can be upgraded to Windows 2000 Terminal Services, but the MetaFrame components will be broken unless MetaFrame 1.8 for Windows 2000 is also installed. If you are not planning on installing MetaFrame 1.8 for Windows 2000 right away, Microsoft recommends removing the MetaFrame component from NT 4.0 Terminal Services before attempting the upgrade.

Terminal Services Tools

Windows 2000 Terminal Services has an extensive tools suite that allows the remote administration and maintenance of Terminal Services connections. Several new tools have been added since NT 4.0 Terminal Services edition, and administrators familiar with those tools may struggle to find what they need in Windows 2000 Terminal Services. The following is a list and short explanation of each tool and its role in managing Windows 2000 Terminal Services.

Terminal Services Connection Configuration (TSCC) This utility is the first that administrators should familiarize themselves with. From within the TSCC, the administrator has the ability to create connection types, change supported protocols, set encryption levels, and even set access security for each server on a connection-by-connection basis. The TSCC also is where the remote control properties of a connection are set. Currently, Terminal Services supports Microsoft's RDP and Citrix's ICA protocols. Figure 1.7 shows the Terminal Services Connection Configuration tool.

Terminal Services Manager (TSM) The Terminal Services Manager can be used to manage users, sessions, and processes on every Terminal Services visible in the domain. Within the TSM, an administrator can initiate a shadow session with a user, check the current license count, and even see on a process-by-process basis what each user is accessing. In the day-to-day management of Terminal Services, this will be the tool most often used for monitoring and troubleshooting. Figure 1.8 shows the Terminal Services Manager.

Figure 1.7 Terminal Services Connection Configuration.

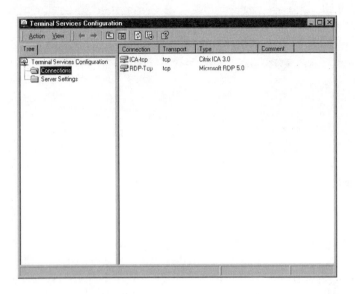

Figure 1.8 Terminal Services Manager.

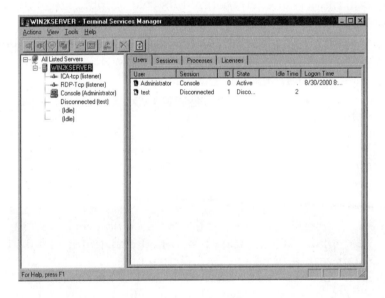

Terminal Services Licensing We have already discussed this tool extensively. Basically, it allows for the management of all Windows 2000 license servers in your environment. Figure 1.9 demonstrates the Terminal Services Licensing screen.

Figure 1.9 Terminal Services Licensing.

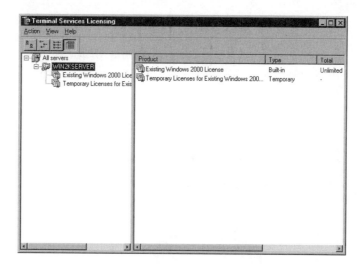

Application Security Registration (ASR) The AppSec tool for Windows 2000 is available through the Windows 2000 Server Resource Kit. With this tool, administrators have the ability to restrict execution of applications based on the list entered in the ASR. Any attempt to execute application in the ASR will result in an error message for non-administrator users. Applications listed must be on a local drive. Applications on network drives will not be available when AppSec is enabled.

In addition, there are two other tools that are common to Windows 2000 but have some additional configuration options when Terminal Services is installed:

Windows 2000 Terminal Services User Manager for Domains This special version of User Manager gives administrators access to the expanded fields for configuring a Terminal Services user. The standard User Manager for Domains that ships with NT 4.0 and Windows 2000 is not capable of displaying or modifying these fields. Here you can set many of the Terminal Services variables such as timeout settings, local drive and printer mapping, and whether that user can be shadowed. Many of these new fields are found under the Terminal Services Profile tab, where you can set specific Terminal Services profiles and home directories. Figure 1.10 shows the new fields available in Terminal Services User Manager for Domains.

Windows 2000 Active Directory Users and Computers When Terminal Services is installed, it adds additional properties to the Active Directory tools that are specific to Terminal Services. The four tabs that contain

Terminal Services information are: Environment (used to configure how client devices are handled on login), Sessions (sets timeout and reconnect settings for a user's TS session), Remote Control (configures how that user will be remotely controlled), and Terminal Services Profile (gives a specific Terminal Services profile and home directory path). Many of these properties are duplicated in other tools, and all of them can be overridden on the Terminal Services.

Figure 1.10 Terminal Services User Manager for Domains.

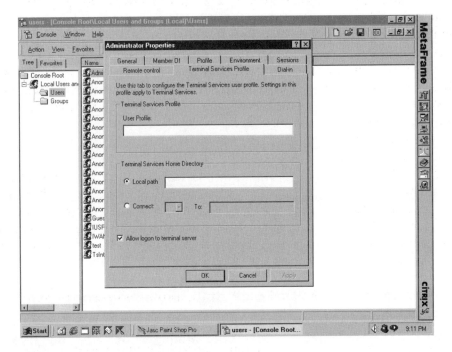

The Virtual Memory

Windows processes require a virtual address space to function. This space is divided between the kernel and user address spaces. Kernel threads are capable of accessing both the user space and the kernel space, while user threads can only access user space. The kernel space is divided among all processes and each process also receives its own user space. This is where the problem lies. If multiple user sessions try to access the single kernel space, there are considerable problems with the kernel sharing. To counteract this problem, Microsoft developed a third type of address space known as the session address space.

The session address space is unique to Terminal Services. Each session places a copy of the kernel space within its own session address space. Each session then has access to its own Windows Manager, Graphical Device Interface (GDI), display, and printer drivers. Used in conjunction with the changes to the Win32 API calls we mentioned earlier, this session address space allows Windows 2000 to present a multi-user environment.

Remote Desktop Protocol (RDP)

We've mentioned RDP several times already in this chapter, and now we're going to take a more detailed look at what it is. Remote Desktop Protocol is the backbone of Microsoft's thin-client package. Capable of controlling the transmission of information between the client and the Terminal Services, RDP is responsible for both graphical data transmission and mouse/keyboard transmission. RDP is based on the T.120 standards and was originally shipped as RDP 4.0 in Windows NT 4.0 Terminal Services edition. Windows 2000 includes the updated RDP 5.0, which allows many of the new features of Windows 2000 Terminal Services.

RDP handles graphical information transmission through a special RDP display driver that is separate for each user session. Since each session has its own Win32 kernel and display drivers contained in a session address space of the virtual memory, the RDP display driver is able to receive commands from the GDI and pass them to the Terminal Services device driver. The device driver then encodes the data in the RDP format and sends it to the Transportation layer, which sends it off to the client. At the client end, the data is decoded and the display is updated with the new information.

The other key role that RDP plays is the transmission of mouse and keyboard data from the client to the server. Every input message (keystrokes or mouse movements) generated by the client is captured and encoded in the RDP format, then sent to the Terminal Services. There, the RDP packet is decoded and processed as normal in the user's session address space and the screen updates are returned to the client to reflect the changes. Input messages can be cached for better bandwidth management. We'll discuss that under the client portion of this chapter.

RDP Encryption

RDP also has three encryption levels available to ensure secure communications between the client and the Terminal Services. You can choose which encryption level fits the needs of your organization. UDP utilizes the RC4 encryption algorithm to secure the RDP packets. The available encryption levels are:

- **Low Security** Data is encrypted in one direction only, from the client to the server. Server to client data is left unencrypted. A Windows 2000 RDP client will use a 56-bit encryption key, while older clients will use a 40-bit encryption key.

- **Medium Security** Data is now encrypted in both directions. However, the key types remain the same.

- **High Security** This option uses a 128-bit security key to encrypt data to and from the server. Currently, this option is only available in the United States and Canada.

NOTE

Recent relaxations of the export laws regarding security technologies may allow you to use 128-bit connections with countries other than the United States and Canada. Check with Microsoft or your local software resellers to obtain the latest encryption export regulations.

RDP Functionality

RDP 5.0 has greatly increased the functionality that came with the RDP 4.0 that shipped with NT 4.0 Terminal Services. With the Windows 2000 Terminal Services Client, users and administrators have expanded capabilities to map local printer, clipboards, and session remote control. The following is a list of some of the new and improved features of RDP 5.0:

- **Local/Remote Clipboard Usage** Prior to RDP 5.0 and the Windows 2000 client, there was no way to copy information between the local and remote clipboards in a Terminal Services session. This meant that text copied from Notepad in a remote session could not be pasted locally. Clipboard mapping is enabled through the Terminal Services Configuration.

- **Client Printer Mapping** With RDP 5.0, local printers will now be remapped as a network printer connection when a session is established to Terminal Services. This enables clients to maintain their default printers and saves administrators from having to define every printer in the network that could be used by the client as a printer on the Terminal Services. However, the printer drivers must exist on the Terminal Services for it to map correctly. Client printer mapping is only enabled in the 32-bit version of the

Windows 2000 Terminal Services client. Mapped local printers are available only to that client's session. Bi-directional printing is not supported in auto-created printers.

- **Remote Control** Prior to RDP 5.0, administrators were unable to remotely control a Terminal Services session. With the introduction of RDP 5.0 to the environment, administrators can now connect to and passively or actively interact with another user's session. This tool is invaluable to support personal for troubleshooting and user education. There are some restrictions on the remote control session however. The video resolutions must be the same or higher on the machine used to control another client. The person attempting the control must have the necessary privileges to control a session. You must be logged in to the same Terminal Services as the person you are attempting to control. In addition, you may only control one user at a time and only one person may control the user.

- **Bitmap Caching** RDP 5.0 uses persistent bitmap caching to store common bitmaps on the local hard drive to speed up user sessions. When a connection is made between the Windows 2000 Terminal Services client and the Terminal Services itself, the client sends a list of keys corresponding to its cached bitmaps to alert the server what it needs to send and what it can substitute the key for. The bitmap cache size is fixed at 10MB and cannot be altered.

The Terminal Services Client

Windows 2000 currently supports two installations of the RDP 5.0 client for Terminal Services. The 32-bit client for Windows 95/98/2000 and NT provides the full functionality of the RDP 5.0 standard to any of those clients listed. The 16-bit client for Windows for Workgroups 3.11 is missing key features such as the client printer auto creation. There are additional clients available through third-party vendors for operating systems such as UNIX, Macintosh, and DOS. A separate Alpha client is available for the Windows NT Alpha platform but is not included with Windows 2000.

The Terminal Services client must be installed on every client machine that will connect with Terminal Services. Consisting of the Client Connection Manager and the Terminal Services Client, the client allows the creation of connections to Terminal Services, shortcuts for those connections, and configuration of the client connection options. Properties such as bitmap caching and default screen area can be defined that will be defaulted to for any connection created. These settings can be overridden at the Terminal Services configuration options we discussed earlier.

Terminal Services Client Installation

There are several methods of installing the Terminal Services Client on a workstation. The method you choose will depend on how exactly you plan to distribute your Terminal Services environment and the types of operating systems you are distributing it to. Here are the choices available:

- **Diskette Installation** You can use the Terminal Services Client Creator program that is located under the Administrator tools off the Start menu to create client diskettes for either a 16-bit or 32-bit installation.

- **Network Installation** Sharing the Winntsystemroot\system32\clients\tsclient\net will allow you to perform network installations of the Terminal Services client. Local machines should map to this and choose either the win32 or win16 directories to run the SETUP.EXE from.

- **Windows CE Installation** This client is available on the Windows 2000 CD under the valueadd\msft\mgmt\mtsc_hpc directory. It requires you to have already installed the CE services on your PC. The next time your CE device synchronizes with the desktop, it will transfer this client over to it.

Using the Terminal Services Client

Training new Terminal Services users can sometimes be a difficult task. Most users are at least familiar with the Windows desktop and have a general feel for how to accomplish certain tasks. Everyone has their own personal preferences and shortcuts for getting where they want to go. In Terminal Services, common tasks require a somewhat different method of execution. For instance, the most common keyboard command CTRL-ALT-DELETE will cause the client to open the local Windows Security screen, as opposed to the Windows Security screen on the Terminal Services. This can cause confusion among users, and it is common to have new users log out of their local session when they really meant to exit the remote session. Table 1.5 lists some common local keyboard commands and their Terminal Services equivalents.

Table 1.5 Common Shortcut Keys

Common Desktop Shortcut	Terminal Services Shortcut	Function
Alt-Tab	Alt-Page Up	Move forward between programs
Alt-Shift-Tab	Alt-Page Down	Move backward between programs
Alt-Spacebar	Alt-Delete	Bring up the selected window's Control menu
Alt-Esc	Alt-Insert	Cycle through all open windows
Ctrl-Alt-Delete	Ctrl-Alt-End	The most frequently used shortcut. This displays the Windows Security box.

Unfortunately, these keys cannot be remapped in Terminal Services. It is important to note that at a console session, the normal keyboard shortcuts apply. It is only when a user is connected through the Terminal Services client that they must remember to use these new keyboard shortcuts. Out of all of the adjustment users have to make to using Terminal Services, this is perhaps the hardest.

In addition to a change in the keyboard shortcuts, the Start menu is slightly different in a Terminal Services session. Instead of a Shutdown option, a standard user connected to Terminal Services is presented with the choices of Disconnect or Logoff. When a user Disconnects a session, all of their processes continue running on the server until the timeout period specified in the connection configuration. If the user reconnects before the timeout period is reached, they will be presented with their session exactly how they left it. If a user chooses to Logoff, then their session is shut down as normal.

TIP

Disconnected sessions can be the bane of a Terminal Services administrator. Users often fail to understand the difference between Disconnect and Logoff, so they choose the Disconnect option. Clicking the X in the upper right hand corner has the same effect as the Disconnect option. A company called Softblox has developed a third-party application that prevents users from using the X to close windows. Called AppScape Utilities, it functions as a System Policy Editor extension and allows you to turn off the close-window button. More information can be found on their Web site at www.netblox.com.

Local Drive Mapping

One of the most requested features that comes with Terminal Services is the ability to autocreate local drive mappings on login. Unfortunately, Microsoft does not provide it with RDP. In a typical situation, the local client will have a C:\ and perhaps D:\ drive that are local to their workstation. On the Terminal Services, there will also be a C:\ drive. When users connect to a Terminal Services session and attempt to save a file to what they see as the C:\ drive, they will be attempting to save it to the local drive of the Terminal Services and not their client machine. Most likely, this operation will fail because they will have inadequate rights to write to the Terminal Services local drive. Users should be taught to save files to a common network location that can be consistent for both the local and Terminal Services sessions. In the next section of this chapter, we'll talk about the Citrix ICA client that does support local drive mappings.

Network Load Balancing for Windows 2000

Scalability of Windows NT products has been a key concern for network managers in the past. With Windows 2000 Advanced Server, Microsoft has provided Network Load Balancing (NLB) to alleviate some of the scalability concerns of their customers. NLB provides TCP/IP-based services as a component of Windows Clustering. Although intended primarily to support Web applications, NLB can also be used to provide reliable, scalable redundancy for a Terminal Services environment. An NLB cluster can be as large as 32 servers, but they must all be on the same subnet.

NLB is completely transparent to the TCP/IP stack. Functioning as a network driver on the load-balanced server, NLB keeps track of client requests and host status within the cluster. A distribution algorithm determines how the load will be distributed and which client in the cluster will respond to a client request. When a host within the cluster fails, all NLB servers in the cluster enter a state called *convergence*. In convergence, the connection load is redistributed to remove the failed host from the list of potential cluster machines. Terminal Services connection information is not maintained across multiple servers, however. If the connection fails, all data within the connection will be lost and the user will be forced to logon again.

NLB allows administrators to define a load weight parameter to determine how the load will be split among member servers. This formula is based solely on network connections and cannot monitor processor utilization, memory utilization, or other system metrics. Servers within a cluster could in fact be running at maximum processor usage while others sit nearly idle because of the type of user session connected.

NOTE

There are several other packages that can provide load balancing in a Terminal Services environment. Windows Load Balancing Service, NCD ThinPATH Load Balancing, and Citrix Load Balancing are all capable of providing varying degrees of load balancing services.

Citrix MetaFrame

Citrix MetaFrame is an extension of the Windows 2000 Terminal Services. Designed to expand on the features that Terminal Services presents to its users, MetaFrame relies upon Citrix's proprietary thin-client protocol known as ICA (Independent Computing Architecture). The ICA protocol is completely separate from Microsoft's RDP and was in fact developed prior to Microsoft's implementation of RDP. The protocols can coexist on the same server, but Terminal Services exclusively uses RDP while MetaFrame uses ICA. Many of the RDP 5.0 functions are based on the ICA protocol. In this section, we will explore the features and functions of MetaFrame 1.8 for Windows 2000 and the advantages it provides over Terminal Services.

The ICA Protocol

The ICA protocol gives users and administrators many new and improved features that RDP 5.0 and Terminal Services do not offer. Specifically, ICA provides full client device mappings such as stereo audio, COM and printer mapping, and local drive remapping. In addition, ICA supports its own load balancing system known as Citrix Load Balancing. The ICA client is available for many non-Windows platforms such as Macintosh and UNIX. ICA also allows expanded shadowing of remote sessions. In general, the ICA protocol fills most of the gaps left by Terminal Services.

As a result of the agreement in 1997 between Citrix and Microsoft, Citrix licensed MultiWin to Microsoft but retained ownership of their ICA protocol. Although Microsoft would develop the RDP 4.0 protocol, Citrix's ICA protocol was much more advanced and provided increased functionality. Every management and scalability feature in MetaFrame is based on and integrated into the ICA protocol. This makes ICA the foundation for all Citrix technologies.

What makes ICA so robust is its small size. The typical ICA pipe will require no more than a 20 Kbps connection speed. This number can be increased based on some of the client options chosen, but a standard user can run an ICA session on a 28.8 Kbps dial-up connection at near-local speeds. This helps add to the seamless remote environment that MetaFrame is capable of creating.

The ICA protocol is first and foremost the presentation protocol that provides remote computing capabilities to users with a MetaFrame session on a Terminal Services server. At this layer the RDP and ICA protocols are almost identical. Both provide graphical and input information between the remote client and the local server. Much like other remote control software, only screen updates and input is passed to lessen the bandwidth requirements to the client. The ICA protocol has a much wider role in the Citrix environment than just a presentation protocol.

SpeedScreen2

SpeedScreen2 is a MetaFrame feature of the ICA protocol that offers considerable speed advantages over other thin-client protocols. SpeedScreen2 cuts the average packet size by 25–30 percent and can reduce total transmissions by up to 60 percent! SpeedScreen2 can improve performance over a low-speed dial up, but at up to four times the normal transmission rate. SpeedScreen2 requires no special installation and is automatically a part of the ICA technology.

The ICA Browser

Each MetaFrame server runs an ICA Browser service in addition to its other presentation duties. This service communicates status information to a central repository server known as the *ICA master browser*. The master browser is responsible for keeping track of the status information for each Citrix member server and maintaining the connection information for each protocol. Master browsers are elected based on certain characteristics such as operating system type, server role, etc. There may be separate master browsers for each protocol that is enabled, or a single master browser can handle multiple protocols. If a Citrix server is not the master browser, it is known as a *member browser*.

Each subnet requires a separate master browser. The ICA master browser election is conducted through broadcast messages that typically are not allowed to cross routers. A master browser election is initiated when a MetaFrame server is started, the current master browser stops responding to member server requests, the current master browser doesn't respond to ICA client requests, or multiple master browsers are detected for the same protocol. The election process will take the following into consideration in an order of precedence, highest to lowest:

1. Which ICA browser has the highest version number?
2. Which MetaFrame browser has been explicitly configured to run as a master browser?

3. Is the server a domain controller?

4. Which server has had the ICA browser service running the longest?

5. Which MetaFrame server has the lowest name in alphabetical order?

For instance, Server A, Server B, and Server C are all MetaFrame servers on a new subnet. Server A and Server B are both explicitly configured to be the master browser, and Server C has a newer version of the ICA browser. Server C will be elected as the master browser, despite the fact that Server A and Server B were both explicitly configured to be the master browser. This ensures that the latest browser version is always configured as the master browser.

TIP

If possible, it is always best to have a dedicated master browser for each subnet. This machine will be completely and solely responsible for maintaining the ICA browser information and should not be used as an applications server. One common way to make a dedicated master browser is to install MetaFrame and let the license expire without activating it. This will limit logons to the administrator console only, but the box can still function as a master browser. Manually configure this machine as the master browser, and make sure you update it first with any new Citrix updates to keep its ICA browser version current.

The ICA master browser is responsible for maintaining a lot of information from the member servers. Because its role is so crucial to the success of ICA, the master browser is often configured with backup master browsers. These are often the machines that are next in line for the master browser position, based on the election criteria. We'll discuss configuring the number of backup master browsers later in the chapter. The list of information a master browser must track includes:

- Pooled license count

- A list of all known Citrix servers

- A list of all published applications

- A list of disconnected user sessions and the servers they are connected to

- Load calculations if Citrix Load Balancing is installed
- Information on the backup master browsers

TIP

Use the QSERVER command to return a list of all Citrix servers and their status information. As part of this information, you can tell which servers are master or backup browsers by looking for the M or B character on the far right.

ICA Gateways

Since an ICA master browser can only manage its own subnet, Citrix developed ICA gateways to allow multiple master browsers to communicate with one another. The master browsers share published application information between themselves via TCP/IP or IPX packets, and any routers between them must pass that traffic. Gateways are independent of each other. A gateway between A and B and a gateway between B and C will not allow A to speak with C.

Establishing an ICA gateway requires a local server and remote server. These do not have to be the master browsers for their subnet. When gateway communications are requested, the local machine will contact the local master browser that will then contact the remote master browser. Gateways can only be established across multiple domains if the appropriate Windows trust relationships also exist.

SecureICA

MetaFrame provides only minimal encryption support for its ICA connections straight out of the box. The only available encryption levels are *basic* or *none*. Basic encryption uses an algorithm of less than 40 bits in size. To achieve more secure communications with the ICA client, Citrix has an option pack known as SecureICA for MetaFrame. SecureICA gives the licensee 40-, 56-, or 128-bit encryption capabilities using the RC5 standard developed by RSA. When a client uses SecureICA, a 128-bit key is always used during the authentication process, regardless of the session key. With the recent release of Feature Release 1, Citrix has provided SecureICA capability to all of its Subscription Advantage holders. They no longer are forced to purchase a separate SecureICA license.

Interaction Between the Browser and the Client

The ICA master browser is a crucial component to the ICA client. Without the ICA master browser, ICA clients would be unable to initiate a session with a MetaFrame server. The ICA client retrieves a list of available servers and applications from the master browser and uses that list to determine the server with which to connect. The client will attempt to locate the ICA master browser by querying an explicit list entered in the client connection configuration, or issuing a broadcast and querying the first Citrix server to respond. Since all Citrix servers know their master browser, either method will return the correct information. However, if there is no Citrix servers on the client's submit, an explicit list must be provided to locate a master browser.

With Feature Release 1, Citrix has included the ability to use TCP for ICA browsing instead of UDP. This greatly facilitates ICA browsing through a firewall, which was a serious problem with the UDP browser service. It also allows communication with the new Citrix XML Service. The XML Service can provide published application data to ICA clients through either the TCP-HTTP network protocol or NFuse-enabled Web servers.

Application Publishing

Application publishing is an important concept with Citrix MetaFrame. It is the key to the seamless integration of MetaFrame servers with your existing desktops and one of the many ways in which Citrix tries to make ICA connections transparent to the end user. Basically, application publishing is the process by which an administrator can configure an application to be visible to the ICA master browser. When the application is "published," the member server will update the master browser with the status of that application. ICA clients can make a direct connection to that application rather than to a desktop environment.

This is invaluable for administrators who want to integrate published applications into an existing environment. Because applications can be published using an anonymous credentials requirement, users will merely double-click the shortcut on their desktop and initiate a connection to the application. All of the ICA connection processing is done in the background and a seamless window can be opened with the published application. We discuss seamless windows more later in this chapter. Application publishing is managed by the Published Applications Manager (PAM) which we talk more about under the MetaFrame Server Tools section.

The ICA Client

The Citrix ICA client contains a wide variety of desktop integration features that allow administrators to seamlessly integrate published applications to remote PCs. Although many of the features in the ICA client are now available with RDP 5.0 and Windows 2000, the ICA client offers improvements and additions beyond the capabilities of RDP 5.0. Different versions of the ICA client provide differing levels of features, but here are some of the features that ICA has improved or added:

- Client device mapping
- Seamless Windows
- Application Launching and Embedding (ALE)
- Program neighborhood
- Improved session shadowing

Client Device Mapping

In addition to allowing the autocreation of local printers as RDP 5.0 allows, the ICA protocol also allows the client to map COM ports and audio devices. Audio can be enabled or disabled in the client setup or in the Terminal Services Connection configuration. COM ports are not mapped automatically, but can be mapped using the **net use** command. For instance, COM port 1 on client machine Test would be mapped as \\Test\COM1. There is also a **change client** command that is native to MetaFrame that can be used to accomplish this mapping.

NOTE

Enabling COM or audio mapping increases the bandwidth requirements of the ICA protocol. Pay careful attention when using these features to make sure that you do not overload the connection.

Perhaps the biggest improvement to the ICA protocol's local device mapping is that unlike RDP, ICA allows the mapping of local client drives. This improvement allows users to easily transfer data to and from their local machine without having to exit the MetaFrame session and connect to a network drive. Citrix accomplishes this by remapping the local drives on login and making them available to the client. There are several ways this can be implemented. The most common is to remap the local Terminal Services drives to letters other than the common C:\ or D:\. When MetaFrame is installed, you will be asked if you would like to remap the local drives and what letter you would like to map them to. The default is M:\.

If you choose to remap the local drives, then all client drives that are autocreated will map on a one-to-one basis. So C:\ on the MetaFrame session will be the local C:\. If the server drives are not remapped, then the client will autocreate the local drives starting at the letter V:\ on the server and moving backwards. In other words, C: will be mapped to V:, D: will be mapped to U:, and so on. This is partly to keep from conflicting with Novell's Netware search drive mapping conventions. If a drive letter is already mapped on the server, it will be skipped and the next one will be used.

This automatic mapping can be turned on and off on a per-user basis through the User Manager MMC or at a connection level in the Citrix Connection Configuration tool discussed later. Disabling client drive auto-creation does not prevent users from manually mapping drives. A careful look at the security policies in place may be required to prevent this manual user access.

Client printers can also be autocreated with the ICA client, much like in the RDP client. The connection can be set to default to the local printer as the default for the client. When the client logs out, the printer is deleted. Careful consideration needs to be paid to printer autocreation. Although it is immensely handy, it can encumber a network. When a job is sent through a client mapping, the job must be sent from the MetaFrame server down to the client to be spooled, and then back across the network to the printer. If the printer is mapped on the Terminal Services, the job can be spooled directly on the server and sent to the printer without having to spool at the client. This can save a considerable amount of bandwidth in an environment with a lot of printing. Figure 1.11 shows the difference between autocreated and manually created printing.

Seamless Windows

In developing a seamless environment, one of the chief concerns is keeping users unaware of the details of how a remote program is executing. By using a seamless windows connection, an administrator can publish an application shortcut directly to a client's desktop that will launch an ICA session in a window no different than what they are used to seeing for a local application. Seamless windows are only available with the 32-bit ICA client. Each window is resizable, appears in the task bar, and responds to the ALT-TAB shortcut. A user can open as many seamless windows as they want on a desktop. Figure 1.12 shows a seamless window open on a user's desktop.

Figure 1.11 Printer spooling in MetaFrame.

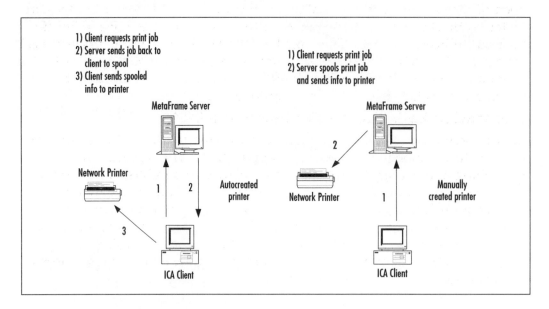

Figure 1.12 Seamless window integration.

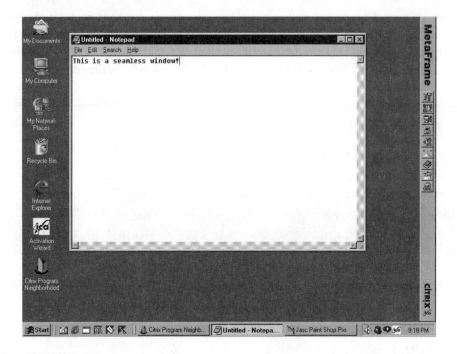

The ICA Connection Center keeps track of all connections currently open or disconnected with MetaFrame servers. The Connection Center can be found by clicking on the ICA icon in the lower right-hand corner of the task bar. If license pooling is enabled on the MetaFrame servers, seamless windows will only require one client license regardless of the number of windows open. If license pooling is not enabled, each separate server to which a connection is opened will require a license.

Application Launching and Embedding (ALE)

Another key feature of the ICA client is the ability to use a Web browser to launch either embedded or seamless applications. The Application Launching and Embedding (ALE) feature allows Web publishers to create a published application and link to it in a Web page. That application can then be launched in a seamless window or run embedded in the Web browser. There are ActiveX controls and Netscape plug-ins to allow those two browsers to use ALE links. Additional ICA support is available for Java- or MIME-based browsers, but these do not have all of the features of the Netscape or Explorer browser clients.

TIP

Be careful when using embedded applications. If the user hits the browser's forward or back buttons, or loads another Web page, the connection to the MetaFrame server is lost. In cases where users will need to be able to surf the Web while using the application, seamless windows is recommended.

Program Neighborhood

Clients that use the Win32 or Java ICA clients have the Citrix Program Neighborhood available. Program Neighborhood provides a single sign-on for all published applications a user has rights to in a Citrix Server Farm (we'll talk about Server Farms shortly). The user is required to log on to the Program Neighborhood, which then uses those credentials to authenticate him to any server from which they launch an application. Additionally, users can be configured with specific application sets. These application sets are defined by the administrator and act as a program group that can be automatically added to the client's desktop or Start menu. Users can also create custom ICA connections that exist independently of the application set.

Session Shadowing

The shadowing options that ICA provides go far beyond the capabilities of RDP 5.0. If you recall, the RDP client will only allow shadowing on a one-to-one basis and only of users on the same server. ICA on the other hand allows one-to-one, one-to-many, or many-to-one shadowing. This could allow multiple users to be trained by a single administrator. Shadow sessions are controlled through the Shadow taskbar, which we will discuss later this chapter. Security privileges are crucial to initiating a passive or active shadow session. There are some properties of shadow sessions you should be aware of:

- Like RDP, ICA shadowing requires that your session be operating at the same or higher video mode as the session you wish to shadow. This applies not only to color, but also to desktop size.

- Users will be prompted to accept the shadow session unless you have configured the shadow to be done without user acceptance.

- Unlike RDP, ICA shadowing can be done across servers.

- Each session must be using the same client (ICA or RDP) for the shadow session to connect.

- Console users cannot be shadowed but can shadow other users.

- Published application sessions can be shadowed.

The MetaFrame Server

So far, we've concentrated mostly on the ICA protocol and its services. Obviously, none of the ICA features would do you any good without a MetaFrame server with which to connect. Citrix MetaFrame provides true enterprise scalability, expanded management tools, and a much broader client support base than Windows 2000 Terminal Services. MetaFrame is a server-based computing model that allows both "fat" and "thin" clients to access hosted applications in a multiuser setting. All client processing is handled by the MetaFrame server, which means that a heterogeneous environment can still take full advantage of all of the features of MetaFrame. PCs with processors as old as the 286 can still take advantage of the MetaFrame environment and MetaFrame fully supports thin-client terminals like Wyse or fat clients like the typical desktop computer.

Thin-client terminals are also known as a Windows-based terminal (WBT) because they run an embedded operating system like DOS but use the ICA or RDP protocol to connect to a multiuser windows environment. There is no local execution since the machines are little more than a keyboard, display, and very basic operating system. WBTs are used as point-of-sale terminals, bank terminals, order entry terminals, and any situation where the user will require no processing capabilities outside of the MetaFrame session. In a MetaFrame environment, WBTs can work side-by-side with normal desktop PCs.

Since the machines require much less hardware than their PC counterparts, they are considerably cheaper and easier to maintain than a traditional fat client. In addition, WBTs help centralize the management concerns for network administrators by allowing user sessions to be tightly controlled. Since many WBTs do not even have a disk drive, they can be incredibly secure devices when data security is a concern. This is an ideal solution for organizations that need to grant specific access types based on the user's job function and security level. Figure 1.13 shows a typical MetaFrame environment with both desktop PCs and WBTs.

Figure 1.13 The MetaFrame environment.

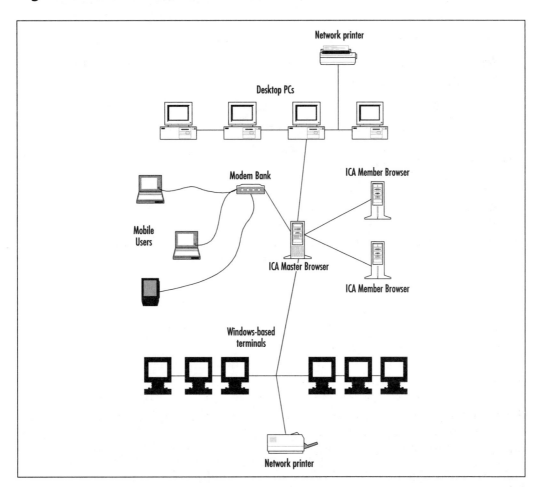

MetaFrame and the Enterprise

We talked about Microsoft's Network Load Balancing (NLB) earlier in this chapter. NLB allows up to 32 Windows 2000 Advanced Servers to form a cluster and load balance Windows 2000 services. The problem with NLB is that it is not RDP-aware and therefore cannot take advantage of some of the key RDP features, such as client reconnection to disconnected sessions, without some sever limitations. In addition, NLB is incapable of balancing the load based on any factor other than connected users. Thankfully, Citrix resolves these issues with the Citrix Load Balancing (CLB) component.

CLB is an add-on feature to MetaFrame that allows any number of servers to make a published application available to ICA users. Load balancing is transparent to the user because applications are accessed by the name, not the server information. The CLB uses load calculations that can be set per server to determine where to pass a client session request. Figure 1.14 demonstrates a load-balanced environment and the steps a client will take to connect to a load-balanced application.

Figure 1.14 Load-balanced environment.

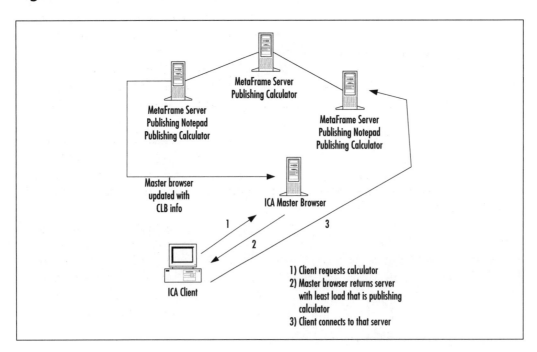

Citrix Load Balancing requires an individual CLB license for each server that will be load balanced. In addition, any application that will be load-balanced on more than one server must be installed on each additional server that might host it. Servers can be added or removed from the load-balanced environment on the fly, letting administrators do routine mainte-nance on one machine while the other servers continue to provide the load-balanced application. If a machine is removed from the load-balanced list for an application, current users will be unaffected but no new users will be connected to that machine for that application.

Citrix Load Balancing is also much easier to implement than NLB. Turning CLB on merely requires activating the appropriate license on that machine, installing an application, and adding that server to the list of servers running a particular published application. No additional hardware or software is required to implement CLB in a MetaFrame environment. CLB is administrator-friendly and can greatly expand the reach of your environment.

Server Farming with Citrix

To further promote the enterprise scalability features of MetaFrame, Citrix introduced Citrix Server Farms. A Server Farm is a group of servers that typically publish the same applications, can be logically grouped together to centralize application management, and can easily deploy a large number of published applications to a variety of users. Citrix Server Farms eliminates multiple logins by authenticating the user when they sign on to the Program Neighborhood and carrying those credentials to any server to which a session request is made.

In addition, Citrix Server Farms allow administrators to easily dis-tribute application sets to users based on their access rights. Once the user logs in to Program Neighborhood, they will be presented with short-cuts to any application that they are authorized to access in that Server Farm. Administrators can also use Citrix Server Farms to automatically publish the shortcut to a user's desktop or Start menu. User credentials are established through Windows trust relationships when a Server Farm spans multiple domains. Server Farms can only span multiple domains if ICA Gateways have been established.

Multiple Server Farms can exist side by side, but each is completely ignorant of the other. Users must authenticate to whichever Server Farm they are trying to access and MetaFrame servers may only belong to one Server Farm at a time. Multiple Server Farms can be necessary in environ-ments with large geographical distances between sites, or multiple-domain environments where Windows trust relationships cannot be established.

MetaFrame Server Tools

MetaFrame has an expanded tool set to manage the ICA environment. These tools allow an administrator to manage the server connections, create client disks, and publish applications. Here is a list of the manage-ment tools available and a brief description of their functions.

Activation Wizard To activate a Citrix license, you must obtain the proper activation code from Citrix and enter it in the Citrix Licensing utility. Most Citrix products have a grace period in which you are allowed to use the license before activation (35 days for a base MetaFrame license). You can use the Activation Wizard to connect to a published application running on Citrix's own servers to obtain the activation codes for your licenses.

Citrix Connection Configuration The Citrix Connection Configuration (CCC) provides the same functionality as the Terminal Services Configuration utility in Windows 2000. MetaFrame installs additional features that allow you to configure alternative protocols and ICA direct dial in.

Citrix Server Administration Citrix Server Administration is an expanded version of Terminal Services Manager for Windows 2000. Although the two look remarkably similar, CSA adds additional tabs at the bottom of the screen to access Published Applications properties, view Server Farms, and display ICA video connections. Additionally, the CSA is used to configure the master browser settings for each server. Notice the differences between the CSA and the TSM in Figure 1.15.

Figure 1.15 The CSA.

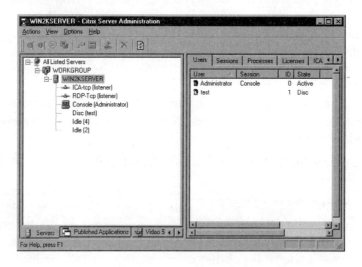

Citrix Licensing The Citrix Licensing tool allows you to add, remove, activate, and manage pooled licenses. This tool is used in conjunction with the Activation Wizard to manage licenses for each MetaFrame server.

ICA Client Update Configuration The ICA Client Update Configuration allows centralized management of ICA client versions. With this utility, administrators have the ability to push new client versions to a user when they connect a session with an older client. Updates can be transparent to the end user, or forced to run before their connection is completed. Additionally, the ICA Client Update Configuration is used to configure the SecureICA clients.

Load Balancing Administration Load Balancing Administration (LBA) can be used to configure the load balancing parameters on any MetaFrame server where load balancing is enabled. Load can be calculated based on six factors, unlike NLB which can only calculate based on connected sessions:

- **User load** This is the only calculation enabled by default on a load-balanced server. User load is figured by calculating the current users in relation to the total number of licenses (local plus pooled), or current users to the total number of users that can be supported by the system. By default, the total number of users that can be supported is set to 10,000. This number should be adjusted to reflect your server's maximum capacity if you choose to load balance based on this criterion.

- **Pagefile usage** This is the ratio of the current pagefile size to the minimum amount of free space left in the pagefile. You configure the minimum free space number yourself.

- **Swap activity** This is merely a measurement of the number of times per second that the pagefile is accessed.

- **Processor usage** This is a combined average of the percentage of processor utilization.

- **Memory load** Memory load is calculated by a ratio of available memory to total memory.

- **Sessions** Much like RDP, this is a ratio of the current number of ICA sessions compared to the total number of sessions available.

WARNING

Citrix Load Balancing does not take RDP connections into account when figuring load balancing based on user load or sessions. To include RDP connections into the equation, things such as processor usage or memory load should be considered.

Published Application Manager (PAM)   The PAM is the tool responsible for managing published applications and their configuration. PAM is used to manage Server Farms, set load-balancing features for published applications, and create the ICA and HTML template files to publish applications to a Web page. Most of the features of PAM use a wizard interface to simplify the application publishing process.

Shadow Taskbar   This tool allows control over the shadowing features of the ICA client. A simple taskbar allows the user to create shadow sessions with one or more ICA sessions and manage the sessions they have established.

Citrix and the Internet

Back when we were looking at remote control versus remote node computing, we talked about how remote node computing was expanding across the Internet. Organizations are allowing home users to establish a connection across the Internet to access resources from their home PC. There are problems inherent to this model, the most pressing of which is the security risk of allowing these remote users access to internal assets. These security holes can lead to hacker attacks if not properly managed.

Citrix has tried to address this problem by making applications more Web-friendly through application publishing. Since applications can be embedded or launched in a seamless window from a Web page link, administrators can use their Web servers to grant WAN access to these remote users. However, this still doesn't directly address the security issues. SecureICA can be used to encrypt the traffic between the client and server, but the holes that must exist in the corporate firewall to allow the connection to take place will still be vulnerable.

To counteract this, Citrix has gone one step further and introduced NFuse. This add-on for Citrix servers is a two-part system that makes a Web version of Program Neighborhood available as a dynamically generated Web page. The front end sits on the Web server and authenticates users against an NT Domain database. Once the user's credentials are established, a MetaFrame server that has the back end of NFuse installed provides the user's applications sets in a Web format. NFuse can use SSL for communication security, which helps to secure the connections from outside interference. Figure 1.16 shows how a home user would connect across the Internet to a MetaFrame server behind a firewall.

NFuse is not required to create an Internet connection to a MetaFrame server; it is merely one of the easiest and most secure methods. A direct connection can be established if your firewall administrators are willing to open the appropriate ports for users to establish the connection through.

Often, this possesses too great a security risk and most administrators will be unwilling to take it.

Figure 1.16 Citrix across the Internet.

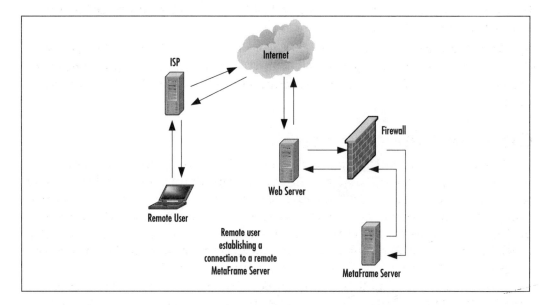

Choosing Terminal Services or MetaFrame

The choice between using just Terminal Services and adding MetaFrame to your Windows 2000 server can be a difficult one. A careful analysis of your needs and future goals needs to be done before a decision can be made either way. Table 1.6 lists some of the key features of thin-client computing and which package utilizes those features.

Table 1.6 Key Features of Windows 2000 Terminal Services and Citrix MetaFrame

Feature	Terminal Services	MetaFrame
Local Printer autocreation on login	Yes	Yes
Clipboard synchronization between client and server	Yes	Yes
Local drive mapping	No	Yes
Session shadowing	Yes (one-to-one only)	Yes, one-to-one, one-to-many,

Continued

Table 1.6 Continued

Feature	Terminal Services	MetaFrame
		many-to-one
Load balancing	Yes, but not RDP aware	Yes, fully integrated into ICA
40-, 56-, and 128-bit encryption	Yes	Yes, but only with SecureICA or Feature Release 1
Application publishing	No	Yes
Direct dialup	No	Yes
ALE for Web publishing	No	Yes
Wide client availability	Yes, with third party products	Yes
Client video depth of up to 24-bit color	No	Yes

Bottom Line Value of Using Thin-Client Technology

One of the chief benefits of thin-client technology is the improved total cost of ownership (TCO) that it provides. TCO can be pretty easily figured for an organization when you divide the costs into hard costs, such as hardware and software prices, and soft costs, such as maintenance and upkeep. Soft costs are most commonly associated with support issues such as user training and problem solving. Of the two, soft costs are the harder to calculate. The goal of TCO is to achieve the maximum return on investment (ROI) with the minimal cost involvement.

Calculating Hard Costs

To calculate the hard costs, you must first determine the hardware and software that will be used in a project and then total that number. In a thin-client project, this means looking at the existing hardware and determining if it can still meet your needs as a client for the new server. For instance, old 386 and 386 machines running Windows for Workgroups 3.11 can still be utilized as 16-bit clients with Terminal Services and MetaFrame. UNIX workstations that have been sitting in the closet could function as ICA clients for MetaFrame. All of these are factors to be considered when calculating hard costs.

The easiest way to decide whether Terminal Services or MetaFrame is a cost-effective solution is to look at a comparison between a traditional desktop upgrade and a MetaFrame solution. In Table 1.7, an example is given where a company with 500 employees wants to present all users with a Windows 2000 desktop. Of the existing computers, 350 are capable of running Windows 2000 Professional and the other 150 would have to be upgraded. Additionally, the network managers determine it would cost $110,000 for the new software and licenses that would be required to bring all 500 users up to Windows 2000 Professional. The number of concurrent users would likely be somewhere around 300.

Table 1.7 Cost Analyses

Desktop upgrade		Thin-client solution	
150 PCs at $1400	$210,000	3 servers (125 users each) at $30,000	$90,000
Software for 500 users	$110,000	Software for each server	$45,000
Total	**$330,000**	**Total**	**$135,000**

If the above numbers were accurate, it would make a lot of sense for this company to consider moving to a thin-client solution rather than upgrading each PC individually. The total cost savings in hard costs would be $195,000. But what if all the existing PCs were already capable of running Windows 2000 Professional? In that case, it would be more cost effective merely to purchase the new software licenses and upgrade the PCs directly. Unfortunately, hard costs alone do not determine which path is better. Soft costs have to be considered as well.

Calculating Soft Costs

Soft costs are much more difficult to quantify than hard costs. Soft costs cover things like user training, troubleshooting and support, and future project considerations. Soft costs are typically the long-term support costs that end up being the most expensive piece of a project. Some considerations to look at when trying to determine soft costs would include:

- **Frequencies of upgrades** How often will the software packages need to be upgraded? How long will the current system specifications be supported for new software versions?

- **Types of users** Will users be frequently connecting from remote locations to central servers? If so, what type of connection speeds will they have?

- **User training** Will users require training on the new packages? How many users will need to be trained and what kind of training will new users need to receive?

- **Hardware maintenance costs** What will you spend to maintain the hardware you have and the new hardware you will need?

The easiest soft cost to consider when planning a thin-client implementation is hardware maintenance. Terminal Services and MetaFrame both allow the reuse of existing older hardware to serve as client machines for users. Because of that support, users will less often require a desktop replacement. Since application processing and data storage will occur almost exclusively at the server level, the workstation will be under less of a load. In addition, the time to install a new workstation is drastically reduced. An administrator can easily take an older machine and install the appropriate client and have the user back up and working far faster than if they had to completely reinstall all the local applications of a typical worker.

Because Terminal Services and MetaFrame provide a consistent desktop to the end user, it is possible for them to switch workstations if the need should arise and not require any retraining. All of their shortcuts, programs, and files will be right where they were on the old workstation. This is key for faster support, and also for users whose jobs include roaming around the facilities to different locations. A user is no longer tied to a specific workstation to maintain their common computing environment.

NOTE

Because of this feature, users who utilize Terminal Services or MetaFrame exclusively should be encouraged to store their files on network drives rather than local ones. This will provide constant availability of their files regardless of the state of their individual PC or their current workstation location.

The other types of soft costs can be harder to quantify and will require some analysis, both of your current computing environment and the projected future requirements of your users. You need to be realistic about those expectations. How often have you had to upgrade software programs in the past? Are your current systems top-of-the-line, or are they already at the bare edge of the requirements for your current packages? How are your users? Do they require a lot of hand-holding, or are they able to pick up new technology without many problems? All of these factors need to be considered when trying to choose between a thin-client and fat-client solution.

In the end, seeing the benefits of one model over the other can be done with a little work on your part. Inevitably, there will be objections to whichever solution you decide to implement. Careful planning and a good presentation of the pros and cons will go a long way towards quieting those thin-client doubters. In many situations, thin-client computing will be the best and easiest solution to implement.

Summary

We've covered a lot of ground in this chapter. From the dawn of mainframe computing through the thin-client models of today, there have been numerous changes to the world of computing and the requirements of users. Windows 2000 Terminal Services and Citrix MetaFrame both combine a melding of the mainframe computing, distributed computing, remote control, and remote node models that have dominated the network design world.

Thin-client computing has seen a real boom in recent years as administrators search for solutions that centralize both the support and maintenance issues involved in a computer network. The benefits of thin-client computing can be considerable in the right environment. Users work from a centralized server, much like the old mainframe model. Client computer requirements for thin clients are typically far less than those of their fat client counterparts.

Windows 2000 Terminal Services is a thin-client solution developed by Microsoft and based on their proprietary RDP 5.0 protocol. Using the RDP client, remote computers can access a centralized Windows 2000 server system and receive a virtual Windows 2000 desktop. The client is available for older hardware and operating systems, which allows administrators to save on hardware costs and upgrade frequency. Terminal Services requires separate client licensing than the base Windows 2000 server license, and we covered the various license types available for Terminal Services users.

Terminal Services can be an appropriate solution for some thin-client environments. If you need to present your users with a standardized Windows 2000 desktop on various client platforms, then Terminal Services may be enough to handle your requirements. However, it does have some limitations. Microsoft only includes clients for 16- and 32-bit Windows clients. Other operating system platforms require a third-party solution.

Terminal Services also does not offer application publishing or Web integration. And finally, Network Load Balancing for Windows 2000 is extremely difficult to integrate with Terminal Services and limits the maximum cluster size to 32 Windows 2000 servers.

Citrix MetaFrame may be the more appropriate solution if Terminal Services cannot meet your requirements. MetaFrame provides a much wider client software base for its ICA protocol, and has improved capabilities for load balancing and enterprise scalability. MetaFrame also includes full Web integration through its ALE feature of ICA, and has tools to manage published applications and create Citrix Server Farms. All of this goes a long way towards providing a centralized, enterprise-wide thin-client solution.

Administrators need to carefully consider the value of thin-client computing and how it fits into their existing network model. User access requirements, planned upgrades, and current hardware and software platforms are all factors in deciding whether to implement a thin-client solution. The total cost of ownership numbers for thin-client computing can be calculated using some patience and good analysis of your current and future needs. The thin-client model may not be the best fit for every situation, but in many cases it will provide the best total return on investment.

We've just skimmed the surface of Windows 2000 Terminal Services and Citrix MetaFrame in this chapter. The rest of this book will give much more in-depth information about each of the features we've mentioned, as well as many others that we haven't. Hopefully you've got a good sense of where thin-client computing has come from and where it could be taking your network.

FAQs

Q: I updated one of my member servers to a new Citrix service pack, and now it is taking over the master browser duties from my dedicated master browser. Why?

A: The updated server has a newer version of the ICA Browser Service, and will always win the browser election because of it. Upgrade your master browser with the same service pack.

Q: I have users that need to use Macintosh and UNIX workstations to connect to my server. Can I just use Terminal Services?

A: Yes, but you will need to get a third-party RDP client to connect. Microsoft's RDP client is limited to 16- and 32-bit Windows operating systems only.

Q: Where can I find good thin-client resources on the Web?

A: There are some very good thin-client sites. Places like www.thethin.net, www.worldofasp.com, and www.egroups.com/groups/thin all provide excellent resources. In addition, Microsoft (www.microsoft.com/ windows2000) and Citrix (www.citrix.com) both provide extensive documentation on their Web sites.

Q: I am planning an upgrade of my network environment and need to decide between using just Windows 2000 Terminal Services and installing Citrix MetaFrame. I will need an enterprise-wide solution that allows me to provide applications via Web pages to remote users. Which application package or packages do I need?

A: Unfortunately, Windows 2000 Terminal Services does not provide Web integration or application publishing. For this reason, you will need to go with Citrix MetaFrame on top of your Terminal Services environment.

Q: I need to provide my users access to graphical packages that use high-color graphics and designs. Can I use Terminal Services or MetaFrame?

A: At this point, both MetaFrame and Terminal Services are limited to a maximum of 256 colors to a client session. That number may soon change.

Chapter 2

Routing and Remote Access Services for Windows 2000

Solutions in this chapter:

- Designing and Placing RAS Servers on the Network

- Remote Access Protocols

- Installing the Windows 2000 RAS Service

- RAS Upgrade Considerations

Introduction

Remote access servers are utilized by remote users who need access to data and applications that reside on a corporate server. Remote terminals for mainframe computers was one of the earliest methods of connecting and using network applications, but users soon demanded access to the PCs connected to the network. Thus was born remote control.

Remote control of networked computers soon required that dedicated PCs be ready to accept remote control requests from any number of end-users at any time. It wasn't unusual for a company to have racks and racks of PCs and modems just waiting for a dial-up user to connect. Remote access grew out of the same need as remote control, but was more cost effective since only a modem was needed for each remote user (instead of another PC). The modem acted much like a network interface card (NIC). Remote access grew to incorporate the use of the Internet and virtual private networking (VPN) technologies.

Thin-client technology combines the best of both remote node and remote control. To maximize connectivity and functionality, a combination of remote access and remote control are necessary. Application performance can be optimized for older hardware, and even delivered to noncompliant client workstations.

Designing and Placing RAS Servers on the Network

The implementation of remote access on a Windows 2000 network can be very complex depending on your specific needs and requirements. Often, a simple Remote Access Services (RAS) solution will fulfill the requirements of a small organization. As the organization's size and remote user base grows, much more consideration needs to be paid to the overall architecture of the RAS environment, and the services it is designed to provide. In this section, we will focus on the design and implementation of RAS servers in your environment and the methods for projecting both your current and future needs.

Sizing the Servers

The first item to consider when discussing a RAS solution is the role it is being designed to fulfill. Careful analysis of your remote computing needs is required to make sure that you have taken all of the factors into account. Are your users going to work online or offline? Will they require applications to be served to them? Are they going to be moving large amounts of data? Will your RAS server need to provide services to both local and remote clients? Will there be any VPN technology involved? And what size will your user base be? These are all crucial in determining what hardware specifications will be required to meet the role the RAS servers will be expected to fill.

Another key factor is the type of RAS services you will be providing. Clients that will dial directly into a network using Dial-Up Networking (DUN) will require different hardware and software than those utilizing a VPN solution. Windows 2000 RAS offers point-to-point, point-to-local area network (LAN), LAN-to-LAN, and LAN-to-wide area network (WAN) connections. Obviously, without knowing the type of service you are looking to provide, it will be difficult to know how you should scale your environment. That is why all of these factors must be taken in to account when you are designing your RAS solution.

RAM

Random access memory (RAM) is perhaps the most crucial piece of system hardware that is used not only by RAS, but also by the system as a whole. Without sufficient RAM, the entire RAS process can become bogged down in slow-moving system paging. Paging is the process whereby information is transferred from volatile, high-speed storage like RAM to slower, nonvolatile memory on a hard disk. The problem with system paging is that it significantly slows the data retrieval process. If the operating system is forced to page out remote access information to the hard drive because of insufficient storage space in the RAM, it destroys the performance gains RAM can provide. For this reason, it is *strongly* recommended that RAM be your number one consideration when pricing a system.

It's a tried but true saying—you really can never have too much RAM. A minimum of 128 MB is recommended, but much more may be needed depending on the total number of users and other functions the RAS server will perform. Remember, we're not just talking about RAM for remote access. You'll need a sufficient amount for your operating system, for any network routing the server performs, and for any other functions or roles it fulfills. Many organizations use the RAS server as a file and print server as well. This can work, as long as it is realized that inadequate hardware will hurt both roles the server is going to perform. For instance, using your RAS server as a database server would be high on the list of things *not* to do. The amount of RAM a database server typically eats would cripple the RAS performance.

RAM is relatively inexpensive in the grand scheme of computer hardware and can often be a solution to many problems with slow remote access. Faster is always better, and any RAM will be faster than hard drive access. Considering the impact RAM has on your overall system performance, carefully monitoring your memory usage can save you some trouble in the future.

TIP

Use Performance Monitor to keep track of Page Faults/second. If this number is more than a handful, you may need to think about upgrading your RAM. Also pay attention to Available Bytes. If this number is getting low, it's another key indicator that your RAS server is underscaled. Page Faults/second can be found in the Memory object of Performance Monitor.

Processors

Processor power is another key hardware consideration, but not one that is typically a critical component. Dedicated RAS servers use processor power mostly for operating system execution and packet routing. For this reason, having a cutting-edge processor is not essential for the RAS server design. Most entry-level servers will function quite well in a RAS server role. A good processor speed would be a Pentium III (PIII) 450 MHz or higher, although it can function with much less. Keep Microsoft's Hardware Compatibility List (HCL) in mind when choosing server hardware.

Of course, if you are using your RAS server for other applications, then the processor requirements will be much more important. RAS servers that run Terminal Services for instance, will require quite a bit more processing power. And for RAS servers that are mission critical, it might be a good idea to invest in a dual-processor system to provide some fault tolerance. Remember, processor power is always a good thing, but by itself it won't make a lot of difference in a RAS environment. Symmetrical Multiprocessing (SMP) is seldom required for a simple RAS machine.

Storage

Storage considerations can be a tricky area when remote access is concerned. Often, storage is the furthest element from anyone's mind when they are putting together a RAS server. Careful choices with your storage options can have a big impact on the speed of your RAS service, and make the difference between a successful and unsuccessful deployment. Storage on a dedicated RAS server needs to be sufficient to meet your needs for storing user profiles, connection data, and general operating system software.

The storage solution you choose should be fast and reliable, because it will make a difference in your overall connection speeds. Slow disk speeds or a poor throughput speed can diminish the performance gains that faster RAM can provide. Inevitably, there will have to be some transfer between the disks and the RAM. The faster that transfer rate, the better your performance. Let's look at a few different transfer technologies.

RAID

Redundant Array of Independent Disks (RAID) is a disk subsystem often used to provide increased fault tolerance and data transfer speeds. Speed is improved because RAID systems stripe the data over multiple disks, which means that bytes or groups of bytes are written across each disk in the set. This means several disks can perform read/write operations simultaneously. Fault tolerance is achieved through the use of either disk mirroring, where two disks contain an exact copy of each other, or parity checking, where a bit from disk 1 is combined with a bit from disk 2 using a Boolean XOR (a phrase that means Exclusive in programming lingo; a logic operation that is true so long as any of the inputs is true) string, and the result is stored on disk 3. If a disk should fail using either method, the information is either duplicated or can be reconstructed.

There are two flavors of RAID controllers. Hardware RAID relies on special functionality built into the hard disk control. This is usually done with server-class machines, and can come in all shapes and sizes. Some devices allow administrators to hot-swap a failed device, plugging the new drive in without having to take the server down. The information is then automatically rebuilt on the new drive. Hardware RAID is most commonly done with Small Computer System Interface (SCSI) drives, because they usually spin much faster and provide better throughput than their Integrated Drive Electronics (IDE) counterparts. The second type of RAID is a software-controlled solution. This is typically much slower than a hardware RAID controller, and usually is used when a hardware RAID solution cannot be afforded. Software RAID erases many of the performance gains that hardware RAID provides, and is best used only when fault tolerance is a must and software RAID is the only way to achieve it.

Fibre Channel

Fibre Channel is a special transmission technology that is designed to provide extremely fast communications between storage and communications networks. With Fibre Channel, hosts can communicate with a storage system (via SCSI) and each other (over Internet Protocol, or IP) using the same network. Despite its name, Fibre Channel is designed to work over fibre, coaxial, or twisted-pair cabling. Each port with Fibre Channel uses two cables to transmit and receive data. A transmitter (TX) is connected to a receiver (RX) at the other end. The connection can be connection-oriented or connectionless using switched technology. In connection-oriented Fibre Channel, an arbitrary loop can contain 127 nodes. Nodes can be either a storage system or another computer. The biggest use of Fibre Channel technology is in Storage Area Networks (SANs), which we will discuss next. Figure 2.1 shows an example of Fibre Channel in both switched and loop environments.

Figure 2.1 Fibre Channel environments.

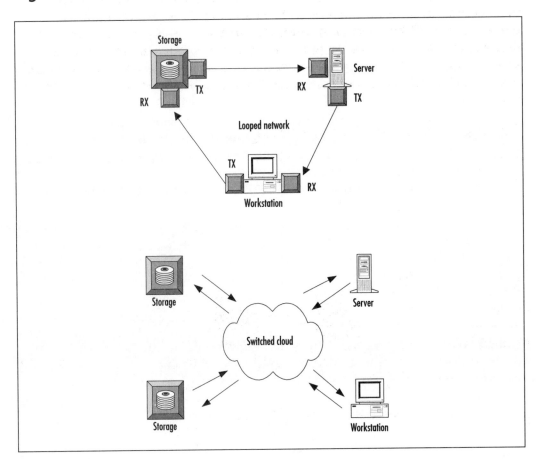

Storage Area Networks (SANs)

With the increased capabilities of transmission technology, the demand for rapid retrieval of data from centrally located and dispersed data storage systems has become much more important. SANs typically utilize Fibre Channel technology to provide transmission capabilities up to 4.25 Gbps each way. A centralized storage system is one in which a large storage device, typically a RAID cabinet with redundant drives and power arrays, is used by many separate hosts. It provides file redundancy, ease of management, and rapid retrieval of data over the Fibre Channel links. Centralized systems are also frequently used in server clustering to provide fault-tolerant solutions for critical applications.

Because Fibre Channel provides extremely fast communications capabilities, SAN nodes can be located centrally, campus-wide, or even over a metropolitan area. With current technology, the Fibre Network can be extended over 20 kilometers. In addition, using a decentralized approach allows nodes to be connected to many different SANs. This means that multiple storage devices can be provided to a network, extending the capabilities of the individual nodes. Figure 2.2 shows a distributed SAN environment.

Figure 2.2 Distributed SAN environment.

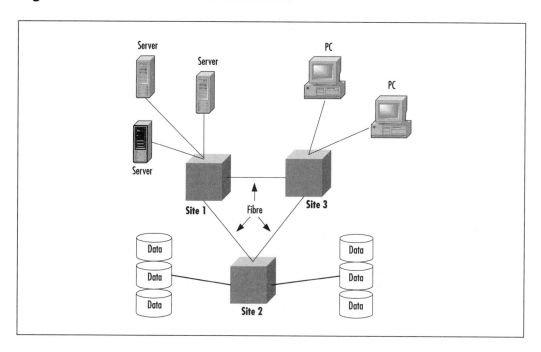

Network Interfaces

Network Interface Cards (NICs) are the hardware used by the RAS server to communicate with the rest of the network. NICs can communicate over several different wiring solutions, depending on design. Common NICs are 10-Megabit Ethernet, 100-Megabit Ethernet, or Token Ring (4 or 16 Megabit). The communications speed of the NIC has no direct impact on RAS performance, but it does affect the connection with the rest of the network. For a self-contained RAS server that hosts its own applications and data, this is meaningless. Few RAS servers are used in such a configuration, however. Most often, remote users will need access to other network resources. At that point, the speed of the NIC becomes an issue.

Choosing a NIC is entirely dependent on the type of network infrastructure already in place. If you are running 10-Megabit switched Ethernet, then a 10/100-Megabit Ethernet card will do you little good beyond the initial 10-Megabit Ethernet capability. In a 100-Megabit Ethernet network, that same card will (theoretically) provide you with 10 times the communication speeds. The NIC will always be based on the type of infrastructure you already have or plan on having.

Another consideration when choosing a NIC is whether to make a machine multihomed or not. A machine is multihomed when it contains two or more NICs that each connects to a network segment. These can be separate segments, or the same segment in the case of multihoming a machine for redundancy or speed issues. Multihomed machines can act as routers if an actual router is not available, but this will eat up the Central Processor Unit (CPU) to provide the routing service. Multihoming a RAS server should generally be restricted to machines that require redundant network access. Some NICs even contain dual network ports on the same card and allow for failover if the first port should go dead.

Clusters

Clustering servers is another excellent way to provide a fault-tolerant RAS solution. In a server cluster, machines are linked together (often by Fibre Channel, which we discussed earlier) to provide constant availability of critical applications and services. If one member of the cluster should fail, others will continue to provide the service for users with no discernable difference. Clusters can typically be load balanced so as to provide good performance between them. Load balancing is dependent upon the type of operating system you are using. With Windows 2000, load-balancing services are somewhat limited in the ways they can balance network load among a cluster. Typically, load in Windows 2000 will be based on the total number of users.

Another important consideration for Windows 2000 clustering is cost. The technology to implement a clustered solution can be expensive, and should be considered only when it is absolutely critical that the service be constantly available. It would be far cheaper to merely provide a rollover service where unanswered or busy lines would roll to another server. Still, clustering can be necessary and even cost effective when the remote user base is large enough to warrant it.

Modems

Choosing modems to fit your needs is the single most critical decision in designing a remote access solution. Before, we discussed the various roles that you might want your server to fulfill. Without the proper modem hardware, your RAS server is just a box in the corner that no one is using. There are many different modem solutions out there, and picking one can really be a challenge. First, you have to consider both the total number of users and the total number of simultaneous users you will have. If this is a RAS solution for two users, then plugging a couple of PCI modem cards into the server will more than fit your needs. But what about those sites that need to provide thousands of available connections? Those need much more specialized hardware that we'll discuss in this section.

There are some basic choices when trying to decide on a modem standard for your environment. First, what hardware do you feel comfortable with? There are plenty of brand name manufacturers for modems (although many modems that are packaged under different names are made by the same company), and picking between them can be a bit difficult. One way to choose is to look at the standards you want to implement. Will all your remote clients have the same modem type to dial in with? Then you might want to consider using the same manufacturer for your RAS solution. Do you need to support various modem protocols? Looking for a manufacturer with a good reputation for inner-connectivity is important.

The key in today's modem technology is 56Kbps connections (56 Kbps stands for 56,000 kilobytes, or 5.6 Kbps per second). This is the maximum connect speed that a traditional dial-up method could support. There were two main standards initially developed for the 56 Kbps modem, X2 and Flex. Both were very popular, and a compromise had to be reached between them. As a result, the V.90 standard was developed. This standard allowed both X2 and Flex modems to talk with each other and still negotiate the 56Kbps speed. Most modems today are 28.8, 33.6, or 56 Kbps. Cheap 56Kbps modems can be as little as 20 dollars. Obviously, you don't want your users dialing in on a cheap modem.

If you are going to provide actual modems to dial in to such as a modem bank (a group of modems stacked together to save space, that typically roll over between each other when one is busy), then be aware that for a user to achieve a 56Kbps connection, you will need to make sure the modems on your end are capable of providing 56Kbps dial-up. Two users with 56Kbps modems that dial each other will never be able to achieve better than a 33.6Kbps connection speed. 56Kbps dial-up requires special modems on the provider's end, and special lines between the provider and the telephone company. Otherwise, a 56Kbps connection will not be initiated.

NOTE

You will never, ever achieve a real 56Kbps connection speed with dial-up modems. Under U.S. FCC regulations, the maximum transmission rate for standard U.S. telephone lines is 53Kbps. Regardless of what your connection speed says it is, you will never really achieve more than 53Kbps transfer.

Modem pools require special connections to the RAS server to allow it to provide access via all the modems. Sometimes this is done through software management of the ports involved. Other times there is a serial solution provided. Regardless, the modem pool should not be located too far from the actual RAS server or network latency can develop.

Serial Cards

Obviously, you can only plug so many modem cards into a machine. There has to be some way of providing hundreds, or even thousands, of connections to a single server. In fact, there are several hardware solutions that will fulfill these needs. The first method is to use a dumb serial card solution. Unintelligent (i.e., "dumb") boards utilize the CPU to handle all processing requirements when sending data through the serial interface. This means that every port on the card will interrupt the CPU every time it has data to send or receive. This can really cut down on the capabilities of your RAS server, but is much more cost effective when the number of users can be small enough to not bog down the server.

The second option is to use an intelligent serial solution. Intelligent boards are capable of performing most of the serial data processing independent of the CPU. Intelligent boards can contain multiple CPUs to support the large number of serial ports they can contain. The system CPU still must be used when data is being transferred from the serial port to the system or when processing that information. Intelligent boards greatly expand the limit of serial ports that can be used by a RAS server. Without an intelligent board solution, a RAS server could easily be pegged at 100 percent usage by as few as 20 users. Unfortunately, without trial and error there is no sure-fire method to determine which serial solution you should use. You could be pegging your processor with 50 users and a dumb board, only to buy a bigger server and still peg the processor. Either use trial and error to determine your load levels, or just invest from the top in an intelligent solution.

Serial Port Hardware

Serial card solutions, whether intelligent or dumb, all have a general hardware scheme. A PCI or ISA card plugs into the RAS server, and generally has a large interface port to which a group of cables called an *octopus* or *fan* is connected. Octopus cables are many 9-pin or 25-pin cables that end in a single interface that plugs into the back of the serial card. This allows you to provide far more connections than would be able to exist on the back of a single card. At a certain point, this solution becomes unwieldy because of the large number of cables involved. When you're talking about 64 serial cables, that's a lot of weight to be put on the back of a server. At that point, you need to consider a serial port concentrator.

A concentrator runs a proprietary cable from the back of the serial card to an external device that can set a certain distance from the actual server. Concentrators can be daisy-chained with each other, so that more ports can be provided. Daisy-chaining the concentrators does contribute to the total distance, however, and should be monitored carefully. Most concentrators have a limit as to the total distance they can be from the server. Traditional concentrators come in 16-port increments. Very often, concentrators are vendor-specific and require the use of special serial cables. There are a wide variety of concentrators available, each of which can provide a different kind of service depending on the services you wish to provide. For instance, some ports can be high-speed connections while others can provide standard service.

High-Speed Connections

More and more users are switching to high-speed connections in today's computing world. These connections can be everything from Integrated Services Digital Network (ISDN) to Asymmetric Digital Subscriber Line (ADSL) and cable modems. ISDN users can connect with either true 64Kbps or 128Kbps connections, ADSL connections can go up to 9 Mbps, and cable modems are capable of 2Mbps connections. All of these require special hardware and wiring at the user's end. Deciding whether to allow these types of connections can be tricky. ISDN users can dial in directly to your network (provided you are capable of receiving the ISDN call), but cable and ADSL users would have to connect through the external network.

This means that some type of hole would have to be opened in your firewall, and might require a VPN connection for security. We'll talk about VPNs and how they work a little later in this chapter. All of this, plus the fact that these high-speed users will be eating up your bandwidth, leads to more costs for the network manager.

ISDN solutions are very popular for remote access today. An ISDN connection consists of an ISDN line and Terminal Adapter (TA) at the client end, and some type of connection on the server side such as a Primary Rate Interface (PRI) or separate ISDN lines to the ISDN card or router. ISDN runs over a special ISDN line called a Basic Rate Interface (BRI), which provides two B channels and one D channel. The B channels are typically 64 Kbps (although some phone lines only support 56 Kbps) and can be used for either voice or data. This means that a user can talk over one channel and still maintain a 64Kbps connection on the other. When they're done with their conversation, the second B channel can be automatically merged to provide 128Kbps speeds. The D channel is used for communications with the phone company. The Terminal Adapter and phone company are always talking back and forth on the D channel, regardless of whether you are using any of the B channels.

Many large organizations use PRIs to provide ISDN connections to their users. In North America, an ISDN PRI is capable of providing 23 B channels and one D channel. This means that 23 users can connect to the ISDN device using one of their B channels, or that 12 could connect using both B channels. Connections for users can typically be limited to a single B channel to provide access to more users simultaneously. ISDN PRIs are typically carried over a T1 line, which at 1.44 Mbps provides the necessary capacity for their 24 channels. Most of the control over the PRI and ISDN lines is done through the ISDN card or router management software you choose to employ.

Placing the RAS Servers on the Internetwork

Now that you have all this great hardware, where do you put it? Some people make the mistake of thinking that you can just tuck your RAS server off in the corner of your network, and there it will hum away for years to come. In fact, if you don't carefully consider where you're putting that RAS server, you could completely congest a network segment, and thus further limit your dial-up users. They are already stuck at a maximum 56Kbps connection. Putting them on a congested segment will further slow their transfer rates. When you consider the RAS placement, you need to keep bandwidth considerations first and foremost in your mind.

It's a simple equation—more bandwidth equals more capacity for productivity (Notice that I didn't actually say *more productivity*. That depends on the user!). If your remote user has to wait five minutes to download the updated file from the RAS server, that's five minutes lost to you. What if a portion of that five minutes was not caused by the dial-up connection, but was instead caused by a poor choice of NICs? The fault then is on you as the network manager. When looking at the RAS server placement, identify what resources your users are most often going to be connecting to. Is there a central file server that they will access regularly? Do they require access to certain print devices, or maybe even CD servers? Knowing what devices they will need to access can help you identify where the bottlenecks in any plan will be.

Take Figure 2.3 for example. In this figure, the Acme Corporation has decided to implement a RAS solution for 30 users. They have decided to locate the RAS server near the network administrator's desk so that he or she can keep a close eye on it. Their typical user will need to access the central file share, as well as a plotter device also located centrally. Notice where the RAS server has been placed in relation to the commonly accessed devices.

Figure 2.3 RAS server placement.

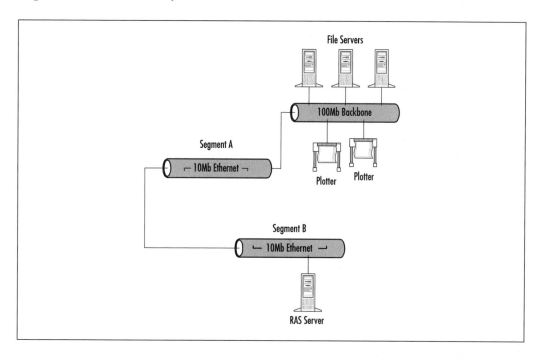

For a user dialing in over the RAS server to connect to the backbone and the network devices located there, they must transverse Segment A (10Mb networks) to reach the backbone (100Mb). This means that any devices on segments A and B will be using some of the available 10Mb, and the RAS users will be limited to whatever they can get. If there are too many other devices on those segments, the RAS performance could drop significantly. You might want to consider placing the RAS server on segment A instead, or even better, on its own dedicated segment. This will allow the remote users to have the full benefit of the available bandwidth. Figure 2.4 shows this kind of RAS placement.

Figure 2.4 Improved RAS placement.

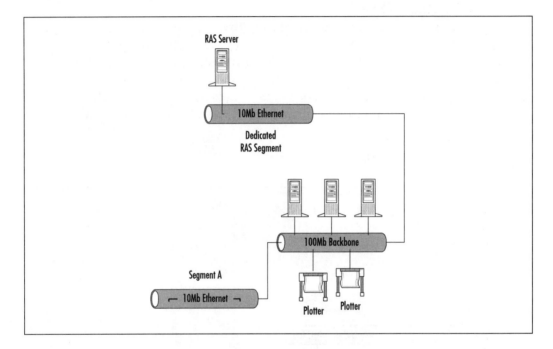

The placement in Figure 2.4 eliminates the congestion of other segments, and provides the full 10Mb of bandwidth to the RAS users. If the resources were not located on the corporate backbone, or not all located centrally, you will need to do some careful figuring to make sure that your bandwidth requirements will be met across all of the segments that remote users will need to access. Good analysis, planning, and an in-depth knowledge of where your network stands and where it might be going will save you and your users time in the long run.

Remote Access Protocols

Remote access today just seems to get more and more complicated. There are hundreds of different modems, at least five flavors of the major operating system (Win95, Win98, NT 4.0, Windows 2000, and now Windows

Millennium, also known as WindowsME), and a multitude of different ways to connect to a remote network. With all of these choices, sorting out what your needs are can be a difficult task. Once you have identified the type(s) of service you would like to provide, you have to figure out how you're going to do that. We've already discussed the hardware considerations and placement. Now you need to look at the various software choices you are going to have to make. The first and most important is the protocol type you will be using.

Dial-up Clients

Dial-up clients are remote users who access the network through a traditional RAS solution. Typically, this means they dial in directly to the local network through a RAS server. Dial-up clients are limited to the 56Kbps connection speeds we discussed before, and require no special hardware or software beyond the dialer and modem. There are two protocols that dial-up supports, Point-to-Point Protocol (PPP) and Serial Line Internet Protocol (SLIP).

PPP and SLIP

PPP and SLIP are the two main dial-up protocols in use today. SLIP is the older of the two protocols. SLIP allows a remote user to make a serial link and transmit IP packets over it. SLIP was once very prevalent as a protocol, but has since been replaced in most networks with PPP because it cannot provide the same security levels that PPP can. SLIP is seen today mostly in older, unsecured network environments where user security is not a consideration.

PPP has become the protocol of choice for remote access providers. Developed in 1991 by the Internet Engineering Task Force, PPP allows you to make a connection over any Public Switched Telephone Network (PSTN) or high-speed connection. PPP does this by encapsulating other protocols in special network control packets. Two examples of this are IP over PPP and Internet Package eXchange over PPP. PPP can also replace the network adapter driver. This means that the user is treated as a node on the network. It also means that PPP can hang up and redial poor connections automatically. PPP supports password authentication of users through both the Password Authentication Protocol (PAP) and Challenge Handshake Authentication Protocol (CHAP) methods.

CHAP and PAP

In PAP authentication, the server has a list of usernames and passwords stored that it compares with the username and password sent by the remote user. This information is not encrypted in any way, and is considered vulnerable. PAP is the most basic authentication protocol available to RAS administrators, and should only be used when the need for password security is low.

CHAP, on the other hand, fully encrypts the username and password by getting a key from the remote server that is used for both the encryption and decryption. CHAP encryption is dynamic, because a user will get a different key each time they connect. This secures the sensitive exchange, and can keep your network secure from attempts to snatch a password. Most RAS networks use a combination of PPP and CHAP for dialup and authentication.

VPN Clients

VPNs are relatively new to the remote access world. The purpose of a VPN is to allow users to make a secure connection to the internal network from outside the network perimeter, such as through their own personal Internet service provider (ISP). With the right software, network administrators can provide this capability to users to defray both telephone costs and hardware requirements. The primary benefit of a VPN connection is that as long as the client software supports it, users can connect to the internal network from *any* external network connection. This means that high-speed devices such as cable modems and ADSL can make the connection to the internal network and still function at their full capacity. This can be a real boon for people who consistently work from home.

There are basically two types of VPNs. The first VPN solution is hardware-based that you manage internally. Usually there is a server-side software package and a client-side software piece that are used to establish the secure connection. Two common solutions are Altiga (owned by Cisco) and RedCreek. The second type of solution is a managed VPN. In this scenario, a major ISP company such as CompuServe or AT&T allows users to dial in to a local Point of Presence (POP) and then establish the secure connection to your internal network. The benefit of this method is that most of the VPN management is handled by the contracted company. The disadvantage is that these solutions are often limited to dialup only, which eliminates one of the major benefits of VPN technology.

VPNs work by using a variety of different secure packet technologies. The purpose of the VPN is to create a secure "tunnel" between the remote computer and the internal network. The tunnel passes the encoded traffic back and forth through the insecure world of the Internet. Using the secure tunnel ensures that communications are as secure between the local and remote network as they would be if the remote network was located locally. This means that two corporate sites can also use a VPN connection to communicate with one another. It operates logically as a WAN link between the sites.

The advantages to VPNs are clear. By providing remote users with the capability to connect through the Internet, scalability is easily managed merely by increasing available bandwidth if the network becomes strained. VPNs save on telephony costs, as users will not have to dial a local modem pool. Instead, they make whatever network connection they typically make (high-speed or dial-up) and then use a client software piece to form the secure tunnel. Additionally, VPNs can give access to network resources that an administrator would never think of otherwise exposing to an outside connection. Security is the key behind VPNs.

When considering a VPN solution, there are several requirements that you need to be able to provide. These include things like:

- **Support for multiple protocols** Any solution you choose must be able to handle the protocols commonly used on the public network (i.e., IP, IPX, and so on).

- **Authentication mechanism** There must be a way to verify each user and restrict access to those users defined for VPN access. Typically, some type of auditing is also desired.

- **Encryption of data** It seems obvious, but the solution you choose must be able to encrypt the data to form the secure tunnel. Otherwise, the solution is worthless from a security point of view.

- **Management of client addresses** Solutions need to be able to assign the external client an internal address so that the network will treat it as a local node. The client's actual network address (supplied by the ISP usually) should be kept secret from the outside world to prevent certain types of hacking.

So under what circumstances would you want to provide a VPN solution? It all goes back to identifying your particular remote access needs. If you have users who constantly travel, who need access to the intranet no matter where they are or how they're dialed in, then a VPN solution might be the right choice for you. If you want those benefits without the management overhead, you can consider a managed solution. Or maybe you just need to provide both a RAS and VPN solution to enable secure communications between campuses, as well as give your users a dial-up solution. Figure 2.5 shows a combination RAS/VPN solution.

In the next section, we'll talk about the various protocols available for a VPN connection such as Point-to-Point Tunneling Protocol (PPTP) and Layer 2 Tunneling Protocol (L2TP). These protocols are the key to ensuring secure, efficient communications between remote systems.

Figure 2.5 RAS/VPN combination.

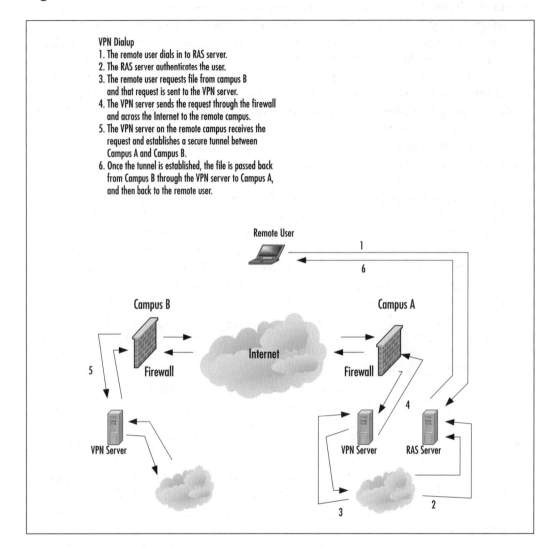

VPN Dialup
1. The remote user dials in to RAS server.
2. The RAS server authenticates the user.
3. The remote user requests file from campus B
   and that request is sent to the VPN server.
4. The VPN server sends the request through the firewall
   and across the Internet to the remote campus.
5. The VPN server on the remote campus receives the
   request and establishes a secure tunnel between
   Campus A and Campus B.
6. Once the tunnel is established, the file is passed back
   from Campus B through the VPN server to Campus A,
   and then back to the remote user.

Remote User

Campus B

Campus A

Internet

Firewall

Firewall

VPN Server

VPN Server   RAS Server

PPTP

PPTP is a Layer 2 protocol that provides security by encapsulating the PPP
frame in an IP datagram to be transmitted over an IP internetwork. PPTP
can be used in LAN-to-LAN or even WAN-to-WAN networking. The original
draft for PPTP was submitted to the Internet Engineering Task Force (IETF)
in June of 1996, and the current proposed specifications are contained in
Request For Comments (RFC) 2637 at the IETF Web site (www.ietf.org).
PPTP uses a TCP connection to perform generic tunnel maintenance, and a
generic routing encapsulation (GRE, documented in RFCs 1701 and 1702)

to encapsulate the PPP frames. The payload can be encrypted and compressed, depending on the requirements of the connection. There is an assumption by PPTP that the internetwork connection already exists.

PPTP uses the same authentication methods as traditional PPP. CHAP, Microsoft CHAP (MS-CHAP), PAP, Shiva PAP (SPAP), and Extensible Authentication Protocol (EAP) are all available over PPTP. PPTP inherits the encryption and compression values of the PPP payload. Payload encryption is done using the Microsoft Point-to-Point Encryption (MPPE). For MPPE to work in Windows 2000, the client must be using MS-CHAP or EAP as its authentication method. MPPE is a link encryption, not an end-to-end encryption solution. For an end-to-end solution, see IP Security (IPSec) later in this chapter.

PPTP can encrypt IP, IPX, or NetBIOS Extended User Interface (NetBEUI) traffic for transmission. Because it is a Layer 2 protocol, it corresponds with the data-link layer of the Open System Interconnection (OSI) standard. Tunnels are established when both endpoints agree to the tunnel and are able to negotiate the configuration variables required for communications. These typically encompass things such as address assignment, compression parameters, and encryption type. The tunnel itself is managed using a tunnel maintenance protocol. Once the tunnel is established, the PPTP protocol performs its encapsulation and the data is sent to the tunnel server. The server strips out the IP header and then forwards the payload up to the appropriate network.

PPTP, like all Layer 2 protocols, includes many useful features that it inherits from PPP. These include things like data compression, data encryption, support for token cards through the use of the Extensible Authentication Protocol, and a variety of user authentication methods. PPTP is available for all current Windows platforms, and supports client-to-server and server-to-server communications. In addition, PPTP supports routed tunnels for both demand dialing and Multilink routing.

Here is an example of a PPTP packet generation in a Windows 2000 environment:

1. The client submits an IPX datagram to the virtual interface that represents the VPN connection. This datagram is typically submitted by the client's Network Driver Interface Specification (NDIS).

2. The data is passed by NDIS to the NDISWAN, where it is encrypted or compressed (or both) and provides the PPP header. This information is then passed to the PPTP protocol driver, which encapsulates it using GRE.

3. The packet is sent to the TCP/IP protocol driver, which encapsulates the packet yet again with an IP header. The packet is then submitted to the interface that represents the local connection using NDIS.

4. NDIS sends it to NDISWAN, which provides the PPP headers and trailers.

5. The final packet is submitted to the WAN miniport driver that corresponds to the connection hardware (i.e., the asynchronous port for a modem). It is then sent across the physical medium to the PPTP server where the process is reversed.

L2TP

PPTP was (and still is) a good idea, but it has been overtaken by other security technologies. Layer 2 Tunneling Protocol (L2TP) is a combination of PPTP and Layer 2 Forwarding (L2F), a proposal put forward by Cisco. The two protocols were very similar in design and function, so the IETF mandated that they be merged into a single protocol design. That design is L2TP, and is documented in RFC 2661. L2TP utilizes the best features of both PPTP and L2F.

L2TP encapsulates frames as User Datagram Protocol (UDP) messages and sends them over an IP network. UDP messages are used for both tunnel maintenance and tunnel data. PPP payload can be encrypted or compressed, or both. L2TP differs from PPTP, however, in that it does not use MPPE to encrypt the packets. Instead, L2TP employs IPSec (which we will talk about in the next section) for the encryption process. It is possible to create an L2TP packet without using IPSec, but it is not secure and is not considered to be a VPN. This is typically only done for troubleshooting purposes to eliminate IPSec as a possible point of failure.

Like PPTP, L2TP utilizes the same authentication methods as PPP. L2TP also assumes the existence of an internetwork between the L2TP client and the L2TP server. Since L2TP tunnel maintenance is performed over the same UDP connection as the data transmission, both types of packets have the same structure to them. The standard port for L2TP on both the client and server in Windows 2000 is UDP port 1701. Windows 2000 L2TP servers will support clients that default to a different port number.

Because L2TP does not use a TCP connection, it relies on message sequencing to ensure the proper delivery order of the packets. The Next-Received and Next-Sent fields within the L2TP control message are used to manage the sequencing of the packets. Packets that are out of sequence are dropped. As you can see, L2TP is very similar to PPTP. So why would you choose PPTP or L2TP?

For starters, while PPTP requires that there is an IP internetwork, L2TP requires only a point-to-point, as the tunnel media establishes a packet-oriented connection. This means that L2TP can be used over IP, Frame Relay, X.25 circuits, or ATM connections. L2TP also allows for multiple tunnels between two end points. PPTP is limited to only a single tunnel. This allows you to provide different qualities of service by using multiple tunnels. L2TP also allows for Layer 2 tunnel authentication while PPTP does not. This benefit is ignored if you are using IPSec however, since it provides the tunnel authentication independent of Layer 2. Finally, the overhead on an L2TP packet is 2 bytes smaller because of header compression.

We've mentioned IPSec a few times already, so now would be a good time to take a look at it.

IPSec

IPSec is a Layer 3 tunneling protocol, and relies on packet technology at the network level of the OSI model. Tunneling in IPSec involves encrypting the IP payload and then encapsulating that encrypted payload in an IP header to be sent across any IP network, such as the Internet. This is an extremely beneficial method, because it allows tunneling to be established across both intranets and the Internet. Any IP-compatible system can support IPSec traffic. However, Microsoft limits support for IPSec to its 2000 platform only. If you need to use IPSec with a Windows 95 client, you will need to get a third-party IPSec client program.

Layer 3 tunneling protocols assume that all of the tunnel configuration issues have already been handled somewhere else. There is no tunnel maintenance phase for a Layer 3 protocol. IPSec functions at the bottom of the IP stack, which allows higher-level protocols to inherit its behavior. There is a security policy that controls each IPSec session. This policy is used to establish the encryption method, tunneling method, authentication types available, and the order of preference for all of them. The IPSec client and server negotiate the tunnel based on that security policy, and all traffic is encrypted using the negotiated result.

Using IPSec in Windows 2000 requires that a computer certificate be installed on both the IPSec server and client. This certificate can be obtained from the Certificates snap-in or the Windows 2000 Group Policy auto-enrollment. Once IPSec negotiation occurs, an IPSec security association (SA) is reached with the exchange of certificates. Encryption over an IPSec connection is either 56-bit Data Encryption Standard (DES) or Triple DES (3DES), where three different 56-bit keys are used for encryption and decryption. 3DES is an extremely secure encryption algorithm at this point, and should be used for particularly sensitive communications.

IPSec is designed for IP networks, which means that packets can be lost or arrive out of order. Each packet is decoded independent of the other packets. The initial encryption keys are established as part of the authentication process, and new ones are generated every five minutes or 250 megabytes of data transferred for DES and every hour or after every 2GB transferred for 3DES. This is more than enough to keep the keys from being decoded and packets decrypted in time to affect the system before it changes the key. Enough with the dry stuff though—let's see about getting RAS installed.

Installing the Windows 2000 Remote Access Service

We've introduced you to all the basic concepts of remote access and VPN technologies earlier in this chapter. Now it's time to take a look at the actual installation and configuration of those technologies in a Windows 2000 environment. If you're already familiar with RAS installation and configuration in NT 4.0, make sure you pay careful attention to where the new tools are. Microsoft has made some major changes to its interface with Windows 2000.

Dial-Up Configuration

When you talk about configuring a dial-up RAS connection, you're talking about the server configuration. This involves the system design, installation, and activation. The client portion of dial-up configuration is not covered in this book because of the multitude of potential dial-up clients that exist. See the individual operating system's documentation on how to configure that client for dial-up networking.

Configuring Your RAS Server in Windows 2000

Before you purchase any new hardware or attempt to install any RAS devices, always check the latest copy of Microsoft's HCL for Windows 2000! It sounds simple, but all too often you can end up with a solution that just won't work because of poor or missing drivers. Assuming you've checked the HCL and are ready to proceed with the installation, let's walk through installing a modem on a Windows 2000 server.

Modem Installation

First, click on the Start button, and then choose Settings/Control Panel. Double-click on the Phone and Modem Options icon. You may be prompted for information such as your area code or dialing system if this is the first time you have used this option. After you've entered all of that information, Windows 2000 will launch the Phone & Modems Options applet. Click on the Modems tab and then click the Add button to launch the Installation Wizard. Figure 2.6 shows the initial Modem Installation Wizard screen.

Figure 2.6 Modem Installation Wizard.

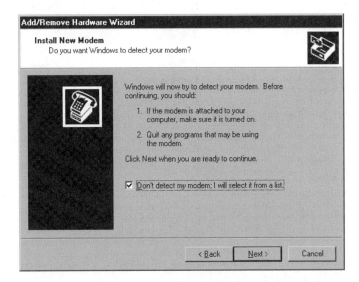

You can have Windows 2000 attempt to identify your modem for you, or define it manually from a list of supplied or manufacturer-provided drivers. If you leave the box labeled "Don't detect my modem; I will select it from a list" unchecked, Windows 2000 will attempt to identify and install the correct driver for it. If your modem is an older model (in other words, not released after Windows 2000 came out) you are probably safe in letting Windows find it for you. If the modem is more recent, you have better drivers for it, or you just want to set all of the options yourself, then check the box and click Next.

If you choose to check the box, the next window you will be presented with gives you a long list of modem manufacturers and models. Search the list to see if your modem is listed there. If it is, you can highlight it and choose Next. If it isn't, or you have more recent drivers, then click the Have Disk button. You will need to tell Windows the location of the driver files, usually either on the A:\ drive or a local hard drive. Highlight the modem driver and click Next.

If you choose to install the modem by hand, you will now be presented with a screen that asks you to choose which port you want to install the modem(s) on. You have the option of choosing any installed port (such as

COM1, COM2, and so on) that your modem is attached to. Or if you have multiple, identical modems that are all attached to multiple ports, you can select the All Ports radial button and the modem drivers will be installed for all of the different ports. Figure 2.7 shows you the port selection screen.

Figure 2.7 Port selection for manually installed modems.

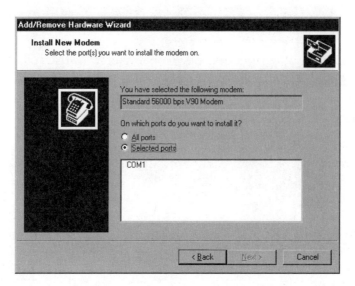

If you choose to let Windows find the modem for you, it will search all of the available ports and present you with a list of modems that it found. Choose the modem that is correct and click Next. Windows 2000 will automatically assign the port and install the correct drivers. You should receive a dialog box indicating that the modem has been successfully installed. At this point, you can use this modem to make dial-up connections. But this is your RAS server—you want them to call you!

RAS Installation

The goal of a RAS server is to accept incoming connections from remote computers and allow those users access to internal network resources. As we've discussed previously, this is typically done through a dial-in connection. Windows 2000 has built-in PPP, which allows it to act as a universal gateway to provide remote access to your users. Any device that can establish a PPP connection can connect to a Windows 2000 RAS server. This list includes Macintosh systems, hand-held devices, and even UNIX hosts. The Windows 2000 server can route connections from those devices to any device internal to your network.

The following must be available for Windows 2000 to accept calls from remote clients:

- Obviously, Windows 2000 must be configured with remote access software to accept incoming calls.

- Any client device that will attempt to connect to the server must be capable of establishing a PPP session.

- Some type of connection device (modem, ISDN line, T1 line, etc.) connected to the RAS server.

- Some kind of connection device connected to the remote client, with the capability to establish a circuit between the two.

- A user account on the Windows 2000 server for the remote user who will establish the connection.

As long as those conditions are met, you should be able to provide RAS services to your users. To start the installation of RAS on a Windows 2000 Server or Advanced Server, click on the Start button and choose Programs|Administrative Tools|Routing and Remote Access. This will take you to the Microsoft Management Console (MMC) and you should see your server listed in the left-hand pane of the MMC window. Right-click your server and select the option for Configure and Enable Routing and Remote Access. This will launch the Routing and Remote Access Server Setup Wizard. After answering yes to the first dialog box, you will be presented with a window like the one shown in Figure 2.8.

Figure 2.8 Routing and Remote Access Server Setup Wizard.

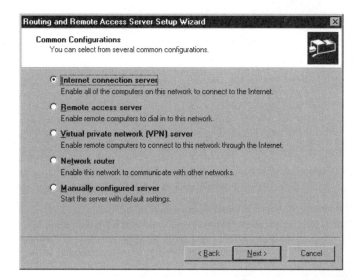

Your first choice in the installation process is to determine what role your server will play. There are several predefined choices, such as a VPN server, RAS server, or Network router. We want to choose the RAS server for right now. Click the Remote Access Server radio button and then click Next. You will be asked whether you wish to configure this server as a basic RAS server (a standalone server with simplified control) or an advanced RAS server (capable of using remote access policies and being a member server of a domain). If you choose to make this server a basic RAS server, Windows will give you a message stating that you must configure the incoming network connection in the Network and Dial-up Connections folder. When you click OK, the RRAS Wizard will end.

If you choose to configure the server as an advanced RAS server, you will be asked to verify that the protocols installed on your server are correct for what you are trying to provide your remote clients. Figure 2.9 shows the Remote Client Protocols window.

Figure 2.9 Remote Client Protocols window.

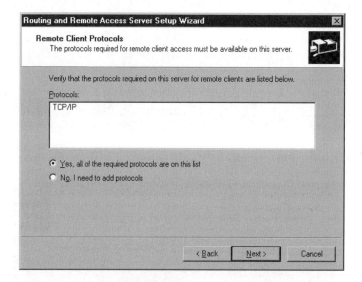

NOTE

Choosing "No, I need to add protocols" will cause the wizard to stop at this step and the configuration process will be aborted. It is recommended that you continue the process and go back later to add the additional protocols you require. The one exception to this is TCP/IP. It is always recommended that you have TCP/IP installed before you attempt the RAS installation.

As you should note in Figure 2.9, it almost appears that you can select which protocols to use with RAS. Sadly, this is not the case. The Routing and Remote Access Server (RRAS) Wizard will assume that you want to use *all* of the available protocols with remote connections. If you want to remove protocols from your RRAS server, you must manually remove them after the setup is complete.

Assuming you have TCP/IP installed, the next step in the RRAS Wizard is to decide how you want to handle the assignment of IP addresses for dial-in clients. Because every device on your network requires a unique IP address, you must have a method of supplying them to your remote users as well. If you have a Dynamic Host Configuration Protocol (DHCP) server active on your network (not necessarily on the same box as the RAS server, just somewhere visible to the network) you can use the DHCP service to automatically assign those IP addresses. This is the default option that the RRAS Wizard will attempt to use. You must have an active DHCP server, and it must have enough available IP addresses for this solution to work.

If for some reason you wish to define the range of IP addresses that the DHCP server will use to assign addresses to remote users, choose the "From a specified range of addresses" radio button and then click Next. You will be presented with a window like the one shown in Figure 2.10, which allows you to define the IP address range. Typically this is done when you have scripts or other routines that are dependent on IP addresses. This would be one method of controlling what scripts and routines run when remote users log in. Once you have defined the IP address ranges you want to assign, click Next.

Figure 2.10 IP address range assignment.

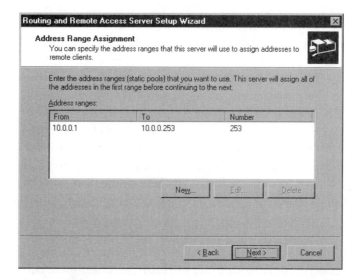

The next screen will ask you how you want to authenticate your users. The two choices you are given are "Yes, I want to use a RADIUS server," and "No, I don't want to set up this server to use RADIUS now." If you don't know what RADIUS is, you're probably going to be very confused at this point. RADIUS is short for Remote Authentication Dial-In User Service, and is used for the authentication and logging of various kinds of remote access. RADIUS provides a security database in which users and devices can be defined for a variety of access levels. If you already have a RADIUS solution in place, you can configure the RRAS service to use it for user authentication. RADIUS setup is outside the scope of this book, so we'll assume you chose the No button. Click Next to continue the installation.

Since you chose not to use RADIUS, you will be presented with a Finish button that will complete the installation of RRAS on this server. At this point, your server is configured to accept the incoming connections, possibly assign them an IP address, verify them against some type of client database (Windows 2000 Active Directory or RADIUS), and let them access the network. But wait, we haven't defined who can use remote access yet! We don't want just anyone to have the ability to dial in whenever they want, do we?

The next step in granting your users remote access is to give them dial-in permissions in your Active Directory tree. Click on the Start button, and choose Programs|Administrative Tools|Active Directory Users and Computers, and navigate to the user you want to assign the permissions to. Right-click on the user and select Edit to get to the properties sheet for the user. Select the Dial-in tab at the top of the Administrator Properties sheet to configure this user for dial-in access. Figure 2.11 shows the Dial-in properties tab for a user.

By default, the Control access through Remote Access Policy option will be selected. Click Allow access to grant this user dial-in permissions. There are other security options available as well. If your modem and phone line supports it, you can use caller ID to verify that the user is calling from a certain phone line. If they aren't calling from the defined line, they cannot make the connection. Of course, this is useless if your users travel and access the RAS server from many locations. The second choice is to use the Callback Options. When Callback is selected, the RAS server will call the user back at a predefined number to make the RAS connection. Again, this locks a remote user to one number. Another option is to assign this user a fixed IP every time they log in. Typically, you would use this feature when you are trying to configure things like firewall rules that are based on specific IP addresses.

At this point, you should be ready to go! You have installed your hardware, set up the RRAS services, and defined your user's dial-in properties—so start those phones a-ringing! Not so fast...always make sure you test your server to see if you are providing the level of service you want to make available. All too often, administrators rush to get a system in place and are suddenly confronted with the fact that it just won't meet their needs. Think about having a test bed to run the server through its paces. The bottom line is: the more testing you do, the better off you will be.

Figure 2.11 User dial-in properties.

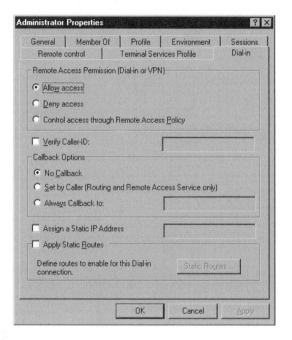

For Managers

Utilizing RADIUS

RADIUS is a very powerful tool when used in conjunction with remote access. Most VPN solutions support RADIUS as a protocol, and the accounting information that can be gained from a RADIUS accounting server is impressive. Still, a RADIUS implementation needs to be considered carefully before it is implemented.

    RADIUS can be used to secure everything from Web pages to your local network. There are many different RADIUS packages available, but all of them share the basic protocol. Network devices such as routers can send accounting data as part of the RADIUS packet to an accounting server that can provide pages and pages of statistics. Basic RADIUS packages are relatively inexpensive, but the advanced accounting packages can really cost some bucks.

Continued

> Windows 2000 includes its own RADIUS solution called Internet Authentication Service (IAS). This is an optional component that can be installed through Add/Remove Programs. For more information on IAS, see the Windows 2000 help files or Server Resource Kit.

Altering Your RAS Installation

Sometimes, you will need to change the RRAS properties once you have them in place. The RRAS Wizard, while wonderful at helping your installation, makes a lot of assumptions behind the scenes that you might need to alter to better fit your environment. To change these settings at a later date (or just to see what they are!) select your server from the Routing and Remote Access MMC and right-click on it, then select properties. From here, you can alter the PPP controls, change authentication security, and remove protocols from dial-up networking as we mentioned earlier. Figure 2.12 shows the RAS server configuration properties that can be modified.

Figure 2.12 RRAS properties.

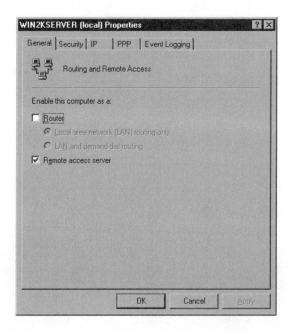

The General tab is used merely to switch the RRAS sever between providing remote access services and acting as a router. A Windows 2000 machine that is multihomed (contains more than one NIC) can route traffic between different subnets just like any router would. RRAS is Routing and Remote Access Services because of the routing capabilities of Windows 2000.

In Figure 2.13, you can see the security and accounting options for the RAS connections. As we discussed earlier, either Windows Authentication or RADIUS Authentication provides security. If you were to later install a RADIUS server in your environment, this is where you would enable it for RAS use. The accounting drop-down allows you to choose Windows Accounting, RADIUS Accounting, or None. The default accounting provided by Windows for RAS connections is far less than what RADIUS can provide. Still, it will give you some basic communications statistics based on the parameters you set in the Event Logging tab.

Figure 2.13 Security and logging.

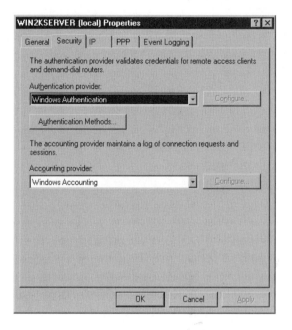

Clicking the Authentication Methods button will bring you to a list of authentication methods that you can use. The common ones are MS-CHAP and PAP, although there are many additional methods such as EAP or even Unauthenticated Access. Setting this correctly is one of the major issues that remote access administrators run up against. Usually, it's just a matter of figuring out what your clients use. Sometimes that involves considering what you will use in the future.

Figure 2.14 shows the IP tab, where you are able to enable IP routing, define how clients receive their remote addressing, and add or remove IP ranges from the address pool. This is also the window you would use to switch your RAS server from a statically defined pool to one provided by DHCP. IP routing must be enabled for remote access clients to be able to access the IP network to which this server is attached.

Figure 2.14 IP configuration.

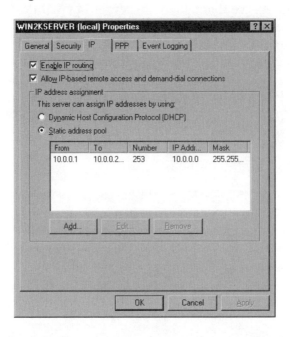

The PPP tab allows you to alter the properties that a PPP connection will try to negotiate with a remote client. You can define whether to allow multilink connections, use software compression, and the link control protocol (LCP) extensions. Individual connection settings are done using the remote access policies. We'll discuss those a little later in this chapter.

The last tab is the Event Logging tab. From here, you can determine what types of events will be logged using the method chosen earlier. Note the option shown in Figure 2.15 to enable Point-to-Point Protocol logging. This check box turns on a separate feature, PPP tracing. If this box is checked, events in the PPP connection establishment procedures are written to the Ppp.log file that is located in the systemroot\Tracing folder. You must restart the RRAS service for this to take effect.

In addition to the configuration changes you might want to make in the RRAS server properties, it is a good idea to look at the ports configured for incoming RRAS calls. The RRAS Wizard assumes that all of your modems are available for dial-in users. It also opens some ports that malicious people could use to try to bring down your server. It is a good idea to remove the ports that you won't be using. Figure 2.16 shows the Ports window in the Routing and Remote Access MMC.

Figure 2.15 Event logging.

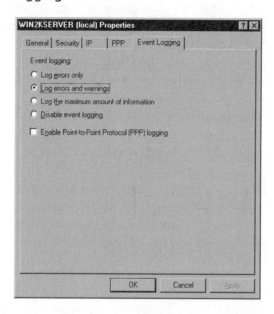

Figure 2.16 Port configuration.

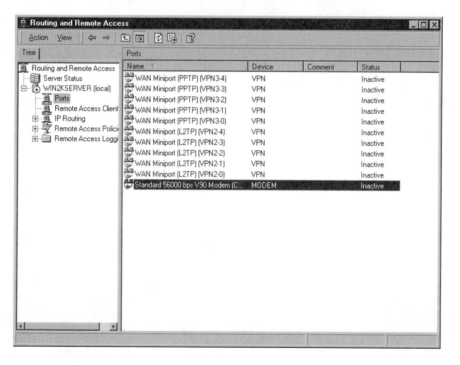

To configure a port for use with remote access, highlight the connection you want to enable and click the Configure button. Check the box labeled Remote Access Connections (Inbound Only) and supply it with the connected phone number (if possible). You should only supply the phone number if you plan on supporting the Bandwidth Allocation Protocol (BAP), which allows you to initiate multiple connections to your server as long as multiple modems and lines are available at each location.

Remote Access Policies

There is one final piece to the remote access configuration. In a native mode, Windows 2000 allows you to define policies that are enforced strictly for remote access connections. If you recall Figure 2.11, one of the options for a user is to Control access through Remote Access Policy. These policies can be configured under the RRAS MMC. Remote Access Policies are important because they allow you to define sweeping policies for all the users who might access your RAS services. One of your policy options is to define remote access by User Groups, which allows you to define remote access strictly by groups.

To create a new policy, select the Remote Access Policies folder, then right-click in the right-hand pane and choose New Remote Access Policy. You will be asked to name the new policy, and will then be asked to configure the conditions for the policy. There are quite a few choices available, from caller ID settings to specific login times and Windows user groups. These settings will determine the policies that are applied to remote logins. Figure 2.17 shows the list of options available for policy conditions.

We've now successfully configured the RAS server to provide remote access services to your users. Policies are established for the remote users, the hardware is configured, the connections are all set. So bring on the users! Adding users to the equation brings up the next important section: Connection Management.

For Managers

A Note on Remote Access Polices

If you are running your Windows 2000 RAS server in a mixed mode domain, the option to manage remote access by policies is not available. NT 4.0 RAS servers are incapable of receiving the remote access policy. For this reason, all users who need to access the RAS services must be set to Allow access in their individual user properties, and the default remote-access policy must be deleted.

Continued

There is one trick that you can use to allow or deny access on a per-group basis. By creating a policy using the Windows Groups condition that has a constraint which cannot be met, that group will not be allowed access. The common constraint is to enable the Restrict Dial-in to this number only and use a fictitious number. Make sure you test this solution before implementing it on a system-wide basis.

Figure 2.17 Remote access policies.

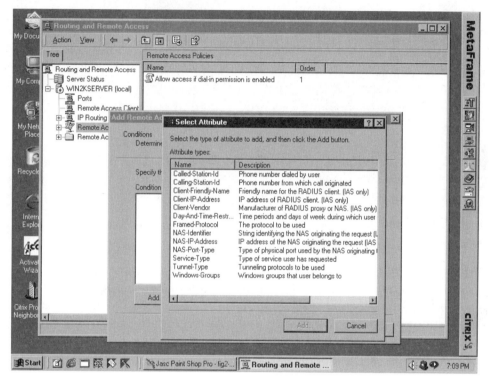

Managing Connected Users

Network administrators like to keep tabs on users. To troubleshoot problems, the ability to monitor a user's session can be an invaluable tool in managing your remote access environment. Thankfully, Windows 2000 comes equipped with several built-in tools that allow you to at least begin to keep an eye on those users.

The first tool is of course the Routing and Remote Access MMC. Highlighting the Remote Access Clients subheading for your RAS server gives you a list of all of the dial-in users currently connected. It also provides some statistics for each user, including length of connect time, current IP address, and even data transfer volume. Clicking on an individual brings up their property sheet where this information can be found. Clicking the Hang Up button on the properties sheet can also break individual connections.

Another handy feature is the ability to message users who are currently connected to the system. This tool can warn users of impending shutdowns, inform them that they need to exit the system, or even tell them to get off their phone so you can give them a call! The message pops up like a basic Net Send command, and identifies who was the originator. Users do not have the option to message you back, however.

Another handy tool is the Performance Monitor. Several RAS-related alerts can be set that will allow you to gather information about the RAS service. These logs are stored with the normal performance monitor logs, and can be accessed through the perfmon utility. Don't forget, RRAS supports its own logging system, which we talked about earlier. Those logs can give you a great look at how things are working with your RAS service.

Windows 2000 also includes a very useful command line utility called netsh. At a command prompt, type **Netsh RAS** to display a list of available netsh commands that apply to your RAS service. Netsh is a query tool that basically checks the availability of services and their current status. It takes a little getting used to, but it can be a real boon to network administrators.

TIP

Netsh can be used for a lot of different queries in Windows 2000. It's a good tool to become familiar with, not just for RAS but for server management in general. More information on netsh can be found in the Windows 2000 help files.

VPN Configuration

Installing the VPN software on a Windows 2000 server is very easy once you've gone through the steps to install the RRAS services. In fact, you've already done about 75 percent of the work. When you added the Remote Access Service, Windows 2000 automatically added support for five L2TP and five PPP connections as part of the default installation. If you haven't already added RAS support, you'll need to go back to the section titled "RAS Installation" and start from there. We're going to assume from this point forward that you've already completed those installation tasks.

The first step in the VPN installation process is to make sure that your ports are actually installed. If you recall from the previous section, you can do this from the RRAS MMC. Click on Start|Programs|Administrative Tools|Routing and Remote Access. When the RRAS MMC comes up, you should be able to find your server in the left-hand column. Double-clicking it brings up the details for that server. Right-click on the Ports listing, then select Properties to give a list of available ports. Figure 2.18 shows the Ports Properties sheet.

Figure 2.18 Ports Properties sheet.

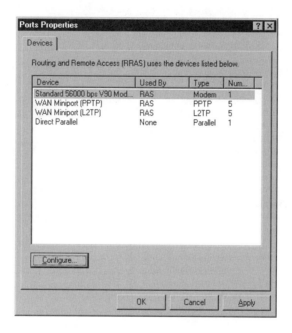

From here, you can edit your ports and protocols according to the needs of your RAS environment. Remove ports that you will not need to use, as these can be security holes in your network. To configure a particular port of VPN use, highlight it and click the Configure button. Figure 2.19 shows you the Configure Device screen for a port. Make sure that the Remote Access connections (incoming calls only) box is checked, and for the phone number of the device supply the public IP address of this server. Clients will connect to this IP address using the VPN client software.

Figure 2.19 Port configuration.

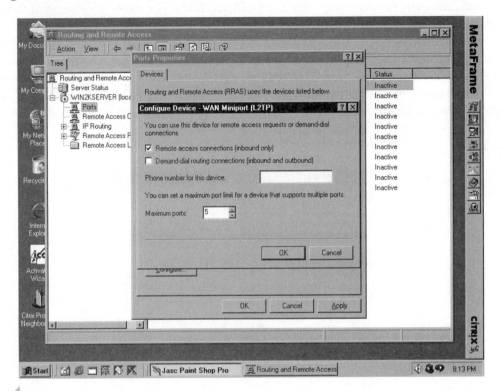

NOTE

The public IP address is used only when you attempt to connect to this server from outside the network perimeter. Usually, this is done through some type of Network Address Translation (NAT) so that your internal IP address scheme is not exposed to the outside world.

This window is also where you will configure the maximum available ports for this service. This number should be scaled based on the maximum number of users your server can support in a VPN role. When you are considering this number, keep in mind issues like Internet latency, the connection to your RAS server, and the typical connection your clients will be making to their ISP (high-speed, dial-up, and so on). Although it may seem like you can just open a bunch of ports and let it go, there are some performance issues to be aware of.

It is very important to note that due to the complex nature of a VPN packet, performance can be degraded from 10 to 50 percent! A lot of this is because of the encryption/decryption process that has to be handled at both ends, as well as the increased packet overhead involved with VPN networks. On a T1 connection at both ends, this might not be so noticeable. But for a dial-in client, a 50 percent reduction could be devastating. If it is at all possible, your users should always dial in directly to your RAS server instead of making a VPN connection. That method will provide the best connection speed and transfer rate.

PPTP

By default, the Windows 2000 RAS installation automatically enables five PPTP ports. These ports can be used to support older dial-up networking clients who are not capable of making an L2TP connection. As we discussed earlier, PPTP encrypts the packet, sticks a PPP wrapper around it, and then shoots it off to the PPTP server. PPTP is based on the shared secret model of NT4.0, which is far less secure than L2TP or IPSec.

The primary benefit to PPTP is that it's cheap and easy to implement. PPTP traffic is compatible with a NAT system, can support multiprotocol and multicast environments, and is much less expensive than public key systems that are used with L2TP and IPSec. And as we mentioned before, many older clients are not able to make an L2TP connection and rely on PPTP for VPN access. For all of these reasons, PPTP is here to stay.

IPSec

IPSec is used to provide enhanced security for VPN traffic in IP unicast situations. It uses a public key infrastructure to encrypt and decrypt VPN traffic, and gives actual end-to-end security in the connection. There are two levels of IPSec tunneling. The first is a combination L2TP/IPSec tunnel, and the second is pure IPSec tunneling. IPSec tunneling is not recommended for VPN connections because it fails to provide some basic services that remote users will require.

IPSec utilizes the on-demand security negotiation and automatic key management services through the IKE (Internet Key Exchange) standard established by the IETF. Group Policy can be used in Active Directory to provide IPSec policy assignment and distribution to Windows 2000 domain members. Security can be established through public/private key signatures using certificates, passwords (but only to establish the trust), or the Kerberos 5.0 authentication that Windows 2000-based domains use. Kerberos is the easiest choice for deploying an IPSec solution.

Windows 2000 *only* supports L2TP over IPSec connections. IPSec is implemented in Windows 2000 through the use of policies. Several policies come predefined with Windows 2000, or you can create your own policy. To manage IPSec policies, use the Local Computer Policy snap-in for the MMC. Highlighting the IP Security Policies on Local Machine subheading will give you the three existing security policies in the right-hand pane. These three default policies are:

- **Secure server** A machine set as a secure server will always try to negotiate security with any client that sends it traffic. If security cannot be negotiated, the server will cease to respond to the client.

- **Client** A client policy will make the machine query the server to establish secure communications. If the server does not have a secure server policy, no data encryption will be performed.

- **Server** A machine with a server policy will attempt to establish secure communications, but if it cannot it will default back to sending packets in the clear.

IPSec does have some limitations, which is why it should always be implemented in combination with L2TP. The primary fault in IPSec is that it does not provide any user authentication. Instead, authentication is handled on a machine basis. This means that there is no way to identify who is using that machine. Another key limitation is that it has no method of managing tunnel address assignment. Also, it does not support NAT technology, multiple protocols, or multicast environments.

L2TP

Like PPTP, L2TP is automatically configured with five ports by the default Windows 2000 RAS installation. L2TP, as we discussed before, is a Layer 2 protocol that is a combination of the L2F and PPTP protocols developed by Cisco and Microsoft. Windows 2000 uses L2TP in conjunction with IPSec to provide the functions of VPN management that IPSec alone cannot provide. Since L2TP is a payload inside the IPSec packet, it can gain the benefits of IPSec (end-to-end secure communications, replay protection, and data integrity) without sacrificing the important features that PPTP can provide (user authentication, multiprotocol support, and tunnel address assignment).

L2TP management is performed in the same RAS MMC port configuration tool we discussed previously. Remember to set the number of L2TP ports to correspond with the correct number for your environment. L2TP is superior to traditional PPTP because it can support multiple tunnels between end points and will work over any packet-oriented network. Also, tunnel authentication is provided by the IPSec layer, which gives far better security than PPTP can provide for its tunnel. L2TP also operates with slightly less overhead than a PPTP packet. L2TP headers can be compressed to 4 bytes, as compared to 6 bytes for PPTP. This may not seem like a lot, but remember the performance issues we discussed before for VPNs.

There are of course some drawbacks for L2TP/IPSec. As we mentioned before, IPSec cannot transverse a NAT solution. This still holds true when L2TP is added to the equation. Additionally, older clients will not support an L2TP solution. This means that many clients will need to be able to utilize the PPTP connection type instead. In the end, L2TP over IPSec is the solution that Microsoft strongly recommends with Windows 2000. It is a bit more complicated to configure than plain old PPTP, but the enhanced security it provides is well worth it.

RAS Upgrade Considerations

There are quite a few older RAS solutions in existence. Windows 2000 far surpasses all of Microsoft's previous attempts at creating a RAS environment. With more and more RAS users flooding the marketplace, the systems themselves have become considerably more robust. One of the potential dilemmas you may run up against is whether to upgrade your existing RAS solution or just do a clean install of Windows 2000. From an administration level, if it is at all possible to do a fresh installation of Windows 2000, that will always be your best bet. Microsoft has improved their upgrade process, but it can still hiccup.

If you have to upgrade, there is very little information available from Microsoft on upgrading your RAS service. Whether this is an oversight on their part or because they don't think anyone will be upgrading those services, we're not sure. Regardless, since it is possible to do a direct upgrade from several previous versions of Windows, this may be an issue for you. Although most field-level administrators recommend a clean installation, Microsoft continues to insist the upgrade process is fine. This section covers the important considerations when choosing to upgrade from a previous Windows version.

A big consideration when looking at RAS migration is your hardware configuration. The hardware you are currently using must be compatible with Windows 2000. For older configurations, this will not be a problem. Microsoft supplies thousands of drivers in the Windows 2000 installation. However, some vendors may not have supplied Windows 2000-compliant drivers before the software shipped. Check your hardware vendor's Web sites to make sure you have the most recent drivers for any hardware or software you will install on the RAS server.

Upgrading from Windows NT 4.0 RAS

Windows NT 4.0 RAS is very similar to the RAS service provided in NT 3.51. Both rely on Windows dial-up networking to establish a connection from the client to the RAS server. Users are enabled for RAS connections using the Dial in button under the individual properties in User Manager for Domains. When you upgrade to a Windows 2000 server, all of this information is theoretically moved to the Active Directory. Users that are configured for RAS access under NT 4.0 will also be configured for access under Windows 2000.

In reality, the upgrade process is not always that clean. Many administrators recommend removing Remote Access from the NT 4.0 installation before attempting the upgrade. Then, once the Windows 2000 server is up and running, reconfigure the RAS service cleanly. It is a bit more work, but can save you a whole lot of headaches down the road. Even if you choose to let Windows automatically complete the RAS upgrade, you'll want to go back and check the assumptions that it made to bring them in line with your RAS expectations.

Upgrading from Windows NT 3.5x RAS

Windows NT 3.51, like NT 4.0, can be directly upgraded to Windows 2000. Like NT 4.0, the user information should theoretically be migrated as well. Again, you're left to trust the migration wizard to get it right. All too often, it won't. As with NT 4.0, the recommendation for upgrading the RAS server is to uninstall RAS before attempting the migration. Yes, it can work and work successfully. It can also damage your Active Directory if it doesn't.

NOTE

Although Citrix WinFrame is based on NT 3.51 technology, you *cannot* directly upgrade it to Windows 2000. A clean installation of Windows 2000 will have to be done. You could, in theory, upgrade the server to NT 4.0 Terminal Server Edition prior to upgrading it to Windows 2000. The odds of it working without anything breaking are probably about 50/50.

Migrating from a Third-Party Remote Access Service

There are quite a few third-party products that provide RAS services to Windows NT administrators. Not surprisingly, many of these rely on the basic features of NT RAS. Some of them *may* migrate the data correctly into the Active Directory, but with a third-party solution you are usually looking at starting over or getting the appropriate version for Windows 2000. It is not recommended that you try to upgrade a RAS server with a third-party RAS solution in place.

Summary

With Windows 2000, Microsoft has really paid a lot of attention to remote access. Windows 2000 has improved RAS configuration, native support for many VPN technologies, and a good help system. Microsoft really seems to be taking RAS seriously as a technology, which is a good thing for anyone who has to support remote users. In this chapter, we've discussed the design and placement of your RAS system, the various protocols associated with RAS and VPN technology, installing and configuring your RAS and VPN server in Windows 2000, and finally some things to think about when considering whether or not to upgrade your RAS server from a previous version of Windows.

Design and placement of your RAS server is key to the success of your entire remote access offering. Poor placement or inadequate hardware considerations can cripple user productivity over your remote connections. Don't just stick your RAS server off in a dark corner and forget it's there! Make full use of your bandwidth and place the RAS server where it's going to do your users the most good.

Remote access has a lot more protocol choices available in Windows 2000. Trying to decide between PPTP, L2TP, or IPSec can be difficult. We went through each protocol and talked about what it did and how. We also discussed where they were appropriate to use, and the way to find more information on each of them. Protocols are the heart and soul of Windows 2000 remote access. Choose them wisely.

Installing Windows 2000 RAS services is made much simpler by the inclusion of an RRAS Wizard. This powerful tool is very helpful for quickly setting up your RAS environment, but makes some assumptions you may not want it to make. Always make sure you go back through the options after the wizard is done and make sure what it assumed accurately reflects what you want. We also went through setting up the VPN technology, including configuring the IPSec policies for each machine.

Finally, we looked at the upgrade considerations for your current RAS environment. The best practice is to always do a clean installation. But if you can't do that, at the very least you should uninstall RAS services before attempting the upgrade. This will save you time down the road when you might otherwise be searching through the Active Directory trying to figure out where it all went wrong. By now you're fast on your way to becoming a RAS and VPN expert.

FAQs

Q: I'm trying to upgrade my Citrix WinFrame server to Windows 2000 and provide RAS services to my users. What's the easiest way to do this?

A: Unfortunately, there is no direct upgrade path from WinFrame to Windows 2000. To make the installation work, you'll need to do a fresh installation of Windows 2000 on the server.

Q: I want to enable an IPSec policy that will challenge *all* of my clients for secure communications and not make the connection unless they can negotiate a secure connection. How do I do that?

A: You can use the default IPSec policy Secure Server to provide that level of systems security. Be warned, remote clients who cannot negotiate a connection will never be able to make a connection to your server.

Q: I'm trying to design my RAS server and want to save a little money. RAM doesn't seem very important to a RAS server, does it?

A: On the contrary, RAM is perhaps *the* most important piece when you consider the design of your server. Besides the modem connection, your RAM will have the greatest impact on your user's session speed.

Q: I want to message all of my currently connected users to warn them that I am about to boot the RAS server. How do I do that?

A: The RRAS MMC gives you the option to message all connected users. In addition, for those that don't get off you can highlight them, right-click, and choose Hang Up.

Chapter 3

Designing Terminal Services for Windows 2000

Solutions in this chapter:

- Designing and Placing Terminal Services Servers on the Network

- Implementing Terminal Services Protocols

- Analyzing the Environment

Introduction

The chief impact on the performance of thin-client applications is the design of the servers. Windows 2000 Servers provide the basis for Citrix MetaFrame thin-client technology with Terminal Services. Terminal Services is provided as a native component of Windows 2000, so businesses can deploy it out of the box.

Designing Windows 2000 Terminal Services requires an accurate sizing of the servers that provide the thin-client application service. Placing the servers on the internetwork can impact the performance of the applications that are supplied. This is an important step on the path to a successful Terminal Services deployment.

Designing and Placing Terminal Services on the Network

The initial design and placement of Windows 2000 Terminal Servers is a critical step in your thin-client deployment strategy. Incorrectly sizing servers cannot only cause your deployment to fail, but can be costly to fix. The first step in the design phase is to determine the hardware requirements and the number of servers necessary for proper deployment. This is done through a discovery process to determine the number of maximum users estimated for the system as well as the requirements of the applications to be used.

The number of users and the types of applications that will be available for use will have a great impact on the performance of the system. You should start the sizing of your server according the requirements of Windows 2000. A dual 450MHz processor with 128 MB of RAM will give you a good starting point for supporting a stand-alone Windows 2000 Server. From there we can start to size the servers upward, adding incremental resources to support users and applications. Starting your server sizing with these base requirements will help ensure proper operation after adding users and applications. This would be considered a small server and would be appropriate for a very limited number of users or in a distributed environment. A larger server should have four 600MHz processors and 512 MB of RAM. A large server would be ideal for running intensive applications and for distributed environments. If you plan on using a server with more than four processors, you'll have to purchase the Windows 2000 Datacenter Server. Regular Server and Advanced Server only support up to eight processors while Datacenter supports up to 32.

NOTE

Windows 2000 Servers that will be designed for Terminal Services should only be loaded with user support programs. They should not be doing other services such as print server, firewall, Structured Query Language (SQL) server, or any other database services. These services should take place on other servers. Extra, unnecessary services will slow the server down and possibly contribute to instabilities.

Sizing the Server— User and Application Analysis

As a general rule, add 20 MB of RAM per user, per server. For example, if you plan on having a Terminal Services server and 50 users, multiply 20 by 50. This will give you 1000MB, or approximately 1 GB of RAM. Take your base model with 128 MB of RAM and add another 1 GB to it. This does not include the RAM that some memory intensive applications will need. Further testing is required to find this amount. If you plan on using MetaFrame with your Terminal Server your memory requirements will differ. Citrix recommends 4 MB of RAM per user.

Your ultimate goal here is to ensure that memory doesn't become a bottleneck in your Terminal Server's operation. Some clients will use less than 20 MB of RAM while others will use more. If you know that you're going to have more application intensive users on your system, you may want to allocate more memory per user. Most of these resource needs will be met once you complete the next step in your server sizing. The next step takes application type into account.

The next step in the sizing process involves the discovery of the processor and memory requirements of the applications to be deployed. The steps for this phase are outlined below. Before beginning, make sure users understand that this is a pilot program necessary for server sizing and that application performance now does not necessarily reflect application performance in the final deployment. Also, be sure to select user test groups that accurately reflect the percentage of normal users to power users, users that work with many applications at once in a multitasking fashion that will be present in the final deployment. Failure to do so could negatively affect server performance.

- Set up your test server with the requirements you have come up with from the user analysis.

- Install the programs you wish to make available via terminal services. The types of application you plan on using will determine the type of server you purchase.

- For testing, start with 15 users and use Performance Monitor to gather test results. Performance Monitor should be set to gather results at 15-second intervals. You should keep track of processor utilization, memory utilization, and pagefile utilization. Figure 3.1 shows an example of Performance Monitor.

Figure 3.1 Performance Monitor screen.

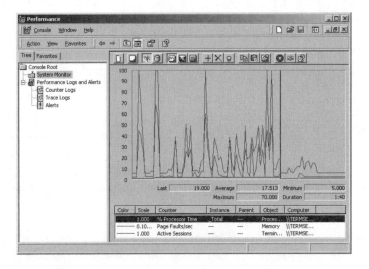

- Keep adding users in 10-user intervals until CPU utilization reaches 70–80 percent.

- Add RAM, if necessary, until you reach this plateau of CPU utilization. You will know you need more RAM when your pagefile usage increases and your system slows down.

TIP

The rule of thumb is to estimate approximately 25 simultaneous users per processor. If you start there and then test your server's capacity against your application usage, you may find you can have more users per processor, and, sometimes, if your application is particularly CPU-intensive, you will need less.

- Once you've reached 70–80 percent CPU utilization, count the number of concurrent users. This is the number of users a single server can handle while running applications, or you can add more processors if your server is capable. You'll then continue testing until you reach the 70–80 percent CPU usage.

- Now you can determine how many servers you will need to support your user and application load. For example, if you determine that one server can handle 50 users running applications concurrently without using more than 80 percent CPU for an extended amount of time (more than 15 seconds), and you know that you'll be supporting 2500 users who are online simultaneously, you can conclude that you need 50 servers with the hardware requirements that you've established through testing. You'll want to have extra servers available as well as hot backups. Not only will they reduce the current load on all of the available servers, but you'll have built in some redundancy. Users won't be too affected by server loss if you have other servers to pick up the workload.

NOTE

When you determine the number of servers, you may wish to determine how many CPUs you need and then purchase Symmetrical MultiProcessor (SMP) servers to reduce the total number of servers you support. When you reduce the number of supported servers, you will reduce the Total Cost of Ownership (TCO), because you will have a reduced need for administering those servers. Be aware that you should select servers that include redundant hardware—RAID arrays, redundant power supplies and error correcting memory—so that the servers are less likely to fail. A failure with fewer number of servers can be catastrophic if there is no backup server or not enough cycles available on the remaining server CPUs to support the users online.

Storage is a consideration when deploying servers, and the same is true of Terminal Servers. Microsoft recommends putting your Terminal Server Operating System and your application files on separate physical devices on separate channels. You can use a mirror set or RAID array for the operating system (OS) disk. You should, however, use a Redundant Array of Independent Disks (RAID) array for the applications disk at a minimum. Fiber Channel may be necessary if conventional RAID arrays do not provide

fast enough throughput to launch and run applications in a timely
manner.

TIP

There are various programs available for stress testing servers. One good
one is WinBatch. WinBatch is ideal because it uses virtually no system
resources. This allows for a clean stress test without the stressing program skewing the results. I recommend using Windows 9*x*, NT, or 2000
Professional to set up multiple user connections. You can use one of
these workstations to create multiple connections, thus allowing you to
stress test without requiring user intervention. That should make both
the users and management happy. Follow the same strategy when using
this form of stress testing as you would if you were using users for performance monitoring.

Network Interfaces

The type of network interface cards (NICs) you install in your server will
be determined mostly by the number of users you will be hosting and the
types of applications you will be deploying. In any case, it is recommended
that you connect all of your NICs directly to a switch. Cut-through
switches will give better performance due to lower latency. Most Cisco
switches use cut-through (fragment-free) switching by default. Fragment-
free switching is a switching method in which the packet is "switched" (forwarded to the destination port) soon after the destination is read in the
header. This is the most efficient type of switching. Some switches read
and buffer the entire packet before "switching" it, a process known as
store-and-forward. This method involves a lot of latency and can reduce
performance significantly when burned with lots of traffic.

TIP

When considering the placement of servers, the servers should be placed
closest to the resources—preferably on the same broadcast domain—
instead of being placed closest to the users.

The Terminal Services client protocol is designed to run over very limited bandwidth, such as 28.8Kbps modems, but you can still run into bandwidth issues when serving several users at once on a Terminal Server. You should design the portion of your local area network (LAN) that borders your Terminal Servers so that you have plenty of leftover bandwidth. Clients will most likely want to transfer files from their workstation to the server, or servers may need to transfer or open files on another server. Printing large files can utilize large portions of bandwidth as well. The type of activities and the total number of users and servers will determine the amount of bandwidth you'll need. If we use Microsoft's recommendations, then we can assume that Remote Desktop Protocol (RDP) needs 30 KB of bandwidth for efficient operation. We can assume this because Microsoft claims that Terminal Server runs efficiently over 28.8 Kbps modem lines. Next we'll want to multiply the number of users we'll be supporting times the amount of bandwidth that will be taken up. So if we need to support approximately 200 simultaneous users, we would multiply 200 by 30. This gives us 12,000 KB, or approximately 12 MB. This already exceeds networks built around 10baseT technology at 10 MBs. If this is the case, as it is in our example network, then infrastructure changes are necessary.

If you had 50 users on a server with 10MB NICs in the clients and a 10/100MB NIC in the server all connected through a hub, you would experience lots of latency with today's bandwidth-hungry applications. You'll have 50 users fighting over the 4 MB of useable bandwidth. There are a couple of ways to remedy this problem. Replacing the hub with a switch will drastically improve bandwidth and throughput. Switches will increase the number of collision domains (network segments in which packet collisions can occur), thus reducing the number of devices contending for bandwidth per segment. This allows for more useable bandwidth on each segment. If each client and the server were on its own segment, the client would monopolize bandwidth within its own segment. You can see an example of a single collision domain in Figure 3.2.

In Figure 3.2, all of the clients must contend for the available 10MB. Everything inside the cloud is inside the same collision domain. With 50 clients constantly sending information back in forth (keystrokes, mouse movements, screen updates) a lot of contention takes place and unacceptable latency will occur.

Many LANs were built with stackable hubs on shared 10BaseT Ethernet. In these LANs, several hubs were connected together to create a single collision domain. As new hubs were added, throughput was reduced because all the client workstations were in contention for access to the 10 MB bandwidth. When designing your network, you can easily increase throughput by splitting the stack and adding an Ethernet switch, which is illustrated in Figure 3.3. This will effectively create several collision

Figure 3.2 A single collision domain.

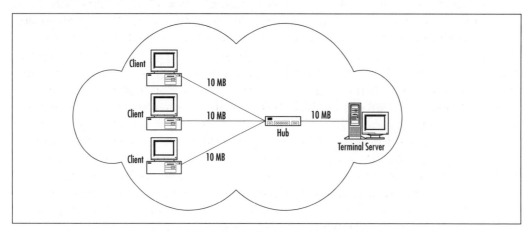

Figure 3.3 Load-balancing bandwidth between the NICs.

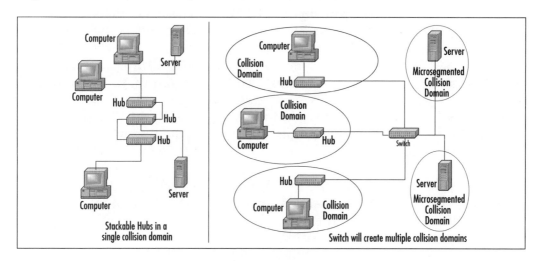

domains. Because servers typically receive a large percentage of traffic, you can microsegment those servers by dedicating a single switch port to each server. Some switches will allow both 100 MB and 10 MB collision domains. With intensive server traffic, you can further increase performance by installing a 100 MB network adapter into the server and dedicating a 100 MB port to the server.

It is not unusual to place users on a hub and connect the hubs to a switch in order to reduce the contention, especially by breaking up a set of stacked hubs and switching through them. The rule is to keep 80 percent of the traffic within a collision domain, so all the local services for those users should be on that hub. You break this rule when you switch, because the former stacked collision domain shares the same resources.

Dedicate one or more segments on the switch to the servers, and dedicate the rest to a hub. This will provide much greater bandwidth to everyone.

Some networks use a combination of hubs and switches to segment networks. When using this method it is recommended, but not required, that you place resources that the users on that hub are likely to use the most as shown in Figure 3.4. The resource (Terminal Servers in the figure) is placed in the same collision domain as the clients that will use it the most. The model shown is cheaper, but not better or faster. Your switch requirements will include a lower port density, which will significantly lower the cost of the switch and hubs (although they aren't expensive compared with other networking equipment). This is not always possible as users may use and share multiple resources. In this case, connecting resources (such as servers) directly to the switch and hooking user hubs to the switch as shown in Figure 3.5 will give you the best results possible. In this case, the assumption is that all of the clients use all of the resources comparably.

Figure 3.4 Using a combination of hubs and switches to segment networks.

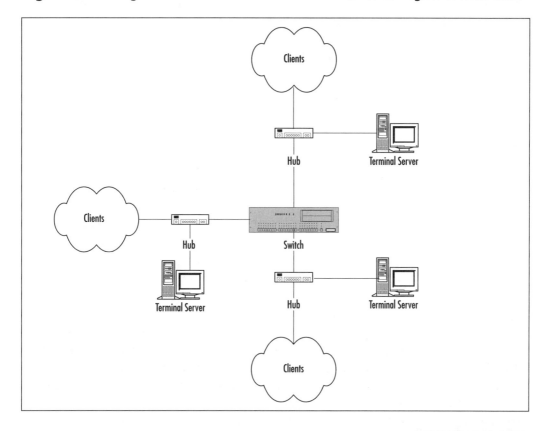

Figure 3.5 Connecting resources (such as servers) directly to the switch.

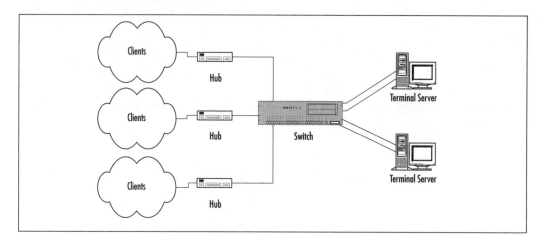

Clusters

Terminal Server is not suitable for clustering services. The best load-balancing solution is achieved using Citrix's Load Balancing product for MetaFrame (see Chapter 4). You can use DNS resolution and its round-robin fashion of resolving Internet Protocol (IP) addresses between load-balanced servers, but this doesn't give true load balancing, which is balancing user load based on server resource usage. In addition, you must disable the session disconnect feature as there is no guarantee that a user would be reconnected to a disconnected session. The session disconnect feature allows users to reconnect to a session that is still running without anyone connected to it.

If you cannot use Citrix's Load Balancing product, Microsoft has a feature called Network Load Balancing that is based on IP affinity. This is only available on Advanced Server and Datacenter Server versions of Windows 2000. Users will be able to reconnect to a disconnected session as long as they do not change client machines (or IP addresses!). Using Dynamic Host Configuration Protocol (DHCP) for client machine addressing doesn't create a problem as long as the machine is not down for so long as to lose its lease. Therefore, if you are using DHCP with Network Load Balancing, keep the lease length high. Three days should be sufficient. If you're using session disconnect timeouts, you'll want to set the DHCP lease period to be at least twice that. Not following this rule may cause your client's IP address to change and the disconnected session to timeout. You will want to store user profiles in a central repository, somewhere that is available to all of the load-balanced servers. This will keep the user's desktop environment the same regardless of which server they connect to. Roaming profiles work great for this.

Modems

If you're going to use modems attached directly to the Terminal Server for remote access, be sure to select modems that don't rely on the system's CPU. Many 'winmodems' work in this fashion. Also, the fastest speed you can achieve is 33.6 Kbps unless you have special digital 56 Kbps modems and the proper digital lines.

Impact from the Number of Users

Obviously, the number of users on the system is the largest contributing factor to system hardware requirements. For each connection made to a Terminal Server by a user, a new session is initiated. Each of these sessions consumes system resources. The previous testing was done to find the amount of resources consumed be each session. By estimating 20 MB of RAM for each user on the system, we are staying at the liberal end of the pool. Microsoft recommends 13–20MB of RAM, but it never hurts to have additional resources. You will want to add extra servers for redundancy. For example, in a distributed environment with 20 servers, it would be advisable to have at least one extra server to help redistribute the load if a server or two were to become inoperative. Without this extra server, user load across the remaining servers could possibly stretch system resources beyond what they were designed to handle, and server performance would suffer. Users' applications could become unresponsive or sluggish. As always, redundancy is a consideration of the criticalness of the application/server versus cost. Only you and your company can make this decision. Just one server can make a world of difference in load distribution if another server crashes.

For Managers

The Learning Curve

IT managers must take into account the learning curve users may encounter when using Windows Terminal Services. The learning curve users experience will be directly related to the type of Operating System (OS) that they are used to using. Clients may currently be using Windows 2000, Windows 9x, or Windows NT 4.0.

Those users accustomed to Windows 2000 will make the transition rather smoothly. Be careful not to assume that they won't need any training. They will need to be trained on how to use the Terminal

Continued

Services Client as well as being informed of restrictions on functionality of Windows 2000 Terminal Services, such as the inability to install programs at will.

Users of the other OSs will have a much more difficult time. The Windows 2000 interface is different enough from Windows 9x and NT to cause a stir among unseasoned computer users. Users should be trained on Windows 2000 and the Terminal Services Client before they are thrown into its unmerciful jaws. Proper training will ease user anxiety and frustration over not being able to complete tasks in Windows 2000 that they could do in Windows 9x or NT and make you look like a hero instead of a tyrant of all things computer.

Making users capable of easily working with the programs and OSs they are dealt are part of reducing your total cost of ownership and raising your return on investment, which as an IT manager should be some of your top priorities. Making users "happy" and capable of completing work faster and easier will make you look good to both the users and your managers. What more could you ask for?

Placing Terminal Services Servers on the Network

Placement of your Terminal Servers inside your internetwork should not be taken lightly. You can't just plug them in somewhere and expect them to work efficiently, or at all in some cases. Firewalls, bandwidth, and security considerations can all affect where you place your Terminal Servers. These issues must be considered and dealt with before deploying your Terminal Servers.

It is recommended that you place your servers in your LAN somewhere on the private side of your internetwork. If you wish to allow access to your Terminal Server from clients through a firewall, then you must allow RDP traffic to pass through. RDP uses port 3389. Firewalls can be used to secure your Terminal Servers. Most firewalls will allow you to determine by host address, network address, or any combination of the two, who is allowed to make connections to the Terminal Servers. Anybody outside of the address range you specify will be blocked at the firewall and not allowed to connect. You could use this design inside your internetwork to keep clients in accounting, who are allowed to connect to Terminal Servers that offer accounting applications, from connecting to Terminal Servers that offer Information Technology applications. Figure 3.6 gives an example of this. Be careful what type of firewall you choose.

Firewalls come in two basic flavors: application-filter based and packet-filter based. Application-filter based firewalls may not have filters set up to handle the RDP protocol. You'll have to contact the firewall vendor to have a filter set up. Packet-filter based firewalls allow you to create rules based on protocol and port or socket. You'll be immediately able to set up filters for RDP.

Figure 3.6 This router is segmenting the network.

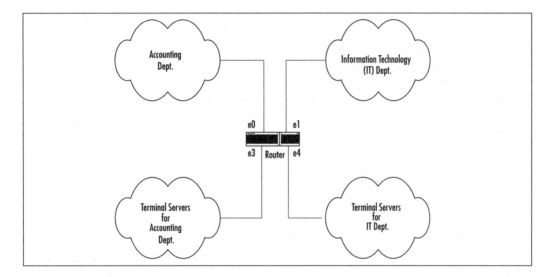

In Figure 3.6, we have a router segmenting different portions of the LAN. This can be done physically or logically. To filter traffic you would create and assign access lists to the various interfaces of the router, however, not all routers have this functionality. Most Cisco routers do have firewall capabilities. An example of an extended access list would be as follows:

```
Router(config)#Access-list 101 TCP Permit {source IP} [wildcard bit mask
{destination IP} eq 3389
Router(config-if)# access-group 101 in
```

This would tell the router to only allow packets with a source address originating from the IT department's LAN segment into the LAN segment that houses its Terminal Servers. This technique can also be used in large offices where different companies share the same network.

Allowing access to your Terminal Servers from the Internet can be accomplished by placing your servers in a 'Demilitarized Zone' (DMZ). A DMZ is a separate segment from your firewall that is not directly connected to your internal network or the Internet. Figure 3.7 shows you what a DMZ will look like.

Figure 3.7 A firewall separates the LAN, Internet, and the DMZ from each other.

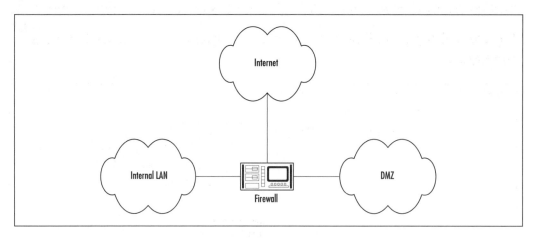

For a DMZ to be effective in securing your Terminal Server and your internal LAN, it must be set up correctly. This is how you should configure your firewall rules to effectively implement a DMZ:

- Traffic from the Internet should be allowed to pass to the DMZ on port 3389 only.

- Traffic from the DMZ should be allowed to pass to the Internet on port 3389 and any other that might be required to be open (such as port 80 for Web browsing).

- Traffic from the DMZ to the LAN should be limited to port 3389, and possibly ports necessary for domain authentication, as well as ports necessary to support other functions, such as WINS. This rule should be bidirectional.

This is a minimum secure setup for a DMZ and is not designed to be inclusive for all situations. You may have to modify these settings to suit your environments and needs.

Bandwidth issues on the LAN can be dealt with in three ways. Each has its own advantages and disadvantages. The simplest way is to throw more bandwidth at the network by upgrading NICs and wiring. Most organizations choose to go the more effective route and segment the network using switches, which we covered earlier. Here, we'll explore this concept more deeply. You can choose to use more finesse and use traffic-controlling techniques such as priority queuing.

Many of today's switches support gigabit Ethernet and there are a few NICs that support gigabit Ethernet. It is highly unlikely that you'll need gigabit Ethernet to your servers, but it certainly wouldn't hurt to imple-ment it between your switches if you're running 100Mb everywhere else and you're in a large environment. Figure 3.8 gives an example of this.

Figure 3.8 A gigabit Ethernet connection between two switches improves throughput.

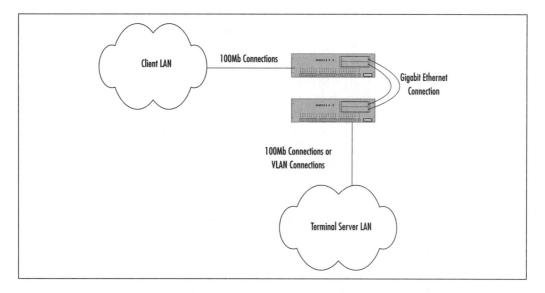

There are a few traffic-shaping techniques that can be employed to improve responsiveness and give the bandwidth necessary to run a ter-minal server session. Exploring all of these fully would be outside of the scope of this book. As an example, we'll quickly cover priority queuing.

Priority queuing is a technique used on routers and switches to prioritize traffic according to application type (or port number). We can use the routers and switches we have in place in our internetwork to control traffic. We would set the devices to give RDP a higher priority than, say, HTTP traffic. When traffic begins to back up in the queue in the device, the queuing priority rules will become effective. This way we can assure that mission-critical application data reaches its destination in a timely manner. In this case, RDP is our mission-critical data, so we would want to set TCP 3389 as high in the priority.

Not only is the logical placement of servers within the internetwork's address structure important, but its placement in the Windows Domain is important as well. Microsoft has specific recommendations depending on the domain model your organization incorporates.

No Domain In this structure, users will have to be created and maintained locally on each terminal server, thereby increasing administration. The lack of fault tolerance and redundancy will severely limit scalability and hamper administrative tasks as the number of servers increases. Load balancing will be difficult to achieve in this format.

Add Windows 2000 Terminal Servers to an existing Windows NT 4.0 domain In this model, you will be able to take advantage of and use the new features available in Windows 2000 Terminal Server. However, keep in mind that you will be limited by the NT 4.0 domain model limitations as well as its SAM. You have more Terminal-Server–specific options available to you in Windows 2000 than you did in NT 4.0. In multidomain models, place your terminal servers in the same domain as the users that you want it to serve.

You might want to distribute your Terminal Servers to specific domains for security, business model, or any number of reasons. There's nothing wrong with this approach if it makes sense and is achievable, which it is with proper planning. Most likely your Terminal Servers won't communicate or interact with Terminal Servers outside of their own domain, so you won't need to worry about setting up any new trusts. They will probably interact with other servers in the domain though. They'll need to communicate to your file servers, databases, groupware servers, and printers. You'll have to create autonomous groups of Terminal Servers in each domain that you wish to have Terminal Server access.

Add Windows 2000 Terminal Servers to the existing Active Directory structure In this model you will have all of the advantages of running Active Directory on your network. You will be able to host thousands of users, take advantage of user and group policies and remote installation services, as well as tons of other features. This is the most feature-rich environment for running your Windows 2000 Terminal Servers. If you already have NT 4.0, you can start from an NT 4.0 domain structure and slowly convert to a Windows 2000 Active Directory model. Otherwise, you can implement a Windows 2000 Active Directory structure with your first Windows 2000 server. When using Active Directory, it is recommended that you place all of your Terminal Servers in a separate organizational unit (OU). This is because you are likely to manage your Terminal Servers differently than other servers or workstations. They are different and should be treated as such.

Add Windows 2000 Terminal Services to other environments This can be a bit more complicated than some of the previously mentioned processes. In a Novell Netware environment, user information can be extracted and entered into Active Directory using a migration tool from Microsoft. Other environments are probably going to require a lot of manual user information input. Microsoft does have a utility in its resource kit, adduser.exe, which might be very helpful in some situations. There are also third-party software products, such as metadirectories, that can synchronize between two or more directory services. Depending on your business requirements, you should consider how automatic this process should be and make an appropriate selection based on which product best meets your requirements.

Implementing Terminal Services Protocols

Windows 2000 Terminal Server services use a proprietary protocol, RDP, to communicate. RDP was designed to use just about any protocol as a transport, but currently supports only TCP/IP. According to Microsoft, if customer demand is great enough, then they may choose to support other protocols in future versions. RDP is a fast, efficient protocol that uses virtual channels to accomplish the great feats that it does. Virtual channels exist logically within the protocol. There are separate 'channels' for different I/O functions, such as mouse, keyboard, video, and client redirectors.

RDP

Remote Desktop Protocol (RDP) was first introduced in Windows NT 4.0 Terminal Server edition. At the time, it was a new protocol based on the International Telecommunications Union (ITU) T.120 standards. RDP 4.0, while effective in servicing thin-client needs over fast LAN-like connections, has failed to provide the necessary speed under slow dial-up links. Although RDP included great components, such as disconnect support and encryption, it lacked other features that consumers wanted that required them to purchase third-party products to make up for RDP's shortcomings.

With the release of the Windows 2000 Server line came RDP 5.0, a much-improved thin-client protocol based on the original. RDP 5.0 incorporates several new features that reflected consumer demand. RDP 5.0 also included new compression technologies and lower overhead, along with the ability to run over wide area network (WAN) and dial-up links.

Architecture RDP is a multichannel-capable protocol that carries the keystrokes, mouse movements, and display data in an encrypted format, as well as session and presentation information from the server. It has the ability to use 64,000 channels, which gives it plenty of room for growth in the future and for third-party add-on products.

RDP on the server side uses its own driver to render and "packetize" display information sent to clients. Clients receive the display information and RDP gives the information to the Win32 Graphical Display Interface (GDI) Application Program Interface (API) for local display. RDP on the client side intercepts keyboard and mouse strokes and sends them to the server. The server uses its own virtual keyboard and mouse drivers to interpret these commands.

Better Encryption All versions of RDP have always had encryption as a feature. However, in Windows 2000 you can choose 56- or 128-bit encryption. Encryption is necessary for secure environments. Without encryption, packet sniffing by hackers would give them access to all user names and user passwords on Terminal Server. RDP uses Rivest-Shamir-Adleman (RSA) Security's RC4 cipher. RC4 is a cipher stream designed and streamlined for encrypting small and varying blocks of data. RC4 is also used in other protocols such as SSL. It's a reliable technology.

Lower Bandwidth Requirements RDP 5.0 needs less bandwidth than its predecessor, RDP 4.0. RDP 5.0 uses many features to reduce overhead and bandwidth requirements. Better compression, disk-based bitmap caching, and caching glyphs and bitmaps in memory allow for smaller packets and fewer bitmaps being sent across the wire. The algorithms for determining screen update intervals were optimized for low bandwidth connections without sacrificing application responsiveness. Round-trip latency was reduced by 50–80 percent per keystroke with this technology. This allows RDP 5.0 to perform well over low-bandwidth connections such as dial-up. This is a major improvement for RDP 5.0 over RDP 4.0.

New features Those of you familiar with MetaFrame 1.8 for Windows NT 4.0 Terminal Server Edition (TSE), will be familiar with new features available to RDP 5.0. RCP 5.0 now has clipboard mapping. Clients can cut and paste between local and remote applications as well between sessions. It also has printer redirection. Clients will be able to print to local devices from remote sessions.

Upgrading from RDP 4.0 to RDP 5.0

Upgrading from RDP 4.0 to 5.0 will be a breeze. RDP 5.0 was designed to be backward compatible with Windows NT 4.0 TSE, and Windows 2000 Terminal Services was designed to be backward compatible with RDP 4.0. So you'll be able to slowly upgrade portions of your thin-client network without too much hassle on the client side.

Windows 2000 ships with the RDP 5.0 client. When you have Terminal Services installed in applications mode, you can use the Terminal Services

Client Creator in the Administrative Tools folder to create client disks. The RDP 5.0 client only supports Windows 3.11b, Windows 9x, Windows NT, and Windows 2000. You can also install clients from the network. The setup files the Terminal Services Client Creator uses to make install disks are located in %systemroot%\system32\clients\tsclients\net. You can share this directory directly or copy its contents to a share elsewhere. You can then instruct clients on how to install the software.

When upgrading your clients, their current connection configurations should remain intact. If you wish to deploy new connection configurations with the client, there are a few ways to accomplish this. The first option we'll describe is probably the preferred method because it doesn't require user intervention. Before you deploy the new client to users, create the connections that users will be using in the RDP 5.0 client. Once you have the connections configured, export them to .CNS files. You can then either put them on the first disk of the installation set or in the shared install directory you created earlier. When the install program is run it will check for the existence of these .CNS files. If they exist, it will use them to create the connection settings specified in the file. The other possible deployment method is to send the .CNS files to users and have them manually import them using the '-import' switch from the command line for the RDP 5.0 client or using 'import' from the 'file' drop-down menu.

TCP/IP

TCP/IP is the transport protocol used by RDP. If you plan on implementing Terminal Server on a routed network, you will need a thorough under-standing of TCP/IP, which is a complicated protocol. Addressing and routing are more complicated in TCP/IP than other routed protocols.

The combination of IP addresses, address classes, and subnet masks determine routing. Each one of these attributes will be discussed separately.

TCP/IP addressing occurs in the IP portion of the protocol at the net-work layer of the OSI model. IP addresses are 32-bit addresses. You can view them in either dotted decimal format or in binary format. It is impor-tant to be able to convert between the two. Dotted decimal format has four octets separated by decimals. The dotted decimal format is shown below.

```
10.10.12.35
```

Binary format is displayed as a string of 1's and 0's. Think of the 0's as standing for 'off' and the 1's standing for 'on'. The position of the 1's and 0's in the string determines its numeric (decimal) value. To convert a binary IP address to a dotted decimal address you must first split the string into four octets. The position of the bits, starting from left to right, line up with a power of two starting at 2^7 down to 2^0. Positions (or powers of two) that have corresponding bits of 1 will have that number *active* in the octet. Add all of the active numbers together in an octet to get the decimal value for that octet. This same procedure is followed for the remaining three octets to get the full 32-bit dotted decimal address.

Here's an example of how it's done.

Let's assume you have a binary IP address of:

```
11011010100110111000110011110010
```

Break this into four groups of 8 bits:

```
11011010 10011011 10001100 11110010
```

Each bit corresponds to a power of 2 in this manner:

(2^7) (2^6) (2^5) (2^4) (2^3) (2^2) (2^1) (2^0)

128 64 32 16 8 4 2 1

The active numbers in the first octet (the leftmost) are:

128 + 64 + 16 + 8 + 2

This equals 218. The first octet of this address is 218. Simply follow this same procedure for the remaining 3 octets.

Once you finish converting, your dotted decimal address will be 218.155.140.242. You reverse this procedure to convert from dotted decimal to binary.

IP addresses are used to uniquely identify a computer on a network. The addresses are logically divided to identify the network that the computer is on and the host of that network.

```
218.155.140.242

|--------------| |----|

Network        Host
```

You can identify the network portion of the address from the host portion of the address by looking at the first three bits in the first octet (leftmost). In our example the first three bits are 110. This is significant because those bits will determine what class that address belongs in.

Class A = First bit is always a 0	default subnet mask = 255.0.0.0
Class B = First two bits are always 10	default subnet mask = 255.255.0.0
Class C = First three bits are always 110	default subnet mask = 255.255.255.0

Using this, we can see that our IP address (218.155.140.242) is a Class C address. Class A addresses use the first octet to denote the network and the remaining three for the host. Class B addresses use the first two octets to denote the network and the remaining two for the host. Class C addresses use the first three octets to denote the network and the last octet for the host. Subnet masks, in binary, will show you which bits are part of the network portion of the address. Those bits with a 1 corresponding to the bit in the IP address are part of the network portion of the address. Those bits with a 0 corresponding to the bit in the IP address are part of the host portion of the address. 255 is an octet with all 1's.

The class can be augmented further by changing the default subnet mask. Let's assume we want to create two networks with the address range of 218.155.140.0. By adding bits to the subnet mask we gain more bits for the network portion, and thus allow for more networks. This does, however, reduce the number of available hosts on each network (fewer bits are available for the host portion of the address). You would use a subnet mask of 255.255.255.192. This will allow you to have two subnets with up to 62 hosts each.

Routing decisions are based on the network portion of an address. This is why correct addressing and subnetting are important. If you don't have the proper address scheme in place, then packets may not get routed to your servers, effectively shutting them down.

Other Protocols

RDP currently only supports TCP/IP as a transport protocol. IPX/SPX, NetBEUI, or any other protocol cannot be used. However, Microsoft has designed RDP to be transport independent. So if consumer demand calls for it, they can quickly and easily adapt it to other transports.

Analyzing the Environment

You should examine your environment before beginning your deployment or testing. You should know what your network currently looks like and its traffic trends. You should know what other kinds of servers your environments host, as well as the types of clients you currently support and the kinds of clients you wish to support after deployment. You should also have a thorough understanding of how Terminal Services will affect your network. Applications hosted by the Terminal Server could affect network performance. We touched on this issue earlier and will expand on it now.

Knowing the current physical layout of your network will help you deal with bandwidth issues, anticipate problem areas, and quickly plan new layouts. Combining this knowledge with traffic trends will help you to identify network bottlenecks. Being able to identify and correct these bottlenecks will help ensure that proper bandwidth is available for the Terminal Server client and other applications.

Knowing and tracking client types in use before installing your Terminal Servers will help you identify possible problems with upgrading to Windows 2000 Terminal Servers. For example, let's say you currently support DOS and Macintosh clients using the ICA client and Citrix MetaFrame on your servers. You're going to have a problem when you upgrade to Windows 2000 Terminal Server unless you upgrade your MetaFrame as well. Windows 2000 Terminal Services will not support DOS or Macintosh clients so you must upgrade MetaFrame or you will no longer be able to support those clients. It's up to you to determine whether or not this is acceptable.

Predicting how Windows 2000 Terminal Services will function can be accomplished during your testing phase. You can use a Network Monitor as seen in Figure 3.9 to capture network statistics while testing your Terminal Servers. This information should give you a pretty good idea of what kind of and how much traffic the new server will add to the network. Keep in mind that you may be taking the older servers offline as you bring the new ones online. So the traffic generated by them will disappear. Don't forget to include that in your calculations. You can get traffic statistics for the old servers in the same way you did for the new servers.

Figure 3.9 Use Network Monitor or another package to check network usage.

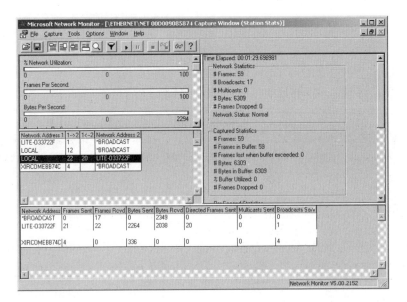

Some applications, such as Internet Explorer or Netscape, will generate other traffic as well. You should know which applications will be accessing the Internet and attempt to predict their bandwidth needs. This may be impossible with applications such as Internet browsers. Others may be more cooperative.

Three-tier applications add a whole new dimension to thin-client bandwidth issues. When the Terminal Server needs to connect to another server, such as SQL, your best bet is to create a new segment with another NIC over a VLAN directly to the SQL server through the switch (Figure 3.10). Packets passing between the Terminal Server and the SQL server within the VLAN will not contend for bandwidth from the clients or the other NIC. VLANs (802.1q) allow the switch to logically segment networks based on tags added to packets traversing the internetwork.

Figure 3.10 A VLAN between the Terminal Server and a SQL server.

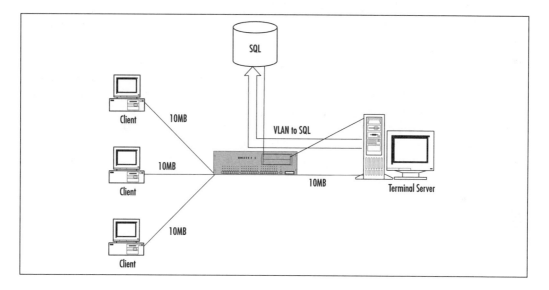

Network Requirements for New Installations

You may find yourself in a situation in which no network infrastructure currently exists. There are many decisions to make when designing your new infrastructure to properly handle a Terminal Services environment. You'll want to consider bandwidth issues, point-of-entry issues, and external application integration issues.

We covered bandwidth issues earlier, but let's go over it again to reinforce the important concepts. You'll first need to determine how much bandwidth you'll need to accomplish your goals. Let's assume that your primary goals are the following:

- Provide necessary bandwidth to clients on the LAN
- Provide Internet access to all clients via Terminal Servers
- Provide access to a SQL server via Terminal Servers
- Provide access to file and print servers residing on the LAN via the Terminal Server

Let's also assume that you'll be supporting 5000 users simultaneously on the LAN with sporadic access via the Internet. We'll take these requirements into account individually to come up with a solution.

LAN

For the sake of discussion and ease, let's assume that all the extra services the clients need are on the LAN. First, you need to provide the necessary underlying bandwidth for the clients. As stated before, we need approximately 30 KB of bandwidth per user. For 5000 users, that's going to be 150 MB. Now let's build your network. First, you'll need to get the clients connected to the network. For a network this large, you'll need a lot of hubs: 107 10/100Mbps 48 port hubs will provide you with enough network drops to accommodate all of the users and still give you plenty of bandwidth in each collision domain. All of the computers attached to a hub will contend for network access with each other. Even with all 47 computers sending and receiving RDP packets, it will only take about 1.4 MB of bandwidth to satisfy their needs. Uplink the hubs to a large, fast switch capable of handling lots of data on its backplane. Many vendors offer large switches with the port density that you'll need to accommodate your users.

For this environment, get a switch with a 10/100 port density of 120 (120 10/100Mbps ports) so that you can connect all 107 hubs to the switch over 100MB links and have 14 ports left over for connecting the Terminal Servers and the Internet connection. If you find through application testing that you need more Terminal Servers than the switch currently supports, you may need more ports later to connect more Terminal Servers.

I recommend getting a switch that works in a modular fashion with a chassis containing the backplane and modules or cards that have the actual interfaces on them with different interface types and densities. Let's just assume that through application testing you've determined that you only need 13 Terminal Servers to serve all 5000 clients efficiently. Use 100Mbps NICs in the Servers to connect directly to the switch. This will lower bandwidth needs on the Terminal Servers and give users the necessary bandwidth to access the Internet. A 150Mbps NICs need for bandwidth evenly distributed between 13 servers works out to about 11.5 Mbps per server, plenty of left over bandwidth for the Internet. The Internet connection can connect from a router directly to the switch via a firewall. You can use the firewall to direct RDP traffic from the Internet to the Terminal Servers.

Now let's connect the Terminal Servers to file and print servers. For this, we'll add a Gigabit uplink module to the switch and link it to another, smaller, switch. This switch will connect to file and print servers and allow access directly from the client or via the Terminal Server. For the SQL server, we'll add a second NIC to all of the Terminal Servers and connect them to a third switch at 100 Mbps and connect the SQL Server to the switch as well. With this, our LAN is complete. Figure 3.11 gives an example of what the LAN would look like.

Figure 3.11 Network example.

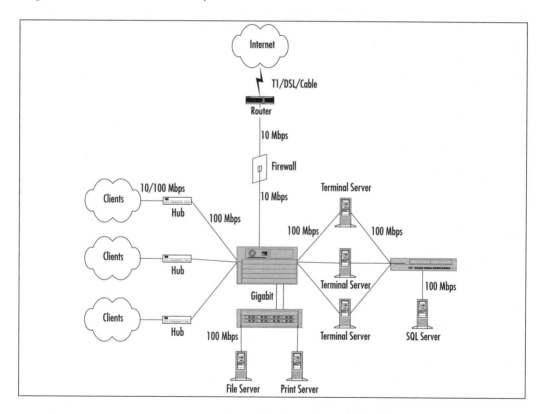

This LAN was designed to accommodate 5000 Terminal Services users as well as Internet access, file and print services, and a SQL application. The SQL application can only be accessed via Terminal Services.

WAN

When connecting to Terminal Servers over a WAN, follow the guidelines set forth earlier. For a good connection, you'll need 30 KB of bandwidth per user. If your clients will be accessing external applications like SQL server, place the Terminal Servers near the application server, not the client. Terminal Server-to-application server traffic will be significantly higher than client-to-Terminal Server traffic.

Internet Connectivity

A connection to the Internet is highly recommended if for no other reason than to make licensing easier for you. A dial-up Internet line would serve that purpose. Users may want to surf the Internet for various reasons or you may want to allow connections to your Terminal Server via the Internet. In either case, I highly recommend a firewall to protect your LAN. For Web surfing purposes, you'll have to open port 80. You'll have to open port 443 as well if you wish to allow SSL-encrypted web traffic. For RDP traffic to your Terminal Servers, you'll have to open port 3389. You may wish to create a DMZ as stated earlier for increased security.

Upgrade from Windows NT 4.0 Terminal Services Considerations

There are many considerations to keep in mind when upgrading from previous versions of Terminal Server, Citrix MetaFrame, or Citrix WinFrame. You must consider the version you are upgrading from and the type of migration you are planning. You will have to purchase Terminal Server Client Access Licenses. You must check your current applications for compatibility. All this must be done before upgrading your servers.

Here are some of the questions you should ask yourself:

- What OS am I running currently?
- How do I plan on upgrading to Windows 2000: Direct upgrade or clean install?
- How will I upgrade my current OS if I choose a direct upgrade?
- Are my servers currently set up to handle a clean install smoothly? If not, what do I need to do to handle a clean install smoothly?
- Will my current applications run on Windows 2000?
- Which applications will need to be upgraded?
- Which applications will not need to be upgraded?

- How many Terminal Server Client Access Licenses (CALs) will I have to purchase?
- How will my applications be affected by the upgrade?

In a best-case scenario you will want to do a clean install of Windows 2000 Terminal Services for your upgrade. Upgrading current servers involves overcoming lots of problems. From having to upgrade applications on production servers to trying to meet the new hardware requirements, you'll definitely have your work cut out for you. You should also realize that Windows 2000 stores its OS files in the default \WINNT directory and user specific information in the \Documents and Settings folder. Windows NT 4.0 TSE uses a default OS directory of \WTSRV and stores its user-specific settings in \WTSRV\PROFILES. I'm sure you can see the inherent problems that might arise from this change in structure. You'll be able to avoid this by doing a clean install of Windows 2000 on a separate server.

Doing a clean install will allow you to test applications and make mistakes without affecting production environments. A clean install, however, requires you to have the proper Terminal Server environment. User profiles should be roaming profiles and documents should be stored on network resources such as a central file server in home directories. If this is not the case, you should start to migrate from whatever your current setup is to accommodate these prerequisites. You should also only install Windows 2000 Terminal Services on member servers. Setting them up as domain controllers will require additional memory, CPU, and network bandwidth usage.

Check your applications for compatibility with Windows 2000. If an application is not compatible with Windows 2000, you will have to upgrade it to a version that is. This will most likely have already been accomplished when you sized your servers. Keep in mind that Windows 2000 ships with Internet Explorer 5.01. So if you have Web-enabled applications that run on Terminal Server, make sure that they work with this version of Internet Explorer. You will also want to find out if any application compatibility scripts exist for your applications. Most programs that have a Windows 2000 Compatibility Logo will be compatible with Terminal Services. You can find some application compatibility scripts in %systemroot%\Application Compatibility Scripts\Install. You can also find some on the Windows Update Web site.

If you elect to go the direct upgrade path then here are some guidelines you should follow. The requirements for upgrading depend on your current OS.

WinFrame, Any Version

Upgrading from any version of Citrix WinFrame requires you to first upgrade to Windows NT 4.0 Terminal Server Edition. Then you can upgrade to Windows 2000 Terminal Services. You should follow the guidelines for upgrading from Windows NT 4.0 Terminal Server Edition once you have it installed over WinFrame.

Windows NT 4.0 Terminal Server Edition

Upgrading from Windows NT 4.0 Terminal Server Edition (TSE) is rather easy compared to WinFrame. When you run the Windows 2000 Setup, it will recognize Windows NT 4.0 TSE as the installed OS and automatically enable Terminal Services in application mode during setup. You must have Service Pack 4 installed before upgrading to Windows 2000.

MetaFrame 1.0 or 1.8

Upgrading from MetaFrame 1.*x* is very similar to upgrading from NT 4.0 TSE. However, a few additional steps are required. MetaFrame 1.0 and 1.8 are not supported on Windows 2000. Citrix has an upgraded edition of MetaFrame 1.8 that will run on Windows 2000 (we'll refer to this edition as MetaFrame 1.8a). There are a few ways to take care of this situation. You can uninstall MetaFrame before upgrading to Windows 2000 and then install MetaFrame 1.8a, or you can simply upgrade to Windows 2000 without uninstalling MetaFrame 1.*x* and then install MetaFrame 1.8a once the upgrade is complete. Understand that MetaFrame and the ICA protocol will not function if you choose not to uninstall MetaFrame 1.*x* until you upgrade to MetaFrame 1.8a. Of course, you can also upgrade MetaFrame 1.*x* to MetaFrame 1.8a before you upgrade to Windows 2000. Just as with Windows NT 4.0 TSE you must have Service Pack 4 installed before upgrading to Windows 2000.

Here's an example of how you would upgrade your MetaFrame server to Windows 2000 Terminal Services.

1. You should log onto the console. You must log in with an account that has administrator privileges.

2. Disable logins on the server by using the **change logon /disable** command. Wait for all users to disconnect and make sure that no more users are using the system. If necessary, close disconnected session using Citrix MetaFrame Administration.

3. Ensure that you have at least Service Pack 4 installed. If not, then install it or another higher version.

4. Uninstall MetaFrame. Be sure to use Add/Remove Programs in the Control Panel. If your drives were remapped during the MetaFrame installation, I recommend simply upgrading your MetaFrame installation to MetaFrame 1.8a instead of removing it.

5. Insert your Windows 2000 CD-ROM and when asked whether you want to upgrade to the new version of Windows select Yes.

6. You must accept the end user license agreement (EULA) to continue.

7. You will be informed of potential upgrade problems if they exist. You should accept the recommendations of the system.

8. Files will be copied to the system and it will reboot. This will start the text mode setup. Setup will reboot again once this portion is done. (This part can take a long time, so be patient.)

9. After rebooting, the server will enter the graphical setup portion. Terminal Services will automatically be enabled in application mode. Once this section is complete the server will reboot for the last time. (When doing a clean install you will have to manually select Terminal Services.) Figure 3.12 shows Terminal Services and Terminal Services Licensing in the Windows Components Wizard. You will reach this screen during setup. If you elect not to install Terminal Services, you can go back to this screen later by running Add/Remove Programs in the Control Panel as seen in Figure 3.12. When you install Terminal Services, you will be prompted with a screen asking you to select either Remote Administration or Application Server as shown in Figure 3.13.

10. You can install MetaFrame once the system is back up.

Figure 3.12 Add/Remove programs screen in Control Panel.

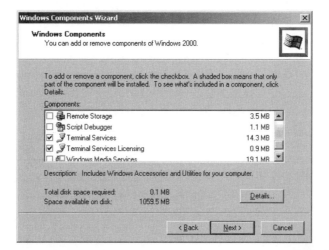

Figure 3.13 The Terminal Services Setup screen: Choose between the Remote administration or Application server mode.

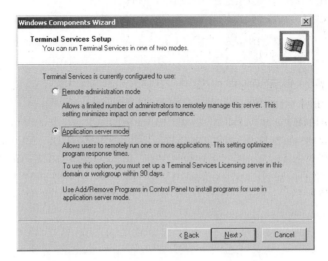

Windows NT 4.0

When upgrading from the standard Windows NT 4.0 server, you must manually select Terminal Services and select application mode. This will install Windows 2000 with Terminal Services.

Upgrading your servers to Windows 2000 can seem like a daunting task after exploring all of the issues that must be considered. However, you can have a successful upgrade experience if you follow the guidelines set forth previously.

Integration with Citrix MetaFrame or WinFrame

I can't imagine why anyone would want to integrate Windows 2000 Terminal Services with MetaFrame or WinFrame. You'll give yourself more headaches than it's probably worth. However, if you do need to, for political reasons maybe, then there are some things you should consider. You'll have to maintain client software for two systems, one for MetaFrame and WinFrame and one for Terminal Server. You'll also have to open ports for both systems in your firewalls. It can be done. Just keep in mind the added difficulties you'll face.

Summary

Designing and placing your Terminal Servers on your network is the basis for a productive and successful deployment. How you design your servers will have a big impact on performance and usability of the servers. Incorrectly sizing your servers could doom your project to failure or simply plague you with user complaints.

Placing the servers on the internetwork will more often than not determine bandwidth availability. Because of this, proper placement is required for the most efficient use of bandwidth. Overutilized bandwidth will give users poor performance. Remember that you need to avoid performance problems in order to successfully deploy Terminal Services and reduce your overall Total Cost of Operation (TCO).

Understanding your environment will help you make decisions for server placement. Knowing your network in advance of placing your servers will greatly help you to make informed decisions. Following the guidelines set forth in this chapter will help you to successfully size and deploy Windows 2000 Terminal Services for any size environment.

FAQs

Q: Can I force my users to only have access to particular applications when they logon to the terminal server?

A: The short answer is yes. Accomplishing this is a little bit more complicated than that, however. You can configure the Terminal Services client to launch an application after logon, but clients can change this setting. However, you can force an application to launch when a user logs on by specifying the application in the user's properties in Active Directory Users and Computers. Figure 3.14 shows this screen. By checking the "Start the following program at logon:" box you can specify an application to start when the user logs on.

There is an inherent problem with this strategy. You can only specify one application, and if the user is forced to open that one application only, they will also not have access to the desktop. Therefore, you would need multiple user domains and Terminal Servers to accomplish the same thing MetaFrame can do with just one of both—multiple published applications on a single server.

Figure 3.14 The Environment tab in Guest Properties.

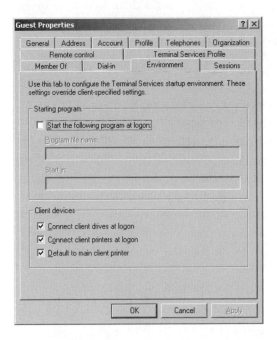

Q: Are the sizing requirements set forth for Windows 2000 Terminal Services the same as those set forth for Citrix MetaFrame on Windows 2000?

A: No, they are not. See Chapter 4 for further explanation on sizing requirements.

Q: What client operating systems does Windows 2000 Terminal Services support?

A: Windows 2000 Terminal Services supports Windows NT, Windows 9*x*, and Windows 3.1. Citrix MetaFrame 1.8 for Windows 2000 supports a greater number of client operating systems.

Q: Is RDP better than Citrix's ICA?

A: No. Citrix's ICA supports more functions and is a faster protocol. However, increased functionality means increased complexity. There are more configurable options with ICA that can increase administration demands.

Q: On a network with 40,000 users, I need to have 100 Human Resources people using Peoplesoft at the same time. We have the Peoplesoft server in New York; where do we put the Terminal Servers, and how many do I need?

A: You should put all the Terminal Servers on the same network segment (literally attached to the same hub or switch) as the Peoplesoft servers. Using the 25 users per processor rule, you can have a single Terminal Server with four or more processors, or you can have two or more servers for redundancy—making certain to have at least four processors and sufficient RAM among them.

Chapter 4

Designing a Citrix MetaFrame Internetwork

Solutions in this chapter:

- Designing and Placing MetaFrame Servers on the Network

- Designing an Internetwork with Multiple MetaFrame Servers

- Implementing MetaFrame-Supported Protocols

- Analyzing the Environment

Introduction

Citrix MetaFrame is not identical to Windows 2000 Terminal Services. It is a set of applications, utilities, and a proprietary Citrix thin-client protocol that is installed on top of Windows 2000 Server, which already has Terminal Services installed.

While the Citrix MetaFrame design has many of the same requirements that Windows 2000 Terminal Services design has, there are many differences, which dictate different design considerations. These differences are based on the protocols and client operating systems that are supported. Citrix MetaFrame also has the ability to provide load balancing of applications, which can impact the design and placement of the servers.

Designing and Placing MetaFrame Servers on the Network

Most technology projects follow the same process. First you have a business requirement that drives a vision. The vision then gives rise to the method with which the company seeks to satisfy the business requirement with a process and/or technology change. This leads to a design stage, followed by testing and development. Then there is a pilot, and finally a full-production deployment of the process and/or technology. At some point in the future, there may be another business requirement requiring this process to begin all over again, so it is somewhat cyclical in nature. This process is illustrated in Figure 4.1.

Figure 4.1 Project cycle.

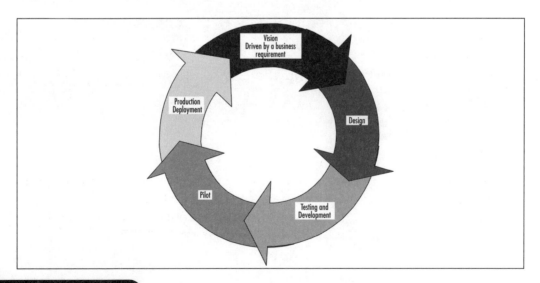

When you begin designing your Citrix MetaFrame environment—that is, the server and the network on which it will communicate—you should already have one or more business requirements and a vision that the MetaFrame server should satisfy. You should do your best to ensure that these business requirements are considered whenever you make a decision.

For example, if your business requirement is to eliminate viruses on the network and you discovered that they are being spread mainly through users bringing floppy disks in from outside your network, you could deploy Citrix MetaFrame to control the spread of viruses, but that would be successful *only if* you did not have floppy disk drives mapped to the Citrix MetaFrame sessions, and/or you replaced PCs with terminals that did not include floppy disk drives.

On the other hand, if your business requirement is to enable access to a SQL application on a global network where there are slow, unreliable links in places like Barrows, Alaska and Moscow, Russia, then you could deploy Citrix MetaFrame to provide a near-real-time access to the application. However, that would be successful *only if* you placed the MetaFrame server on the same subnet as the SQL Server (or on a well-connected subnet in the same location, if the same subnet is not feasible) and if you provided dial-up lines to back up those unreliable network links.

No matter what, you should always let the business requirement drive the technology vision, and then your project will be successful.

Sizing the Server

The first step of your design should be to specify the size of one of your MetaFrame servers. This process is called *capacity planning*. Many Citrix MetaFrame projects begin with a single server. Then, as more users get acclimated to the system, they stay online longer and the administrator ends up having to acquire more licenses and to either add more power to the existing server or add more servers into a pool. Accounting for growth and usage patterns is easier if you simply start with a larger size than you need, and plan to have a pool of servers, *even if* you begin with a single server, for your initial project.

The size of the server will depend on two factors:

1. How many users will be online concurrently
2. What types of applications will be used

These two factors will be used to determine what size components you need within your server—memory, processors, and storage.

To determine how many users will be online concurrently, you first need to know how many users will need access to the server at all. For example, if you have a Citrix MetaFrame server deployed so that the 40 people in Human Resources (HR) and the 30 people in Information Technology (IT) can access the PeopleSoft application from anywhere in the world, then your total users are 70. If half of those people are in London, England, and the other half are in Los Angeles, California, then the mere time zone difference would drive the concurrent usage to a maximum of 35. You'll probably find that there will be closer to 20 (about 60 percent of the maximum number) concurrent users at any one point in time. There is an easy way to manage the maximum concurrent users—simply purchase that number of licenses and no more will be able to logon! Users may not be happy about this in crunch periods, though, so be aware of what limits you want to impose and how they will affect the business.

Applications drive the way that the MetaFrame server will be used. If you are deploying the MetaFrame server to provide a PeopleSoft application, for example, you should take a moment to consider what other applications the users will need to have available while they are using the PeopleSoft application. Do they need a calculator? Do they need a word processor? Do they need a spreadsheet? Each additional application that is used by a user will increase the stress on the server components.

For Managers

Accounting for Growth

Expect the unexpected and double up the size of your server. Growth and change in usage of your MetaFrame server is going to happen. This story follows the typical pattern I've seen:

1. One business unit in the company needs the server to provide one application.

2. They start to use it and find that it would also be great to have their new MetaFrame server provide another application, too.

3. Somehow, some other business unit discovers that the MetaFrame server exists and decides that it would work well for their own application.

Continued

4. Then the server is maxed out on licenses, or storage, or memory, or processing power, so they augment the server and add another, larger server.

5. The next thing you know, there are multiple servers on the network with different applications.

6. After that, someone decides they should pool all the resources and then all those servers need to be added to a MetaFrame Server Farm.

7. It's around this time that someone discovers that MetaFrame can share applications over the Internet. This leads to new applications and possibly a second Server Farm on a demilitarized zone (DMZ) to service Web users.

8. Then, they implement VideoFrame to provide better video integration on the Web site with another MetaFrame Server.

Unexpected? To others, yes. To you, not anymore!

RAM

Windows 2000 Server uses a 32-bit address space. This means that the operating system can address up to 2^{32} bytes of memory that can be accessed at any time. 2^{32} is equivalent to 4 Gigabytes (GB) of random access memory (RAM). This 4GB is divided such that half (2GB) is assigned to each user-mode process and the remaining half (2GB) is assigned to the kernel, handling system data structures. What this means is that the maximum RAM you can have that will affect the way the kernel works is 4GB. With a MetaFrame Server, you will notice when you hit that RAM limit on the kernel by odd errors, such as Out of Paged Memory. If you ever hit this maximum and you have 4GB or more of RAM, your best bet is to scale out by adding more servers to a pool of MetaFrame servers, rather than to scale up the single server with more RAM.

If you have need for more RAM, you do have options. Windows 2000 Advanced Server supports up to 8GB of RAM on servers that use Intel's Physical Address Extensions (PAE). Windows 2000 DataCenter Server supports up to 64GB of RAM, however, these servers must be built and configured by an Original Equipment Manufacturer—you can't get the DataCenter Server version off the shelf.

The user-mode process side is interesting. When a user logs onto Citrix MetaFrame and executes an application, if that user is the only user online, the system lets that user have all the RAM available. When the second user logs on, the new user uses some RAM, and then there is less available to each user. As more users are added, the available RAM is divided by the usage of the session and the applications used during each session until all users experience a performance reduction.

The minimum requirements for a Windows 2000 Terminal Services server running Citrix MetaFrame is 64MB, although a minimum of 128MB is recommended. This 128MB minimum is recommended for the *operating system only.* That's enough to boot up the server and logon without crashing into a variety of blue screen of death (BSOD) errors. However, to actually run Terminal Services for multiple, simultaneous users, you need to add RAM.

You should determine what type of users will be on the system before determining how much RAM you need. There are two basic types of users:

- **Clerical Users** These users mainly enter data into applications or run a set of basic tasks. Their main applications are word processing, e-mail, Web browsing, and spreadsheets.

- **Knowledge Users** These users are creative. When it comes to applications, they use a lot of graphics and mathematical equations, and they will run multiple applications at a single time. In the Microsoft world, they are also known as "Power Users."

Clerical users will use approximately 4MB of RAM each. Knowledge users will use at least 8MB of RAM and probably more, depending on the types of applications that they use and whether they use several applications simultaneously, and will continue to do so on your MetaFrame server. You can run scripts on a test system to simulate how much RAM these applications will use, and with a third-party utility, you can even simulate the same number of users. While executing these tests, you can run Performance Monitor to determine how much RAM is needed for the knowledge user. Or you can estimate at the upper end that each knowledge user should be granted about 20MB of RAM.

You should discover how many of each type of user you intend to have on your system simultaneously. If you have 200 users, but you expect only 40 of them will ever be online at the same time using the Terminal Server, you should estimate enough RAM to accommodate 40 total simultaneous users. Now, if there are 80 knowledge users and 120 clerical users in the original 200, then you can estimate that of your 40 simultaneous users, that there will be an average of 16 knowledge users and 24 clerical users online simultaneously. Then you execute the formula with these simultaneous users and RAM:

((# of Knowledge users) × (Knowledge RAM))+((# of Clerical users) × (Clerical

RAM))+(Base Operating System RAM)= Lower limit Minimum RAM required

So, given that you have 16 knowledge users that you determine need 20MB of RAM, and 24 clerical users that need 4MB of RAM and 128MB of RAM for the OS, the minimum RAM you will need is 544MB.

If you run a system with that 544MB RAM (this is hypothetical—there is no way a system can have 544MB on it, but please bear with me), and all 16 knowledge users get online and all 24 clerical users get online, you will have a system that will perform slowly. Let's say that you have that system up and running and those users online at once, and all the clerical users log off and then are replaced with knowledge users—then you have trouble. So, you should consider that your upper limit minimum (for emergency's sake) is:

((# of Total simultaneous users) × (Knowledge RAM))+ (Base OS RAM)= upper limit minimum

In our example, the upper limit minimum is 800MB + 128MB RAM = 928MB RAM. Your next task is to round up the upper limit to the next amount that the system can accept—in this case, 1GB of RAM, and consider that the minimum amount that you will install in the server. You can never have enough RAM, so do add more if you have the budget for it.

WARNING

Growth of the number of users on your system can impact performance significantly. If you have sized a server for 40 users and are then requested to enable 60 simultaneous users, then you have a problem. Try to look ahead into the future and determine whether more users will demand access to the Citrix MetaFrame server. You should consider whether your corporate culture promotes adoption of technology at a quick pace, and whether your business is experiencing a high growth rate. With this knowledge, you should try predicting whether you will need more hardware to support additional users, or simply plan to add more servers.

Processors

The version of Windows 2000 Server that you are using will determine your maximum number of processors. Windows 2000 Server allows up to four processors using Symmetrical Multiple Processing (SMP). Windows 2000 Advanced Server allows up to eight SMP processors. Windows 2000 DataCenter Server (from an OEM) supports up to 32 SMP processors.

TIP

One of the methods for estimating your server's requirements is to char-acterize the resource usage of a typical user on a sample system. Use Performance Monitor to scrutinize the Processing, Memory, Paging File, Storage, and Network Interface utilization characteristics of that user. Based on this, you should be able to determine how many users can be supported simultaneously on a server.

The minimum number of processors you need is dependent upon the number of users and types of applications. If you have users who run simple data-entry applications (clerical users), you can squeeze up to 50 concurrent users on a single processor server. On the other hand, if you have users who are running Office suite applications and a few other spe-cial applications (knowledge users), you can only put about 20 concurrent users on a single processor server. If you have high-end knowledge users that need processor-intensive applications, you may be able to have only 10 concurrent users on a single processor server. Most businesses have a group that includes some of each type of user, and on average, can get about 25 users per processor.

The type of processor that you use will affect how many users can be supported as well. For example, a Pentium II 450MHz will not support as many users as a Pentium III 933MHz. You may be able to fit between 5 percent and 10 percent more users per processor when you invest in faster processors. If you can fit 25 users on a Pentium II 450MHz processor, you could then get as many as 28 users on a Pentium III 933MHz.

Now, let's assume that you have the need to provide 400 users access to Citrix MetaFrame with 250 of those being online simultaneously. Of these 400 total users, 300 are clerical users, 75 are standard knowledge users, and 25 are high-end knowledge users. This is equivalent to 75 percent clerical, 19 percent knowledge, and 6 percent high-end. You use a test system and discover that you can put about 23 clerical users with 6 knowledge users and 1 high-end knowledge user on one processor (30 total users)—approximating the same percentages of users you will expect overall. If you need to have 250 users online simultaneously, you must have a minimum of:

$$\frac{(\text{\# of concurrent users})}{(\text{\# of users on a single processor})} = \text{minimum processors}$$

So in the above example:

$$\frac{250}{30} = 8.3$$

There is no such thing as a third of a processor, so you will need to round that figure up to nine processors as your absolute minimum processors.

To figure your minimum number of processors, you will need to determine how many processors it will take to support all of the knowledge and high-end knowledge users online with any remaining spots filled by the clerical users. If you test out that you can have ten high-end users on a single processor, 20 knowledge users on a single processor, and 55 clerical users on a single processor, then you will figure this formula:

$$\frac{((Total \text{ \# of high-end users})}{(\text{\# of high-end users per processor}))} + \frac{((Total \text{ \# of knowledge users})}{(\text{\# of knowledge users per processor}))}$$

$$+ \frac{(((Total \text{ concurrent users} - (high\text{-}end \text{ users} + knowledge \text{ users}))}{(\text{\# of clerical users per processor}))}$$

= upper limit minimum processors

So in our example:

$$\frac{25}{10} + \frac{75}{20} + \frac{(250\text{-}(25+75))}{55} = 8.977$$

As you can see by this formula, you will again need to round up and you still only need to have nine processors. Now your decision is how to divvy up those nine processors and whether to add more processors for growth. You have several options available to you. Option 1 and option 4 are depicted in Figure 4.2:

1. You can obtain a single DataCenter server with 16 processors. This will provide you the capacity for growth, but will not provide any redundancy if that one server fails.

2. You can obtain two Advanced Servers with eight processors each. This will provide you the capacity for growth, and reasonable redundancy in case of failure. (The redundancy is very good in this scenario because each server is nearly able to handle all the 250 users by itself.)

3. You can obtain one Advanced Server with eight processors, and a Windows 2000 Server with between one and four processors. This will provide you small capacity for growth, and a small amount of redundancy. (Redundancy here is skewed—if the Advanced Server goes down, then the standard Windows 2000 Server will not be able to provide the processing power required. But if the Windows 2000 Server fails, the Advanced Server can provide the processing power.)

4. You can obtain three Windows 2000 Servers with four processors each. This will provide some capacity for growth, and a good amount of redundancy. (Redundancy is better here, since if a single server fails, there are still two left—rather than one, as in the other scenarios. Plus, there will be eight processors left online if one server fails.)

Figure 4.2 Distributing processors among servers affects capacity and redundancy.

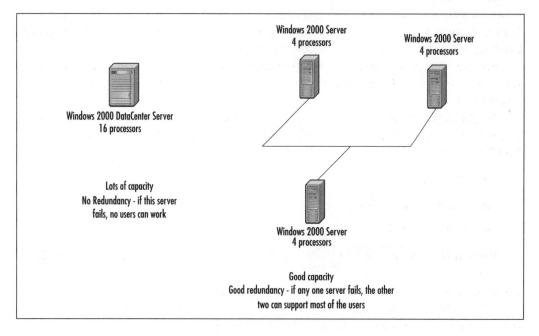

Storage

Storage on the Citrix MetaFrame server includes the hard drives, floppy disk drives, CD-ROM drives, and tape backup systems. In some cases, a Citrix MetaFrame server may need access to a storage area network (SAN) for mission critical data. Some of these storage design decisions are simple—you would most likely purchase a server that already had a floppy disk drive and a CD-ROM drive in it. In addition, if you did not place a tape backup system directly on each of your Citrix MetaFrame servers, at least you would have one available on a server somewhere on the network that could back up the MetaFrame server over the network links.

File System

One of the easier decisions that you will need to make when you deploy the server is which file system to use. Windows 2000 supports:

- FAT (File Allocation Table)
- FAT32 (32-bit File Allocation Table)
- NTFS (NT File System)

FAT is a file system available in many operating systems—DOS, Windows 3.*x*, Windows 9*x*, Windows NT, and OS/2, for example. Because it is common to so many operating systems, it is usually selected for multi-booting. FAT has a 2GB limitation for partitions.

FAT32 is new to Windows 9*x* systems. It was not accessible by Windows NT, but Windows 2000 does support it. FAT32 supports partitions larger than 2GB.

NTFS is the native file system for Windows 2000. It also supports partitions larger than 2GB. In addition, NTFS offers several things that FAT and FAT32 don't:

- Fault tolerance
- Optimized disk space
- Advanced security

Redundant Array of Independent Disks (RAID) support provides fault tolerance that you must configure. NTFS also includes built-in fault tolerance. Log files help recover files that are changed but not written when a failure of the system occurs. NTFS also automatically handles bad sectors on the hard drive without displaying errors.

File compression is one of the ways that NTFS optimizes disk space. You can also set disk quotas for individual users to prevent them from storing more than their fair share of files.

Security on Citrix MetaFrame is extremely important because end users are running their applications from the server console. Without applying strict security measures, users can completely obliterate files on the server. NTFS allows an administrator to apply local security on a file-by-file basis. Table 4.1 lists the access control list (ACL) rights that can be assigned.

Table 4.1 NTFS ACL Rights

Right	File or Folder?	Function
None	File and folder	Cannot access the file or folder
Read Data	File	Open and view the file contents
Write Data	File	Change the file contents
Execute Data	File	Run an executable program or batch file
Delete	File	Delete a file
Change Permissions	File and folder	Change the ACL on a file or folder
Take Ownership	File and folder	Become the owner of a file or folder
List Folder	Folder	View the folder contents
Create Files	Folder	Add files or subfolders
Traverse Folder	Folder	Open up a subfolder

In Windows NT systems, many people installed FAT for the boot drive because there was no other way to access the hard drive if the system failed and it was formatted with NTFS. With Windows 2000, however, there is the Recovery Console that enables you to access the NTFS partition and manipulate files on it. The Recovery Console is available by booting the original Windows 2000 CD-ROM. Or you can install the Recovery Console to be available on the Boot Menu by executing WINNT32/CMDCONS from a command prompt at any time after the server has been installed.

Because NTFS has so many advantages over both FAT and FAT32, it is the optimal selection for a file system on Citrix MetaFrame.

RAID

Windows 2000 supports software-based RAID natively. Software-based RAID means that if you have enough hard disks installed on the system, you can create a custom RAID configuration without needing to install a special array interface card. The types of software-based RAID that Windows 2000 supports are listed in Table 4.2.

Table 4.2 Types of RAID Supported by Windows 2000

RAID level	Type	Tolerance	Minimum number of disks
RAID 0	Disk striping	No tolerance—if a disk fails, the system fails	3
RAID 1	Disk mirroring	Good tolerance—if a disk fails, the other can be configured as the boot disk	2
RAID 1	Disk duplexing	Good tolerance—if a disk fails or if a disk controller fails, the other disk can be configured as the boot disk	2
RAID 5	Disk striping with parity	High tolerance—if a disk fails, the array can be rebuilt while the server is running	3

You should, if possible, implement RAID 5 for fault tolerance. If possible, you should select hardware-based RAID. Hardware-based RAID 5 is superior to software-based RAID 5 because there is no overhead within the operating system. Aside from that, most hardware-based RAID systems work with hot-swappable disk drives so that if one drive fails within an array, another can replace it without the server being brought offline. Hardware-based RAID, from the viewpoint of the operating system, looks like a single hard disk.

Fibre Channel

The most common storage interface method is Small Computer Systems Interface (SCSI). However, one of the newer technologies is Fibre Channel. Fibre Channel is faster than SCSI and scalable in speed. It also has a Fibre Channel-Arbitrated Loop (FC-AL) that allows multiple devices to be connected on one interface to a single computer.

When you install applications on the local hard disk for a Citrix MetaFrame server, you will probably want the application to load up as fast as it can. This will improve performance. When you select your storage system, keep in mind that the faster the access, the better perception by your end users.

Storage Area Networks

Fibre Channel is used by SANs because of its speed and scalability. Fibre Channel Storage systems are attached directly to a storage network and all the servers on that network are configured to access the data on that storage system. This is illustrated in Figure 4.3.

Figure 4.3 SAN architecture.

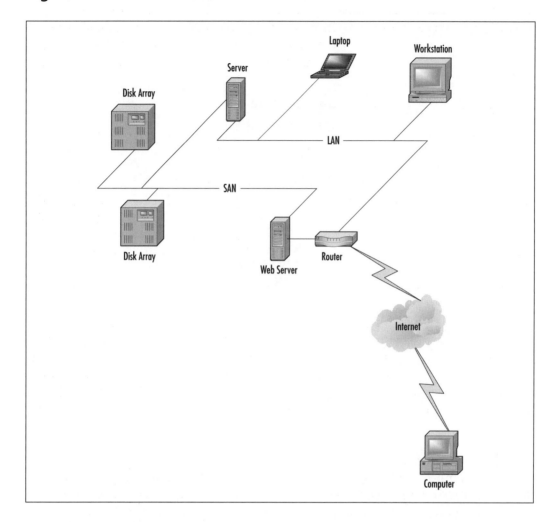

SANs are scalable to terabytes (TB) of information. There is reduced LAN bandwidth utilization because a separate conduit is used for data access. SANs are critical to Internet systems because of their scalability. Multiple Internet and intranet servers can all access the same database. In comparison to a traditional storage system, where each server carries the data on its own hard disk, the SAN will allow a centrally managed store for data. This translates to not having to consider which file server has that file stored on it, and not having multiple instances of the same file. Plus, there is real-time data access from both internal users and external Web users.

If you have a SAN implemented in your network, you should consider what type of data access your users will need, and whether your Citrix MetaFrame server should be directly connected to it. However, since the Citrix MetaFrame server traditionally acts as a client to other servers, it is far more likely that you will not have that server interact directly with the SAN.

Network Interfaces

Some vendors offer server hardware that supports multiple network interface cards (NIC) that can either split up the traffic sent to the server from the same network segment (load balancing), or that can come online if the main NIC fails (failover redundancy). If you have a server that supports many concurrent users, you may discover that the network interface card is a bottleneck. To avoid this, you should select a server that can load balance the traffic between two or more NICs. If you wish to avoid the disastrous cost of a NIC failure, you should select a server that supports failover redundancy.

When implementing a Citrix MetaFrame server with more than one NIC, where each NIC is on a separate subnet and separate IP address (a *multihomed* server), you should ensure that the server is not the ICA Master Browser. If you do install a multihomed MetaFrame server that is an ICA Master Browser, the ICA Browser service can broadcast on one segment. It will then switch to the other segment, interfering with performance of the other Citrix MetaFrame servers. The ICA Browser service uses directed packets to communicate with other servers. If you wish to link up multiple Citrix servers on two different networks, an ICA Gateway that connects two different ICA Master Browsers is the appropriate configuration.

In order to reconfigure the ICA Browser service, start by opening the Citrix Server Administration tool. Select the ICA Browser tab. Select a server, configure the ICA Browser to not attempt to become the master browser and click the Apply button. Finally, open the Services utility in the Administrative Tools menu and Stop and Restart the ICA Browser Service.

Modems

One of the business requirements that Citrix MetaFrame may provide is remote access to mission-critical applications. If so, there is the question of whether to have dial-up users call a Citrix MetaFrame server directly, or to call a Remote Access Server (RAS) elsewhere on the network.

If you already have a RAS server in place, you may not need to consider modems at all. If you do not, or feel that there is a need for users to access the Citrix MetaFrame directly, then you should select your modems. Citrix MetaFrame should be configured to support the number of concurrent dial-in users you expect. If you need 15 people to dial in and only eight of them will be dialing in concurrently, then you need a minimum of eight modems in your modem pool. You should include more than your minimum to be able to handle periods of high demand and for redundancy in case of modem failure. To handle multiple modems, you can purchase modem cards that support multiple modems, or even external modem pools that are rack-mountable.

Up to this point, the word *modem* refers to analog modems. In some areas, such as Europe, you may find that you need an Integrated Services Digital Network (ISDN) modem pool. ISDN provides digital access over copper telephone wires. There are two configurations:

1. **Basic Rate Interface (BRI)** A total of 144 Kbps bandwidth using one data (D) channel at the rate of 16 Kbps and two bearer (B) channels at the rate of 64 Kbps. D channels carry overhead traffic, while B channels carry voice and data. BRI runs over standard copper telephone cables.

2. **Primary Rate Interface (PRI)** A total of 1.54 Mbps bandwidth using one D channel at the rate of 64 Kbps and 23 B channels at the rate of 64 Kbps. PRI uses a T1 leased line and does not run over standard telephone cable.

When your users dial in, they will most likely be using a BRI configuration, and in some cases will only be using a single B channel. However, you can have a PRI configuration at your site that allows up to 23 concurrent users dialing into separate B channels. In most cases, this will require special hardware—perhaps an ISDN router that accepts the incoming calls separately from the server. If you do purchase an interface card that installs into your server, you will most likely need to add the ISDN card using the manufacturer's provided drivers and the Control Panel's Add/Remove Hardware Wizard, depicted in Figure 4.4.

Once that has completed, your next step is to create the connections that will be available to incoming calls. To do so, right-click on My Network Places and choose Properties, then double-click Make New Connection. When the wizard appears, select the option to Accept Incoming Connections as shown in Figure 4.5.

After clicking Next, select the interface on which the calls will be dialing in. The dialog depicted in Figure 4.6 will enable you to accept virtual private connections through the Internet.

Next, select which users in the Active Directory can connect. The next screen lets you choose which protocols are enabled for connecting. On the final dialog, you can name the connection and click Finish to add it.

Figure 4.4 Add Remove Hardware Wizard.

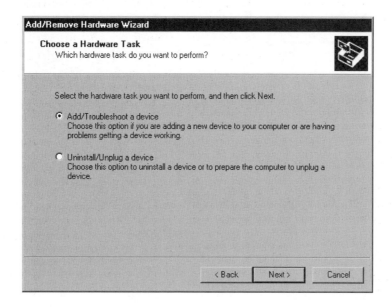

Figure 4.5 Adding an incoming connection.

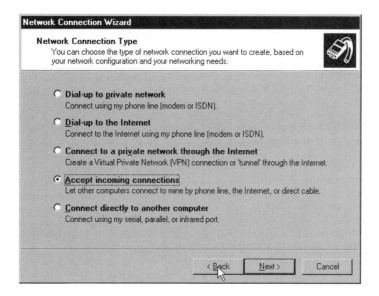

Figure 4.6 Enabling incoming virtual private connections.

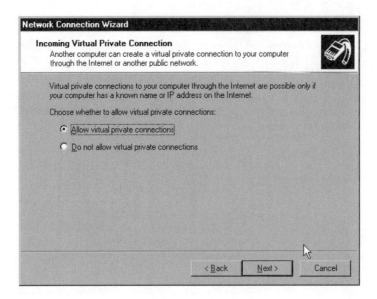

Placing the Server on the Network

Server placement will affect the performance of applications on the network. Normally, when you select the placement of the servers, you try to keep the server as close to the majority of its users as you can in order to manage bandwidth. What is interesting in the Citrix MetaFrame model is that you do not need to consider how close the users are to the Citrix MetaFrame server, as long as you verify that there is a path to the server from the users' stations. Instead, your main concern is how easily that Citrix MetaFrame server can access the information that exists on other servers on the network. Therefore, you would place those servers on or near the backbone of the network.

Before you design the placement of your servers, you should measure the performance of the network. An accurate measurement of the network's capacity will indicate the network's stability, which is critical to application deployment. To start, you should diagram your network. This diagram should include the following elements:

- Network segments with designated speeds
- Network devices—routers, switches, servers, bridges, firewalls
- Network protocols running on each segment, with applicable address ranges

- Problem areas in the network where there are multiple errors or the link has reached capacity

Figure 4.7 is an example of this type of logical diagram.

Figure 4.7 Sample network diagram.

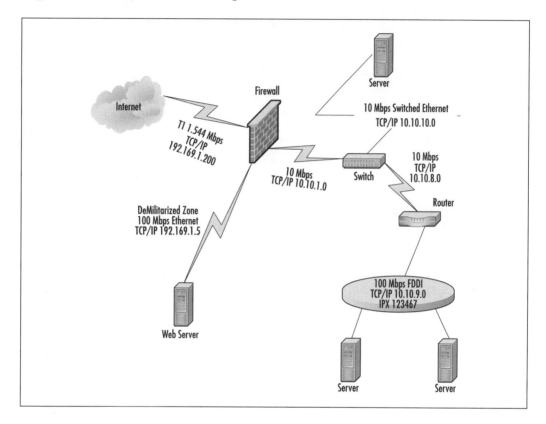

Designing an Internetwork with Multiple MetaFrame Servers

When a Citrix MetaFrame server is deployed, it quickly becomes a mission-critical server on the network. Some users may depend upon the server for their entire desktop. Some Internet users may depend on it for delivery of Web applications. All users depend on it for certain applications to be delivered to their desktop. Because of the critical nature of the server, you need to reduce the risk of failure. This is done through having multiple servers that are all configured to deliver the same set of applications. This is the process of *scaling out* the servers on the network, in place of *scaling up* an individual server, as illustrated in Figure 4.8.

Figure 4.8 Scaling out versus scaling up.

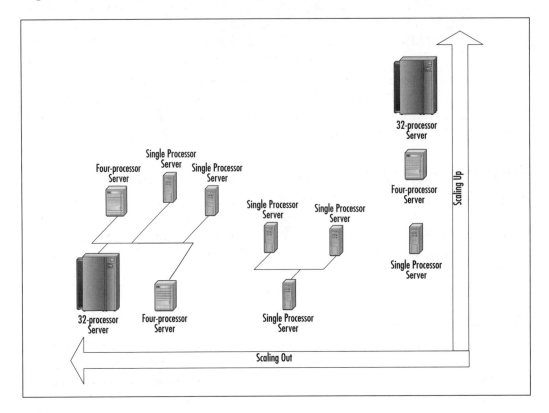

Placing Servers on the Network

When multiple Citrix MetaFrame servers are providing multiple applications, they should be placed close to the backbone, in addition to any data source servers. For example, let's look at a network which has a Lotus Notes server in Sarasota, Florida; a SQL Server in Boston, Massachusetts; and an Oracle server in Tokyo, Japan. There are three options for deploying these servers to provde applications to the network:

1. Dedicate a Citrix MetaFrame server to providing each application. In this scenario, there would be a Citrix MetaFrame server in Boston to provide the SQL application, a Citrix MetaFrame server in Sarasota to provide the Notes application, and a Citrix MetaFrame server in Tokyo to provide the Oracle application. The advantage to this configuration is optimal performance. The disadvantage to this configuration is that one server could be maxed out while the others are not being used at all, so there is not a good balance of resources.

2. Place all servers—the SQL, Notes, and Oracle servers as well as the three Citrix MetaFrame servers—on the backbone and load balance the MetaFrame servers. The advantage to this configuration is in its resource management. The disadvantage to this configuration is that performance will be driven by the utilization on the backbone.

3. Move all the servers to one location on a single segment and deploy the Citrix MetaFrame servers on that same segment in a load-balancing configuration. This scenario has the advantage of both resource management and optimal performance.

Implementing Load Balancing Procedures

Load balancing distributes the amount of processing that a computer is required to do among two or more similar computers. This results in more work being done in the same amount of time, alleviating bottlenecks. It also ensures efficiency and uptime for server farms (also known as clusters).

TIP

One of the benefits of implementing a load-balancing system is that most load-balancing systems also include failover capabilities. Because load balancing requires multiple servers all performing the same function, if one server goes offline, the others can automatically take over at the time of the failure.

There are several ways to implement standard load balancing. The first method is called *software-based load balancing* whereby you install a software application, which receives all traffic, then it will redirect it to other servers on the network.

The next method, *hardware-based load balancing*, usually consists of a computer, a switch, or a router that redirects traffic to other servers on the network. You can also purchase preconfigured clustered servers that automatically load balance between the servers that are attached to that particular cluster.

Most of these solutions are dependent on a network addressing translation of sorts. The traffic is sent to a single network address and then distributed from there. This method does not work well with Citrix MetaFrame servers because it is likely that some servers will provide different applications than others.

The third method, *application load balancing,* provides a slightly different approach. Citrix developed Citrix Load Balancing services to be used with multiple WinFrame and MetaFrame servers. This load-balancing process starts by the client requesting the use of an application. The server that is contacted by the client determines which servers on the network are configured for that application. Next, that server discovers which MetaFrame server is the least busy. The algorithm used to determine which server is least busy creates a load factor. The load factor consists of the Central Processing Unit (CPU) utilization, the measure of the page file utilization, how many users are currently online, plus other system variables. Each server's load factor is compared and the one with the lowest load factor is selected. Then the Load Balancing Service transparently routes that client's session to the least busy server.

Citrix Load Balancing Services is hardware independent, which means you can use any hardware platform that will run Windows 2000. It is also application independent. Any application that can be run on a Citrix MetaFrame server can be load balanced, and any ICA client can connect to a load-balanced application. Load Balancing Services are unlimited, so you can configure as many servers as you wish into a load-balanced configuration. It is also network independent, so you can configure load balancing across a local area network (LAN) or a wide area network (WAN).

WARNING

When you use Direct Asynchronous connections to a particular server, you will not be able to take advantage of load balancing. The server that accepts a Direct Asynchronous connection will not be able to move that connection to another server. If you need dial-up services, you should provide a dial-up RAS server.

Applications, however, are not automatically provided with failover services. If a server fails, users can logon to the load-balanced application and begin working again. When you design multiple servers, you should always have user data stored on non-MetaFrame servers, so that a single Citrix MetaFrame server failure will not interrupt data access. For example, let's look at a case with two MetaFrame servers—Meta1 and Meta2—that are configured to load balance an application. If a user, Jill, stores her data files on Meta1, and Meta1 goes down, Jill may be able to connect to the application, but she will not be able to access her data. Even if Meta1 is still online, but Jill connects to Meta2, she may not be savvy enough to find her data or it may be inaccessible because she may have saved it to a local drive on Meta1 rather than to a shared volume.

On the other hand, if data is stored on Data1, and the administrator JoAnn has scripted a drive mapping for Jill so that wherever Jill connects to the application, she will always see her data on the J: drive, then it doesn't matter if either server fails. Jill will still be able to work on the application and have access to her data files. The only thing that Jill will have lost is her session data. When a server fails, the session vanishes and a new session must be established. Should Jill have been working on a file and had not saved it, she cannot reconnect to the session to see the changes on that file.

TIP

When you store data on file servers rather than MetaFrame servers, data integrity is maintained without sacrificing performance. In addition, you will reduce the time it takes to backup the server, thus enabling access to the MetaFrame server for longer periods of time.

Utilizing License Pooling

License pooling is not the same thing as application load balancing. License pooling does not redirect a client to the least-busy server. Instead, when a server is configured with license pooling, it can accept a client connection even if its own licenses are currently being used but another MetaFrame server in the pool has an available license. When a server is involved in license pooling, it does not need to share out all its licenses. An administrator can reserve some licenses for the server itself and the remaining for the license pool.

For example, let's look at two servers, Pool1 and Pool2 that are configured with license pooling, and each has 20 licenses. If Pool1 is completely out of sessions, and a client requests access to Pool1, under normal circumstances, the client would be denied access. However, in a license pool, Pool1 just borrows one of Pool2's free licenses and allows the client to connect.

Implementing MetaFrame Supported Protocols

Specifying the size and number of the servers is half the job of configuring a network. The other half is specifying how clients are going to connect to their applications. This requires selecting a protocol or method for the ICA client to run on. The types of connections that Citrix MetaFrame supports are:

- Direct Asynchronous Dial-In
- Internet
- Remote Access Service as a remote node
- Workstation connected across a LAN
- Workstation connected across a WAN

The only type of connection that does not depend on a network layer protocol is the direct asynchronous connection. This configuration requires that the Citrix MetaFrame server has modems installed that answer ICA-only connections to that particular MetaFrame server. Direct asynchronous connections do not provide remote node functionality; Citrix MetaFrame servers also support several protocols.

TCP/IP

Transmission Control Protocol/Internet Protocol (TCP/IP) is the protocol stack used on the Internet. Most LANs and WANs also use TCP/IP to connect to the Internet. TCP/IP supports Point-to-Point Protocol (PPP) as well. The session protocol selection for Citrix MetaFrame allows the administrator to create either TCP or IP connections. TCP connections will have the overhead of the TCP header in the packets, whereas the IP connections will have ICA providing connection-oriented services. In fact, of all the methods that you can use to connect to a Citrix MetaFrame server, the only one that cannot use TCP or IP is the direct asynchronous dial-in connection.

Because of the versatility of TCP/IP, it is a prime candidate to use as the session protocol, and if you intend to connect over the Internet, you must use it.

IPX/SPX

Internetwork Packet eXchange/Sequenced Packet eXchange (IPX/SPX) is the protocol stack used by Novell NetWare servers. Citrix MetaFrame allows either IPX or SPX connections to be created for sessions. IPX/SPX can be used over PPP connections, so if you have a RAS server that is configured to support it, you can use IPX or SPX connections. However, an IPX or SPX connection is *not* appropriate for use over the Internet.

If you use NetWare servers, you do not have to use IPX/SPX for your connections as long as your workstations support other protocols. For example, if a workstation supports both IPX/SPX and TCP/IP, it can connect to a NetWare server via IPX/SPX and connect to the MetaFrame server via TCP/IP.

NetBEUI

NetBIOS Extended User Interface (NetBEUI) is a protocol stack that was used widely on Windows NT servers. The NetBEUI protocol stack is non-routable, not viable to be used across WANs, and NetBEUI cannot be used across the Internet. However, it can be used on LANs and over PPP remote node connections.

NetBEUI has been slowly weaned out of the Windows NT (and now Windows 2000) line of products. In the Windows NT 3.5x days, NetBEUI was the default protocol, and then Windows NT 4.x began making TCP/IP the default protocol. With Windows 2000, TCP/IP is required—no longer just the default protocol—if the computer is going to access or otherwise interact with the Active Directory.

When you are planning your session protocols, you should avoid adding protocols that you do not already use on your network. If you've already upgraded to Windows 2000, you may have already removed NetBEUI or you have the opportunity to do so. In the interest of reducing the numbers of protocols on your network to only those that you need, you should probably avoid the use of NetBEUI as a connection protocol.

ICA

ICA is the protocol that enables the remote control session between the client and the Citrix MetaFrame server. ICA is the only protocol that runs on the direct asynchronous connection. ICA runs over the TCP/IP, IPX/SPX, and NetBEUI protocols for all the other remote control sessions.

ICA is a uniquely flexible protocol. Whereas it provides the full protocol stack services on a direct asynchronous connection, it only provides the protocol services needed above the protocol that is running. For example, if you create a session over IP, a network layer protocol (Layer 3), ICA will provide the transport, session, presentation, and application layer services. On the other hand, if you create a session over TCP, a transport layer protocol (Layer 4), ICA will provide the session, presentation, and application layer services. ICA simply fills in the protocol layer gaps for session traffic, as shown in Figure 4.9.

ICA browsing traffic is different from session traffic. Browsing traffic is what occurs when a client requests a Citrix server for a list of published applications or a list of Citrix servers. When using TCP/IP, this is executed over User Datagram Protocol (UDP) port 1604. The session traffic over TCP/IP uses TCP port 1494. When XML is installed on the server, and when using MetaFrame Feature Release 1, the browsing traffic can be performed over strict TCP/IP instead of UDP.

Figure 4.9 ICA protocol flexibility.

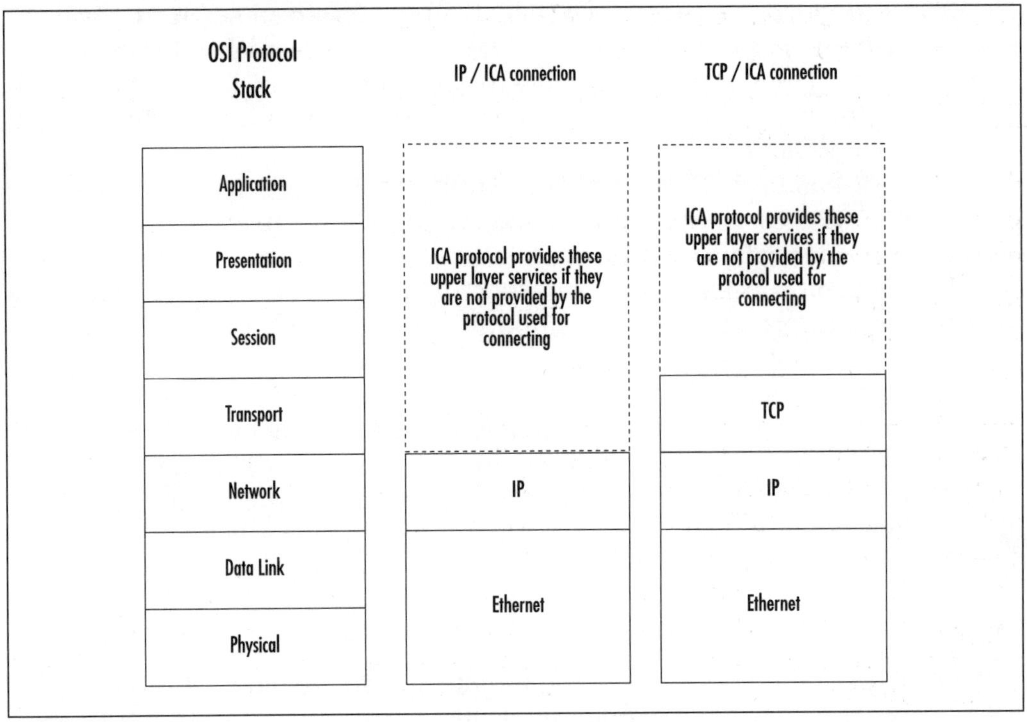

When you are designing your use of ICA, you should consider your need to reduce bandwidth utilization and enhance user-perceived performance. In order to do so, you can configure the clients to use caching and compression. You should also consider the need for local printing and how that will impact your network and user-perceived performance. Local printing will increase the ICA traffic.

Analyzing the Environment

In deciding where to place a Citrix MetaFrame server, whether to use multiple servers, and what types of protocols to implement, you need to consider the aspects of your project listed in Table 4.3. These questions and answers should offer you some guidance in your design decisions.

Table 4.3 Design Questions

Design Question	Purpose
What is the business requirement that the Citrix MetaFrame server will solve? (Remember, the most successful projects use the business requirement to drive the technology configuration.)	This question will tell you to which servers and data the Citrix MetaFrame servers should be placed closest.
How are the users going to connect to Citrix?	This will tell you what protocols to implement and whether to provide dial-in via RAS or direct connection.
What applications will be used on the Citrix server?	This will also tell you what servers the Citrix MetaFrame servers should be near, as well as what requirements your MetaFrame servers need to be able to support—such as memory requirements for the application.
What network data or services will the Citrix MetaFrame server need to access as a client?	This will tell you what configuration your Citrix MetaFrame server will need. For example, if the data that an application needs to access is located on a NetWare server, then you will need to have IPX/SPX compatible protocol and a NetWare client configured on the Citrix MetaFrame server.
Where do those network servers reside?	If some servers are placed on different segments, or even in different buildings, this question will tell you whether to redesign the placement of other servers on the network.
Are there any bandwidth utilization problems that exist on the links between those servers' and the users' locations?	This question will tell you how to configure the clients as well as indicate some of the bandwidth utilization reduction goals your project can have.
What impact will the Citrix MetaFrame server have on the security policy of the network?	This question will provide you with whether you need to access Internet services through a proxy from the MetaFrame server, whether you need to reconfigure a firewall to enable TCP ports for the ICA protocol, and how to configure user security on the server.

Continued

Table 4.3 Continued

Design Question	Purpose
What is the Active Directory design and which domains contain the data servers that Citrix MetaFrame needs to access?	This question will provide you with the domain that Citrix MetaFrame should be placed as a member. (Best practices are such that a MetaFrame server should not be a domain controller.)
Are there multiple segments that all need to access the Citrix MetaFrame server, but are not connected to each other?	This question will provide you whether you need to install a router. You should not multihome a Citrix MetaFrame server because the ICA Browser service is not able to be bound to a single NIC and you would suffer problems.
What workstation names or naming conventions are used?	If the names or naming conventions are not unique for all workstations, a new naming convention should be devised and implemented. ICA clients must have unique names in order for printing to function.
What user names are used?	If user names are unique, then scripts can use the %username% variable to individualize a user's experience. Otherwise, you should consider whether the naming convention will cause a security breach.
Will the user's experience be seamless with a desktop?	The answer to this question will guide you to select drive letter assignments that integrate with the user's desktop. Best practices are to remap the server hard drives starting with the letter M:. However, if there is a conflict, you should select other drive letters, contiguous for each partition on the Citrix MetaFrame server. The client drives will appear as the same drive letter it normally is—so the C: drive is still the C: drive.

Continued

Table 4.3 Continued

Design Question	Purpose
Where will user data be stored?	If you maintain user data files on separate servers, then application load balancing is more easily implemented on top of the facts that backup time is reduced for the application server and server performance is increased.
What client hardware and software will be used?	The answer to this question will tell you which clients to download from http://download.citrix.com.
How will remote users connect?	The answer to this question will determine whether you need to implement Direct Asynchronous connections or if you can use existing remote access services on the network.
What are the users' requirements?	This question will help decide what applications or services you may need to install that are not part of the initial business required application that the MetaFrame server was implemented for.
Will some users be given different security requirements than others?	This question will assist in deciding the groups of users and the security to apply to each of the groups. For example, you can prevent one group from printing or copying data, but grant those rights to a different group.
Will users need to use their local COM ports or have sound and color enhancements?	This question will help in configuring the sessions for users so that they will be able to use their applications in the way that they are familiar.
What are the users' printing requirements?	Printing is usually a critical aspect of the project, so you should gather detailed information and test printing repeatedly.
What criteria will determine if the project is successful?	If you list these criteria and are able to check them off the list as accepted when you deploy your project, then you are successful!

Designing the Internetwork

Many aspects of the internetwork will impact how you design client access from various points of entry on the network. The following scenarios will illustrate how to design client access taking into account LAN, WAN, and Internet connectivity.

LAN

The LAN scenario is a single Token Ring network owned by an insurance agency called Finance Advantage. Finance Advantage has 100 people in its agency, although 60 of them are agents that work out of home offices. Finance Advantage has both a NetWare server and a Windows NT server. They are running both IPX/SPX and NetBIOS on their network.

They are planning on adding an Internet line to the network at some point in the next six months, but they have experienced little growth in the size of their company and do not expect to add more than one agent per year over the next three years, so it is not a priority.

They want to install a Citrix MetaFrame server running on Windows 2000 right away so that their agents can access a new insurance application from telephone lines, and the administrative staff can access it over the LAN in the office. The data source of the application will reside on the Windows NT Server that Finance Advantage currently owns. All data files will also be stored there. The new insurance application is a data entry application, and with testing, a single processor can handle 45 concurrent users with the application, and each session only requires 4MB of RAM. Figure 4.10 displays the Finance Advantage network.

In this LAN environment, you have only one place to put the Citrix MetaFrame server—directly attaching it to the Token Ring LAN. Although you have the option of installing a router and placing the Citrix MetaFrame server on a different segment, there is no reason to do so. Because agents are intermittent users, it is likely that of the 100 total users, you would never have more than 60 online simultaneously. This means that you need at least two processors, and a minimum of 368MB RAM (60 users × 4MB RAM + 128 Base RAM = 368MB RAM), which is rounded up to 512MB RAM.

Since there is no existing remote access method, and because the protocols that are used on the network will eventually change, a direct asynchronous connection for the remote users is preferable. The direct asynchronous method ensures that there is no bandwidth utilization on the LAN consumed by users coming through a RAS server, which means that local printing is not going to interfere with network performance. This will also ensure that there will never need to be a change on the remote user's end when the protocols are switched over, reducing administrative efforts in the future.

Figure 4.10 Finance Advantage network.

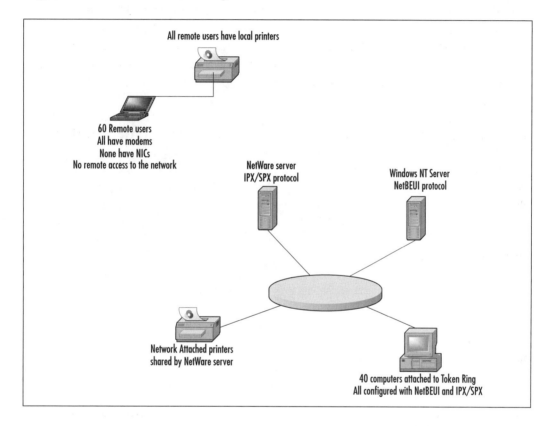

This means that a single server with two or more processors is the better choice, because that will ensure that the agents only need to dial one server since load balancing is not supported with the direct asynchronous method. In using a single server, Finance Advantage selects a 20GB hardware-based RAID array with hot-swap hard disks and dual power supplies, so that there are some redundancy and failover capabilities. They also select a rack-mounted modem pool of 30 modems that connects directly to the Citrix MetaFrame server.

The LAN can be accessed through either NetBEUI or IPX/SPX for now, with a change to TCP/IP in the future. Or the administrative staff can work through it now and deploy the Microsoft TCP/IP client during this project. Finance Advantage decides to use NetBEUI because the Windows NT server that houses the new application also uses NetBEUI. The design for the future Finance Advantage network will resemble Figure 4.11.

Figure 4.11 Finance Advantage network design with Citrix MetaFrame.

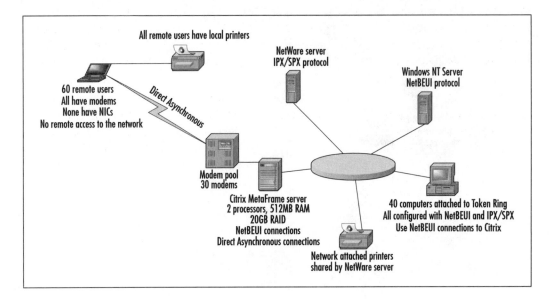

WAN

Affluenz is a banking and credit company with over 60,000 employees worldwide. The headquarters is in New York City, and two other large locations with 5000 or more users are in Sydney, Australia and Munich, Germany. There are 20 locations throughout the world that are connected via various types of links, some satellite, some Frame Relay, some leased lines. Affluenz only uses TCP/IP across the backbone network since having upgraded their Novell NetWare network to be IP-only. Affluenz has two mainframe computers at their headquarters, and 235 Windows 2000 servers across the global network participating as member servers and domain controllers in a two-domain Active Directory forest.

Affluenz has encountered an increased amount of credit card fraud over the past two years, and has a need for a better tracking system. They have purchased a security tracking system that runs on a SQL Server platform, and have also hired programmers to customize the client for their security department. In each location, there are between three and 30 security personnel who will need access to that database, and these users may change in numbers because the number of security personnel increases at the same rate as Affluenz, which is expecting to double in the next two years. Affluenz has decided to implement Citrix MetaFrame to provide that application without taxing some of the slow links.

There are 250 security personnel who will run the application, and an estimated 200 will run it all day long to track the provided security alerts. Taking time zone differences into account, the number of concurrent users will be about 175 during high usage periods. The application tested out that 20 users could run simultaneously on the same processor, and 8MB of RAM is required for each session on a Citrix MetaFrame server. No data files will be stored on the server, so the Affluenz standard RAID array with 30GB of space is considered more than acceptable for servers. The new security application will be placed on a database server in the New York headquarters because it will exchange some data with the mainframes located there. Figure 4.12 illustrates Affluenz's current network from a high level.

Figure 4.12 The Affluenz WAN.

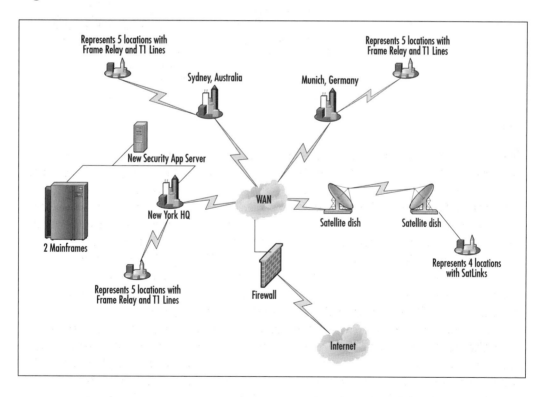

When designing the Citrix MetaFrame servers for this network, it is apparent that we will need nine processors for the concurrent users. The servers will need 8MB RAM × 175 users + 128 Base OS RAM = 1528MB RAM (or 1.5 GB). A 30GB RAID array will provide ample storage. Because Affluenz will be doubling over the next two years, we can account for growth by doubling the processing and memory numbers to 18 processors and 3GB RAM. To allow for redundancy, and because all users will connect over the network, Affluenz will implement application load balancing with five four-processor servers, each carrying 1GB of RAM. All of these servers will be placed on the same segment as the security application SQL database server in New York. Clients will access the server through TCP/IP connections.

Internet

In this scenario, we have a publishing company called BookMill. BookMill has a single location in Raleigh, North Carolina with 20 employees. BookMill also employs 10 freelance editors and copywriters who work out of their homes across the United States and Canada. In addition, BookMill hires authors to collaborate on book projects from all over the United States and Canada. While BookMill has over 150 authors that have collaborated on books, only 20 to 30 are working on projects at any one point in time. BookMill sells books from their Web site and they use Internet e-mail to communicate with their remote editors, copywriters, and authors. They are now contemplating deploying Citrix MetaFrame to share out their project application with their editors, copywriters, and authors over their Internet connection.

The BookMill network is an Ethernet LAN connected to the Internet via a T1 line. There are two servers that provide Web services on the Internet. These servers are placed on a demilitarized zone (DMZ). The project application is located on a database server on the Ethernet LAN, which uses TCP/IP as its only protocol. The project application has been tested so that 20 users can access it simultaneously on a single processor server, and it requires 6MB of RAM per user. It is expected that there will be no more than four concurrent users for average usage, but as deadlines approach, there may be as many as 10 concurrent users. BookMill has experienced a huge growth over the past three years, and may expand into more e-book business during the next two. BookMill expects to double the number of projects it can support in three years. BookMill wants to make certain that all users can access this application even if a server fails. The BookMill network is depicted in Figure 4.13.

Figure 4.13 BookMill network.

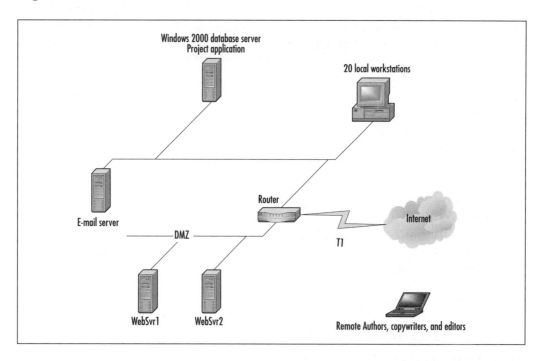

The server will require one processor, even after growth doubles. It will require 20 users (after growth) × 6MB RAM + 128 Base OS RAM = 248MB RAM, which rounds up to 256MB RAM. The project data will exist on the database server, so a RAID array of 10GB should be sufficient. To support the failover requirement, BookMill will need two servers that meet the 1 CPU, 256MB RAM and 10GB storage minimums. These two Citrix MetaFrame servers will be placed on the DMZ. They will be configured to provide the application through an Internet Web page. BookMill's administrator intends to apply security both at the Database server and at the Citrix MetaFrame server to ensure that only authors, editors, and copywriters currently working on any particular project will be able to access its data. The local workstations will have the application installed directly, and will not go through the Citrix MetaFrame server to access the data. The BookMill network design is illustrated in Figure 4.14.

Figure 4.14 BookMill's network design.

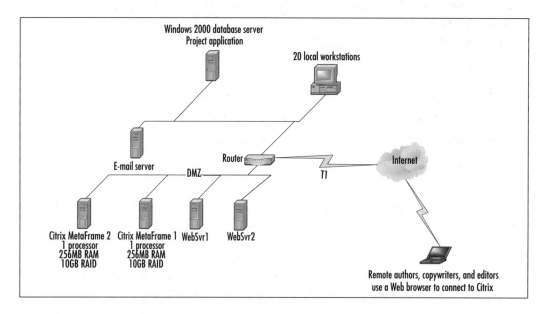

Upgrading to Citrix MetaFrame 1.8 for Windows

If you are planning to upgrade to Citrix MetaFrame 1.8 for Windows 2000 from an existing Citrix MetaFrame for Windows NT 4.0 Server, Terminal Server Edition or even an earlier version of Citrix WinFrame, you can do so while conserving the existing user settings and installed applications. The one thing that you should be aware of is that the hardware for older versions of Citrix WinFrame or MetaFrame may not be compatible with Windows 2000 Server. You can check the hardware compatibility on Microsoft's Web site for the Hardware Compatibility List, located at www.microsoft.com/hcl/default.asp.

When you are ready to perform your upgrade, you should start with a full backup of the server. The backup should include the registry and all system files.

TIP

A server recovery plan can save the day if there are problems with your upgrade. You should create an emergency repair disk, have a full backup, and original installation disks for all the applications on hand, just in case. Then, you should test a rebuild process in the lab and write down the successful steps prior to beginning your upgrade.

After your backup is completed, logoff all the users and any disconnected sessions. Then disable connections so that no users are able to connect to the server.

Document all your server requirements, including:

- Disk partitioning configuration
- Paging file configuration, if you've specified one
- Protocols to be installed and configured
- Memory requirements, if they've changed
- Special drivers, such as those for network interface cards that are not included in the base operating system

Obtain all the software installation disks, drivers from the manufacturer, service packs, and hotfixes and have them available during your upgrade procedure.

As with all Windows 2000 installation processes, you should determine whether the hard disk partition is sufficient for the system files, paging file, and any other applications that need to be installed on that partition. If the partition is not sufficient, you will need to repartition the hard disk. You may be able to use a third-party utility like Disk Image Pro to repartition. If that is not available to you, you will need to delete the existing partitions, as well as all the data, and repartition the disk.

If you have sufficient space, or you have successfully repartitioned the disk without losing data, then you can start the installation program. Windows 2000 will automatically detect the existing operating system and offer to upgrade. By following the dialog screens and referring to your server requirements document for configuration details, you will complete your upgrade.

If the old partition is retained, and it was formatted with FAT, you should convert the file system to NTFS. Once you have converted the drive, you cannot convert it back. If you have upgraded from a Windows NT 4.0 server and then converted to NTFS on Windows 2000, you cannot go back to Windows NT 4.0 without repartitioning the server. Windows NT 4.0 does not understand the new NTFS 5.0 file system included with Windows 2000. This is done with the following command, where you replace the <drive letter> with the letter of the drive that you are converting at a command prompt window.

```
CONVERT <drive letter>: /FS:NTFS
```

After the upgrade to Windows 2000 Terminal Services, your next task is to install Citrix MetaFrame 1.8 for Windows 2000 using its standard installation process.

Summary

When you design the Citrix MetaFrame environment, you should start by determining what your minimum requirements are for the server components:

- Number of processors
- Amount of RAM
- Storage

These requirements are based on the number of concurrent users and the applications used by those users. To ensure that the server requirements will be sufficient for some time going forward, these requirements need to be adjusted for the growth that the company might experience. Once the minimum requirements are determined, these are then parceled out among one or more servers. Scaling up is preferable when using direct asynchronous connections; scaling out is preferable for all other situations because of the redundancy it offers.

The Citrix MetaFrame server needs to be placed nearest to the data sources that it will be providing to end users. If multiple servers will be load balanced, all the servers that are providing a single application should be placed on the same network segment as the data source server.

MetaFrame supports multiple protocols for connections, as well as direct asynchronous connections. When you design your protocol, you should use the protocols that are in use currently, or that may be used in the near future. For each client that connects, the server needs to have a connection waiting that uses the protocol that the client has installed. Therefore, if a client uses TCP/IP, it could not connect to an IPX/SPX connection waiting on the server, it would need to find a TCP or IP connection.

FAQs

Q: We have an Oracle application in the New York office that we are planning on implementing with Citrix MetaFrame. We also have a PeopleSoft application in Paris, France that we are also going to use with Citrix MetaFrame. There are 30 users of each application. Both of these applications' users reside in New York and in Paris. Where should we place the Citrix MetaFrame server?

A: You should consider deploying two Citrix MetaFrame servers, one in New York to deliver the Oracle application and the other in Paris to deliver the PeopleSoft application. Otherwise, you might want to move one of the servers to the other office on the same segment as the first server, and then place a Citrix MetaFrame server on that same network segment.

Q: We don't have the resources to test how many of our users a processor will take on. Most of our users are clerical and about 20 percent of them are knowledge users. How many processors should we put into our server(s) if we have 100 users?

A: If you estimate about 25 users per processor, then you will be fairly close to the true number of users per processor. However, you should consider the growth of the network usage of the Citrix MetaFrame servers, and double up on your resources. By starting with two four-processor servers, you will have more than enough resources for the 100 users, and you can test the number of users your processors will withstand.

Q: We have a NetWare server from which our Citrix MetaFrame server will be accessing a Btrieve application via IPX/SPX. All the workstations on the network support TCP/IP only. Do we need to add IPX/SPX to the workstations in order to connect to MetaFrame IPX/SPX sessions or can we use IP connections?

A: You do not need to add IPX/SPX to the workstations, and yes, you can use IP connections. What will happen is that the application data will travel from the MetaFrame server to the client in the form of compressed draw commands over the IP connection. However, the data that passes between the Citrix MetaFrame server and the NetWare server will travel over IPX/SPX so you will need to configure the MetaFrame server to support IPX/SPX as well as TCP/IP, but the workstations can remain with a single protocol stack.

Chapter 5

Deploying Terminal Services Clients

Solutions in this chapter:

- Limitations of the Terminal Services Client

- Client Considerations

- Installing the Client Manually

- Deploying the Client Using Automation

- Using the Client Software

Introduction

When you connect to a Windows 2000 Terminal Services server, you need to have an application to act as the terminal or shell for the applications that you will be accessing. In addition, you need a protocol that can transport the remote control information. This is provided by a Terminal Services client.

There are three Windows 2000 Terminal Services clients:

- Client for Windows for Workgroups 3.11
- Client for Windows 95, Windows 98, Windows NT 3.51, Windows NT 4.0, and Windows 2000
- Client for Windows CE

In addition, Microsoft released the Terminal Services Advanced Client to be used with Internet Web browsers. To connect to Terminal Services, your client must be running one of these types of operating systems.

When deciding on a server-based computing solution, many administrators implement Windows Terminal Services with the addition of Citrix MetaFrame. MetaFrame is an add-on product that installs on top of Terminal Services. MetaFrame will provide enhanced features and functionality to your Terminal Services Server. The Independent Computing Architecture (ICA) protocol used by Citrix MetaFrame is what allows for this increased functionality. It is up to you to decide if your organization can function sufficiently with just Terminal Services or if Citrix MetaFrame should be purchased.

Limitations of Terminal Services Clients

Windows 2000 Terminal Services is a much more robust product than Terminal Server 4.0 was. It has much more functionality, and allows for more flexibility. In spite of its advancements, Terminal Services does have its limitations. One way to overcome some of these is to add Citrix MetaFrame. We will briefly go over some of the limitations of Terminal Services and what advantages can be gained by adding Citrix MetaFrame.

Licensing

Licensing, of course, is a big issue. Microsoft has taken a new approach to licensing when it comes to Terminal Server. Licensing is broken into different components:

Microsoft Clearinghouse This is a database used by Microsoft to activate license servers and to issue client license key packs to license servers that request them. It also keeps track of and stores information about all activated licenses. Your life will be immensely easier if your license servers have access to the Internet.

License Server These Windows 2000 servers have the "Terminal Server Licensing" option installed. Their job is to track the licenses installed for Terminal Servers and the licenses that have been issued to clients. Terminal Servers must be able to communicate with License Servers before clients can connect and be issued a license. Only one License Server is required for multiple Terminal Servers.

Terminal Server Not only do these servers dish out applications, but they also check client licenses with the License Server on behalf of the client. If the client doesn't have a license, it is issued one by the License Server through the Terminal Server.

Client Licenses Every client that connects to a Terminal Server must have a valid client license. Clients store client license information locally and present it to Terminal Servers when they log on. The Terminal Servers then validate the license and allow the client to connect. Client licenses are outlined later in this chapter.

License servers can be set up in one of two modes: Domain License server or Enterprise License server.

Domain License Server This mode should be selected if you are using a workgroup or Windows NT 4.0 domains. It can be used in Active Directory if you wish to have separate license servers for each domain. Terminal Servers must be in the same domain as a license server set up in Domain License server mode. This is the default setting.

Enterprise License Server This mode is used for Windows 2000 domains and can serve many domains in the same site. You must use Add/Remove programs to install Terminal Server License Server in Enterprise mode.

You must activate License Servers 90 days from the date of install or client connections will be refused. You will need not only Windows 2000 server CALs, but also Terminal Services CALs for each client device. This is not a user basis, but a client basis. If you have a user who connects to Terminal Services from a PC in the office and a different computer at home, you will need two CALs for that user because the connection is coming from two different client devices. Windows 2000 Professional comes with a Terminal Services license installed, so you won't need to purchase additional CALs for users connecting from a Windows 2000 Professional client. To see how these pieces fit together see Figure 5.1.

Figure 5.1 Representation of Microsoft's licensing scheme.

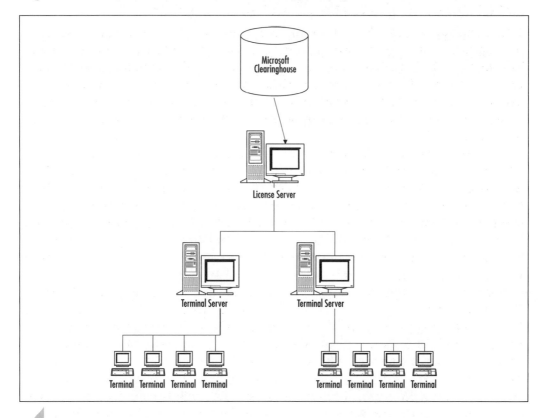

> **TIP**
>
> Be careful where you put your Terminal Servers in your domain when using Domain License servers. Terminal Servers use broadcasts to find the License Server. In a Windows 2000 domain with Enterprise License servers, the Terminal Servers will query the Active Directory for the location of the License Server. So, if you have a network device (such as a router) that does not forward broadcasts, you may have a problem. Most devices will let you configure them to forward broadcasts.

A Windows 2000 Terminal Server will keep track of all of the License Servers in its broadcast domain if it's a Domain License server. It will check to ensure that its primary license server is available every one to two hours. If its License Server doesn't respond, then it will switch to another License Server in the domain. For this reason, you should have a backup License Server in each broadcast domain.

Licensing a Terminal Services Client

Users connecting to a Terminal Services session will need a separate license from the one required to connect on a file and print sharing basis. Windows 2000 Terminal Services requires the configuration of a Licensing Server. When a Terminal Services client wants to connect to a Windows 2000 Terminal Services server, it must first contact a License Server. The License Server will then assign a license to the client, and the connection will be allowed.

The licenses on a License Server are obtained from the Microsoft Clearinghouse. The Microsoft Clearinghouse is a database maintained by Microsoft that keeps track of the licenses that have been purchased. The Clearinghouse will be contacted by your Terminal Server when you start the licensing process. When a Terminal Services Licensing Server requests license packs, the Microsoft Clearinghouse will assign the appropriate licenses to the server. The server is then free to distribute these licenses to the clients that request them.

There are two types of client licenses that are available for Windows Terminal Services: network client licenses and Internet client licenses. The licensing for network clients can be done on a per-server or a per-seat basis; usually it is done on a per-seat basis. This means that a client access license must be purchased for every user that will connect to a Terminal session. The Internet connection licenses follow a per-server scheme. It is what you would consider *concurrent licensing*. Licenses must be purchased for the maximum number of users that will be simultaneously connected to your server. The reason for the use of per-server licensing is because you have less control over what users access your server over the Internet. There is no way for you to ensure that all clients who access your server through the Internet have a client access license.

TIP

Microsoft Terminal Services Servers can be run in application mode for up 90 days without being licensed. This will give you some time if you want to evaluate the product before you purchase it.

Operating System Limitations

There are a limited number of clients available for Windows 2000 Terminal Services. Microsoft offers Terminal Services clients for Windows for Workgroups 3.11, 32-bit Windows clients (Windows 9*x*, Windows NT, Windows 2000), and Windows CE clients. These are the only operating systems supported natively by Windows 2000 Terminal Services. The limitation of client software available from Microsoft is, in part, due to an agreement signed between Microsoft and Citrix. The addition of Citrix MetaFrame to your server will provide support for a wider variety of clients. In addition to the operating systems supported by the Terminal Services clients, Citrix MetaFrame also supports Macintosh, DOS, Java, UNIX, Linux, and various Sun clients. Many organizations choose to install Citrix MetaFrame solely because of the need for access by operating systems not supported natively by Terminal Services.

Protocol Limitations

Windows Terminal Services only supports client connections using TCP/IP and the Remote Desktop Protocol (RDP). The new Terminal Services clients use RDP 5.0, whereas older Terminal Server 4.0 clients used RDP 4.0. The new version of the RDP protocol enables faster connections. It also allows for more secure connections. The RDP 5.0 protocol is backwards compatible with RDP 4.0, therefore, your newer clients will be able to access your older Windows NT 4.0 Terminal Servers. The addition of Citrix MetaFrame will provide support for IP connections, as well as IPX/SPX and NetBIOS connections, using the Independent Computing Architecture (ICA) protocol. Citrix developed the ICA protocol specifically for the purpose of remote computing.

Other Limitations

There are several other Terminal Services limitations that can be overcome with the addition of Citrix MetaFrame. Citrix MetaFrame provides multimedia support, which is not supported with the Terminal Services client. MetaFrame allows you to map to local audio devices. This does, however, consume a lot of bandwidth. Citrix MetaFrame also provides support for local client devices. Using Citrix MetaFrame, clients can access their local drives while they are attached to the Terminal Server. Citrix MetaFrame also allows for COM port redirection. The ability to map to a local clipboard is another feature that is added by Citrix MetaFrame. This can come in very handy.

Client Considerations

Terminal Services was designed to require minimal processing from the client. Because of this, the client requirements for the installation of the Terminal Services client software are very minimal. As long as you have the hardware to run the operating system, you have suitable hardware to run the Terminal Services client. The following chart shows you what hardware requirements are required for each operating system.

Table 5.1 Terminal Services Client Hardware Requirements

Operating System	Processor	Memory
Windows for Workgroups	386	16MB
Windows 95	386	16MB
Windows 98	486	16MB
Windows NT 4.0	486	16MB
Windows 2000	Pentium	32MB
Windows CE	Any Windows CE device	Dependent on device

NOTE

Remember that minimal requirements are just that, minimal. In order to increase your performance, you should try to exceed the minimal requirements for the operating system that you are using.

Once you have installed your client software, you should take the time to fine-tune your client settings. Taking time to fine-tune your client settings can allow you to have increased performance in client workstations. The key to increased performance in remote computing is to speed up the communication between the server and the client. This is where the bottleneck will usually occur. In most cases, you cannot increase bandwidth. So, in order to improve performance, you will have to make your communications as efficient as possible.

Enabling data compression is one method you can use to increase performance. When compression is enabled, data will be compressed before it is transmitted. This allows you to send more data in each transmission. Compression is especially useful over slow links where bandwidth is limited.

Caching bitmaps will also help increase performance. Frequently accessed bitmaps can be cached locally, so they are not being constantly transmitted over the link. Eliminating the need for large bitmaps to be continually sent over the link will allow more bandwidth to be dedicated for useful data.

> ## NOTE
>
> Microsoft created the Terminal Services Advanced Client (TSAC) in response to demand from clients to be able to launch 32-bit applications from within a browser. The TSAC provides this functionality from within the Microsoft Internet Explorer using an ActiveX control.
>
> The TSAC ActiveX control plus a set of sample Web pages are available for download from www.microsoft.com/windows2000/downloads/recommended/TSAC/default.asp.
>
> You can test the client online at www.trylive.co.uk/demo/.

Installing the Client Manually

Manual client installations can be done in several ways. The client installation files are stored in the Terminal Services Server in the following directory: \\%systemroot%\System32\Clients\TSCLIENT\Net.

You can create a share to this directory. Clients can then attach to this directory in order to install the client software. You can also create the installation disks, which is what we will now cover.

32-bit Windows

In order to manually install the 32-bit Windows client, you must first create the client installation disks. We will briefly go through this process.

1. Select Start | Programs | Administrative Tools | Client Creator.

2. You will be presented with the Client Creator menu.

3. Select Terminal Services for 32-bit x86 windows and press OK as shown in Figure 5.2. This requires two disks.

Figure 5.2 Create Installation Disk(s) window for 32-bit x86 windows.

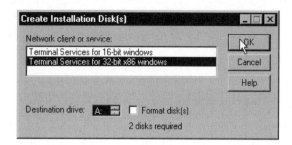

4. You will be asked to insert a floppy disk as illustrated in Figure 5.3. The client disk creation process will then begin.

Figure 5.3 Prompt for 32-bit x86 windows installation disk.

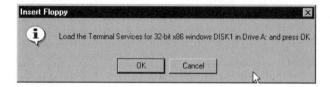

5. During the disk creation process, you will be presented with a copy status screen (Figure 5.4).

Figure 5.4 Copy status screen for 32-bit x86 windows.

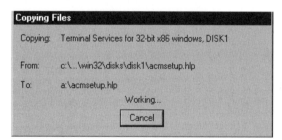

6. After the client disks have been created, you will receive the message shown in Figure 5.5.

Figure 5.5 Message indicating successful client disk creation.

The next process is the actual installation of the client software onto the workstation. The following procedure will guide you through the installation of the 32-bit Windows client on a Windows 2000 Professional workstation.

1. Start by double-clicking on the Setup icon, or typing **(source drive):\setup** at the command prompt.

2. Next, you will get the installation welcome message seen in Figure 5.6.

Figure 5.6 Terminal Services installation welcome message.

3. Then, you are asked to enter your name and organization (Figure 5.7).

Figure 5.7 Name and Organization Information prompt.

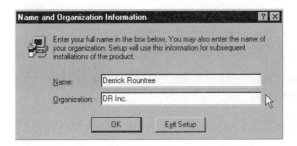

4. You must then accept the standard License Agreement shown in Figure 5.8 in order for the installation to continue.

Figure 5.8 License Agreement prompt.

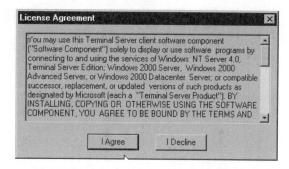

5. Click on the Setup button and the installation process will continue. You can also select the Change Folder button to change the folder where the client will be installed.

6. Next, you are given a choice of whether you want the client installation for use by all users or just the current user as shown in Figure 5.9. Selecting Yes will make it available to all users. Selecting No will make it available only to the current user.

Figure 5.9 Client software settings.

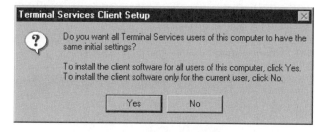

7. Now click OK to complete the installation.

16-bit Windows

The manual 16-bit client installation process is very similar to that of the 32-bit client. We will start with the creation of the client disks and then load the client on the workstation.

To create the client disks:

1. Select Start | Programs | Administrative Tools | Client Creator.

2. The Client Creator menu will appear.

3. Select Terminal Services for 16-bit windows and press OK, seen in Figure 5.10. This will require four floppy disks.

Figure 5.10 Create Installation Disk(s) window for 16-bit windows.

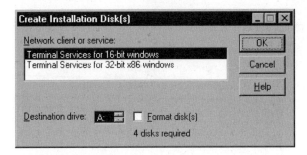

4. You will be asked to insert a floppy disk (Figure 5.11). The client disk creation process will then begin.

Figure 5.11 Prompt for installation disk for 16-bit windows.

5. During the client creation process, you will be given a status display as seen in Figure 5.12.

Figure 5.12 Copy status screen for 16-bit windows.

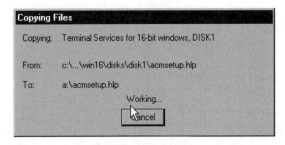

6. You will be given a display message, shown in Figure 5.13, letting you know when the client creation process has ended.

Figure 5.13 Message indicating successful client disk creation.

Next, the client must be installed onto the workstation. This is very similar to the installation process for the 32-bit Windows client.

1. Either double-click on the Setup icon or type **(source drive):\setup** at the command prompt.

2. The Client Setup screen will appear. Select OK and the installation process will begin.

3. You must then input your Name and Organization.

4. After that, you must agree to the License Agreement.

5. On the client services installation screen, click the large Setup button.

6. You can then select a program group where you would like the Terminal Services Client icons to reside.

7. Finally, click OK to complete the installation.

Windows CE

The Windows CE client installation is a little different than the installation of the 16-bit and 32-bit clients. The Windows CE client is not available from the server or through the Client Disk Creator. In order to install the Windows CE client, you must download the software from the Microsoft Web site. At the time this book was written, the Windows CE client software was available for download at www.microsoft.com/mobile/downloads/ts.asp. The file will be a self-extracting executable. Simply double-click on the file to start the installation. Make sure you check the information on the Web site to be sure that the client is compatible with your version of Windows CE.

When upgrading your clients, their current connection configurations should remain intact. If you wish to deploy new connection configurations with the client, there are a few ways to accomplish this. Generally, the first option we'll describe is the preferable method because it doesn't require user intervention. Before you deploy the new client to users, create the connections that users will be using in the RDP 5.0 client. Once you have the connections configured export them to .CNS files. You can then either put them on the first disk of the installation set or in the shared install directory you created earlier. When the install program is run, it will check for the existence of these .CNS files. If they exist, it will use them to create the connection settings specified in the file. The other possible way to deploy it is to send the .CNS files to users and have them manually import them using the '-import' switch from the command line for the RDP 5.0 client or by using 'import' from the 'file' drop down menu.

Deploying the Client Using Automated Installation Methods

The simplest way to install your Terminal Services clients is to install them manually. Unfortunately, this is also the most tedious method. Automated installations can be difficult to configure at first, but once you have it configured correctly, installation will be quick and easy. After configuring automated installation, you won't have to go to each workstation and install the client manually. This will save you a great deal of time. We will briefly go over some practices that can help you to automate your client installations and ease your administrative burden.

32-bit Windows

In order to set up your automatic install, you must first find some way for the client to automatically launch the installation program. This can be done by simply adding the installation command to the logon script. Every computer that logs onto your server can process logon scripts.

The next step in automating the client installation process is through the use of the 'quiet' setup program. A 'quiet' setup minimizes the amount of user interaction needed during a setup. The 'quiet' setup program can be started with three switches:

- /Q will suppress user prompts. The user won't be asked any questions about the installation. They will only see the Exit box after the installation has completed.

- /Q1 suppresses all user prompts and hides the Exit box.

- /QT suppresses all user prompts, and hides any signs of the installation. The user will not even see the copy gauge or the turquoise installation background.

You can also have your client connections automatically created during installation. This is done by creating the connections on a workstation that already has the client software loaded. The connections can then be exported into a .CNS file. The .CNS file should be placed either on the first installation disk or in the directory from where the client software is being installed. The installation program automatically checks for the existence of a .CNS file. If the file exists, the connections are then imported during the installation. Using the quiet installation switches in conjunction with a .CNS file will allow you to totally automate the installation of your Terminal Services clients.

Sample Automated Installation

To begin a sample automated installation, perform the following steps:

1. Start by creating your .CNS file.

2. In the Client Connection Manager on a client workstation, select Export All from the File menu.

3. You will then be asked for a file name. Name the file *conn.cns*.

4. Copy the file to the \\%systemroot%\System32\Clients\Tsclient\ Net directory on the Terminal Services Server.

5. Next, create a share to the \\%systemroot%\System32\Clients\ Tsclient\Net directory. Name it *tclients*.

6. Add the following line to the logon script of the users you want to have the 32-bit Terminal Services client: \\servername\tclients\ win32\setup /qt.

Now, whenever a user logs on, the Terminal Services client will automatically be loaded and configured with a default connection. The user doesn't have to do anything, as everything will occur automatically.

Using the Client Software

After loading the Terminal Services client software, you will see two new applications. One is the Terminal Services Client. The other is the Client Connection Manager. Both allow you to connect to a Terminal Server, but the Client Connection Manager is a more robust application with added features.

Terminal Services Client

The Terminal Services Client is a very simple application that provides connectivity to a Terminal Server. There are few configurable parameters, as you can see in Figure 5.14. You can choose which to make a connection to. You also get a choice of screen sizes. Data compression can also be enabled. So can bitmap caching. These are your only configurable parameters. This application is simply used for connecting to a Terminal Server. If you want more control over your environment and the ability for added features, you must use the Client Connection Manager.

Figure 5.14 The Terminal Services Client.

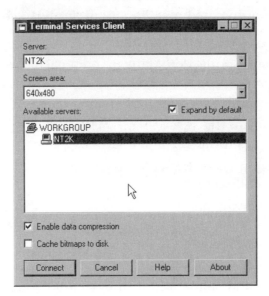

For IT Professionals

Terminal Services Advanced Client

Microsoft is currently working on the Terminal Services Advanced Client, or TSAC. It is the next generation of Terminal Services client. The TSAC will replace the existing Terminal Services clients. The TSAC currently supports all of the features that are available in the current clients, with one important addition. The TSAC allows the ability to run a Terminal Services client session through a Web browser.

Users can now access a Terminal Services Server and run applications directly over the Internet by simply pointing to the correct URL. Previously, this was only available with the addition of Citrix MetaFrame. In fact, this was one of the more coveted features of Citrix MetaFrame. With the introduction of the TSAC, Microsoft is taking strides to take back a portion of the remote computing market.

Microsoft will continue to support the older versions of the Terminal Services clients, but no new features will be added to them. All future Terminal Services client updates will be in the form of TSAC client updates, since Microsoft wants everyone to move to the TSAC. The TSAC, however, is a 32-bit product. This means that it is not supported by Windows for Workgroups. Windows for Workgroup users will have to

Continued

use the older 16-bit version of the Terminal Services client. Microsoft has no plans to make a 16-bit version of the TSAC for Windows for Workgroup clients. This means that you will soon have to upgrade your WFW clients if you want to use the added features of the current version and future releases of the TSAC.

The Terminal Services Advanced client can be downloaded from the Microsoft Web site. Currently, this is the only way to obtain the TSAC. To install, you simply run the self-extracting executable file.

Client Connection Manager

The Client Connection Manager can be used to manage all of your connections. You can save connection configurations for later use. The Client Connection Manager is also what you would use to create the .CNS file used for automated installations. Let's start by creating a connection.

1. Start by choosing New Connection from the Client Connection Manger File menu.

2. You are then taken to the Client Connection Wizard (Figure 5.15). First you must enter a connection and either a server name or IP address. You are also given the option of browsing the network for a Terminal Server.

Figure 5.15 Client Connection Manager wizard.

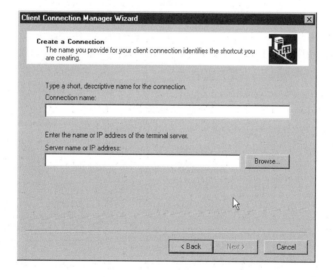

3. Next you are the given the option to input logon information (Figure 5.16). If you input the logon information here, you will not be prompted when you attempt to make a connection. Inputting logon information here can cause two problems. First, it could cause security issues, because anyone who has access to the machine can log on to your Terminal Server without having to input a username and password. Second, if your account passwords periodically expire, the user will receive an error when trying to make a connection after his or her password has expired.

Figure 5.16 Logon information.

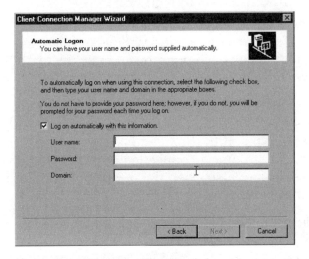

4. Next you are asked to input a screen size (Figure 5.17). The screen sizes available to you are dependent upon the resolution of your current windows session.

5. Next, you must decide if you want to enable bitmap caching or data compression as shown in Figure 5.18. Both of these will help to increase the efficiency of your connection.

6. Now you are given the opportunity to specify a program that will be launched when your session is connected as illustrated in Figure 5.19. This is useful is the user will only be running one program. You can specify this program to launch automatically and then lock down the rest of the desktop. If no program is specified, the user will see a Windows desktop when the session is connected.

Figure 5.17 Screen size settings.

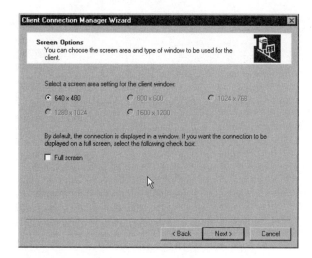

Figure 5.18 Connection properties settings.

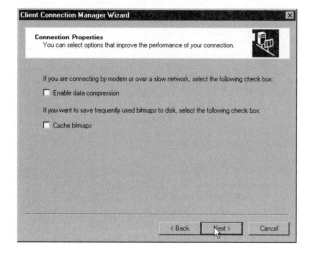

Figure 5.19 Launch specifications.

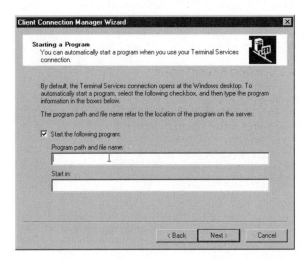

7. You are then given the opportunity to choose an icon for your connection and specify a program group where the connection will reside (Figure 5.20). Your connection is then complete.

Figure 5.20 Icon and program group settings.

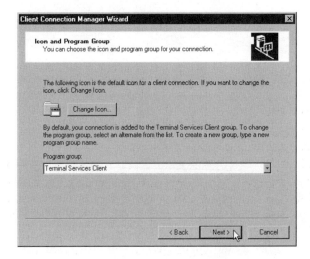

After your connections have been created, you can go back and modify the properties for each connection. These properties are the same properties you were asked about when you added the connection. If you select Properties from the File menu, you are given a three-page property sheet. The first page is the General Information tab seen in Figure 5.21. The

General Information tab allows you to set the connection name. You can also change the server name or IP address to which you are connecting. You are also given the opportunity to specify logon information to be used when making the connection.

Figure 5.21 General Information tab.

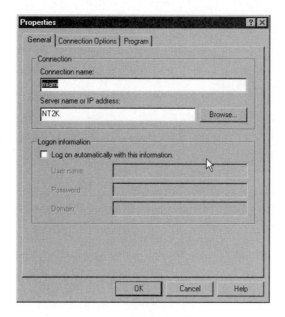

The second page is the Connection Options tab shown in Figure 5.22. The Connection Options tab allows you to set whether your connection will be seen as full screen or in a window. If you choose window, you can set what size window you would like to use. You can also enable data compression and bitmap caching in order to increase the amount of useful data that can be transmitted during your session.

The third tab is the Program page (Figure 5.23). This is where you can specify a program to start upon session connection. You can also change the icon used for your connection or the program group where your connection would appear. If you wanted to set up your user desktop with one folder for all of the applications they will need to use, you could place your connection there. This would keep users from having to search through the Start menu to find the Terminal Services client software and the appropriate connection.

Figure 5.22 Connection Options tab.

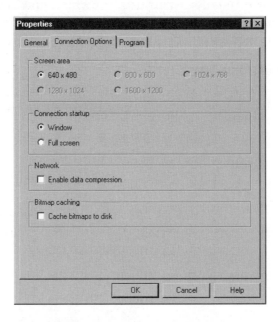

Figure 5.23 Program tab.

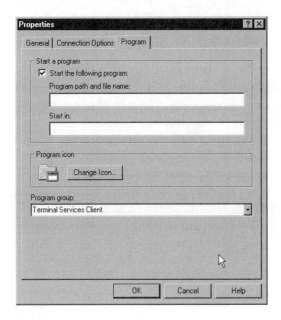

As mentioned previously, the Client Connection Manager also allows you to build a .CNS file that could be used during an automated installation. This is done by selecting Export from the File menu. You can export a single connection or all of your configured connections. The file menu also allows you to import a .CNS file. This can be used to populate the Client Connection Manager with a set of preconfigured connections, so you won't have to recreate the connections on a multitude of workstations. You can simply import the .CNS file that contains all of the connections.

Summary

Windows 2000 Terminal Services comes with an expanded set of features, as compared with the previous NT 4.0 Terminal Servers. Terminal Services, however, does have its limitations. Many of these limitations can be overcome with the addition of Citrix MetaFrame. It is an administrative decision to determine if the added features of Citrix MetaFrame will be worth the additional cost.

Windows 2000 Terminal Services has clients available for 16-bit Windows operating systems, 32-bit Windows operating systems, and Windows CE. These clients can be installed manually, or in some cases you can do an automatic installation. Once the client software is installed, you can attach to either a Windows 2000 Terminal Services Server or a Windows NT 4.0 Terminal Server.

The Windows 2000 Terminal Services client software includes two components: The Terminal Services Client and the Client Connection Manager. The Terminal Services Client offers the ability to make a simple connection to a Terminal Server. The Client Connection Manager allows you to create multiple connections that can be used later. You can save all of your connection configuration parameters, so that you don't have to set them each time you want to log on. You can also import and export connections. Importing and exporting will save you from having to manually create connections on multiple workstations.

FAQs

Q: My environment currently has Windows 95 workstations, Windows 98 workstations, Windows NT workstations, and Sun workstations. Will all of these clients be able to attach to my Windows 2000 Terminal Services server using the Terminal Services client?

A: No, Windows 2000 Terminal Services clients are available for Windows for Workgroups, Windows 95, Windows 98, Windows NT 4.0, Windows 2000, and Windows CE. There is no Sun client software. You may have to consider using Citrix MetaFrame in order to service your SUN clients.

Q: What protocol is used by Windows 2000 Terminal Services clients to achieve the remote desktop?

A: Terminal uses the RDP protocol version 5.0.

Q: What protocol is used by Citrix MetaFrame clients to achieve the remote desktop?

A: Citrix MetaFrame uses the ICA protocol.

Q: My environment consists of Pentium 100MHz desktops with 32 MB of RAM. They are currently running Windows 98 and the Terminal Server 4.0 client. I plan to upgrade my environment to Windows 2000 Professional. I also want to run the Windows 2000 Terminal Services client. Is this possible with my existing hardware or will I have to upgrade?

A: Yes, this is possible. Windows 2000 Professional clients require a Pentium PC with 32MB of RAM.

Q: Where are the licenses on a Windows 2000 License Server obtained from?

A: The licenses on a License Server are obtained from the Microsoft Clearinghouse.

Q: I have just upgraded half of my Terminal Server 4.0 servers to Windows 2000 Terminal Services. I have also upgraded my clients to the new Terminal Services client using RDP 5.0. Will these workstations still be able to attach to my older Terminal Server 4.0 servers?

A: Yes, Terminal Services clients running RDP 5.0 can attach to Terminal Servers running RDP 4.0

Q: Where would you create a CNS file that can be used during an automated client installation?

A: .CNS files are created using the Client Connection Manager.

Q: What installation switch should I use if I want to make the client installation totally invisible to the user?

A: The /QT switch will hide everything from the user, including the Exit prompt and the Copy Status window.

Q: If I am building a Windows Terminal Services server that will be accessed exclusively through the Internet, should I use per-server or per-seat licensing?

A: You should use per-server licensing. Per-server licensing is governed by simultaneous connections. Per-seat licensing would be too hard to keep track of because you would have to know every client that would ever attach to your server. This is difficult when your server is readily accessible through the Internet.

Chapter 6

Citrix MetaFrame Clients

Solutions in this chapter:

- Selecting a Protocol
- Installing MetaFrame Clients
- Deploying MetaFrame Clients Using Automated Installation
- Configuring the MetaFrame Clients

Introduction

Citrix MetaFrame clients can run virtually any type of operating system. It's not that Citrix developed every type of client for each operating system. Although they did develop several clients, Citrix also developed a client for Web browsers. With this client, applications can be provided over the Internet.

Not only are standard workstations supported, but so are specially manufactured ICA terminals. These terminals are the original "Net PCs." The idea is to deploy applications remotely (and not be required to support an operating system remotely) and maintain all data on a server located somewhere across the Internet. Regardless of the method of connection, application servers like Citrix MetaFrame can greatly reduce administrative overhead and support costs.

Selecting a Protocol

When first considering a Citrix MetaFrame solution, the first question many clients ask is "How do I connect to a MetaFrame server?"

There are two main presentation service protocols available for connecting to a Citrix MetaFrame server: Remote Data Protocol (RDP) and Independent Computing Architecture (ICA). RDP works only over TCP/IP. ICA provides for connectivity using a variety of transport protocols including the following:

- Transmission Control Protocol/Internet Protocol (TCP/IP)
- Sequenced Packet Exchange (SPX)
- Internetwork Packet Exchange (IPX)
- NetBIOS Extended User Interface (NetBEUI)
- Direct Asynchronous

NOTE

Direct Asynchronous is different from a typical asynchronous modem or Remote Access Server (RAS) connection, which the MetaFrame server also supports. A "Direct" asynchronous connection is typically done with a direct serial-to-serial or "null modem" cable. The Direct Asynchronous connection is capable of approximately 230 kilobytes per second (Kbps) data transfer rate.

Your existing or planned network infrastructure and client connectivity options should be the primary factors in deciding which protocol or protocols to use. Other factors to consider are as follows:

- Available bandwidth

- Local area network (LAN) or wide area network (WAN) routing

- Security

- Direct dial or analog modem access

- Server hardware limitations

Let's discuss some of these factors and determine how they may help you decide which protocol or protocols to use. The first factor, available bandwidth, may not be important if you are connecting to your server on a brand new 100MB Fast Ethernet LAN. However, if you are connecting to servers across the Internet or via a dial-up connection, bandwidth issues become very important, and you will find that the ICA protocol gives better performance in a limited-bandwidth environment.

The second factor, routing, is probably not an issue if you are communicating exclusively in a LAN environment. Install a protocol that is compatible with your server and you are ready to connect. If you are connecting over the Internet or a company WAN, then TCP/IP is by far the most widely used and effective protocol for routing over remote networks. Security using the MetaFrame client is an improvement over most other types of remote connections in that all communication is encrypted. While the default client uses only a weak XOR encryption, the SecureICA client allows 40-, 56-, or even 128-bit RC5 Rivest-Shamir-Adleman (RSA) encryption. Performance may suffer slightly with the higher encryption, but companies that require high encryption should be used to that.

NOTE

The SecureICA encryption is currently available only with the following clients:

- 32-bit Windows clients

- 16-bit Windows clients

- DOS

- Windows CE clients

- Web clients (Netscape plug-in and Microsoft ActiveX)

Future SecureICA support for UNIX, Java, and Macintosh is planned but not currently available.

While many restrictions for exporting "high" encryption products have been lifted, be sure to check the most current regulations before exporting to clients outside the United States or Canada. Current foreign trade relations prohibit exportation to Cuba, Iran, Iraq, Libya, North Korea, Sudan, Syria, and Yugoslavia. Check the Citrix Export FAQ at the following address or consult with your attorney before exporting to avoid potential legal conflicts.

www.citrix.com/products/sica/introfaq.asp

Another important issue is modem access. Many administrators place a single modem on their server for emergency back-up access. However, if you are going to be providing dial-up access for numerous users, you are better off providing a separate RAS, Remote Authentication Dial-In User Service (RADIUS), or other dial-up authentication resource. Installing a multimodem interface card is a viable solution if you don't have a lot of users or heavy usage, but this extra overhead can place an unnecessary burden on a high-usage server and possibly increase security risks and exposure. Having a separate RAS, RADIUS, or other type of authentication server adds an additional layer of security an intruder would have to break through. This reduces the load on your Citrix MetaFrame server. Most large companies already have an existing dial-up infrastructure in place that can be used with little or no modification.

Other server hardware factors besides modems can take a toll on server resources. The more protocols, services, applications, and users that you add to a server or client system, the more resources they take up. Keep this in mind when you are calculating your client and server hardware requirements. A weak client system that was just barely staying afloat may sink when you add "just one more" protocol to its network stack.

Still another factor is what type of client interface you want. Both ICA and RDP now offer Web based ActiveX type clients. Both offer a Connection Manager-like interface. RDP has a new RDP plug-in for the Microsoft Management Console (MMC). ICA has the seamless desktop. We will discuss many of the details in using these different options later in the chapter. One may be better suited to specific applications than the other in certain environments. If you are connecting to a remote machine located across a WAN or other external network, only one type may be supported.

NOTE

There actually are two versions of RDP, RDP4 and RDP5. RDP5 provides a significant performance increase (although still not equal to ICA performance) and an increased feature set over version 4. Both RDP versions are backwards compatible with each other, so both are capable of connecting with Windows NT4 Terminal Server Edition, Windows 2000 Terminal Services, or Citrix MetaFrame servers. We will consider the versions to be the same protocol, and will refer to features from version 5 for our purposes in this chapter.

The ICA protocol provides the greatest variety of client connectivity options. ICA clients are currently available for all types of Windows operating systems including Windows CE (Windows Based Terminals and Handheld PCs), Windows NT Workstation, Windows 95/98, Windows 2000 Professional, Windows for Workgroups, and Windows 3.x. ICA clients are also available for non-Windows-based operating systems including DOS, Mac OS, Java, and EPOC. Many flavors of UNIX are supported, including HP/UX, Solaris/Sparc, Solaris/x86, Solaris/SunOS, SCO, Tru64, SGI, IBM AIX, and Linux.

The ICA protocol makes more efficient use of bandwidth. ICA is conceptually similar to the UNIX X-Windows protocol. This protocol allows an application to execute logic on the MetaFrame server while the user interface executes with minimal resource consumption on the client's PC. ICA is implemented at the system-level Graphics Device Interface (GDI) and is very efficient and compact. This architecture allows applications that normally consume large amounts of bandwidth to run at near-LAN speed over low-bandwidth phone lines.

What this means is that all the high bandwidth and processor intensive "work" is done on the MetaFrame server while only the screen updates, keystrokes, and mouse-clicks get transmitted over the wire to the client. As a result, even a lowly DOS 386 machine can run programs and the latest compatible software as if it were the Dual or Quad processor server machine with 1 or 2GB of RAM! The MetaFrame server can also provide connectivity for Windows-based terminals, so all users can run the same applications. Running applications from a centrally controlled server can ease a great deal of administrative headaches.

Let's say, for example, that you have 1000 users. They are all ready to be upgraded from Microsoft Office 97 to Microsoft Office 2000. Using this thin-client model, your support staff would only have to upgrade the MetaFrame servers hosting the Microsoft Office 2000 application instead of visiting each desktop. After a weekend upgrade of your servers, all 1000 users could come in Monday morning and begin using their new version of Microsoft Office 2000! This can save a great deal in time, effort, and licensing costs. Many companies can purchase "concurrent use" licenses. In concurrent use licensing, software is installed on a central server with usage monitoring. You then only need to purchase licenses for the amount of users simultaneously using the software. This could add up to big savings. If you have 225 employees, but only 25 at a time ever use a particular program, that's 200 fewer licenses just for one software package. If the software cost $500 per license, that's a savings of $100,000 for the one software package alone!

For IT Professionals

ICA Bandwidth

According to Citrix, the ICA protocol only consumes an average of 20 KB of bandwidth. While this may be true for terminal type sessions, graphical applications or applications using a high screen refresh setting can consume far more. While ICA was designed and functions well for most applications even over a 14.4 modem connection, if more bandwidth is available, it will use it.

I conducted testing from a Dual ISDN (4–64Kbps B channels) dialed directly into a T1-PRI on our network and found that normal terminal applications and even Microsoft Word and Excel used about the average stated, sometimes spiking up to 60–70 percent utilization of two B channels (128Kbps). However, bringing up Internet Explorer, browsing to the Citrix home page, and then quickly scrolling up and down repeatedly to view the home page kept three B channels (192Kbps) at a near constant 75 percent utilization.

By comparison, I decided to connect to the same server using RDP5. There wasn't a lot of difference in just moving the mouse around or using terminal applications. When I got to the Internet Explorer test, browsing to the Citrix home page and then constantly scrolling, I found that the RDP5 brought up all four B channels (256 Kbps), maxed it out at 100 percent, and was still sluggish refreshing the up and down scrolling. I continually had to wait on the screen to refresh, just to click to Page Up and Down in the scrollbar. This was a distinct difference from

Continued

> the first test where I could barely scroll the ICA connection fast enough to keep the bandwidth usage up. As with anything else, I'm sure Microsoft will continue to improve the RDP5 protocol, but for now, ICA won out hands down on my "real world" test based purely on speed and bandwidth utilization.
>
> Network administrators need to keep this in mind if depending on ICA technology to solve all their network bottlenecks. ICA will certainly help, but it is not a cure-all for poor network design or inadequate bandwidth.
>
> While both types of connections performed well under normal conditions, and I have used both successfully on dial-up connections, administrators beware! Plan for the unusual. That way, you won't be surprised when a user says to you, "What do you mean, I can't open 10 Word documents, five large spreadsheets, play Solitaire, and surf the Web without performance issues?"

An administrator or client does not necessarily have to limit him or herself to making one choice. For instance, a client could use RDP to connect to a MetaFrame server on the local LAN but use ICA to connect to a remote server at a business partner's location. Most MetaFrame administrators will have multiple connectivity protocols available; however, they may not be available to all users. Many administrators reserve one or more protocols for use only by other administrators and restrict their client usage to only one of the available choices. Choosing a single protocol for client connectivity can result in a more effective support structure and lend itself more readily to automated client installation configurations. Connectivity options are determined by the server administrator. Be sure to check with the person operating the server or with their help desk to determine the most efficient client settings for connecting to their equipment.

The ICA protocol used with Citrix MetaFrame has a much more robust feature set than the RDP protocol.

The key differences are as follows:

- ICA provides a 16-bit client for connectivity from older, less powerful systems.

- ICA provides for connectivity using a variety of transport protocols: SPX, IPX, NetBEUI, and Direct Asynchronous are all supported, while RDP works only over TCP/IP.

- ICA provides audio support by default.

- ICA provides accessibility to local drives by default, as does RDP (with add-ons).

- ICA provides "seamless windows" allowing remote server-based applications to resize and minimize similar to local applications.

- ICA allows advertising of server-based applications directly to client desktops.

- ICA protocol makes more efficient use of available bandwidth.

- Other features such as Load Balancing, Remote Control, and Bitmap Caching, while provided on both protocols, may be implemented differently.

For more detailed information on ICA and RDP, including a feature comparison chart, visit the site at the following link: www.microsoft.com/ntserver/terminalserver/techdetails/compares/rdp.asp.

Installing MetaFrame Clients

As we discussed previously, the first step to installing a MetaFrame Client is deciding which client operating system (OS) and which MetaFrame client and protocol you will be using. You should contact the system administrator of the server or servers you will be connecting to and already determine which client and protocol is correct for your needs. We will discuss several options and present the methods of installing each.

One factor that is common to all clients is the need for a unique client name. The client name is one of the methods that the MetaFrame server uses to track individual connections, drive mappings, printer mappings, and so on. Most ICA clients are available in several different languages including English, French, German, Spanish, and Japanese (to host multiple languages, a separate Citrix server is required for each language). All of the numerous current client software installations are available from the Citrix Web site download page (http://download.citrix.com).

DOS

Citrix provides two DOS clients for MetaFrame, a 16-bit and a 32-bit. The 32-bit version consumes a great deal less conventional memory space by using a DOS-protected mode. This new version requires the use of DOS 4.0 or greater and runs on systems with a 386 processor or higher. The 16-bit version runs on older 286-based machines. Citrix will not be applying any future feature enhancements to the 16-bit DOS ICA client. Technical support

For IT Professionals

Where the Client Names are Stored

By default, the MetaFrame Client Setup uses your computer name during initial installation as the Client name. If your computer name is something common, like John, Mary, client1, and so on, you must either change your computer name or enter a custom name in the client configuration. Having duplicate client names connecting to the MetaFrame server can have undesirable effects.

If you change your computer name later, the MetaFrame client does not automatically recognize the change but continues to pass the original name chosen during the install process when connecting to a Citrix MetaFrame server. To manually modify the name passed to the Citrix server, you must modify the Wfcname.INI on the client machine. The file is usually located in the system root directory (C:\). If you have trouble locating it, use the search feature of your respective operating system.

Here is a partial example of contents from the Wfcname.INI file where the client name is stored:

```
[WFClient]

ClientName=K3
```

Change the value of the client name to the new one you wish to use (.K4), and save the file.

from Citrix for the 16-bit client will also be limited. The 32-bit version will perform better, be more stable, and provide more features than the 16-bit version and is recommended if you meet the minimum hardware requirements. At the time of this writing, there is no Java or Automatic Linking and Embedding (ALE) client available for DOS.

To install the 32-bit Citrix DOS ICA client, perform the following steps:

1. Download the most current version of the client software from the Citrix Web site: http://download.citrix.com.

2. Copy the downloaded file (EE000779.EXE) to a temporary directory on your hard drive and then double-click it to extract the client files.

3. Take care to close or exit all programs running on the PC.

4. Run Install to install the client software from either the floppy disk (A:) drive, the temporary directory where you extracted the files, or from a network share created by your administrator.

Creating DOS ICA Client Installation Floppy Disks

To create installation floppy disks, use the following command to begin extracting client files:

```
EE000779.EXE -d
```

The -d option recreates the original installation directory structure so that the client files can be moved or copied directly to floppy disks.

1. The MetaFrame DOS client installation requires more than one disk. Make certain to have two blank, formatted 1.4MB floppy disks prepared before you begin. You should label the floppy disks as follows to keep track of them:

    - ICA 32 DOS Disk 1
    - ICA 32 DOS Disk 2

2. Copy the file EE000779.EXE (or most current version) to a temporary directory (in our example, we use C:\temp, but you can use any directory name that you please), and then extract the client files using the following command:

```
EE000779.EXE -d
```

3. The extraction process should create the new directory structure as follows:

```
c:\temp\README.txt
c:\temp\disk1\
c:\temp\disk2\
```

Here, C:\temp is our example temporary directory and location where the client files were extracted to.

4. Insert floppy disk number 1 and copy the files from the \disk1 subdirectory to the floppy disk by typing the following at a command prompt:

```
copy c:\temp\disk1\*.* a:\
```

5. Insert floppy disk number 2 and copy the files from the \disk2 subdirectory to the floppy disk by typing the following at a command prompt:

```
copy c:\temp\disk2\*.* a:\
```

6. Make certain to close or exit all applications currently running on the client machine.

7. Insert floppy disk number 1 and type **install** at a command prompt to install the client.

8. Follow the on-screen instructions and answer, when prompted, to complete the installation.

Windows 16-Bit

Installing the Windows 16-bit client begins with downloading the most current version of software from the Citrix Web site (http://download.citrix .com). Your network administrator may also supply you with a set of installation disks created from the server, or a network share where the client installation files are located. The most current file name for the 16-bit client as of this writing is we000779.EXE. Floppy installation creation and installation is the same as with the Windows 32-bit client. Simply substitute the we00079.EXE (W16-bit) filename for the ne00079.EXE (W32-bit) filename when creating the floppy installation diskettes. For detailed instructions, refer to the section on Windows 32-bit client installation. The Windows 16-bit client is also used for installation on OS/2 systems. Special instructions must be followed for use with OS/2. See the OS/2 client installation section for details on use with this specialized operating system.

Windows 32-Bit

Installing the Windows 32-bit ICA client begins with downloading the current version of software from the Citrix Web site (http://download.citrix .com). After selecting your choice of client from the download page, you are presented with a license agreement. After reading and accepting the license agreement, you are able to proceed with the download. Once at the download page for the correct client, you are presented with the choice to download the client software itself, the README file, a Windows Quick Reference guide, and a Windows Client Admin Reference guide.

The current client and the one used for the screenshots in this chapter are version 4.21.779, which has a filename of ne000779.EXE. Many IT Professionals simply refer to the last three digits in common discussion of the client version: in other words, "client 779," "client 741," or "client 727." This is a self-extracting .EXE file with a size of approximately 2.57MB. This means it will not fit on a single floppy diskette.

After downloading the file to your hard drive and double-clicking on it, you will be presented with a DOS window where the file is described and you are given an option to extract the files. When you choose Yes, the files are extracted to the same directory where the ne000779.EXE file resides. The client can either be installed from this directory, from a shared network drive containing these files, or from installation floppy disks that you can create if needed. The floppy installation method requires three formatted floppy disks and is slower than a local hard drive or network install.

Creating Windows 32-Bit Client Installation Floppy Disks

To create installation floppy disks for the Windows 32-bit client, perform the following set of instructions:

1. Instead of (or in addition to) double-clicking the ne00079.EXE file, open a command prompt and type: **ne00079.EXE –d**

2. The –d switch will extract the directory structure below (where temp = the directory the .EXE file resides in):

   ```
   C:\temp\README.txt
   C:\temp\disk1\
   C:\temp\disk2\
   C:\temp\disk3\
   ```

3. Be sure you are in the c:\temp directory. Type **CD C:\temp** at a command prompt and press Return.

4. Put the first floppy disk, disk number 1, into your floppy drive and copy the files from the C:\temp\disk1 subdirectory to the floppy disk by typing: **copy C:\temp\disk1*.* a:**.

5. When disk 1 has finished, put the second floppy disk, disk number 2, into your floppy drive and copy the files from the C:\temp\disk2 subdirectory to the floppy disk by typing: **copy C:\temp\disk2*.* a:**.

6. When disk 2 has finished, put the third floppy disk, disk number 3, into your floppy drive and copy the files from the C:\temp\disk3 subdirectory to the floppy disk by typing: **copy C:\temp\disk3*.* a:**.

7. * Files could also be copied using Windows Explorer or another method if you prefer.

8. After disk 3 has finished, close or exit all other running applications, then put the disk number 1 back into the floppy drive and type **A:\setup** to begin the install process.

9. Follow the on-screen instructions and answer when prompted to complete the installation.

Once we have the client software extracted, we are ready to begin the actual install process. The installation choices will be the same no matter which method you choose to use (of course only the floppy method will prompt you to replace and insert the multiple disks you created in that method).

1. To begin the install, use Windows Explorer to browse to the directory you extracted the client files to (we will use C:\temp as an example), and double-click on SETUP.EXE. Or, from the run menu or command prompt, type **c:\temp\setup**. This will begin the client install program.

2. After double-clicking SETUP.EXE or running from the command line, the Citrix MetaFrame client install begins. You should see the following screen welcoming you to the MetaFrame client install.

3. Clicking on the Next button presents the Citrix Licensing Agreement. You must choose Yes to continue. Choosing Back takes you to the previous screen, choosing No ends the installation process.

4. If you have previously installed the MetaFrame client, or an earlier version of the client, you will be presented with the option to upgrade your existing client or install it to a new location.

5. Choose Next and you are given an option for the Client Name as shown in Figure 6.1. This is the only critical step that requires actual user input during the install process. All client names connecting to the MetaFrame server must be unique or unexpected errors may result. Your Windows machine (NetBIOS) name is placed in the box by default. If using a common name or one that may be easily duplicated by someone else, change it here during the install process. It can also be changed later as part of the configuration options, but if two users from different computers connect with the same client name, many configuration settings can be corrupted. This could include drive mappings, printer mappings, timeouts, and other critical system resources.

Figure 6.1 Applying a unique client name.

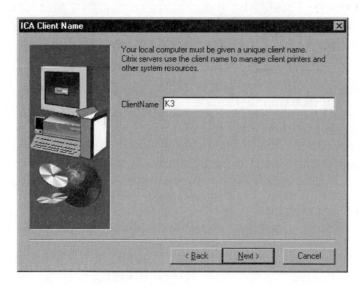

6. Clicking Next then begins the actual process of installing files to your local hard drive.

7. Congratulations! If you followed the steps correctly, you should see the completion message. Be sure to reboot your machine to ensure that the desktop icons for program neighborhood and other system settings are finished correctly.

8. Now you should have successfully installed Citrix MetaFrame client and rebooted your machine. You should have a new icon on your desktop called "Citrix Program Neighborhood."

9. You're all ready to connect and start using MetaFrame, right? Not so! Unless you are connecting to an ICA or NFuse enabled Web page, you must tell the client how to connect to the server. In an upcoming section, we will actually configure the client settings. This portion *must* be successfully completed to proceed any further. If you had any error messages or difficulty, start the procedure over and make sure to follow the instructions very carefully. If you still have problems, contact your system administrator or Citrix support for assistance.

Macintosh

Installing the Citrix MetaFrame client on a Macintosh system is a very straightforward process, similar to that of the Windows 32-bit client. Prior to the install, download the appropriate client version from the Citrix Web site download page (http://download.citrix.com). The Citrix MetaFrame Macintosh client is available in five languages, English, French, German, Spanish, and Japanese. The files are in compressed *.HQX format and must be decompressed after downloading with a compatible utility, such as StuffIt. StuffIt is available from the Aladdin Systems homepage (www.aladdinsys.com) or numerous other sources. Refer to the StuffIt README or help files for instructions on decompressing .HQX files. After decompressing, open the Citrix ICA Client 4.1 folder created by the decompression utility and double-click on the installer icon. Follow the instructions given on-screen to finish installation. After installation, refer to the configuration section to adjust the client settings for connecting to a server, published application, or server farm.

The Citrix ICA Macintosh Client will *not* support asynchronous connections to a WinFrame or MetaFrame server. Although this limitation exists, a Macintosh user is able to establish a point-to-point connection to a PPP server—such as a Remote Access Server (RAS)—using other utilities, and can be provided with a virtual TCP/IP address. In layman's terms, a "virtual" IP address is one that is assigned to the dial-up adapter at connection time. This then "pretends" to be a network interface card that is assigned the given address. The computer is then allowed to send and receive traffic as if it were really directly connected to the same network it is dialed into, using the "virtual" IP address as its identifier. After this is accomplished, the Citrix ICA Macintosh Client can successfully initiate an ICA session with the Citrix server.

PPP dialers for Macintosh include:

MacPPP (freeware) While still available on some Web site archives, a similar version is now included with Mac OS 8.0 and above. Check your Macintosh user's manual for configuration guidelines.

FreePPP (freeware) Rockstar software: www.rockstar.com/ppp.shtml.

Open Transport/PPP (works with Mac OS 7.5.3 and later; shipped with Mac OS 7.6 through 8.1) Open Transport seems to be the most widely used and easiest, since it is now included with the OS.

Apple Remote Access Version 2.1 shipped as an optional extra with Mac OS 8.1; Version 3.1 shipped with Mac OS 8.5.

There is a Macintosh Java and ALE plug-in also available from the Citrix download site listed above; however, these may require additional configuration on the Citrix Server, the Web Server, or the Macintosh client for proper functionality. Check with the system administrator to determine if this has been enabled on the server you wish to connect with. Check out the Citrix Java Client Admin Guide at http://download.citrix.com/ftpweb/bin/java/v411/en/javagde.pdf more information on copying the Java classes, installing the applets, and creating Macintosh launching scripts.

OS/2

There is no OS/2 MetaFrame Client available from Citrix. The only client versions known to function on OS/2 are the DOS and Win16 versions on OS/2 version 4 systems. The following connectivity methods are supported on the MetaFrame clients.

DOS TCP/IP, IPX, NetBIOS, Async(direct), and Async(modem)

Win16 TCP/IP, NetBIOS, Async(direct), and Async(modem)

Note that neither one includes SPX, and only the DOS client supports IPX.

Setting up a MetaFrame client on OS/2 is no task for the inexperienced or timid. I have seen or read of several users attempting to do so ending up with a Blue Screen of Death (BSOD) or other seemingly unrecoverable errors. Many of them ended up simply rebuilding their OS/2 machine as the path of least resistance.

I would *not* attempt this unless you have backed up all of your data, and are willing and able to restore your machine from backup or completely rebuild the operating system. The Citrix Support Forum is your best resource and you would be wise to read through it before launching in on such an endeavor. You may wish to also have one hand on the phone and the Citrix support number handy on the wall. That said, if you still wish to continue, good luck.

OS/2 Installation

Prior to beginning OS/2 installation of the Citrix MetaFrame client, first install the operating system using the standard install procedures for OS/2 Warp version 4.0. You should install the correct networking support for your environment (File and Print Client Services, Novell Netware, TCP/IP, Netware Client.) You should verify that your network adapter is functional and that all settings are correct. If using TCP/IP, specify the hostname, IP address, subnet mask, domain name, and default gateway or router address. You may also use Dynamic Host Configuration Protocol (DHCP) to configure your client machine, if there is a DHCP server active on your local area network (LAN).

Refer to your OS/2 installation guide for instructions to install the proper network protocols for your system. The networking software for the virtual WIN-OS2 and the virtual DOS sessions are automatically added during the install process.

TIP

Your client name and password must be an exact match on the OS/2 machine and the MetaFrame server. Login is attempted automatically upon connection and mismatches will result in failed logins. Depending on your server settings, this could result in the account being locked out temporarily, or permanently (until reset by the administrator).

Win-16 OS/2 Installation Procedure

If you wish to use Dynamic Data Exchange (DDE) and the clipboard with the Win-16 OS/2 client, you must make the following adjustments to your system settings *before* installing the MetaFrame client:

1. In the OS/2 system folder, click on System Setup, then Win-OS/2 Setup.
2. Select the Data Exchange tab.
3. On the Data Exchange window, select Public for both selections. This enables the DDE and Clipboard functions.
4. Close all open windows, saving settings.
5. In the OS/2 system folder, click on Command Prompts.
6. Right-click on either the Seamless Win-OS/2 icon, or the Full screen Win-OS/2 icon and choose Settings.
7. Select the Session tab and modify the All DOS and Win-OS/2 radio buttons that are highlighted and click on OK.
8. Change WIN_RUN_MODE to 3.1 Enhanced Compatibility.
9. Change WIN_CLIPBOARD and WIN_DDE to On.
10. Close all open windows, saving settings.
11. If you are going to use NetBIOS, or think you may need it in the future, use your favorite text editor and add the following line to your autoexec.BAT file:

    ```
    C:\ibmcom\ltsvcfg n1=1
    ```

    C is the OS/2 system drive letter. This enables NAME_NUMBER_1 support that is required for NetBIOS network connections.

You may now run Setup from the MetaFrame client installation floppy disk (drive A:) or from the directory on your hard drive or network drives where the client installation files have been copied. You should have the server hostname available and all desired networking protocols already installed. During installation, you will be prompted for dial-in options. I recommend that you not select this option during installation, but wait until installation is complete and you are setting up properties for the local user.

DOS OS/2 Client Installation Procedure

To install the DOS OS/2 client, perform the following steps:

1. Download the DOS MetaFrame client software from the Citrix Web site (http://download.citrix.com).

2. After extracting the files to floppy disk or your hard drive, run the Install program.

UNIX

Installing the Citrix MetaFrame client for UNIX-based systems can be done using two different methods. The first is a normal extraction and text mode install method. The second method uses the graphic user interface (GUI), Red Hat-Package-Manager (RPM)-based installation procedure on any UNIX-style OS that supports it. Citrix has specific clients for HP-UX, Solaris (Sparc, Sun, x86), Tru64, IBM AIX, SGI, SCO, and Linux. Current OSs and versions supported are shown in Table 6.1.

Table 6.1 Supported UNIX Operating Systems

OS	Versions Supported
Digital UNIX	3.2 or above
HP-UX	10.20 or above
IBM AIX	4.1.4 or above
Linux	Red Hat 5.0 or above, Caldera 1.3 or above, SuSE 5.3 or above, and Slackware 3.5 or above
SCO	UNIXWare 7, UNIXWare 2.1*, OpenServer 5*
SGI IRIX	6.3 or above
Sun Solaris	1.0** (SunOS 4.1.4), 2.5.1 (SunOS 5.5.1), and Intel Platform Edition 2.6 (SunOS 5.6) or above

Note in the table that the SCO client requires the Binary Compatibility Module to run under UNIXWare 2.1 and OpenServer 5 and that Sun Solaris 1.0 requires OpenWindows patch 100444-76.tar.Z.

WARNING

The Citrix MetaFrame client for UNIX requires an "X Window" session and cannot be run from a "plain" Telnet prompt.

System Requirements for all UNIX systems running the ICA UNIX Client are as follows:

- 12MB free disk space for installation
- TCP/IP Networking
- 16 or 256 color video display and adapter

Check the Citrix Web site download area (http://download.citrix.com) to see if your OS type and version are supported. Red Hat Linux has widely promoted the RPM installation package and arguably has one of the largest installed bases of "UNIX" end-user systems. The UNIX installation and configuration screen captures used in this chapter were taken from the Red Hat Linux 6.2 operating system.

TIP

The UNIX (Linux) client machine name must also be unique just like the Windows, DOS, and all other client machine names. The UNIX client name can be configured, though not through the user interface. A 'ClientName=' entry can be placed in either the [WFClient] section of wfclient.INI, in the relevant description section of appsrv.INI, or in both. An appsrv.INI entry takes precedence over any wfclient.INI entry. If no name is specified, the default name is the host name.

Steps to Perform a Text-Based UNIX (Linux) Client Installation

Follow these steps to perform a text-based UNIX client installation:

1. Login as root at the client machine.

2. Open a command window.

3. Be sure you have enough free space on the hard drive to complete the installation.

4. Download the appropriate MetaFrame client from the Citrix Web site.

5. Unzip the downloaded archive file, gzip –d linux.tar.gz (yours may differ).

6. Uncompress the resulting tar .TAR file and extract the contents into a temporary directory, tar –xvf linux.tar (again, your filename or command may differ somewhat).

7. Run the setup program by typing **./setupwfc** and press ENTER.

8. If setup fails, check filenames for upper/lowercase and re-enter accordingly.

9. An option menu should appear with three choices: Install, Remove, and Quit.

10. Enter **1** to choose Install and press ENTER.

11. You will be given a choice where to install the client. Press ENTER to accept the default of /usr/lib/ICAClient or type in a different path and press ENTER.

12. The installation will ask you to confirm. Type **Y** and press ENTER to continue or **N** and press ENTER to cancel the installation.

13. The Client Software License Agreement is displayed and you are again prompted for confirmation. Answer the same as in step 12.

14. When installation is complete, the client should be integrated with the Netscape browser (if installed) and the main installation menu is displayed again. Enter **3** and press ENTER to exit from the program.

15. That's it! You can now configure the client to connect to a server. Start the client by typing **/usr/lib/ICAClient/wfcmgr** and pressing ENTER.

TIP

To remove the Citrix ICA Client for UNIX (Linux):

1. Log on as root.

2. Run the setup program as we did during install by typing **/usr/lib/ICAClient/setupwfc** and press ENTER.

3. If you installed the ICA client to a different directory, enter that path and press ENTER.

4. The menu will be displayed. Type **2** and press ENTER to remove the ICA client.

Using the Red Hat Package Manager (RPM) to Install the Client

Using the Red Hat Package Manager (RPM) to install software has become one of my favorite ways to install almost any software. Although frowned upon by some UNIX purists, the RPM has some useful features not available from the "normal" tarballs or gzip files. RPM can be used to install software from either the command line mode, or using the GUI interface. In the GUI interface, it acts almost like a "Windows Setup" program, eliminating the need for long README files or lengthy texts on proper compilation techniques. It can also be used to uninstall, verify, update, and perform other useful features, including acting as a poor man's security tool by verifying the installed binaries to check against Trojan horse installation. A detailed discussion of RPM is beyond the scope of this book, but I encourage you to research it; I find it a useful and timesaving tool. If you have RPM installed but are unfamiliar with it, try the MAN pages or type **rpm – help** at the command prompt for the switch syntax.

The RPM Installation steps are as follows:

1. Login as root.

2. Start X-window session (for Red Hat Linux users, type **Startx** and press ENTER).

3. Click on the Start button in the lower-left corner and go to System, then click on GnoRPM as shown in Figure 6.2.

4. This opens the Gnome RPM window.

5. Click on the Install button.

6. This opens a new Install window.

Figure 6.2 Starting GnoRPM.

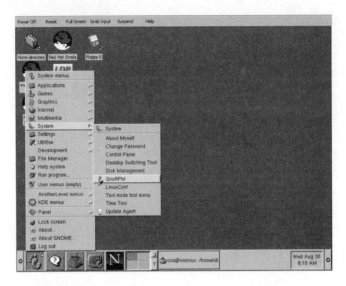

7. Click on the Add button.

8. This opens the new Add Packages window shown in Figure 6.3.

Figure 6.3 Adding new software.

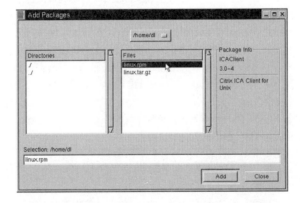

9. Browse to the directory where you downloaded the linux.RPM installation file.

10. Select the linux.RPM file and click the Add button.

11. You should see that the ICAClient-3.0-4 (or current version) has been added to the Install window opened in step 6.

12. Close the Add window, and return your focus to the Install window.

13. The box next to ICAClient-3.0-4 should be checked, then click
    Install at the bottom of the window as shown in Figure 6.4.

14. The RPM should begin copying and installing files.

15. That's it! Close the RPM Install windows and you're ready to run
    the client and configure it to connect to your servers. Start the
    client by typing **/usr/lib/ICAClient/wfcmgr** and pressing ENTER.

Figure 6.4 Installing RPMs.

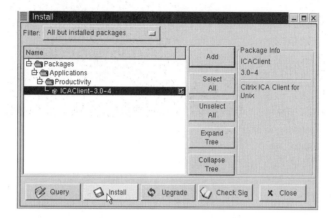

TIP

A shortcut on the Red Hat Linux GUI desktop can be created for the
MetaFrame Client. To do so, click the Start button. Go to Panel, then click
on Add New Launcher. Assign the properties as follows:

    Name: MetaFrame Client

    Command: /usr/lib/ICAClient/wfcmgr

    Type: Application

    Click on the icon button if you wish and browse for a custom icon.

    Click OK to save and create the new launcher.

    The new icon should appear on the taskbar.

Deploying MetaFrame Clients Using Automated Installation

Experienced MetaFrame administrators are always looking for ways to make the administration and user support tasks more effective. One of these ways is to automate the installation process of the MetaFrame client. In a previous section, we have discussed installing the MetaFrame client. In another section we looked at configuring the MetaFrame client to operate efficiently in your environment. Wouldn't it be great if we could combine these tasks, so that users would not be tasked with all the complicated screens and configuration options?

In this section, we will show you the steps needed to create customized installation disk sets that can contain all the configuration options your clients need to connect with your servers. Once you have configured these installation disks, users need only run through the installation steps given earlier, then connect to the server. All the complex configuration options have been done ahead of time by the administrator, so you know they are done correctly. Many administrators will place these custom configured install disks as a link on their Web sites to more easily support clients, or maintain an FTP site with the most recent available. While it does take a little extra time to configure the custom disks, they are well worth the time it takes to avoid having to walk multiple users though the manual configuration process.

WARNING

Use caution when implementing a customized client install. Installing a customized MetaFrame client on a system for the first time should never create a problem. Using a customized client install on a system that already has a configured MetaFrame client could overwrite their previous settings. This could adversely affect settings they had for connecting to other company's servers or overwrite special firewall or proxy configurations their system administrators have designed for them. Always have the user check for a previously installed MetaFrame client and, if it exists, determine if there are settings that exist which differ from the one in your custom install. If so, the best method is to always do a generic upgrade or install, then configure the client manually. Also, be sure to check the custom install to make sure it contains *only* what you want before distributing it. You probably don't want 100 or more users connecting with your administrator's username and password preconfigured in their client.

Steps to Create Preconfigured Client Install Disks

Follow these steps to create preconfigured client install disks:

1. To create the custom preconfigured installation disks for your clients, you must first create normal installation disks, either from the server client install creator or using the latest version downloaded from the Citrix download site (http://download.citrix.com).

2. You should then install the client software normally as described previously.

3. Configure your custom connections, settings, and preferences that you wish to be distributed to your clients.

4. After saving your custom settings, copy the following files from the workstation you just modified to the floppies containing the original installation files, overwriting the existing files:

    Module.INI → **A:\module.SRC**

    Wfclient.INI → **A:\wfclient.SRC**

    Apsrv.INI → **A:\appsrv.SRC**

5. These files should be located in the C:\Program Files\Citrix\ICA Client directory. If you have trouble locating them, use the search feature of your operating system.

6. You may now use your customized installation disks to streamline your client installation process. Installation should now require no user input to install the software and configure the settings needed to connect to your server.

After the above steps have been completed, you can distribute the custom installation disks to your clients and decrease your setup and support time. An even greater time-saving measure is to configure the server and client for Automatic Updates. Using the Automatic Client Update utility on the MetaFrame server, you can automatically distribute this custom client and any others you create automatically when the clients connect to your server. In order for this to function properly, the client setup must allow automatic update. This feature is enabled by default on the client (see the client configuration section) but requires special setup and configuration on the server.

Creating a New Client Update Database

If you support many users, you will find the Client Auto Update feature to be one of the most indispensable tools on your server. It will save you many hours of both installation and troubleshooting effort if you put in just a little time to learn how it works and take advantage of the many powerful features it has to offer. Here's the way it works:

- You store new versions of the MetaFrame client software (from Citrix, or your own custom) in a central database on the Citrix server (or a network share).

- When clients connect to your server, it compares the client version with the version in your database and then automatically downloads the new version to the client if needed and upgrades their installation.

- You have full administrative control of update options for each client.

- You can restore old client versions in case of programming errors, corrupt files, and so on (providing the client can still connect, of course).

- Auto Update works on all supported ICA transport types, including TCP/IP, IPX, NetBIOS, and serial connections.

As with anything else, there are a couple of "gotcha's" with the Client Auto Update feature.

- Client Auto Update only works with the "newer" versions of the client. Versions 727 and above should function properly. If the client is not yet at that level, they will have to update manually before Auto Update will function.

- Client Auto Update can only update clients to a newer version of the same client. For example, it can be used to update the Citrix ICA Win32-bit Client 741 to the ICA Win32-bit Client 779. It *cannot* be used to update a Win16-bit client to the Win32-bit Client or the DOS 16-bit client to the Win32-bit client.

Configuring MetaFrame Clients

In the previous sections, we have discussed choosing protocols, downloading the correct client, and installing various MetaFrame clients on many different operating systems. In this section, we will begin configuring the clients. You will see that while there are some cosmetic differences, most of the important required parameters are pretty much the same from one operating system to another. Some clients may not have all of the same features available to them that are found in the others, but other than that, the differences are minor. I think that you will find that the Win32-bit client has the most robust feature set and provides the most customized user experience.

For IT Professionals

Steps to Create a New Client Update Database

The following are the steps to create a new client update for a database. Realize that these steps must be performed on the MetaFrame Server.

1. To enter the client database utility, click on Start | Programs | MetaFrame Tools | ICA Client Update Config.

2. From the Database pull-down menu, click on New.

3. Enter a path and name for the new client update database. By default, it creates a file called DBConfig.INI in the \systemroot\Ica\Clientdb folder.
   For NT4 and MF1.8, this would be C:\wtsrv\Ica\Clientdb\ DBConfig.INI where C: is the root hard drive. For Windows 2000 and MF1.8, this would be:
   C:\Winnt\Ica\Clientdb\DBConfig.INI.

4. If you wanted to configure multiple Citrix servers to share the same database, place the file in an accessible shared network folder.

5. Once you have added the database, you must add client versions you wish to use Auto Update.

6. From the Client pull-down menu, click on New.

7. You should see the Description dialog box.

8. Browse to the client installation file (Update.INI located on disk1 of the Citrix Clients or on your custom installation disk set) or enter the full path and file name.

9. The client name, version, product, model, and icon are displayed. You can modify and customize comments you wish for this client. After adding your comments, click Next.

Continued

10. The Update Options tab should now appear. This is where you have the choice to: pick client update mode (ask user, notify user, or transparent), do version checking (update older client version only, or update *any* client version), force disconnection or allow background download, and add a custom message to be displayed on the client console.

11. After choosing Next, you are presented with the Logging tab; you may select Log downloaded clients and Log errors during download. I suggest you should at least log all errors. This will give you some idea whether your Auto Update is functioning correctly or not.

12. After choosing Next again, the Enable Client box should appear. Check the box to update your clients to the version of software stored in your database. The database can store multiple versions of the same client model but only one version per model can be enabled at the same time. When you enable one version, all other versions for that model will be automatically disabled.

13. Click Finish and your Auto Update setup is now complete for this client version. If you wish, right-click on the new client icon you created and look at the properties again; you should now see an additional tab called Client Files. This is a listing of the filenames and sizes that will be automatically downloaded to your clients the next time they connect to your server.

14. You may now sit back and enjoy the fruits of your labor as several thousand clients are upgraded while you do nothing but watch.

Configuring the UNIX Clients

The UNIX client has many of the same features available as the Win32-bit client. We will go through the steps involved in setting up an initial desktop connection and then discuss customizing options.

If this is your first UNIX install and you followed the directions outlined previously, you should have a working UNIX client. Since TCP/IP is the most widely used protocol and the most compatible across platforms, we will use that for our examples. If you use a different protocol, substitute those settings needed for your environment. Any IP addresses that you see listed are either private, nonroutable IP addresses or others used in our testing environment.

Please substitute your own IP addresses for any shown. If you are unsure of which IP addresses and subnet masks to use, check with your network administrator. In order for you to use a specific protocol, it must be a valid protocol for your operating system and network, be supported by the MetaFrame client version you are using, and be correctly configured and bound to your network interface card (NIC). Please consult the manual for your operating system or ask for assistance from your network administrator if you are unsure of these settings.

To begin using the UNIX Client:

1. Login to your system and start up an Xwindow.

2. Open a command window and type **/usr/lib/ICAClient/wfcmgr** then press ENTER.

Or, you can do the following.

3. Click on the Launcher button we created earlier.

4. The Citrix Client for Linux (UNIX) Main window should open.

5. You should see five buttons and two pull-down menu items.

6. Click on the Entry pull-down menu, then on New as shown in Figure 6.5.

7. The new entry properties window should open as shown in Figure 6.6. By default, it starts on the Network tab.

Figure 6.5 Linux client configuration.

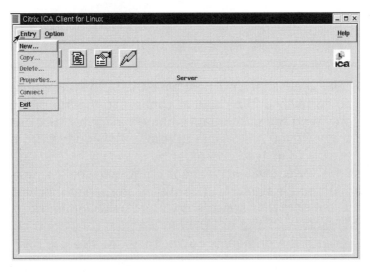

Figure 6.6 Network tab.

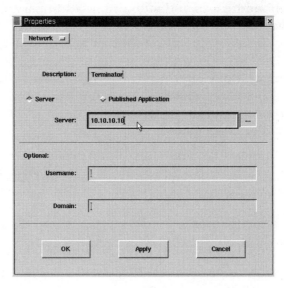

8. Type in a name for the connection. This does not have to be the server name, just a name you wish to use to refer to this server or application.

9. Type in the IP address or the Fully Qualified Domain Name (FQDN), e.g., **server1.foo.com**, of the server you wish to connect with.

10. If you click OK, you now have the bare minimum necessary to connect to the Citrix MetaFrame server.

TIP

To use FQDNs, your machine must have the Domain Name Service (DNS) configured correctly and be able to connect to the Internet or intranet servers, providing the authoritative name service for that domain to resolve names. If you are unable to resolve DNS queries from your workstation, you could instead add an entry manually by editing the /etc/hosts file (or equivalent) on your client machine. Using a FQDN is the preferred method if available. This way, if the server machine changes IP addresses, only the DNS server entry must be changed, not all the clients. Many companies will also use DNS to automatically point clients to a backup server if the primary is down. They can also use DNS as a crude form of load balancing, with a technique called "Round Robin" that assigns incoming client requests first to one IP address, then the next, then the first again, and so on.

Other options available on the Network tab are spaces for UserName, Domain, and Password. Enter these to automatically connect to the Citrix MetaFrame server when the connection document is run.

NOTE

If users save their usernames, domain, and passwords, they are stored in the appsrv.INI file. This file will be found in a hidden directory called ICA Client located beneath the users' home directory. The username and domain are stored as plain text, while the password is encrypted. With the power of today's computers and the current atmosphere of cracking, some individuals (myself included) may consider this a security risk. I would recommend *never* saving any passwords, be they for Web site access, MetaFrame access, FTP, or whatever. If you can save it, then it's stored somewhere on your system and if your system is ever compromised, a determined cracker can eventually break it, especially if you don't use complex passwords. If you don't save it, there's nothing there for them to crack.

Connection Tab

If you then click the small button next to Network, you will see the other tabs available (Figure 6.7).

Figure 6.7 Connection property options.

Let's click on the Connection tab and look at the options there. In Figure 6.8, we see the options for Data Compression and Bitmap Cache and Sound.

Figure 6.8 Connection sound and compression options.

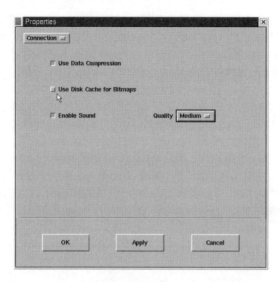

Data compression should be on by default; I usually recommend turning on the Disk Cache for Bitmaps, and turning off the sound unless you have high bandwidth available or a definite need for sound. The Sound tab has three settings. They deserve an extra look.

High This setting uses 1.3 Mbps of bandwidth to play clearly. This amount of data can result in increased Central Processing Unit (CPU) utilization and network congestion. Clients can play a sound file at its native data rate, but at a cost. Bandwidth must be plentiful, so don't try this over a shared T1!

Medium Sounds sent to the client are compressed to 64 Kbps. This results in a moderate decrease in the quality of sound played at the client computer. The host CPU utilization will decrease due to the reduction in the amount of data being sent over the wire. This is the recommended setting for most LAN-based connections.

Low This setting is recommended for most modem connections and other low-bandwidth connections. Sounds sent to the client are compressed to a maximum of 16 Kbps. This results in a significant decrease in the quality of the sound. The CPU requirements are similar to the Medium setting, but the lower data rate allows reasonable performance for low-bandwidth connections.

I still recommend turning the sound completely off if you are on a dial-up connection. Sometimes, even on a network, there are bandwidth or congestion issues. This can also be controlled by the server administrator globally, so all options may not be available to you.

Window Tab

Let's move on to the Window tab, shown in Figure 6.9, where we can set the color, size, and appearance of our virtual desktop. Note that the maximum color setting is 256, as this is all the MetaFrame 1.8 server and client will support. This is supposed to be upgraded in the release of MetaFrame 2.0. I know a lot of administrators who have been itching to try some high-end graphic applications and games on their MetaFrame servers but have been restricted by these limitations.

Figure 6.9 Color and resolution options.

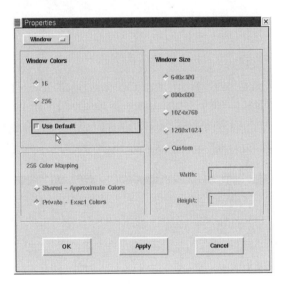

Application Tab

The last tab is the Application tab shown in Figure 6.10. This is where you can run a published application. If you specify an application, you do not see the full Windows desktop when you connect, and the connection is closed automatically when you quit the application. Just specify the pathname of an application to run after connecting to a MetaFrame server and the working directory pathname (optional). This option is only available when configuring a desktop connection profile. If you are configuring a published application profile, the Application dialog box will not be available.

Figure 6.10 Application settings.

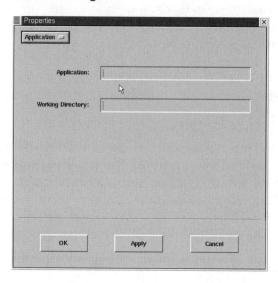

Preferences Tab

The next section is accessed from the Option pull-down menu in the main window. We then click on the Settings tab to open the window. The first tab we see here is the Preferences tab shown in Figure 6.11.

Figure 6.11 Preferences tab.

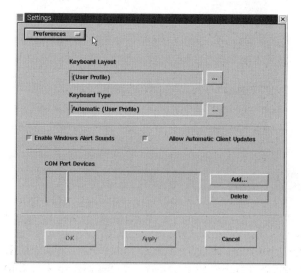

This is one of the more important views because this is where you set the client's ability to accept automatic updates from the server. This is enabled by default and should normally be left that way. The server can then push automatic updates to your client when configured properly, ensuring that you always have the latest client and most robust feature set. Here you can also set the Keyboard Layout, Windows Alert Sounds, and Map Com Ports.

Server Location Tab

Here you set the preferred servers to connect with when using published applications. Type in the IP address (or FQDN) of your MetaFrame application servers, and you should be able to browse the published applications. If non-standard alternate addresses are used by your server, this is where you can change the address ports to correspond with the servers (see Figure 6.12).

Figure 6.12 Server locations.

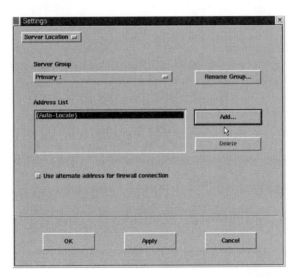

HotKeys Tab

The next two tabs are HotKeys tabs. Here you can set the ALT-F1 to ALT-F12 keys shown in Figure 6.13. These key combinations are used for different functions in X Windows. If you have a client application installed on the MetaFrame server (such as WRQ's Reflection) that remaps these, you should set the clients hotkeys preference to None; otherwise, the Citrix client software will overwrite the special mappings your software made.

Figure 6.13 HotKeys settings.

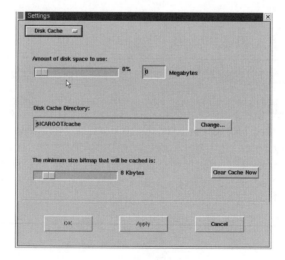

Disk Cache Tab

The Disk Cache tab shown in Figure 6.14 allows you to set the size and location for the disk cache. It also includes a choice for the minimum size at which to cache bitmaps. Some connections may benefit from lowering the default bitmap cache from 8KB to 4KB. You can also clear the disk cache from this tab. Clearing the disk cache is not recommended while connections are active. Be sure to close all active connections before clearing the cache.

Figure 6.14 Disk cache settings.

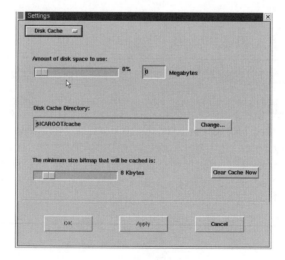

Drive Mapping

Figure 6.15 shows the drive mapping setup screen. Client drive mapping is one of MetaFrame's key features.

Figure 6.15 Client drive mappings.

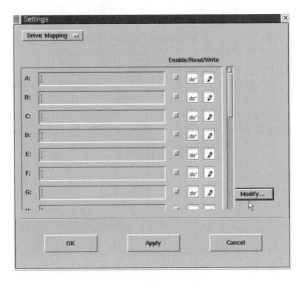

With client drive mapping, any directory mounted on the UNIX client machine, including CD-ROMs, is still available to the user during ICA sessions on MetaFrame servers. When the server is configured to allow client drive mapping, users can still access their locally stored files, work with them, and save them to either their local drive to a drive on the MetaFrame server all within the same ICA session. Simply choose the drives you want mapped and the type of access desired. See Figure 6.16 for a more detailed view showing the paths. This option can be controlled by the server, so you may not have access to all of the features.

After you are finished modifying the connection profile, click OK to save the settings, then go back to the main window and double-click on the entry you created to start the connection (see Figure 6.17). After a few seconds, you should see the familiar login screen. Congratulations, you are now running Windows from a UNIX machine! See the Citrix Client Administrator's guide for further information on configuring the client software.

Figure 6.16 Drive mapping detail.

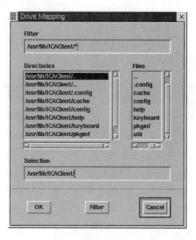

Figure 6.17 Connecting to the server.

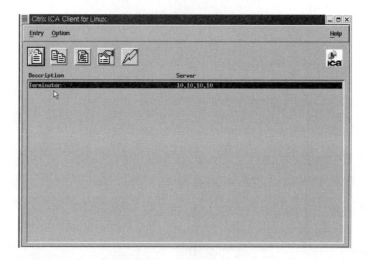

Win32 Client Configuration Overview

Configuring the Windows 32-bit clients is where most of us will spend the majority of our time. This has the most options and is therefore the most complex of all the client configurations. This client contains all the options of the others, so any client not discussed specifically should have the same options discussed in this section, with perhaps some minor differences to the window and menu design. Any client using the Windows 16-bit client should be manually upgraded to the 32-bit if it meets the minimum requirements; Auto Update will not function cross-version.

When connecting to a MetaFrame server, the Win32 Client provides additional features that make remote applications running on a MetaFrame server nearly indistinguishable from applications running on a local desktop. Citrix is constantly upgrading their client software and providing new and exiting features to remote computing. Check their Web site product page for the latest information.

The ICA Win32 adds the following features:

- Video support
- TAPI support
- Program Neighborhood
- Client Device mapping
- Sound support
- Seamless windows
- Dialing prefixes
- Encryption
- Client Auto Update
- Windows clipboard integration
- Low-bandwidth requirements
- Disk caching and data compression
- Wheel mouse support
- Business recovery

A few of these extended features deserve further discussion.

Video Support VideoFrame in conjunction with MetaFrame 1.8 enables you to produce and deploy custom video applications to Win32-bit clients. VideoFrame uses its own compression and streaming extensions to the ICA protocol to accomplish performance equal to or better than some of the most popular methods in use today. This product goes hand-in-hand with the ICA objectives of communicating over low-bandwidth connections, allowing even dial-up modem users to view streaming video content. It has the ability to autosense and adjust for different connection speeds, to provide the best quality available to the user.

Program Neighborhood With this feature, server-based applications can be pushed to the Program Neighborhood client, integrated into the local Windows desktop, or pushed directly to the client's Start menu.

Seamless Windows This feature allows the seamless integration of local and remote applications on the local Windows 9*x*, Windows NT4, or Windows 2000 desktop. By selecting the Seamless Windows option in the configuration setup, a user does not need to access an entire remote desktop to run remote Windows applications. The user is now able to have fully functional keyboard control, switch between local and remote applications from their local taskbar, define remote application icons on their local desktop, and even tile and cascade local and remote Windows applications. This is a favorite feature of the Win32 client among users. Most users can barely tell, if at all, the difference between local and remote applications.

Windows Clipboard Integration Users can cut and paste between local applications and remote ICA applications without using any special procedures.

Encryption The Win32 clients support advanced RSA RC5 encryption (requires server extension and special client). Available in 40-, 56-, and now 128-bit encryption, this provides a substantial increase in the ICA MetaFrame security posture. Anyone serious about his or her network security should be sure to visit the Citrix SecureICA Services page on the Citrix Web site at www.citrix.com/products/sica.

Configuring the Win32 Clients

Now that we've covered the basics of what it can do, let's configure our client software. For this step, we will assume you have already completed the steps covered in the Installation section successfully and are now ready to configure your client and connect to a MetaFrame server.

1. To begin, double-click the Citrix Program Neighborhood icon created on your desktop during the install process or click on Start | Programs | Citrix ICA Client | Citrix Program Neighborhood. This brings us to the main window of the Win32 client program shown in Figure 6.18.

2. Double-click the Add ICA Connection icon.

3. This brings up a dialog box for you to choose the type of connection, shown in Figure 6.19.

4. For our connection, we will choose LAN since this is the most common. (This will also work for connections that use Dial-up Networking to first dial in to a Remote Access Server (RAS) or Internet service provider (ISP)).

5. The next window prompts us for the Connection Name, Protocol, and Server or Published Application name shown in Figure 6.20.

Figure 6.18 Adding a new connection.

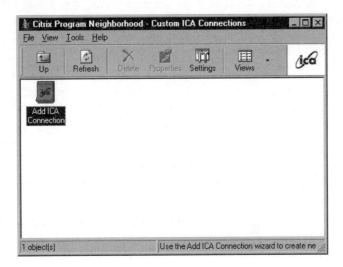

Figure 6.19 Specify connection type.

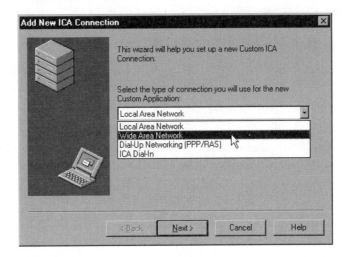

You may call the connection anything you wish; it does not have to match the server name. For the protocol, we will choose TCP/IP. For the server name, enter either the IP address or Fully Qualified Domain Name (FQDN) of the server. Here we chose to enter the FQDN of terminator.foo.com. If the MetaFrame server you are connecting to is located on the same subnet, you may be able to just click the drop-down arrow and have the available servers displayed.

Figure 6.20 Server settings.

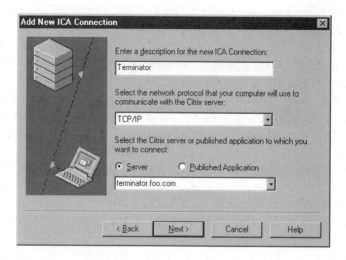

6. Choosing Next brings up a dialog box allowing us to connect via a proxy server, if required. Proxy servers are frequently used when connecting corporate users to the Internet. If you are connecting to a remote Internet MetaFrame server, you may need to use this setting. This is a relatively new feature to the Win32 client. This may require special ports and "Socks" client entries. Check with your network administrator to determine the proper settings.

7. The next box prompts us for User name, Password, and Domain. If left blank, it will prompt you for this information when you connect.

8. Click Next and the new window asks us for the resolution and color settings. If you don't know what to put in here, accept the defaults. MetaFrame 1.8 does not support any greater than 256 colors. This should be improved upon in the upcoming release of MetaFrame 2.0.

9. Click Next and the subsequent box will prompt you for an application name and specified working directory. Leave both these fields blank to run a full remote desktop.

10. That's it for the connection setup. Click Finish and your new connection icon should be added to the main ICA Client window. Simply double-click on the icon to connect to your remote desktop. Later in this section, we will learn about some of the many options available to enhance your remote desktop experience.

TIP

As discussed in the UNIX section previously, to use FQDNs, your machine must have the Domain Name Service (DNS) configured correctly and be able to connect to the Internet or intranet servers providing the authoritative name service for that domain to resolve names. If you are unable to resolve DNS queries from your workstation, you could instead add an entry manually by editing the host's file on your client machine **C:\winnt\ system32\drivers\etc\hosts** for Windows NT or **C:\windows\hosts** for Windows 9x users. Using an FQDN is the preferred method if available. This way, if the server machine changes IP addresses, only the DNS server entry must be changed, not all the clients. Many companies will use DNS to automatically point clients to a backup server if the primary is down. They can also use DNS as a crude form of load balancing, with the "Round Robin" technique.

If we go back to the main ICA Client window and click on the Up arrow, we should see two different icons. We now have Custom ICA Connections, which contains the custom connection we just created, and Find New Application Set. Double-click on Find New Application Set, and begin the steps to connect to published applications.

1. After clicking in the New Application Set icon, you should have a new window giving you a choice of connection types (see Figure 6.21). This time, choose WAN.

Figure 6.21 Connection types.

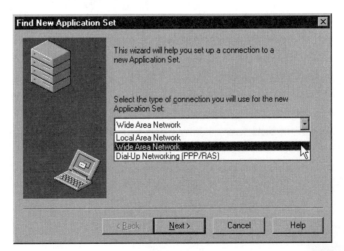

2. A new box pops up, asking you for a description of the new Application Set. You also have a drop-down box to choose applications from and a Server Location button (Figure 6.22).

Figure 6.22 Application sets.

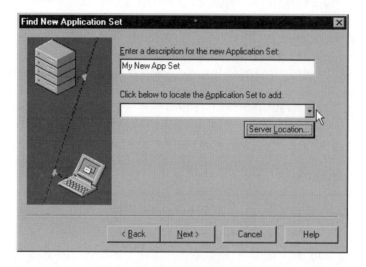

3. If there are no applications to choose from in the drop-down box, it means that your client is unable to browse a list of published applications from the server. This will usually be the case with servers on a remote subnet. To enable your client to obtain the application list, click on the Server Location button and then add the MetaFrame server's IP address or FQDN to the list. You may add Primary server names and Backup server names. You can also mix and match FQDNs and IP addresses as we have done in Figure 6.23.

4. After entering a Primary (and optionally, Backup server names/addresses), you should now be able to pull down a list of the published applications or server farms available (Figure 6.24).

5. The next window (Figure 6.25) shows the options for the Application Set such as sound, colors, and window size. Notice with the newer Win32 clients, besides the standard resolutions, that you now have available: percent of screen size, full screen, and seamless windows. Seamless windows were explained earlier in the section and are really what sets apart the Win32 ICA Client.

Figure 6.23 Adding to the server list.

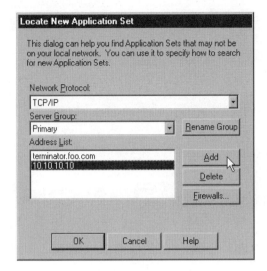

Figure 6.24 Application Set drop-down box.

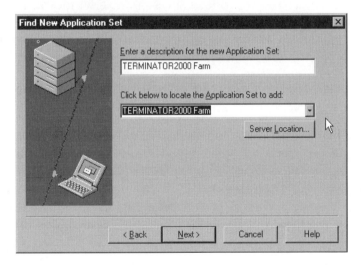

Figure 6.25 Color and resolution settings.

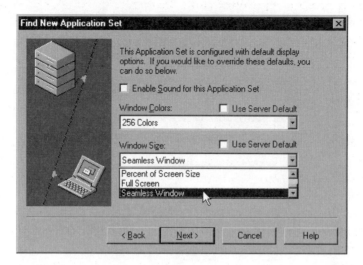

6. That's it for connecting to published applications and server farms. I'm sure you're going to love the seamless windows. Here's a fun exercise: Publish an application that your users also have on their local machines. Create two identical icons on their desktop, one for the local, and one for the remote application. Let your users minimize, maximize, and use the two programs and see if they can tell them apart.

ICA Settings

Now we will get into some of the detailed option screens, performance, and application tuning issues. Let's start with the Tools | ICA Settings pull-down menu from the main menu.

On the General tab, the all-important client name setting is at the top. Another important box is at the bottom—the allow automatic client update box, which is checked by default; I suggest you leave it that way. Deselecting this could be very frustrating to administrators waiting to get everyone updated to a new client version before rolling out a new application. If you turned it off and prevented the administrator from automatically updating your software, they would then have to visit your machine or call you to do a manual upgrade. This may not be a problem if you have a small client base of only five or ten users, but if your administrator is responsible for several hundred or thousand clients, they probably do not want to visit every single desktop to perform a simple upgrade.

The rest of the settings are not as important; the serial number field is only used by a product like WinFrame host/terminal, which requires each client to have a Citrix PC Client Pack serial number in order to connect to the server. Keyboard layout and type are normally left as the defaults unless you are configuring non-English connections.

The next tab is the Bitmap Cache tab. Here you can set the amount of local disk space to use for cache, specify the directory to use, and set the minimum size of bitmap to cache. Many people seem to get slightly improved response by decreasing the minimum cache size from the default of 8KB. Your systems may vary. You also have a button to clear the cache. Citrix recommends closing all active connections before clearing the cache.

In the next tab, the HotKeys tab, we see the table to map Hotkeys. Depending on your applications and client usage, you may need to disable some or all of these by setting them to None. I have seen users and even administrators accidentally overwrite Shortcut keys needed by client applications by leaving the Hotkeys settings at the defaults.

The last tab, Events, is where you can set the event logging parameters and directories.

Those are the settings primarily used in everyday client configuration. For more detailed explanations, see the Citrix Client Administrator Guide available on the Citrix Web site.

ICA Client Mappings

The Win32 ICA Client provides for many services by "mapping" server devices to local devices. One example of this is client drive mapping. Client drive mapping allows drive letters on the MetaFrame server to be redirected to drives on the local client computer, (i.e., drive J: in a MetaFrame user session can be mapped to drive C: of the local computer running the MetaFrame client). A default installation maps drive letters assigned to client drives starting with V: and works backwards, automatically assigning a drive letter to each fixed disk and CD-ROM (assuming the administrator has not disabled client drive mapping in the server connection configuration). Floppy drives are assigned their existing drive letters.

An experienced administrator will normally change the default server installation drives to M:, N:, or some other letter. This method then allows the client to access their C: and D: drives directly, without having to memorize complex drive mapping tables. After all, it can be very confusing to inexperienced users to learn about complicated things like C: drives, D: drives, and so on. Having them get swapped around when they log on remotely is really asking for trouble.

The Win32 ICA Client also supports "auto-created printers." Having auto-created printers means that users find their local printers mapped to their sessions and ready for use as soon as they connect. Client printers are automatically connected when users log on and are deleted when they log off as long as the printers do not contain any print jobs. If print jobs are present, the printer and its jobs are retained.

If users do not want the auto-created printer deleted when they log off, this can be changed. Use the Print Manager in the ICA session to view the Properties dialog box for the client printer. In the Comment field, modify or delete the string that says Auto Created Client Printer. The printer will no longer be deleted at logoff. If your user or connection profile does not specify Connect Client Printers at Logon, you can still use Print Manager to connect to a printer. A printer connected this way will also not be deleted at logoff.

Mapping Win32 Client Audio

Client audio mapping allows remote MetaFrame applications running on the server to play sounds through the client machine (a Sound Blaster Pro-compatible sound device on the client is required). The audio settings can be set or disabled both from the server and from the client. If the two settings are different, the lower of the two is used. The Sound tab has three settings of high, medium, and low. These are essentially the same as the high, medium, and low settings described earlier in the Configuring the UNIX Clients section of this chapter.

There are so many other settings and options available, it is impossible to stay current with them all in one book, let alone one chapter. New options appear with every new release and upgrade of the server and client. Many other options are available by directly editing the Appsrv.INI file. For a more complete description of the power in this file, refer to Appendix A, "Secrets."

Troubleshooting Basic Client Connectivity.

Most connectivity problems between the MetaFrame Clients and servers are due to networking issues. Here are some of the basic questions to ask when your clients can't connect. They may not always fall in the same order, depending on what problems you are having and many other factors.

1. Is the server up? Of course this sounds silly, but sometimes servers and components do fail. Always check to be sure you or someone can connect to the server in question.

2. Has the client *ever* been able to connect to the server in question? This will help resolve whether it is a new setup problem, a transient error, or a configuration error.

3. Do they have the correct client and version required? Many administrators prevent outdated clients from connecting.

4. Is the client on the same network as the server or remote? This may uncover a network or WAN link that is down. It also may point toward firewall or routing issues.

5. Can the client connect to any other MetaFrame server? If so, are they on the client's LAN or remote network?

6. Can anyone else from the clients network connect to the servers? If so, it points to a client-based problem rather than a network, firewall, or routing issue (could still be proxy settings).

7. Can the client ping or connect to any other machines using the required protocols? Maybe the client has a bad or misconfigured network card.

8. Can the client ping the server in question? That is not always an indicator, as there may be a firewall or other filters in place that block ping and other ICMP traffic but allow for the ICA protocol to pass. Still, it's generally a good test to at least try, because if it is successful, you know there is network connectivity.

9. Can the client resolve the FQDN? If the client is using a FQDN in the connection setup, make sure they can properly resolve the name. Check their DNS configuration; also try changing the connection profile to point directly to the IP address instead.

10. Can the client Telnet to the server in question? A better indicator than ping is to have the client machine open a DOS prompt and type **Telnet 10.10.10.10 1494** (substitute the server IP address for the example 10.10.10.10). No, the MetaFrame server does not need to have a Telnet daemon running for this to succeed. This is telling the client to attempt a TCP connection on port 1494, the default ICA port. It looks just like an incoming ICA connection request to the server and firewalls. If successful, a couple of small blocks, followed by "ICA," followed by two blocks, followed by "ICA," repeated over and over should appear on the screen. This is one of the most foolproof methods of testing firewall pass-through because it actually tries to open the ICA session. Many client networks will be configured to pass HTTP traffic through proxy servers with the assumption that the ICA client can also pass through the proxy. This is not usually the case. Proxy servers must be set up specifically to pass the ICA protocol through, and many also require a custom "Socks" application be installed on the client.

11. Have they opened the required ports on their firewall or network filters? The MetaFrame clients require port 1494 TCP open to the server to establish communication (with response allowed back in), then communicate over a negotiated high port (1023 and above, similar to the way Telnet and FTP function). MetaFrame also uses port 1604 UDP to browse for published applications. If you are connecting to published applications or server farms, this will also need to be open. With the new NFuse application, port 1604 UDP will no longer be required. The Microsoft RDP client uses port 3389 TCP instead of 1494; if using the RDP client to connect, this port must be open.

12. If trying to connect to a published application or server farm, can the client instead make a connection to the full desktop? If so, this may indicate a problem with the server address setting in the client configuration or a problem with port 1604.

13. What if the user is trying to watch a VideoFrame streaming video from an Internet server, and the media player starts but then displays a message about not being able to locate the server? When a link is clicked to start a video, the client uses a NetBIOS request to locate the server. If on a different network segment, or the Internet, the client will be unable to resolve the name. One solution is to place a manual entry in the hosts file as discussed in the client setup documentation, or to add the domain suffix to the DNS search path in the client's networking setup.

There are many other troubleshooting tips and white papers available on the Citrix Web site to assist you in solving those connection problems.

Summary

In this chapter, we have covered a number of MetaFrame client connectivity issues, such as selecting a protocol or using multiple protocols, along with choosing and installing the correct MetaFrame client software for your operating system. We described at some length the advantages of the ICA MetaFrame client. We have also discussed configuring and upgrading the MetaFrame client software both automatically and manually to connect to your MetaFrame server. We brought up some common troubleshooting problems and solutions. I hope this chapter has brought you at least some of the answers you were looking for and assists those of you who plan to pursue certification.

After all of this you may be asking, "What next?" Well, if all this wasn't enough, Citrix has come out with MetaFrame 1.8 Feature Release 1 (FR1).

This adds a wide variety of new features and technologies to enhance the user's computing experience and provide more efficient network management. There are more browser-based connectivity options with NFuse 1.5. With the new Citrix Extranet 2.0 server product, you can now incorporate Single Socket Layer (SSL) Certificate and Smart Card authentication using VPN technology across the LAN, WAN, or Internet. The Extranet 2.0 server combines the use of public-key encryption and 168-bit 3DES encryption while utilizing the "standard" firewall ports of 443, 80, and 3845 to provide one of the most secure VPN solutions available. You can read in detail the benefits of FR1, NFuse 1.5, and Extranet 2.0 at the following Citrix URL: www.citrix.com/products/fr1/default.asp.

We will discuss briefly some of the new features found in MetaFrame FR1. Many improvements in performance, usability, and security have been added. Among these are the following:

SpeedScreen 3 An improvement over the SpeedScreen 2 technology used in MetaFrame 1.8, this further reduces latency and improves the "feel" of network applications. It also reduces bandwidth consumption even more, which should show significant improvements on low-bandwidth dial-up connections.

Text-Entry Prediction This is a component of the SpeedScreen 3 technology that removes that "lag" feeling when typed characters lag several seconds before showing on the screen. This allows users to receive instant response to typed data while actual transmission to the server is completed. This has resolved one of the most common complaints from users over low-bandwidth or high-latency connections.

Instant Mouse-Click Feedback Along with the text lag, another primary user complaint was no feedback when clicking on an icon. If an application had a delay while starting, the user often ended up clicking multiple times to be sure it worked, thereby starting multiple instances of an application unintentionally. This provides an immediate change in the appearance of the mouse when an action is pending.

TCP-based ICA Browsing UDP broadcasts are no longer required for discovering published applications. This resolves many issues firewall and security administrators had with not wanting to open UDP-based traffic on their firewalls.

Web-based Client Install Users can now automatically install the MetaFrame client software simply by connecting to a Citrix NFuse-enabled Web server with their browser.

Greater Color Depth Multimedia and graphical applications will be enjoyed more because of the new support for high-color (65,000) and true-color (16 million).

Panning and Scaling This allows users of handheld devices to view the same applications that run on desktops by letting them "pan" a view window over a larger image or applications can be "scaled" to shrink them to an arbitrary client window size.

Pass-through Authentication and 128-Bit Encryption Pass-through authentication allows the workstation to automatically pass the user's desktop password to the server. Seamless connections can be maintained on both local and remote connections without requiring additional logins. 128-bit encryption, which in the past has been a somewhat expensive add-on, is now available as a standard feature of MetaFrame. This is a great improvement over the old basic XOR encryption technology that was standard on earlier versions.

Also new are Multi-Monitor support and "Application Save Position" in which the client "remembers" the application's previous size and position, then opens the application with those stored values the next time the user starts the application.

These are all part of the Citrix "New Product Delivery Strategy" in which they promise customers a new Feature Release two or three times per year that will provide update MetaFrame features, and a new Platform Release every 18–24 months that will provide the underlying architecture for new features.

FAQs

Q: What transport protocols are available for use with the ICA MetaFrame client?

A: TCP/IP, SPX, IPX, NetBEUI, and Direct Asynchronous.

Q: What transport protocols are available for use with the RDP client?

A: Only TCP/IP.

Q: What is the average amount of bandwidth used by the ICA MetaFrame client (according to Citrix)?

A: The average amount is 20 KB.

Q: Will running an automatic client upgrade from a MetaFrame server upgrade your Win16 client to the correct Win32 client automatically?

A: No. Upgrading from Win16 to the Win32 client must be done manually.

Q: What type of ICA client software can you install on OS/2?

A: The DOS and Win16 client function on OS/2. There is no OS/2 client.

Q: Should ICA clients on a dial-up modem use the High audio quality setting if they have a 56Kbps connection?

A: No. The High setting uses approximately 1.3 MB of bandwidth. The Medium setting uses approximately 64Kbps. Modem users should use a Low setting of 16Kbps or disable audio altogether.

Here are some helpful Web pages for you to reference for general questions that you may have on MetaFrame products and their utilization.

Citrix Glossary of Terms: www.citrix.com/glossary.htm

Citrix Online Knowledge Base: http://ctxex10.citrix.com/texpert.nsf

Citrix How To's: http://ctxex10.citrix.com/texpert.nsf/How+To's

Citrix Online Support Forum: http://ctxex10.citrix.com/icaforum.nsf

Citrix SecureICA Web Page: www.citrix.com/products/sica/

Microsoft Exploring Terminal Services:
www.microsoft.com/windows2000/guide/server/features/terminalsvcs.asp

Chapter 7

Installing Terminal Services

Solutions in this chapter:

- Gathering Business Goals and Objectives
- Testing Configurations and Deploying a Pilot
- Rolling Out the Final Configuration
- Using the Training Tools

Introduction

Terminal Services, which delivers the Windows 2000 graphical user interface (GUI), through a server-based computing model, provides shared access to applications and an excellent remote administration capability to administrators.

Before you deploy Citrix MetaFrame, you first need to install the Windows 2000 Terminal Services component. Although Terminal Services is an integral component of the Windows 2000 operating system, it is not deployed by default. Best practices demand that the Windows 2000 Terminal Services deployment is approached as a project in itself.

For IT Professionals

About Terminal Services

All versions of Windows 2000 Server include Terminal Services, as the program is now a component of the operating system.

Before you begin installation, be sure you are familiar with all types of adapters in the computer (check the Microsoft Hardware Compatibility List at www.microsoft.com/hcl/default.asp): the types and quantities of licenses, how the physical disks and partitions will be configured, and all the necessary network information (IP addresses, subnet masks, and Windows Internet Naming Service/Domain Name System (WINS/DNS) mapping).

Note that Terminal Services Licensing only manages Terminal Services licenses. It does not work with or replace other Windows licensing.

Terminal Services client software is used for 16-bit and 32-bit Windows-based clients. If you want to run clients with other platforms, you must install a third-party software package such as Citrix MetaFrame for your Windows 2000 server(s).

Gathering Business Goals and Objectives

Microsoft has introduced Windows 2000 Server to vastly improve the tasks and administrative efforts of the Information Technology (IT) networking professional. Within the Windows 2000 Professional desktop, Microsoft has provided an operating system to succeed the Windows 98 and Windows NT Workstation in a business environment. As an IT professional, you can increase the scalability of your network in two ways by installing the Windows 2000 Terminal Services component—by allowing remote administration and centralizing application management.

Terminal Services increases scalability in your networking environment because it does not require vast changes to the current architecture of your systems. Your clients will remain unaffected by the Terminal Services installation. In addition, the features included with Terminal Services allow you to remotely administer your servers. It will not matter if you are in a satellite office, on the road, or at home; you can gain access to your servers to perform any administrative functions.

In the Application mode, you can often implement the Windows 2000 Professional desktop in your own network without making any hardware upgrades to your clients. This eliminates the substantial costs commonly associated with upgrades while continuing to bring even your simplest clients the latest technologies. This is an excellent solution if you are looking to provide the fastest and least expensive solution to the various problems usually associated with upgrades. In the Remote Administration mode, administrators have the ability to perform many of the same tasks on the server whether they are remotely or locally logged into the server. For instance, while you are in the office you can locally log on to your server and perform any necessary tasks. If you are at home, you can still log on to your server using Terminal Services' remote log-on features.

Terminal Services exists as a part of the Windows multiuser architecture. Any of the following clients can access a Windows 2000 Terminal Services:

- Windows CE-based terminals
- Windows CE-based Handheld Professional devices (H/PC Pro)
- 32-bit Windows-based PCs running Windows 95, Windows 98, Windows NT 3.51, Windows NT 4.0, or Windows 2000 Professional
- 16-bit Windows-based PCs running Windows for Workgroups 3.11 with MS TCP/IP-32
- Third-party software vendors such as Citrix can provide access to clients with non-Windows platforms such as the Apple Macintosh, MS-DOS, and UNIX

Any of these clients can connect through a local area network (LAN), wide area network (WAN), or a dial-up connection. As shown in Figure 7.1, numerous types of platforms can utilize Windows 2000 Terminal Services. The client software can be installed on virtually any operating system or hardware system. If you are trying to establish a more secure, efficient, reliable, and productive work environment in your IT department, you should consider the benefits that Terminal Services will provide you.

Figure 7.1 Terminal Services Client can be installed on virtually any client.

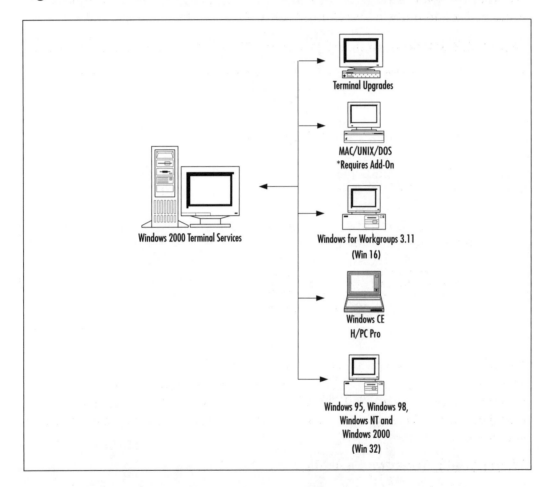

Components of Windows 2000 Terminal Services

Windows 2000 Terminal Services consists of five integrated components. The *kernel* is a fundamental component of Terminal Services that works with your server's hardware. The Terminal Services protocol, *Remote Desktop Protocol* (RDP), is the communication component of Terminal Services. Enacting the *Terminal Services licensing component* on your server is key to allowing your client desktops to gain access to your servers. Installing *Terminal Services Client* on your client desktops allows users to gain access to your servers, and the *administration tool* allows administrators to gain access to your servers. You can see the relationship of these components by studying Figure 7.2.

Figure 7.2 Relationship of the Windows 2000 Terminal Services components.

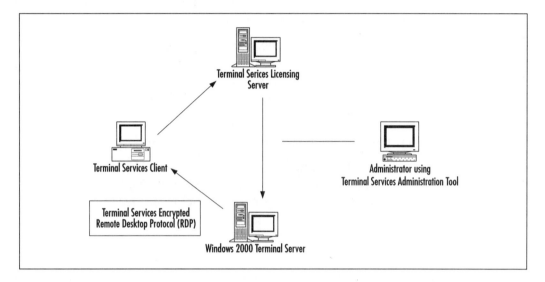

Windows 2000 Multiuser Kernel

The kernel extensions for Terminal Server are fully integrated in the Windows 2000 Server family kernel. Even if Terminal Server is not installed on the Windows 2000 server, these extensions still exist on that server.

Remote Desktop Protocol (RDP)

This protocol can be configured for any type of network that allows local-ization, automatic disconnection, and remote configuration, which makes it the key component of Terminal Server. RDP also supports three levels of configuration. This protocol is ideal for a thin client; the server allows the client in the connection to cache bitmaps and therefore support different bandwidth allocations. RDP is also unique because it provides optional compression for low-bandwidth connections.

TIP

Remote Administration Mode doesn't require the Terminal Services Licensing Service or even use this service. However, you must enable this service if you are serving applications within your network. As devices connect, this service allows Terminal Server to both obtain and manage its Terminal Server Client Access Licenses (CALs) to transmit back to these client devices.

Terminal Services Client

This software, which resides on the client, displays the common and familiar 32-bit GUI for the user. The software is a relatively small application. It maintains the connection, which communicates all client keystrokes and mouse movements to the server, and then displays the information and print streams from the server.

Terminal Services Administration Tool

This feature of Windows 2000 manages Terminal Server through the following software: Terminal Server License Manager, Terminal Server Client Creator, Terminal Server Client Configuration, and Terminal Server Manager.

Terminal Services Encryption

Windows 2000 Terminal Services provides three different levels of encryption: 40-bit, 56-bit, and 128-bit. You can only use 128-bit, or "strong encryption," in the United States or in Canada, as it is not available elsewhere. Strong encryption is defined as a cryptographic operation using keys with 128 bits or larger. An example would be an encrypted browser-to-web server session or even VPN connections in your company. On January 14, 2000, the U.S. government enacted legislation that allows for global shipments of products utilizing strong encryption. In the past, Microsoft was only allowed to ship 40-bit or 56-bit products to international customers (except some financial institutions and medical companies). The United States allows for strong-encrypted products to be delivered after a one-time technical review is performed. More information on this subject can be found at www.microsoft.com/exporting. The encryption pack can be downloaded at www.windowsupdate.microsoft.com.

Remote Administration Mode

Microsoft Windows 2000 Terminal Services runs in two different modes, Remote Administration Mode, and Application Server Mode. The following sections discuss these roles as well as the limitations, advantages, and disadvantages.

The Remote Administration Mode provides the administrator remote access to any server running Windows 2000. The administrator has complete access to any GUI and administrative tools, just as if he were at the server locally. The administrator can be connected through TCP/IP via LAN, WAN, or dial-up. Fortified with Citrix MetaFrame 1.8 for Windows 2000, an administrator can remotely manage forests and trees, mixed domains (Windows 2000 and NT), and clusters from any legacy MS-DOS-based PC, Windows 95, Windows 98, Windows NT, or even non-Windows-based client machine.

Don't worry about taxing your servers by using Terminal Services to facilitate remote administration. Using Remote Administration Mode has minimal impact on your server because it disables application compatibility tools and client licensing functions, and also leaves memory and processor usage unaffected. Visit the following link for more information on processor utilization: www.microsoft.com/windows2000/library/technologies/terminal/tscaling.asp?RLD=62.

Advantages in addition to limited overhead include the ability to install Terminal Services on additional servers in your network that may already have crucial functions such as database applications, Web access, remote access, file servers, and print servers. Because this tool allows you to remotely administer servers and has little affect on system resource, you may consider installing it on many of your servers in your domain—within security limitations, of course. It does, however, limit the number of concurrent connections to two. For increased security, only system administrators can use a connection. Consequently, this disallows the possibility of a user accidentally (or deliberately) gaining access to your server, thereby eliminating attacks. Only two people—both administrators—can be logged in remotely at a time. There are no simultaneous remote users allowed in Remote Administration Mode.

NOTE

You might choose to run Terminal Services in Remote Administration Mode because it allows for two connections—easing recovery. If a problem occurs and you have to reboot or log off your server, you can make a second connection and save configurations or files.

Implementing Remote Administration Mode in your networking environment could help the tasks of field technicians and engineers. For instance, perhaps you have an internal help desk for your sales department. If a remote user calls in requesting help for an application on their laptop, your help desk technicians could gain access to the remote user through Terminal Services and solve the problem.

With Terminal Services running in Remote Administration Mode, an administrator can perform each of the following tasks remotely:

- Collaborate on a session with another administrator—by establishing two shadowed sessions.

- Perform upgrades, reboots, and promotion/demotion of domain controllers.

- Perform application, installation, and execution.

- Provide security from eavesdropping.

- Access local disks and media.

- Access the server over low-bandwidth connections, even at 128-bit encryption.

- Have full RDP privileges, including local printer support, clipboard mapping, and virtual channel applications support.

To remotely administrate a server, install Terminal Services Remote Administration directly on the server by performing the following steps:

1. Double-click on the Add/Remove Programs icon in the server's Control Panel.

2. Click the Add/Remove Components and start the Add/Remove Components Wizard.

3. Scroll through the list to find the Terminal Services and select it. Figure 7.3 shows Terminal Services in the Windows Components list of Add/Remove Programs.

4. Click Details to see the Terminal Services component selection window.

5. Click both of the selections: Client Creator Files and Enable Terminal Services as shown in Figure 7.4.

6. Click OK to return to the Windows Components window.

7. Click Next.

Figure 7.3 Check the Terminal Services box in the Windows Component Wizard window to install Terminal Services.

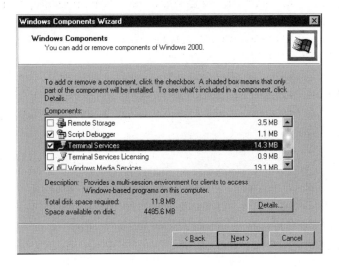

Figure 7.4 Check both selections for installing the Terminal Services subcomponents.

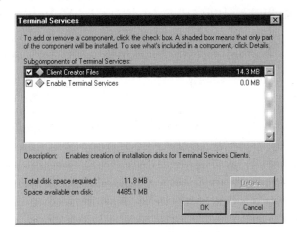

8. As shown in Figure 7.5, select Remote Administration Mode and click Next (you may need to insert the CD).

9. After the files have finished copying, click Finish.

10. Close the Add/Remove Programs window.

11. Reboot the computer.

Figure 7.5 To install Remote Administration Mode, select the radio button and hit Next.

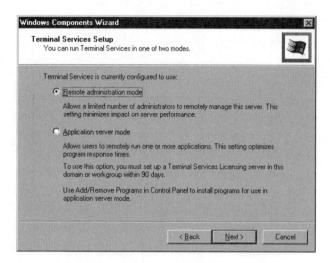

Application Server Mode

With Windows 2000 Terminal Services running in Application Server Mode, users can request applications over the network from the server and the server performs all the necessary processing. Because Windows 2000 Terminal Services utilizes a multiuser architecture, software applications exist on the server allowing for centralized management. For instance, all of your users can work with the same version of an application, such as a proprietary tracking system that your shipping department might use in conjunction with the billing department.

Another benefit to this architecture is the ease in implementing software patches, fixes, and upgrades. As an example, when it becomes time to upgrade software applications, IT professionals will commonly schedule months or weeks for upgrades. When using Terminal Services in Application Mode, you would only need to worry about upgrading the software application on one or more servers, rather than having to make upgrades on each user's desktop individually. Your deployment time would be close to instantaneous and you would not have to schedule months, weeks, or days for necessary upgrades.

This architecture also provides greater control and security over applications. For example, you can be positive exactly which version of an application a client is using—the one you have installed on the server they are accessing. When Terminal Services is accessed, all of the computing for the application is done on the server. The client receives only the presentation part, the GUI part, of the application. Your server must authenticate all users requesting the application, and therefore unauthorized access is not possible. You can restrict access to applications and prevent users from printing, copying, or deleting data.

You can install Terminal Services Application Mode on multiple servers if you want specific servers accessed only for specific applications. You could also install on multiple servers if you wanted to distribute the workload in a busy network environment. Remove all existing applications before installing Terminal Services in Application Mode on an existing Windows 2000 Server. Do not install on a Windows 2000 Domain Controller. Also, Microsoft does not recommend installing on a server which is running crucial infrastructure services (DNS, WINS, or File and Print) or server applications (SQL, Exchange, or Internet Information Service.)

Remember, an application can be accessed from a Windows 2000 Terminal Server through a LAN, WAN, or dial-up connection via any Windows-based or even Windows CE-based client.

WARNING

If you decide to run Terminal Services in the Application Server Mode, make sure that your applications can run in a multiuser environment.

Perform the following steps to enable Application Server Mode on Windows 2000 Terminal Services:

1. Double-click on the Add/Remove Programs icon in the server's Control Panel.

2. Click the Add/Remove Components and start the Add/Remove Components Wizard.

3. As shown in Figure 7.6, scroll through the list to find Terminal Services and select it.

4. Click Details to see the Terminal Services component selection window.

5. As noted in Figure 7.7, click both of the selections: Client Creator Files and Enable Terminal Services.

6. Click OK to return to the Windows Components window.

7. Select Terminal Services Licensing to check the box.

Figure 7.6 Selecting Terminal Services.

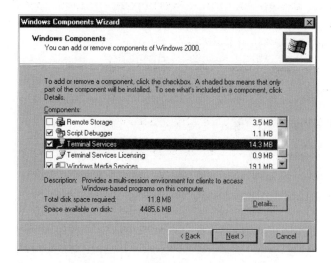

Figure 7.7 Check both selections for installing the Terminal Services subcomponents.

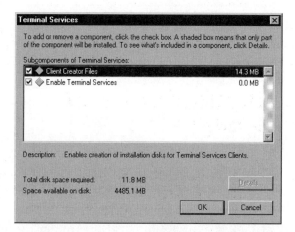

8. Click both selections (Client Creator Files and Enable Terminal Services) to check the boxes.

9. Click Next.

10. Select Application server mode and click Next, as shown in Figure 7.8.

11. At the next screen, the Terminal Services Licensing screen, select Your Entire Enterprise or Your Domain or Workgroup and leave the Install License Server Database at the Location as is. Select

Enterprise when your entire network will be utilizing Terminal Services. Select Domain or Workgroup when a specific group within your network will be utilizing Terminal Services.

12. After the files are done copying, click Finish.

13. Close the Add/Remove Programs window.

14. Reboot the computer.

Figure 7.8 Selecting Application Server Mode.

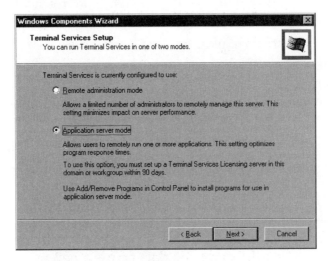

Testing Configurations and Deploying a Pilot

As always, make sure you construct a test environment and deploy test configurations before implementing the real thing in your network. The following sections should help you begin creating a test Windows 2000 Terminal Services environment so you can provide 100 percent accuracy when deploying the final product.

Installation

Before you begin installing Windows 2000 Terminal Services, take the following preparations (just as you would for installing any part of Windows 2000):

- Hardware components: Make a list of all the adapters in your system, including Small Computer System Interface (SCSI), Redundant Array of Independent Disks (RAID), and network cards. Make sure you have all the software drivers for the adapters. Your best bet would be to use the drivers provided in the Windows 2000 Plug-and-Play support, and then upgrade later to the most recent available versions of the drivers.

- Client Access Licenses (CALs): Determine which type of license you will use and how many you will need. Also, record the location of your Windows 2000 licensing server.

- Drives: Construct a plan for configuring your local disks and determining partitions.

- Network: Make a note of your network configurations, such as all IP addresses, subnet masks, and WINS/DNS addresses.

WARNING

It is better to install Windows 2000 and Terminal Services on a separate partition or physical disk from the applications—this helps deployment, security management, and maintenance. You really should not format any of your Terminal Servers with FAT partitions. Share permissions are inadequate security for accessing data across a network.

For security reasons, you should install Windows 2000 on a separate partition from where the applications will reside. By partitioning with NTFS you can provide extra security to your Terminal Services. When selecting the licensing mode, only the per-seat option is valid for Terminal Services in Application Mode (allows multiuser access). You may also choose to install only the basic components of Windows 2000—most components can be installed later. This keeps server utilization and bandwidth at a minimal required level. Table 7.1 shows the suggested components to run in Windows 2000 for Terminal Services:

Table 7.1 Recommendations for Selecting Components in Windows 2000 Setup

Component	Select or Deselect	Why To Select or Deselect the Component
Accessories & Utilities	Deselect Communications, Games, Multimedia, and Wallpaper	These components are not necessary and will only consume space if installed.
Certificate Services	Deselect	This component is for IIS and is unnecessary for Terminal Services to operate. Its primary use is to issue certificates to public users.
Cluster Service	Deselect	A fault-tolerant option that allows for clustering of server-based application redundancy.
Indexing Service	Deselect	This component is for IIS and is unnecessary for Terminal Services to operate.
Internet Information Service (IIS)	Deselect	This component allows for Web and FTP site hosting and is unnecessary for Terminal Services to operate.
Management and Monitoring Tools	Deselect the Connection Management Components. Select Network Monitoring. If you don't need SNMP, deselect this option as well.	These options can dominate space. You can install these features in the future if you find the need to monitor your Terminal Server.
Message Queuing Services	Deselect	This can dominate space. Installing Message Queuing on a server cluster will provide active/active queue failover in case of computer failure or malfunction.
Networking Services	Deselect	None should run in Terminal Services.

Continued

Table 7.1 Continued

Component	Select or Deselect	Why To Select or Deselect the Component
Other Network and File Print Services	Deselect	This option is mainly for a server designated as a file or print server, not for Terminal Services.
Remote Installation Services	Deselect	This option can also dominate space. However, you can use this option to install Windows 2000 Professional on remote computers.
Script Debugger	Windows Scripting Host. If you plan on using it, then select the option.	Can help identify problems in Windows Scripting.
Terminal Services Licensing	Deselect	Use this option to configure a different server for issuing Terminal Services Licenses.
Windows Media Services	Deselect	You won't need this option unless you plan on streaming multimedia to your clients.

The following instructions will help you to install Windows 2000 Terminal Services for a first-time install on a clean server.

1. Place the Windows 2000 Server or Advanced Server boot disk into drive A: and power on your server.

2. Immediately after you see the screen turn blue, you'll have the option of pressing F6 if you have any special SCSI or RAID controller drivers to install.

3. When prompted, insert disks number 2, 3, and 4 to load the core drivers.

4. When the Windows 2000 Server Welcome to Setup window appears, press ENTER to continue the installation.

5. When prompted, insert the Windows 2000 Server CD and press ENTER to continue.

6. Next you will see the End-User License Agreement. When you have finished reviewing and have accepted the terms, press the F8 key to continue the installation.

7. The next screen prompts you to select and configure the system boot partition. You can choose to complete this task after installation through Computer Management.

8. After you have created a system partition, highlight that drive and press ENTER. Next, you will need to format the drive, either File Allocation Table (FAT) or NT File System (NTFS).

9. Your computer will then restart.

10. After the restart is initialized and completed, Windows 2000 Setup starts the plug-and-play detection. This step installs the necessary working drivers for your system hardware. Checking the Windows 2000 hardware compatibility list can help indicate whether your hardware has been properly detected.

11. Next, you'll see Setup open the Regional Settings dialog box. In this box you can determine the specific settings for your region, such as number, currency, and time and date formats.

12. In the next window, provide your name and organization information. Click Next when finished.

13. Next, find the correct product key for Windows 2000 Server on the back of the CD jewel case and type it in. Click Next.

14. You will be prompted to select the right CAL mode. This isn't for the clients that will be accessing your Terminal Services, but is the Microsoft CAL. If you don't have one now, you will need one within 90 days of installation. Per-seat licensing is the only valid licensing option with Terminal Services. Select per-seat licensing and then click Next.

15. On this screen you need to enter the name of the server and the local administrator's password. Click Next.

16. Now you will see the Windows 2000 component box. See Table 7.1 for information about selecting and deselecting components at this stage of installation. When you are finished configuring, click Next to continue.

17. In the next window, confirm the date, time, and time zone. Change if necessary and then click Next to continue.

18. The next window is for Terminal Services setup. Here you will choose whether or not you will run Terminal Services in Remote

Administration Mode or Application Server Mode (see the Gathering Business Goals and Objectives section earlier in this chapter for more details).

19. The network services will begin and you will be asked to either choose Typical or Custom network settings. Choose Typical if you want to use Dynamic Host Configuration Protocol (DHCP) for Transmission Control Protocol/Internet Protocol (TCP/IP) addressing, and Client for Microsoft networking, and file and print sharing. If you want to set the configuration options for your networking services, then choose Custom. Here you can enter static IP addresses.

20. If you choose Custom networking service, you will see another screen, which allows you to view and change the properties for the default networking components that are going to be installed.

21. Determine whether the computer will be part of a domain or a workgroup.

22. After you make this final selection, Setup installs the necessary components and performs the final setup configuration.

Using Table 7.2, compare the cost of upgrading 100 users to Windows 2000 Professional on a PC platform versus a Terminal Services client platform.

Table 7.2 Thin Client vs. PC

Computing Asset	100 PC Network	100 Thin-client Network
Computers	100 PCs and one server	Two servers (plus 100 clients)
Number of Central Processing Units (CPUs)	102 PIII (300Mhz min.)	8 PIII (850Mhz)
Number of CPUs to upgrade	102	8
Working memory	128MB RAM per PC	1GB RAM per server
Total RAM	13,056MB RAM	2000MB RAM
Hard disk storage	6GB hard drives per PC	12GB RAID5 per server
Total hard disk storage	612GB storage	26GB storage

Continued

Table 7.2 Continued

Computing Asset	100 PC Network	100 Thin-client Network
Cost of Windows 2000 Professional software (for PCs) or Terminal Services CALs (for Windows-based terminals)	$31,900	$10,680
Number of Microsoft licenses	100	100
Copies of Microsoft Office maintained	100	2 (1 per server)
Number of locations to visit for upgrades	100	1
Time to upgrade or activate on PC or terminal	90 minutes	10 minutes
Time to implement Windows 2000 at the desktop	19 days	2 days
Number of users with access to operating system software	100	0

Rolling Out the Final Configuration

The various components of Windows 2000 Terminal Services provide many key features such as RDP. RDP works like the Citrix ICA protocol and bundles the data for transmission in small packets and consumes minimal bandwidth—approximately 20 Kbps. Microsoft has improved on the NT 4.0 Terminal Services by adding the following features in the newest Windows 2000 version.

Local Printer Support

Now administrators can connect to the printers attached locally to clients within the network. Imagine how this might help your IT support desk solve customer and/or client printer technical issues. The client is able to maintain their own printers but they are still accessible to the network.

Roaming Disconnect

This new feature allows a user, without logging off, to disconnect from a session, move to another machine and access the same work. For example, imagine a plant operator in a company is documenting a procedure for resetting the boilers within the building. In the north end of the building, the operator opens a company template designed to assist in writing procedure manuals. He records the steps to resetting the boiler in the north end of the building. However, not all the boilers in the building are alike, so the operator walks to the south end of the building, connects to the same session with the document still open and makes an addendum recording the steps to resetting the boiler in the south end of the building.

Enhanced Performance

With the addition of this feature, your users will notice substantial improvements in server performance because of persistent caching, packet utilization, and frame size. Caching is the concept of writing data to a temporary location (local temporary memory or hard drive space allocated for this reason). The processor can then push data out faster to a user. For instance, modern portable CD players cache music data so that if a skip occurs, the player refers to the cached music and the listener never hears the skip. If persistent caching is occurring, your server is constantly storing temporary data and spends less time requesting usage from the processor. In Terminal Services, persistent caching allows for optimal transmission of data packets over the network. Packet utilization refers to the practical use of moving the transmission packets through your network at the highest optimization. Because Terminal Services uses RDP, the frame size is ideal for thin clients.

Multiple Login Support

Microsoft has added this feature to Windows 2000 Terminal Services so that a user has the capability of logging into several servers simultaneously using the identical login at every instance. In addition, it allows the user to log into the server many times so multiple different tasks can be performed on the same server. For example, a user in your Human Resource department may be constructing a report on worker performance. She needs the numeric information in an Excel spreadsheet to construct the slides for the oral presentation she's designing in PowerPoint, and she wants to keep both open while she works. Even if these applications reside on the same server, this client can use both programs at the same time.

Clipboard Redirection

This feature allows users connecting in Terminal Mode to cut and paste between applications running locally on the client and those running on the server. This would be beneficial, for instance, for webmasters wanting to transmit their constructed code and pages between their client workstation and the Windows 2000 Terminal Services running Web services, like Internet Information Server. However, be aware that this can breach security because the cut and paste process of clipboard redirection does not allow for encryption. By default, this feature is enabled. This feature can be secured or disabled by using any of the following methods:

To stop sharing a local ClipBook page, perform the following:

- In the local ClipBook window, click the ClipBook page you want to stop sharing.
- From the File menu, click Stop Sharing.

Perform the following steps to remove a group or user from the ClipBook permissions list. Realize that you must be the owner of the page or have been granted permission to do so by the owner.

- In the local ClipBook window, click the ClipBook page you want to remove permissions from.
- From the Security menu, click Permissions.
- In the Name list, click the name of the group or user whose permissions you want to remove, then click Remove.

To remove ClipBook page auditing for a group or user, do the following. Realize that you must be logged in as Administrator or be a member of the administrators group.

- In the Local ClipBook window, click the ClipBook page you want to stop auditing.
- From the Security menu, click Auditing.
- In the Name list, click the name of the group or user, then click Remove.

Securing ClipBook Pages

You can set the following permissions on individual shared ClipBook pages.

- No Access
- Read
- Read and Link
- Change
- Full Control
- Special

Permissions for shared ClipBook pages are cumulative. For example, if an individual user is a member of more than one group, and each group has a different set of permissions for the same shared ClipBook page, then all permissions granted to the user for that ClipBook page are available. The exception is the No Access permission, which overrides every other permission.

Remember to check the Hardware Compatibility List before installation at www.microsoft.com/hcl/default.asp. The next section lists Microsoft's requirements for installing the Windows 2000 Server family. You will want to increase this hardware scale if you plan on using Terminal Services in the Application Mode.

Windows 2000 Server

Microsoft has a minimum recommendation for hardware when installing Windows 2000 Server. Be sure that your server meets the following hardware recommendations.

- 133MHz or higher Pentium-compatible CPU.

- 256MB RAM—recommended minimum (128MB supported, 4GB maximum) per Microsoft.

- 2.0GB hard disk with a minimum of 1.0GB of free space. (Additional hard disk space is required if you are installing over a network.)

- Windows 2000 Server supports up to four CPUs on one machine.

Windows 2000 Advanced Server

Microsoft has also published a minimum recommendation for installing Windows 2000 Advanced Server. Note that Advanced Server supports up to eight CPUs on one machine, which is twice as many as Server.

- 133MHz or higher Pentium-based compatible CPU.

- 256MB of RAM recommended minimum (128MB minimum support, 8GB maximum).

- 2.0GB hard disk with a minimum of 1.0GB of free space. (Additional free hard disk space is required if you are installing over a network.)

- Windows 2000 Advanced Server supports up to eight CPUs on one machine.

Terminal Services Licensing

Note from Figure 7.9 that you can maintain Windows 2000 Server and Terminal Services licensing onsite using the License Server.

Figure 7.9 Terminal Services licensing.

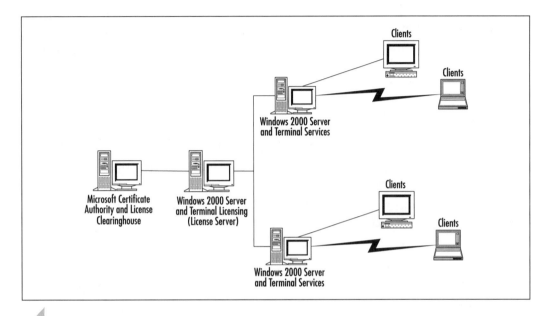

TIP

If you have more than one Terminal Services in your network, configure another Windows 2000 server to act as the licensing server, separate from the Terminal Server requesting licenses. This setup helps with maintenance—you don't have to worry about bringing the machine down.

Terminal Services will issue, from the machine it is installed on, system-event-log messages every six hours until it locates a Terminal Services license server.

Installing the Terminal Services Licensing Component

The following instructions will lead you through the installation of the Licensing Component in Windows 2000. You will then be able to issue licenses within your network.

1. In your server's Control Panel, double-click the Add/Remove Programs icon and then click Add/Remove Windows Components.

2. Scroll down to select Terminal Services Licensing and click Next.

3. Next, setup will inquire which mode you want to operate in. Select Application Server Mode (the default setting) and click Next.

4. In the Terminal Services Licensing Setup window, specify whether the license to cover the server is for the entire Enterprise or for the domain or workgroup. Choose the desired location of the license server database and then click Next.

5. When prompted, insert the Windows 2000 Server CD, or browse to a location for the system files.

6. When the computer shows the Finish Setup box, click Finish.

7. You don't need to reboot your computer.

Activating the Terminal Services License Server

Remember, you have 90 days to activate a license server in your network after your installation of Windows 2000 Terminal Services. After this service is activated, each non-Windows 2000 client requesting a connection to the Terminal Services is issued a temporary Terminal Services Client Access License (TS CAL). The TS CAL gives access to the client for 90 days and is replaced by the permanent licenses when they are purchased and installed on the server.

1. Run the Terminal Services Licensing Program by clicking the Start button, pointing to Programs, pointing to Administrative Tools, and then clicking Terminal Services Licensing.

2. At the Licensing Wizard Welcome screen, click Next.

3. Choose your connection method. If your computer is behind a firewall, you may not be able to use the Internet connection method.

4. Follow the instructions in the wizard.

Once you activate the license server and have finished this process, setup automatically launches the process of obtaining licenses, which can be via Internet, Web, telephone, or fax. If you choose to obtain the information via the Internet, the setup program accesses the Internet from the machine it is running on. If you try the Web, setup will use any computer in the network to gain access.

If necessary, after Microsoft links the server to a digital certificate that validates the identity of the owner, the license server uses this certificate to obtain more licenses for the other Terminal Services servers.

TIP

You have 90 days after installing Windows 2000 Terminal Services to have an appropriate license server in place.

Using the Training Tools

Windows 2000 Terminal Services brings a wide array of tools that can benefit the trainer and the student. As an IT administrator, you won't have late night configurations to worry about. In addition, it won't be necessary to purchase numerous client computers and install expensive equipment. In this environment, you could present everything from certification seminars to bootcamps.

Also, as a central IT administrator in an office in New York, you can teach your field administrators how to perform certain management functions and maintenance by remotely gaining access to their Windows 2000 Servers and using the GUI to provide specific instructions. For example, if you wanted to teach your field engineers how to install a software application on their local desktops, you can gain access to a test desktop while the engineers are watching and remotely install the application. The field engineers would have first-hand knowledge and could actually see the installation process before making their own installations. Field engineers could visually link steps to corresponding text instructions.

Terminal Services Application Mode could help an IT group train several remote users by placing a video on the server to be viewed by the client at any time. Virtually everyone could attach, whether they were in Alaska or downtown New York, so long as the users were Microsoft Windows-based. Other clients would need to connect through a more robust Citrix MetaFrame thin-client solution.

TIP

Citrix MetaFrame features an excellent tool for training—VideoFrame. This feature allows for numerous connections to a trainer's computer so that students can view instructional material in a hands-on environment.

Administrators

Windows 2000 Terminal Services has four Administrative Tools that can be used to manage and administrate functions, users, and sessions. Listed below are the main features and functions.

Terminal Services Manager

The Terminal Services Manager allows you to manage sessions and processes on Terminal Services. Some features are as follows:

- Display connection status
- Display user and client information
- Display user and system processes
- Send a message to a session(s) or user
- Remotely control (or *shadow*) another session
- Process termination
- Disconnect or reset a session

Terminal Services Configuration

The Terminal Services Configuration tool creates, modifies, and deletes both sessions and session sets on Terminal Services. Some features are as follows:

- Add users and groups to permission lists
- Configure a new connection
- Manage permissions for a connection
- Control timeout settings and disconnect settings

Terminal Services Client Creator

The Terminal Services Client Creator tool creates the set of floppy disks used to install Terminal Services Client software. With it, you can do the following:

- Create Windows for Workgroups 3.11 (16-bit) client disks
- Create Windows 32-bit client disks for Intel-based computers
- Create Windows 32-bit client disks for Alpha-based computers

Terminal Services Licensing

The Terminal Services Licensing tool creates a secure way for your administrator to install client licenses, issue the licenses to Terminal Services clients, and also to track and manage CALs for Terminal Services. You can use this tool to perform the following:

- Activate the license server
- Obtain licenses
- View licenses, both issued and available

End Users

Microsoft has also improved on management for the following features:

Load Balancing This component is only available in Windows 2000 Advanced Server and Datacenter server. The Microsoft version of load balancing refers to redundancy of data. For instance, in the event of a failure of one server, the Terminal Services Load Balancing option allows for another server to take over. The Citrix version of this feature can be more versatile since it has the unique ability to dynamically manage and assign sessions based upon multiple server-load parameters.

One-on-One Shadowing Called Remote Control by Microsoft, this software is a tremendous tool for enhancing solutions and providing support quickly. Your own help desk staff gains a view of the customer's desktop and can take joint control of the desktop and troubleshoot problems efficiently and accurately.

Remote Client Administration This application allows administrators to create certain profiles for connecting users. The profiles can dictate specific connections and actions. The profiles are constructed by the administrator and can be deployed individually or in a broadcast. This is the tool at an administrator's workstation that allows him or her to remotely set security and access levels, disable security, set log off and disconnect features if desirable, set permissions, grant licenses, and set user accounts. The administrator also has the ability to send system alerts and set timeout rules for inactive sessions. Setting timeout rules will help conserve and reduce the workload on the servers.

Terminal Services Manager Your administrative query tool designed to manage the sessions, users, and processors on computers running Windows 2000 that are connected to your Terminal Services.

Summary

Microsoft has introduced a component of the Windows 2000 Server family that brings a cost-effective solution to an ever-growing concern in the Information Technology sector. That component is Windows Terminal Services for Windows 2000. An application can be installed easily on any Windows 2000 Server from the Add/Remove Programs icon in the Control Panel.

In its two modes, Remote Administration and Application Server, Windows 2000 Terminal Services provides a versatile component for managing your Windows 2000 servers. Remote Administration runs in minimal space and does not overly tax your server's resources. It also provides two remote administration connections via LAN, WAN, or dial-up.

In Terminal Service's second mode, Application Server, Windows 2000 provides rich scalability for your clients to take advantage of Windows 2000 Professional desktops. With the applications residing on the Terminal Services, and all processes occurring on the Terminal Server, clients can request access via LAN, WAN, or dial-up from any type of Windows-based client, and use the various applications previously installed. This is a low-cost alternative and highly manageable component of Windows 2000, which cuts down on upgrade costs and quickly implements new technologies.

Within Windows 2000 Terminal Services the licensing component eases the administration of licensing both the Terminal Servers in your network and the clients that are accessing them. The wizard allows you 90 days to connect a server license and issues a 90-day temporary license to non-Windows clients as well. You can do this via the Internet, phone, or fax.

Within security constrains, we recommend installing Windows 2000 Terminal Services Remote Administration on many of the Windows 2000 Servers in your network. That way, you can be anywhere within your network and have a connection to any of your servers. It is a secure way to administrate your servers without ever having to leave your desk. Consider Application Mode if you're looking to keep costs low but are striving to bring the latest technologies to your clients and meet their desktop application demands.

Using Terminal Services to Provide Applications over the Internet

An administrator has the ability to bring applications over the Internet to clients, using Terminal Services Advanced Client. An administrator can provide their client with a Web page with a hyperlink pointing to a specific command prompt on a specific server. Once the Web page is built and published, the administrator can give the Web site address to the client and the client can launch the application from the hyperlink as if it were an icon on the desktop.

FAQs

Q: Our company has just acquired a small, remote office in Alaska. Because the office is in a remote section of the country, there are few options for bandwidth upgrades so we are forced to use the existing 56Kbps dial-up connections with the current client running Windows 95. In addition, our company will soon be selling this remote office to another company. Therefore, upgrading hardware would not be very cost effective. What Microsoft solution would be best for us?

A: Install a Windows 2000 Terminal Services in Application Server Mode. Use RDP so that clients can access remote applications in your main office. You can easily remove the clients from your network once your company sells the remote location. Most importantly, there are no client software or hardware upgrades. The only cost will be the Terminal Services Licenses, which you control completely from within your own server farm.

Q: What type of clients can access Windows 2000 Terminal Services?

A: The following clients can access Windows 2000 Terminal Services:

- Windows CE-based terminals

- Windows CE-based Handheld Professional devices (H/PC Pro)

- 32-bit Windows-based PCs running Windows 95, Windows 98, Windows NT 3.51, Windows NT 4.0, or Windows 2000 Professional

- 16-bit Windows-based PCs running Windows for Workgroups 3.11 with MS TCP/IP-32

- Third-party software vendors such as Citrix provide clients for non-Windows platforms such as the Apple Macintosh, MS-DOS, and UNIX

Q: What is the purpose of RDP?

A: As a protocol, it provides the desktop data to the remote client, and carries keyboard and mouse clicks back to the server session.

Q: What is an advantage of using Windows Terminal Services in Remote Administration Mode?

A: An administrator can collaborate with another administrator within a session.

Q: What are two advantages of running Windows 2000 Terminal Services in Application Mode?

A: Users can request applications over the network from the server and the server performs all the necessary processing. Application Mode provides centralized management for administrators.

Q: What are two reasons for installing Terminal Services in Application Mode on multiple servers?

A: To configure specific servers for use with specific applications and to distribute the workload in a busy network.

Chapter 8

Installing Citrix MetaFrame

Solutions in this chapter:

- **Business Drivers for the Selection of Citrix MetaFrame**

- **Installing MetaFrame 1.8**

- **Integrating MetaFrame with the Active Directory**

- **Testing Configurations and Deploying a Pilot**

- **Rolling Out the Final Configuration**

- **Training**

Introduction

Rapid delivery of applications is a tremendous need in businesses today. It reduces the time to production and, if the application is business critical, can increase productivity of network users.

Delivering applications on the Internet can deliver a competitive advantage. These applications can form the basis of business-to-business process improvement and enhance customer relationship management. Citrix MetaFrame can provide a business with a competitive advantage. Installing it is the first step.

Business Drivers for Selection of Citrix MetaFrame

Fast-paced work environments demand flexible access to resources and rapid rollout of new technologies. The ability to offer workers flexibility in where, when, and how they work can provide a competitive edge in business. Increased concern for security requires technical infrastructures that promote flexible access while maintaining security not only to internal employees, but to trading partners and strategic alliances connected via extranets as well. Adding Citrix MetaFrame to Windows 2000 Terminal Services allows IT departments to rapidly deploy applications while centrally maintaining control over version control, user access, and application availability without requiring high technology or platform standardization of end-user interfaces.

Application publishing made possible by Citrix Program Neighborhood allows end users to access applications from virtually any location. Whether running a 2-D Computer-Aided Design (CAD) program via Web TV or office applications on a thin client, Citrix Program Neighborhood deploys applications to users in a consistent and efficient way. Seamless windows are a Citrix feature that allows published applications to be presented to an end user as if it were running locally on the local machine. User shortcuts such as ALT-TAB can be used to toggle between local and remote applications with ease. Seamless windows presents applications to users in a way in which they are familiar, using the Independent Computing Architecture (ICA) protocol that is more bandwidth efficient than Microsoft's Remote Display Protocol (RDP), with additional features to reduce latency and delay in keyboard/mouse response over low-bandwidth connections.

Citrix management tools allow administrators to deploy applications and data security rules to intranets, extranets, and via the Internet with efficiency and consistency, especially when integrated with Active

Directory. A well-developed Active Directory Group Policy can create a seamless user experience, whether the user is working on their office desktop, at home on a PC connected via dial-up, or at a tradeshow kiosk connected via the Internet. Combining the best features of Windows 2000 with the additional features of Citrix MetaFrame allows companies to rapidly deploy, support, and maintain applications to users in a consistent manner across many desktop platforms, operating systems, and network topologies.

Applications deployed via Citrix MetaFrame eliminate the hardware and operating system requirements required by these programs.

The Citrix ICA client can be run on virtually any platform from high-powered UNIX workstations to thin clients and handheld Windows CE devices. Citrix's digital independence program has led to the ability to deploy applications on existing hardware that would otherwise be obsolete, low-cost thin clients, or whatever hardware a potential telecommuter has that can successfully connect to the Internet running a Web browser. Citrix MetaFrame can eliminate the requirement of costly hardware upgrades or stringent standards for telecommuters and extranet-connected strategic partners. The ability to connect securely via the Internet eliminates the requirement to make point-to-point connections with strategic partners in order to share information and applications.

Adding Citrix MetaFrame to Windows 2000 Terminal Services adds flexibility in the deployment, security, upgradeability, and administration of applications deployed to users by Terminal Services. Additional features such as VideoFrame, which distributes streaming video, and server load balancing, which provides scalability to application publishing to a virtually unlimited number of users, extend the capabilities of server-based computing beyond the capabilities of Windows 2000 alone. These added features create an application deployment strategy that provides robust application presentation to the end user, ease of administration to the IT professional, competitive advantage, and improved efficiency of support to management. The features of Citrix MetaFrame can drive down IT costs by extending hardware life and reducing administrative costs, and create a competitive advantage by providing the ability to rapidly and securely deploy applications over intranets, extranets, and the Internet to virtually any client.

For IT Professionals

Running a Successful Testing and Pilot Program

I recently worked on a project that required users to be able to access applications remotely over low-bandwidth connections. Sounds like a perfect scenario for Citrix MetaFrame, right? The immediate response to my recommendation was "Citrix doesn't work, you can't run FoxPro applications over Citrix." It turns out that a previous employee had come to this conclusion, then left the company. This project illustrated up front that failure to properly test applications in the Citrix environment can lead to the project being scrapped for not meeting performance expectations, or perhaps worse, to big headaches down the road when the applications don't work the way you expected them to. By establishing clear guidelines and thoroughly documenting expectations and results, a smooth and productive Citrix implementation can take place.

This project involved enabling a claims processing application to be used by telecommuters. The business drivers for this project were simple. The labor market was tight, workers wanted more flexible hours, and were found to be more productive working from home. The technical issues were not so simple. The application was internally developed and had been piloted using remote control software. The required production standard was 200 claims processed per hour. An initial evaluation of Citrix MetaFrame enabled users to process approximately 100 claims per hour with an unsatisfactory user experience due to delays in keyboard/mouse response. A more thorough testing and pilot of Citrix MetaFrame led to more spectacular results.

1. **Define success** For the project to succeed, dial-up or Web-based connectivity to Citrix MetaFrame had to be reliable (less than two disconnects per day), the rate of claims processing had to meet or exceed 200 claims per hour on average for an 8-hour day, and the user experience had to be acceptable to prevent excessive errors, user fatigue, or other measures of dissatisfaction by the end user.

2. **Baseline** A pure out-of-the-box installation of the Windows 2000 Server, MetaFrame 1.8, and Win32 clients on all test equipment was configured. The application was first run on the local area network (LAN) to benchmark performance in

Continued

four, 15-minute time periods. This same procedure was then repeated via dial-up directly to a corporate modem pool, dial-up to a local ISP (Internet service provider), and over the Internet via a broadband cable modem. Users recorded overall processing speed (number of claims processed per time period) and feedback as to which screens or actions were faster/slower than others.

3. **Compare baseline results with desired results** Local users achieved results comparable to running the application in its standard fat-client configuration. Dial-up users achieved less than half the stated goal rate. Broadband Internet connectivity was better than dial-up, but still fell short of the desired outcome.

4. **Research** Because performance was acceptable over the LAN, and nearly acceptable over broadband, it was assumed that server performance was adequate and focus was placed on increasing the efficiency of bandwidth utilization. Microsoft TechNet, www.citrix.com, www.thethin.net, and www.thinplanet.com are excellent sources of information and opportunities for collaboration with other IT professionals using Citrix technology. Reading the README files for hotfixes and patches was an excellent source of detailed information regarding issues and capabilities of specific Citrix features. Areas researched included:

- Application tuning
- ICA protocol and client configuration
- Connection quality
- Server tuning

5. **Apply changes one at a time** Back up the test system prior to making changes so you can return to a true prechange configuration. For each fix or change that improved performance, at least three left things the same or made things worse. Each fix was applied, then the complete baselining procedure outlined above was repeated. Changes that helped or made no difference were maintained. Changes that hurt performance were discarded. These changes included each client-configurable option for bandwidth management and modifying the default settings for several hotfixes. In this

Continued

application, we found that queuing mouse and keyboard movements hurt performance, and caching bitmaps up to about 100MB helped performance. The biggest improvements came from implementing supercache.

6. **Apply multiple changes together** The changes that enhanced performance were then applied together one at a time and tested after each change. Performance was documented using the baseline procedure above.

7. **The required performance goals are met, tested, and production implementation is approved**

8. **Production hardware configurations are established** Since resource configuration scales linearly on MetaFrame applications, it is easy to use information from the testing scenario to define hardware requirements for production use by multiplying the resource load of single applications by the number of expected concurrent users.

9. **Continue to monitor server performance and research resources** New patches and upgrades, and the experiences of others reflected in user groups and mail lists, may lead to further improvements in application performance.

This process is important due to the fact that it is documented and repeatable. It is easy to report progress to management and to demonstrate cause and effect. The required specification for this project was an average of 200 claims processed per hour. In the current state, production quotas have been increased to 250 claims per hour, with peak performances over 350 claims per hour over dial-up and up to 400 over broadband Internet. A once-discarded solution has now resulted in a 25 percent increase in productivity above the savings realized by moving many workers out of limited office space. Configuring client features is not a simple process of following configuration steps one time. Optimum performance is the end goal, so it is important to evaluate the process regularly.

Installating MetaFrame 1.8

After successfully installing the Windows 2000 Server and configuring Terminal Services, the basic installation of Citrix MetaFrame is relatively quick and easy. It is not unusual to install, configure, and deploy applications via the Internet within a single day to begin a pilot program. The steps below cover the installation process for standard installations of Citrix MetaFrame 1.8 on Windows 2000, Citrix NFuse, and Feature Releases.

Prior to installing MetaFrame there are a few things to consider. You typically want to install MetaFrame on the same drive partition as Windows 2000, you will want to have adequate disk available on this partition to install MetaFrame and have approximately 2x installed RAM available for your page file. If you will take advantage of the drive letter remapping feature, you need to install all applications after MetaFrame installation. Configure all networking protocols you will use for MetaFrame connections before installation for ease of networking configuration.

1. Insert the MetaFrame CD in your server. If autorun is enabled, the installation welcome screen will be displayed. Otherwise, run setup.EXE from the root of your CD drive.

2. Read and follow the prompts for the screens that are displayed, there are a few choices to customize the installation. Note in Figure 8.1 that the server is rebooted at the end of the installation procedure.

Figure 8.1 Note that a system reboot is required during the MetaFrame installation.

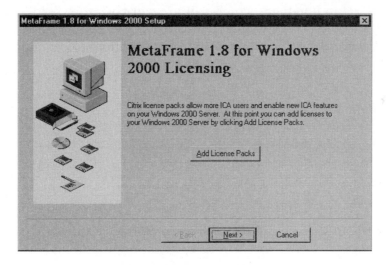

3. The MetaFrame 1.8 for Windows licensing screen allows you to add license packs during the installation. If you add licenses during installation, you will have 35 days to register your server with Citrix Systems. To add license packs during installation click Add License Packs (Figure 8.2).

Figure 8.2 License installation screen.

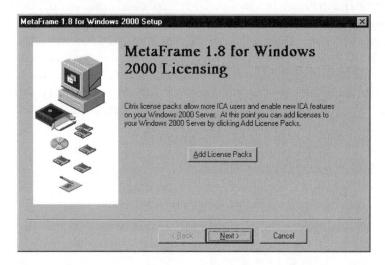

4. To install license packs, click the green plus sign in the licensing window and type the license serial number in the dialogue box as displayed in Figure 8.3. Make sure you use the license key from inside your CD case. The license code on the back of the case has "XXXX" in one field, which will prevent you from installing it as a license key. When registering your license keys with Citrix, you will get the machine code from the license number column of the licensing window. After installation, this screen is opened from the Citrix management toolbar.

Figure 8.3 The Citrix Licensing window.

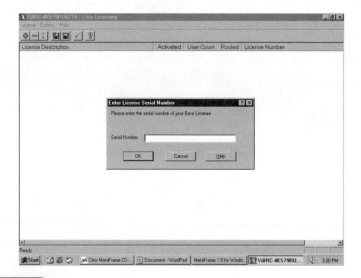

5. Choose the network protocols you will allow to carry ICA traffic. Only the protocols installed on the server will be available during installation. A default ICA connection will be configured for each protocol you select in the window displayed in Figure 8.4.

Figure 8.4 The Network ICA Connections window.

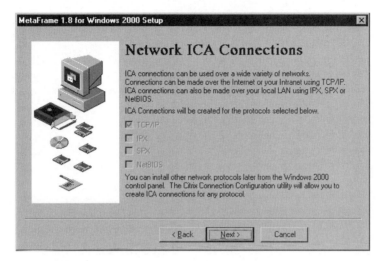

6. If you will utilize ICA dial-up connections you can configure modems during installation from the screen displayed in Figure 8.5. Modems cannot be configured for both ICA dial-up and Remote Access Service (RAS). Modems configured for RAS will not be displayed in the Add Modems dialogue box.

Figure 8.5 The TAPI Modem Setup window.

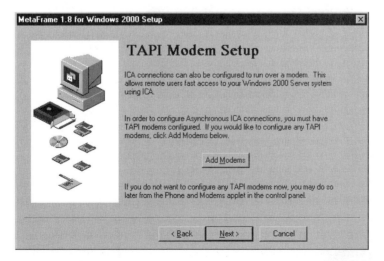

7. Figure 8.6 describes the client drive mapping feature of MetaFrame. If the server drive letters are left in their default configuration (starting with C:, D:, etc.) the client drives will map starting with V:, U:, etc. This does not create an intuitive user experience.

Figure 8.6 The Drive Mapping window.

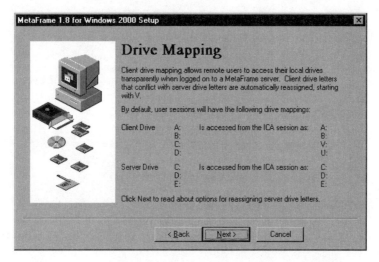

8. A warning box (Figure 8.7) indicates that applications installed before MetaFrame could be affected by the drive remapping feature. Whenever possible avoid this conflict by installing MetaFrame before installing applications on the server. If you already have applications installed, the MetaFrame README file describes the procedure for modifying the registry to resolve any conflicts.

Figure 8.7 The drive remapping warning box.

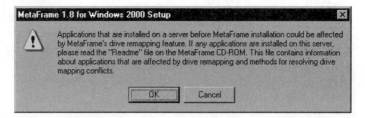

9. The Server Drive Reassignment window (Figure 8.8) enables the drive remapping feature and customization of the initial drive letter. For clustering and load-balancing applications make sure you configure all servers with the same drive remapping configuration to prevent complications in application publishing and administration.

Figure 8.8 The Server Drive Reassignment window.

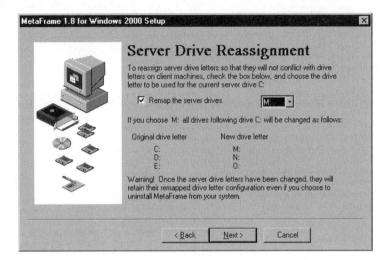

10. Figure 8.9 displays the final window of the MetaFrame installation procedure. Clicking Finish in this window initiates a system reboot. When the system comes back up, you will have successfully installed Citrix MetaFrame.

Figure 8.9 The System Reboot window.

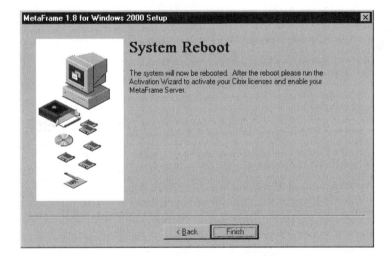

> **TIP**
>
> If you are building a server for a pilot program or configuring multiple servers that will be configured with the same applications, do not install license packs during installation. Following installation, you can install your applications and then conduct a full backup of the server. This allows you to restore the server during a pilot rather than reinstalling if your pilot goes beyond 35 days. Likewise, you can use the configured server with no license packs installed as a master image for multiple servers using Sys Prep and the imaging tool of your choice.

Integrating with the Active Directory

Active Directory is a significant leap forward for administration, security, desktop control, and versioning of configurations. Group Policy advances well beyond NT 4.0 system policies to integrate security and user configuration into roaming policies that can roam between desktop (fat client) and published application configurations. When designing your MetaFrame environment it is best to dedicate MetaFrame servers to application serving only. Installing MetaFrame on a domain controller does not allow anonymous access to applications from that server. Also, the overhead induced by domain controller and/or Active Directory services reduces the number of user sessions that can be hosted by a MetaFrame server. Maximize your investment in MetaFrame by taking advantage of Active Directory services and using your MetaFrame servers for application hosting only.

Mixed Mode

Mixed mode Active Directory is a compromise of features and performance designed to be used during a migration to a pure Windows 2000 server environment. The full features of Active Directory are not available in mixed mode. Group Policy and NT 4.0 policies do not work well together. Mixing NT Terminal Services and Windows 2000 MetaFrame servers is possible, but it is difficult to implement roaming profiles, policies, and applications. In many cases, users recognize the performance difference between a NT 4.0 Terminal Services server and Windows 2000 server, creating a dissatisfying user experience.

Native Mode

Native mode Active Directory can be activated when all domain controllers are running Windows 2000. Native mode allows full implementation of Active Directory features including Group Policy. Group Policy can be configured to control access (not NT security file system) and roaming profiles that can follow a user from PC to remote session. Native mode Active Directory provides the most robust set of features for administering back-end functions and creating the most consistent user experience.

If you are using thin clients or non-Windows-based clients, you will most likely allow your users to run a Windows style desktop from which they will run various applications. This allows non-Windows 32-bit clients to have the look and feel of a Windows 2000-based PC. It also opens the window of opportunity for users to wreak havoc on your Citrix environment. In the default configuration of a MetaFrame desktop an end user can shut down the server, thinking they are simply shutting down their workstation, and this could be the least of your worries. An effective Active Directory structure including implementation of Group Policy can eliminate these and other issues resulting in a safe and effective environment for end users. A thorough examination of Active Directory and Group Policy is best left for another text. A brief discussion of Active Directory features and functions that apply directly to a MetaFrame implementation follows.

Group Policy-based change and configuration management is designed to centrally manage permissions and presentation of network resources to ensure they are available to users when and where they are needed. IntelliMirror is the centralized function that ensures a user configuration is maintained on whatever platform they log on to. This is an evolutionary extension of roaming profiles that permits user files, software, and user customizable desktop and environment settings to be applied to whatever workstation the user logs on to in the enterprise. These features can be used to define policies to restrict user access to areas of the MetaFrame desktop to prevent users from shutting down the server, changing system settings, or otherwise corrupting the configuration you have developed to maximize application performance in your enterprise.

Some best practices for implementing a Group Policy for MetaFrame users include:

- Create multiple groups for users who require different desktop access options (access to a command prompt, and so on).
- Create separate access groups for each of your published applications. In some cases you can nest these to ease administration.

- Use folder redirection to move the default location of My Documents to a separate network share so user files are not saved within the user profile directory. This can replace the old "H: for Home" drive mapping.

- Remove the Shut Down option from the Start menu.

- Remove Control Panel from the Start menu.

- Hide local server drives (M:, N:, and so on, if you remap drives).

- Remove the Run command from the Start menu.

- Remove the MetaFrame Management toolbar.

- Implement disk quotas to limit user disk use.

If you really want to tighten down the environment:

- Prevent right-click on the desktop.

- Clear the Start menu except for Shut Down (with Shut Down server removed) and Printers window.

- Do not allow users to install printers.

- Allow users to only run applications from icons on the desktop. Then publish applications to add an icon to the user desktop.

- Remove My Computer and My Network Places from the desktop.

These are just a few of the user configuration features that can be configured using IntelliMirror and Group Policy. In some cases it may not be necessary to provide users with a Windows desktop. With the introduction of NFuse it is possible to embed Program Neighborhood within a Web page. Using this tool it is often possible to create an acceptable user environment by creating a Web page with relevant content links in addition to icons to a user's applications.

TIP

To keep roaming profile sizes to a minimum, configure Group Policy to redirect My Documents folders, Internet Explorer-related files (temporary Internet files, cookies, etc.) that are stored within the profile by default to a separate file server. This will minimize the time it takes to load the user profile at application launch.

Installing NFuse

NFuse is a free add-on to Citrix MetaFrame that makes publishing applications over the Web easy to the point of making it an essential feature of any MetaFrame deployment. With the release of Feature Release 1 and NFuse 1.5 creating a secure (up to 128-bit encryption) environment for Program Neighborhood, published applications can be implemented in less than an hour using the default installed Web pages. Use of scripting tools and the Web Site Wizard makes creating a customized Web site that includes access to applications through an intranet, extranet, or the Internet a relatively easy task. Using NFuse 1.5 to deploy applications over the Internet creates a method for rapidly deploying applications to remote offices and telecommuters that is very cost efficient when compared to point-to-point connectivity, firewalls, and application redesign. There are two steps to installing NFuse. First, install the NFuse extensions to your MetaFrame server. Next, install Web extensions to a Web server. NFuse supports several types of Web servers. The steps for installing NFuse 1.5 and Web Extensions to Microsoft Internet Information Server (IIS) are outlined below.

1. Insert the NFuse 1.5 CD in your MetaFrame server. Double-click NFuseWizard.EXE to launch the install application.

2. Follow the prompts to install the NFuse files to your MetaFrame server. The window in Figure 8.10 allows you to select the location of the Web Site Wizard.

Figure 8.10 Choose Destination Location window for NFuse.

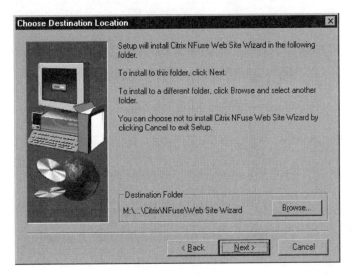

3. Figures 8.11 and 8.12 display some of the screens involved in installing NFuse. Note that there are no customizable options aside from file location for the Web Site Wizard and that reboot is not required following installation.

Figure 8.11 File installation window.

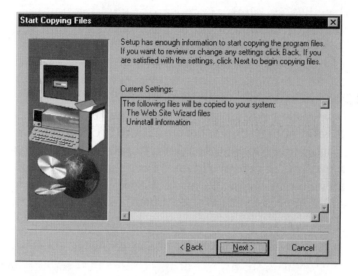

Figure 8.12 The Setup Complete window. Note that reboot is not required following this installation.

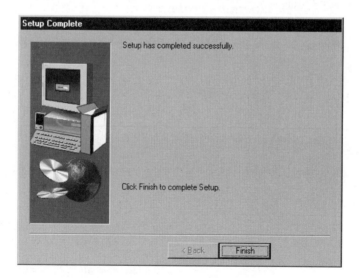

4. Install the Web server extensions to your Web server. Your MetaFrame server can run IIS and host your NFuse Web pages. When possible, use a separate Web server to reduce overhead on your MetaFrame server. When connecting via the Internet, a higher level of security is possible by separating your MetaFrame and Web servers. NFuse 1.5 supports secure sockets layer (SSL) relay between Web servers and MetaFrame servers.

5. Run [insert filename] from the NFuse 1.5 CD. Choose to install the example files if you want to have immediate access to NFuse features (Figure 8.13).

Figure 8.13 Select components to install to IIS.

6. The NFuse objects must be able to connect to a MetaFrame server to establish connections. In the connection dialogue box (Figure 8.14), input the IP address of your MetaFrame server and a Transmission Control Protocol (TCP) port that will be used to establish connections.

7. In most cases you will not want to be able to use port 80 for Citrix XML communications because this will conflict with regular HTTP traffic. When you select a port other than 80 you will see a warning message (Figure 8.15). Make sure you use the same port when setting up your MetaFrame server. You can check the MetaFrame server's port information in the following registry key:

```
HKLM\SYSTEM\CurrentControlSet\Services\CtxHttp\TcpPort
```

Figure 8.14 Configure the port for XML communications.

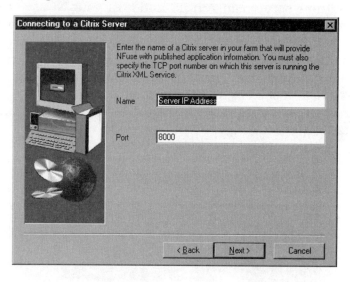

Figure 8.15 Ensure you configure IIS and MetaFrame to communicate on the same TCP port.

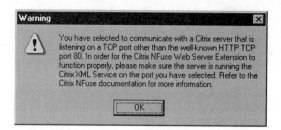

TIP

Citrix and Yahoo! have formed an alliance to combine the features of corporate Yahoo! and NFuse for developing intranets and extranets. This can be an excellent option for rolling out a robust corporate site.

8. Insert the directory for your Web server's root URL (Figure 8.16). If you are creating a different virtual server/directory for NFuse, browse to the desired installation location. Place the files in the root of the Web server to connect to http://server IP address/ NFuse15/default.htm.

Figure 8.16 Define destination folder for sample NFuse files.

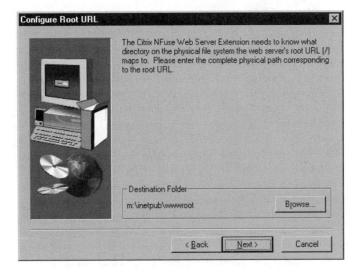

9. To have NFuse automatically install ICA Clients when a user accesses the NFuse Web site, choose Yes from the dialogue box in Figure 8.17.

Figure 8.17 Choose Yes to allow automatic installation of ICA Clients from Web pages.

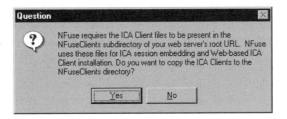

10. Setup then installs Web extensions, example files, and client files to your server (Figure 8.18).

Figure 8.18 NFuse Web server extension installation file copy.

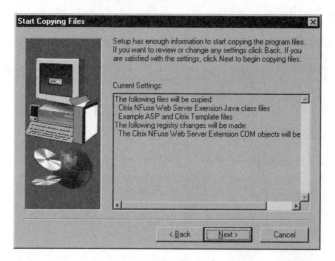

11. NFuse installation will finish and the WWW service will be restarted on your Web server. To test the installation, you can visit http://[IP address of your Web Server]/NFuse15/default.htm. This page has several links to demonstrate the features of NFuse 1.5. These pages can be used as examples for creating your own page that will take advantage of the features that suit the needs of your environment.

Feature Release 1

Feature Release 1 for MetaFrame 1.8 improves upon many existing features and enables several new features, including NFuse 1.5. In addition to the features discussed below, there are several other features that improve the user experience including increased screen resolution, increased color depth, and multiple monitor support.

NFuse 1.5

Feature Release 1 contains an updated XML service that replaces Citrix NFuse services to support communication between a Web server and a MetaFrame server. This new service improves communication by using TCP rather than User Datagram Protocol (UDP) packets, making connections through firewalls much easier to configure. By default, the XML service uses TCP port 80.

RC5 Encryption

Previously Citrix Secure ICA service was sold as an add-on to MetaFrame. The RC5 encryption that is included in Feature Release 1 enables 40-, 56-, and 128-bit encryption for user sessions. When enabled, logons are encrypted at 128-bit. This encryption method uses the symmetric key algorithm from RSA Data Security to encrypt and decrypt data, and Diffie-Hellman key agreement algorithms to generate the secret keys. When enabled, the entire ICA packet is encrypted. Encryption levels can be set for connections or published applications, allowing for flexible deployment of encryption levels.

SSL Relay

When NFuse is installed on a Web server separate from the MetaFrame server, traffic between these servers was previously unencrypted. The Citrix SSL relay uses SSL technology to encrypt data between Web servers and the server farm. By default, this service uses port 443 and requires installation of a valid certificate on the Web server.

TCP-Based Browsing

This feature eliminates the requirement to allow UDP traffic through firewalls to allow NFuse connections to an internal network. This feature eliminates one of the key complaints with NFuse—that it required additional ports to be opened on firewalls. This feature runs on TCP port 80 by default—the same as normal Web traffic.

Web Install

The Web Install feature allows administrators to create Web pages that will prompt users to install the appropriate client software if it is not present. This feature makes rolling clients out much easier, especially for Web-based applications that may be published to public Web sites.

SpeedScreen Latency Reduction

SpeedScreen is one of the core Citrix features that enhances application performance over low-bandwidth connections. SpeedScreen provides instant mouse-click feedback and local text echo to users over low-bandwidth connections. The mouse feedback changes the mouse pointer when an action is pending. Local text echo displays the keystrokes as they are keyed at the client, prior to returning the screen refresh from the terminal session. This feature should be tested thoroughly and applied selectively as it only works on applications that use standard Windows APIs for text display.

Testing Configurations and Deploying a MetaFrame Pilot

After installing MetaFrame and optionally Nfuse, it is time to get down to the business of testing applications and running a pilot project. The procedures for publishing applications and monitoring the performance of your MetaFrame server are covered elsewhere in this book. Use this book to guide your initial installation and configuration, then make changes as necessary to obtain the performance goals and end-user configuration that meet the needs of your environment.

Keys to a successful pilot:

Define success

1. Define the applications that will be included in your initial rollout.
2. Define the connection types and network access that will be used (TCP/IP, IPX/SPX, dial-up, broadband, LAN, WAN, and so on).
3. Define application performance standards.
4. Define cost parameters per user and for the project as a whole.
5. Define any "show stoppers." These would be single, negative outcomes that jeopardize the entire project.

Establish a testing center

1. Dedicate sufficient hardware to a test environment so that it can be modified and taken offline without negatively impacting your production environment.
2. Use sufficient server hardware for three simultaneous users; this should provide sufficient information to determine the effects of users on hardware and scale the production requirements.

   - I typically use a current technology PC with at least 256MB RAM for a test server.
   - I try to have client configurations to match the variety of clients that will be present in production.

Back up, test, research, test some more

1. Back up your test server prior to every change and restore to prechange conditions rather than simply uninstalling or "unconfiguring" changes, especially those that impact the registry.

2. Test each application individually prior to testing server load under multiple users and applications.

3. When performance standards aren't met, research possible solutions. Listserv archives are an excellent resource.

Define your production environment

1. Define how you will present applications to users, using Program Neighborhood or a desktop session.

2. If using a desktop, define Active Directory and group policy parameters and test thoroughly to ensure users have sufficient rights to be productive, but no permissions that could compromise the environment.

Underpromise, overdeliver

1. Be conservative in establishing performance standards and in reporting benchmark results, especially if users will connect via the Internet or dial-up connections.

Once all of your applications are running without issue and to the stated performance goals, it is time to scale your production hardware. For MetaFrame servers, the best rule of thumb is to buy the fastest of everything you can from disk to CPU, and use your baseline application data to ensure you have enough RAM. For each application you tested, measure the amount of RAM in use while the application is running. Multiply by the amount of RAM consumed by each application by the required number of simultaneous users. Total the RAM requirements for each application, plus the amount of server overhead (RAM in use when idle/no connections), and you will have a fairly accurate measure of the RAM requirements for your production environment. I always like to add the construction planning rule of adding 10 percent to the total as a buffer. Other hardware considerations should include disk configuration and CPU. When configuring hard disks, duplexing is the fastest fault-tolerant method for this application. When choosing Intel CPUs, several studies have found that higher cache levels for XEON CPUs does not appreciably increase performance. As with all things, budgets may constrain your hardware options. Compromise on CPU speed if you must, but never on RAM.

TIP

Do not install any Citrix licenses during the MetaFrame installation procedure. After you successfully configure Windows 2000 and Citrix MetaFrame, perform a full backup of the server. This will allow you to restore the server to its original configuration if your test/pilot runs longer than 35 days. You can take this a step further during testing by installing applications/custom configurations prior to installing licenses and backing the machine up. This makes it very easy to maintain successful modifications and eliminate unsuccessful ones while maintaining a relatively clean install of all software. As always, maintain accurate records of all modifications and backups during your testing to maintain change and configuration control.

Application Launching and Embedding

Application Launching and Embedding (ALE) is an exciting feature of MetaFrame for Web-enabled applications. ALE allows applications to either be launched in separate windows or embedded within a Web page. Embedded applications are easily deployed within a Web browser. This feature works great for applications that are run individually and fit within the confines of a Web browser. Launched applications are difficult to differentiate from a locally installed Windows-based application. Users can easily move between launched applications and the desktop of their Windows-based client. ALE technology is a powerful feature that makes Terminal Services a robust and usable feature when combined with MetaFrame.

Rolling Out MetaFrame to the Environment

When you have successfully achieved the goals of your pilot program, it is time to roll MetaFrame out to your production environment. Based upon the results of your pilot you should have the configurations necessary to effectively run your applications on Citrix MetaFrame and utilization information to properly scale hardware and bandwidth to support your expected user load. The key issues in rolling out the product to your users will be how to present the applications to end users, establishing a policy to control user access, and installing the client software.

Presenting Applications to Users

When deploying Citrix MetaFrame to end users, a fundamental question is whether to publish a Windows desktop from which users will run applications or to publish applications only. If users are working from Windows-based clients, running a desktop session in MetaFrame is very confusing, which makes Program Neighborhood with applications published to seamless windows a clear best choice. Other clients may have benefits either way. From an application security/simplicity of management standpoint, publishing applications is less complicated than creating profiles and using Group Policy to define a structured desktop for users. The portal approach using NFuse and a Web page has not taken off to date, but presents an interesting alternative to the conventional desktop. The decision in this case comes down to the needs of the user and what is an acceptable environment.

Defining the Environment

If you will be publishing applications to users using Program Neighborhood and/or NFuse, the task of defining the environment is easy. Hide the server drives, make sure printers are available, change default file save locations, and you are off to a good start. This is a larger challenge if users will be running a desktop from which they run applications. Hopefully you have tested your group policy and Active Directory configurations in your pilot and will roll out one department at a time to your production environment. If you have properly tested in your pilot this will go very smoothly. As corporate intranets and extranets become more prevalent, the use of NFuse and portal-style delivery of applications is likely to grow.

Installing the ICA Client

Citrix has developed clients for virtually every device that can access a data network. Steps for installing and configuring ICA clients were covered in Chapter 6, "Citrix MetaFrame Clients." Here we will discuss strategies for deploying the various ICA clients to production environments. If the machine can access a browser, NFuse 1.5 can be configured to install the appropriate client prior to logging on the MetaFrame server. This feature works by checking for installed clients and then determining the correct client to install. Alternatively, share points can be established to install clients via logon scripts to various platforms, or various software delivery tools can be used to create and deliver the software to the client. Of course, installation disks can be created for "hand install" of the software. Whatever method you use, you will want to test and configure your client, then preconfigure your installation media to deliver a fully configured package to the client.

To create a customized ICA client installation:

- Install the desired ICA client on an appropriate client machine.

- Run the client on this machine and customize it to meet the needs of your environment.

  1. Create remote application entries.

  2. Make firewall/alternate address settings.

  3. Configure user preferences.

- Rename Module.SRC and Appsrv.SRC on your installation point to Module.OLD and Appsrv.OLD.

- Copy Module.INI and Appsrv.INI on the client machine to the location of the installation media, renaming them to Module.SRC and Appsrv.SRC. These two files contain the customized settings for your client. Use the installation media to create your install point, installation package, or installation diskettes to install the client to your target machines.

- Repeat these steps for each client required for your environment.

Citrix MetaFrame Licensing

All Citrix products and license packs must be registered with Citrix within 35 days of installation. Citrix client licenses are sold per concurrent user. Licenses can be pooled across servers to allow multiple servers to have access to all installed licenses for an enterprise. This is especially useful when using load-balancing features. If you take a server down for maintenance the client licenses associated with that server can be used by other servers if they have the resources to support additional user sessions. A user can run multiple applications within a single session. Add-on products such as resource management services and load balancing are licensed per server. Each server must have a valid license for the add-on product that will run on that server.

Repeated registration of the same license key is not recommended and can prompt questioning from Citrix Corporation. For this reason, you want to have your production environment configured and stable prior to registering your license keys with Citrix. The procedure can be most easily completed via a Web browser.

Citrix provides two tools for establishing and maintaining valid licensing for their products, a licensing utility within MetaFrame and the Citrix Activation System (CAS) which can be accessed via the Citrix Web page. The Citrix Licensing utility is used for installing and activating Citrix MetaFrame and add-on components that require a license. The Citrix Web site contains links to the automated license registration pages that provide the information required to activate your MetaFrame servers and add-on products. The first time you access these pages you will have to register for a logon. This makes tracking your MetaFrame products easy as you can access information on all licensed products for your company in one location. Use this Web page to obtain activation codes for your licenses.

Training

As with all new products, some training will be necessary for both the IT staff and end users prior to and during a MetaFrame rollout. For administrators familiar with Windows NT, the administrative tools and customization options of MetaFrame can be mastered with a few hours of hands-on training combined with a reference such as this text. End users familiar with working in a Windows environment will find working with MetaFrame to be very intuitive.

Administrators

As an add-on component to Windows 2000 server, MetaFrame is very easy to administer for those with solid experience with NT. The sites www.thethin.net and www.thinplanet.com provide excellent newsgroups and downloads for collaborating with IT professionals and troubleshooting. Citrix offers several training courses on MetaFrame and its add-on components. The Citrix Certified Administrator and Citrix Certified Enterprise Administrator certifications are fair assessments of an administrator's understanding of the key concepts of installing and administering a MetaFrame environment.

End Users

The ALE features combined with application publishing to Program Neighborhood makes the end user experience very intuitive. Clients able to take advantage of seamless windows will find it difficult to discern between local and published applications on their desktops. Client drive and printer mapping makes running applications within a MetaFrame environment very easy for users trained to work in Windows-based environments who are familiar with navigating within a Web browser. Most users will be able to begin using published applications with no training at all. With a reference card and brief training (conducted in small groups or using session shadowing), users can be trained to manipulate client settings to manage their experience with ease.

Summary

Installing Citrix MetaFrame is a straightforward process that can be accomplished by administrators familiar with NT technology and networking concepts. The business needs of providing flexible access to applications for internal employees, sharing information with strategic partners, exploiting the Internet, managing costs through reduced support and training needs, and extending the life of existing equipment are supported through a MetaFrame implementation. Configuring NFuse 1.5 pushes secure application publishing via the Web to new levels of ease and seamless user experience. Though it is fairly easy to install MetaFrame, a thorough pilot and implementation plan should be developed to ensure MetaFrame is tuned to best support the applications and end-user requirements of your environment. Web-based client deployment and shadowing allow rapid rollout and training of end users. Publishing applications in seamless windows creates a user experience that is familiar to most users and will create an easy migration to server-based computing.

FAQs

Q: Our company is planning on deploying an accounting package and delivering it through ICA to Windows-based terminals located all around the world. When we select the server operating system and configure it, what special configurations of Windows 2000 are required in order to install Citrix MetaFrame 1.8?

A: You must install Terminal Services in Application Mode on top of Windows 2000 Server and install a Terminal Services license server on your network.

Q: End users keep saving files to the C:\ drive of my MetaFrame server; what can I do to prevent users from doing this?

A: During installation MetaFrame gives the option of remapping server drive letters to prevent such a problem. Remapping server drive letters improves the user experience when client drive mapping is enabled. This feature allows MetaFrame sessions to map the client's local C: drive to C:\, etc. creating a more intuitive environment.

Q: Why is Active Directory integration important to a MetaFrame deployment?

A: Active Directory features, especially Group Policy, allow user configuration and administration to integrate desktop and MetaFrame policies to create a consistent user environment. Group Policy features also allow roaming profile management to improve system performance.

Q: What security concerns should be addressed when deploying applications over the Web?

A: When using NFuse the default configuration passes logon information via plain text. Using SSL/secure site for the NFuse log-on screen reduces security risk here. RC5 encryption of 40-, 56-, or 128-bit encryption can be used with NFuse. Citrix Extranet can be used to further increase security.

Q: Can I install MetaFrame on a domain controller?

A: Yes, MetaFrame can be installed on a domain controller, but it is not recommended.

Q: I need to deploy an application over the Internet. I have downloaded NFuse 1.5 from the Citrix web site. What else do I need to do prior to installing NFuse 1.5 in my MetaFrame 1.8 environment?

A: Install and register a valid license for MetaFrame 1.8 Feature Release 1.

Configuring the User Experience

Introduction

Administrators can successfully create a positive user experience by configuring session parameters on the MetaFrame server. One measure of the success of a Citrix MetaFrame deployment is how satisfied the end users are with the ease of use of the applications deployed on it. If they are able to use applications in just the way that they expected, with fast performance and full functionality, then the deployment is considered successful from their point of view. The result, a reduced need for administrative support, makes the deployment a success from the administrators' point of view.

Users are less concerned with *how* the application reaches their desktop than they are with whether it works the way they need it to.

Configuring Parameters with Active Directory Utilities

Many large companies integrate MetaFrame as member servers into their Windows 2000 Active Directory and let the standard Windows 2000 domain controllers handle the Domain Name Service (DNS), replication, and Dynamic Host Control Protocol (DHCP) functions. While MetaFrame will function running on Windows 2000 in a UNIX DNS and DHCP environment, there is less integration effort, more compatibility, and fewer cross-platform security issues by providing those services on dedicated Windows 2000 domain controllers. Windows 2000 DNS and DHCP servers provide new features and functionality, such as "peering" DNS servers and "dynamic" DNS thru DHCP, among many others that place them ahead of most UNIX-based services in the technology curve. Along with the increased and more granular security controls offered, which some say rival or exceed those in UNIX-based systems, I would imagine most shops running MetaFrame Windows products will also want to use Windows 2000-based domain controllers and DNS. Those shops running UNIX-based MetaFrame servers will probably want to stick to their UNIX servers for other tasks as well.

We do not intend to concentrate heavily on Active Directory design or configuration in this book. We will touch briefly on a few key points that are required or recommended specifically for the tasks we need to accomplish. Proper design and implementation of Active Directory is a book topic unto itself, and several good ones have already been written. I can highly recommend the more in-depth documentation of the Windows 2000 Server Resource Kit Deployment Planning Guide at www.microsoft.com/windows2000/library/resources/reskit/dpg/default.asp. There are many more highly informational items included in the Resource Kit documentation, and anyone who is serious about Windows 2000 and Citrix MetaFrame should have the full retail product close at hand.

TIP

For more information on Active Directory, refer to other Syngress Publishing titles including *Windows 2000 Server System Administration Handbook; Mission Critical! Windows 2000 Server Administration;* and especially *Managing Active Directory for Windows 2000 Server.*

Citrix recommends not installing your MetaFrame servers as a domain controller. If you do, dedicate them to that task and do not serve user applications from the same server. This is for performance reasons. If you are going to install a client/server application, such as SQL, you should install the SQL server on a separate, non-MetaFrame server and install only the client portion on your MetaFrame servers. If you want to manage your domain controllers remotely, install Terminal Services in Administration Mode; this places very little extra load on the server and allows you to reduce administrative costs by providing you with the ability to work off-site. MetaFrame can be integrated into your existing or new Active Directory as a member server, only without imposing the system and network performance restrictions that the Active Directory Domain Server services require. If installed as a member server, the Active Directory tools won't be installed by default, and you will have to create a custom Microsoft Management Console (MMC) snap-in to manage the users and groups from the MetaFrame server.

The user object property sheet is where all user-specific settings are stored. If you are logged in to the console of a domain controller, you get there by clicking on Start | Programs | Administrative Tools | Active Directory Users and Computers. Expand the Users folder in the left window, then double-click a user name, or right-click and choose Properties. If you are on a member server or workstation, you will need "domain admin" rights and will have to browse to the domain controller using a custom MMC. See the next sections in this chapter for instructions on creating a custom MMC for user and computer management. This is usually the first place you will start customizing what the user can see and do on your server.

While Citrix MetaFrame will work on NT 4.0 domains and Windows 2000 networks without domains, integrating your server into an Active Directory domain will provide a better way to manage and respond to your users' needs. For our configuration guide in this chapter, we will be using the Active Directory Users and Computers from a MetaFrame server also configured as a domain controller. For those who will be bringing up MetaFrame as a member server, see the section titled "Creating a Custom MMC Console." Once in the Active Directory Users and Groups window, account creation and configuration options will be the same.

WARNING

While an Active Directory domain controller has only "domain" accounts, a member server has both domain and "local" accounts and can be accessed by either one. Don't forget to go back and use good passwords or disable unused local accounts, especially the local administrator account (did you leave it blank during install?), or you could provide an easy target for the bad guys. I've seen more than one member server brought up and immediately joined to the domain that still had a blank password on the default local administrator account!

Many new administrators experience shock, or at least feel some anxiety, after upgrading their first domain controller to Active Directory. One of the first things they are accustomed to doing after upgrading is to open Computer Management and go to Local Users and Groups, shown in Figure 9.1, to see what kinds of new features they have and start adding new user accounts—but they are greeted with that message in the window and that big ugly red X over their most-used utility.

That message, however, is actually no reason for alarm. The Local Users and Groups utility is disabled after upgrading the server to a domain controller. If you remember, domain controllers have no local users or groups any longer, and existing accounts are converted to domain accounts.

Figure 9.1 Local Users and Groups utility.

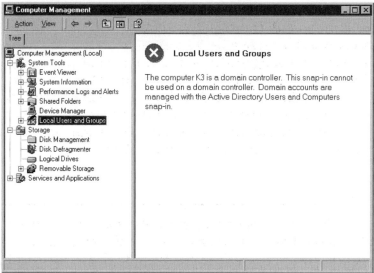

Creating a Custom MMC Console

As we discussed, if you have not installed your MetaFrame server as a domain controller, you will not have the Active Directory Users and Computers added to your Program list automatically. In order for you to manage users and groups, you will have to manually add the snap-in by creating a custom MMC Console. This is a simple process, and once you do it a few times you will probably find that you perform this task quite frequently. Numerous administrative functions can be combined into a "favorites" list of your most-often used tools. To begin, click on the Start button and choose Run. Then type **mmc** into the Open window. This will open a new, blank MMC console window. Next, from the Console pull-down menu, choose Add/Remove Snap-in. This will open an empty Add/Remove Snap-in window. Next, click the Add button, and the Add Standalone Snap-in window shown in Figure 9.2 will open and display the available standalone snap-ins.

Choose Active Directory Users and Computers. Click OK and you can now start configuring your Active Directory. You can save this console using a meaningful name, and it will automatically be added to your Administrative Tools program listing.

Figure 9.2 Adding the Active Directory snap-in.

Configuring the User Properties

Now that you have completed the initial steps, let's move on to actually configuring an account. To begin, we will open the property sheet for a user by selecting Start | Programs | Administrative Tools | Active Directory Users and Computers. Once there, open the user's folder and double-click on a user to bring up the property sheet (this should be a test account you've created). In the next section, we will explore the settings of the property sheet tabs.

The General tab, seen in Figure 9.3, is where you enter the first name, initials, last name, display name, description, office, telephone number, e-mail address, and Web page parameters for your user. The Other buttons allow you to enter additional telephone numbers or Web pages.

The Address tab (Figure 9.4) is where you enter the street, P.O. box, city, state/province, zip/postal code, and country/region parameters.

The Account tab is probably the most-used tab in the user property sheet. This is where you enter the user logon name, the domain, and the pre-Windows 2000 (NetBIOS) logon name and domain. Pressing the Logon Hours button provides a nice graphical user interface (GUI) utility to specify the permitted logon. With a few simple mouse-clicks and drags you can easily restrict an employee's hours from 8 AM–5 PM Monday through Friday as shown in Figure 9.5.

The Log On To button allows you to specify which workstations users can log on to. Just below that is the Account locked out check box. Under normal circumstances, this should appear grayed out. If checked, it means the account has had more incorrect logon attempts than permitted by your

Figure 9.3 The General tab.

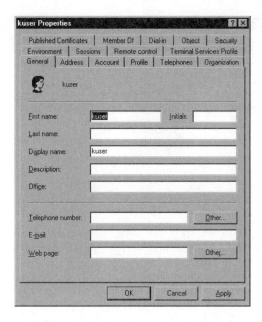

Figure 9.4 The Address tab.

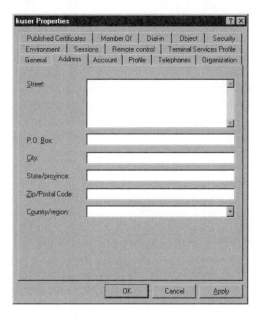

Figure 9.5 Restricting user logon times.

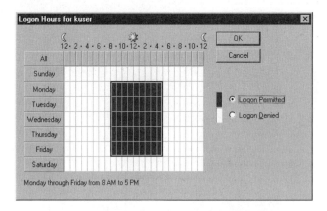

security policy. The user should be contacted immediately, and you should also check your logs to verify whether he or she forgot their password or if there has been an unauthorized access attempt. In a secure environment, the account will stay locked until reset by an administrator. Otherwise, it may reset in an hour or other length of time specified in your policy. In the box below Account locked out there are numerous account options. Forcing the user to change the password at next logon is useful if you need to expire an account immediately, or wish to give out a default password for new rollouts, which then must be changed immediately by the user.

Many companies also use the next Account tab, shown in Figure 9.6, to prevent the user from changing the password. This can be useful if you have a small or restricted environment and wish to assign passwords to users to ensure compliance with minimum standards, or if you have certain users and services that you don't want changed without notice. This should always be set on any disabled accounts (such as guest), and also for any services that need to log on to function. Several known automated "crack" utilities or unscrupulous persons attempting to manually crack your server may attempt to change the password to these services, many of which are already running with "admin" access. If these passwords need to be changed, they are normally done so by an administrator logged into the machine and are almost never done logged in as the service or disabled user.

Setting the password to never expire should not be done. Most companies should have a policy requiring password changes at least every 90–120 days. Even every 90 days is not often enough to prevent a brute-force attack if someone can obtain the SAM file from your server, or go undetected with an unlimited number of logons. Programs exist that allow an individual to crack any Windows password that is created using normal, single keystroke methods (alphanumeric and special characters) within a few days or even within hours, depending on the workstation used, if he or she can obtain the encrypted password file.

Figure 9.6 The Account tab.

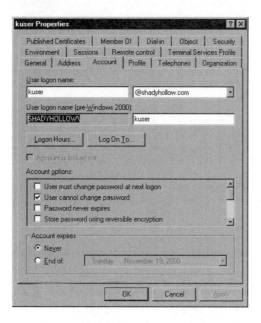

The main reason for requiring changes is that no matter how much we try to educate our users and admonish them not to share their passwords, many will still give their "secret" word out to their trusted coworkers, which leaves your system vulnerable at any time. At least with forced change, there is only a limited amount of time those users can gain access to your system with that password. Other settings in this tab allow you to disable the account. Disabling (rather than deleting) an inactive account allows you to restore account settings instantly in case you have workers on long absences, contract workers, and so on. At the very bottom of the Account tab, you can choose a specific date for an account to expire—a very handy utility. If an administrator knows an employee's last day is September 28th, he or she can set the account to automatically expire on that day and not worry about forgetting to disable it when the time comes.

The Profile tab shown in Figure 9.7 is used to set the profile path for "normal" windows network connections using standard Transmission Control Protocol/Internet Protocol (TCP/IP) or Network Basic Input/Output System (NetBIOS) file and print services. The location of the user's home directory is also set here. These settings do not affect the Remote Desktop Protocol (RDP) and ICA Terminal client settings.

Figure 9.7 The Profile tab.

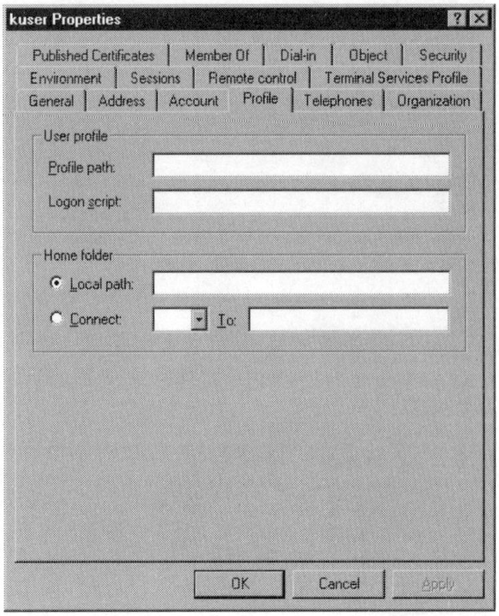

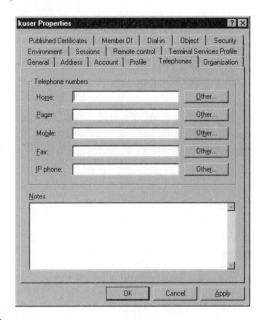

The Telephones tab shown in Figure 9.8 is used to set the user's telephone numbers for home, pager, mobile, fax, and IP phone. It also has a Notes field for comments. Each field also has an Other button for entering multiple numbers of the same type.

Figure 9.8 The Telephones tab.

The Organization tab shown in Figure 9.9 has fields for job title, department, company, manager name, and direct reports. The Manager field has a Change button that allows you to pick users from Active Directory.

Figure 9.9 The Organization tab.

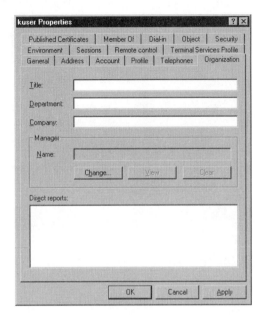

The Remote Control tab shown in Figure 9.10 is used for Terminal Services-type connections only. It contains a check box to enable or disable remote control (shadowing). This is also where you specify the level of control you want to have, either view only or interactive. Most important, this is where you can remove the requirement to obtain the user's permission before shadowing. By default, user permission is required for shadowing. Think about this before you do it, because turning off client notification could have undesirable consequences. Viewing a session allows you to remotely watch the monitored session in real-time. Interacting allows you to take control of the mouse, and directs your keyboard commands to the monitored session.

The Terminal Services Profile tab shown in Figure 9.11 is used to configure the location of the user profiles for Terminal Services users. A home directory for your Terminal Services users can also be specified and mapped at logon by setting the Connect field and specifying a directory share point. This tab also includes a check box to allow or disallow logon to the terminal server.

Figure 9.10 Remote Control (shadowing) tab.

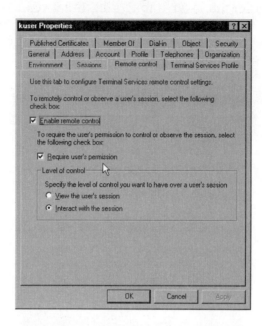

Figure 9.11 Terminal Services Profile tab.

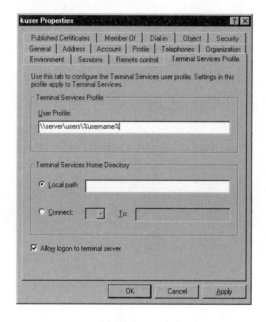

The Member Of tab shown in Figure 9.12 allows you to display and edit group membership for the user. Click the Add button, then choose additional groups from which to add or remove the user.

Figure 9.12 The Member Of tab.

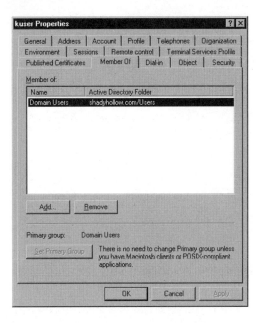

The Dial-in tab shown in Figure 9.13 specifies Remote Access Server (RAS) permissions. You may allow or deny RAS access, allow it to be controlled through Remote Access Policy, set callback options, and define IP Addresses and static routes for RAS clients. These settings do not apply to Terminal Service connections under normal configurations.

The Environment tab, shown in Figure 9.14, is used for Terminal Service connections and allows you to configure the startup environment for your users. In this window, you can specify a starting program for the client to run automatically at logon. If you do so, that will be the only program the user can run, and when the user closes that program, he or she will be logged off the server. You can also specify if you want to allow the client to connect client drives, connect client printers, and default to the main client printer at logon.

Figure 9.13 The Dial-in (RAS configuration) tab.

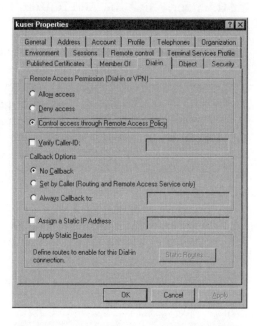

Figure 9.14 The Environment tab.

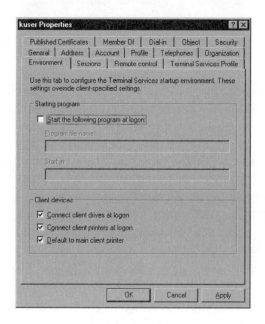

TIP

The settings in the Environment tab override those set on the Terminal Service Remote Desktop Protocol or Independent Computing Architecture (RDP or ICA) client software. This can be a useful feature if you need to restrict clients from saving files to their client machine's hard drives or from printing sensitive information. Mapping client drives is supported only with ICA connections; it is not available for RDP clients at this time. There are some add-ons for the Windows 2000 Server Resource Kit (Drmapsrv.EXE and Rdpclip.EXE) that provide enhanced clipboard, file copying, and client drive mapping capabilities, but they are not fully supported at this time and do not function using RDP (port 3389) only. They may provide some added functionality for some people. I would *not* recommend testing these on a production server. For more information or to download these tools, visit the Microsoft Web site at the following link:

www.microsoft.com/windows2000/library/resources/reskit/tools/default.asp

The Sessions tab, shown in Figure 9.15, is another tab used for Terminal Service connections, and it works for both RDP and ICA connections. The choices allow you to set minimum and maximum times for active sessions, idle sessions, and how long a disconnected session will be retained before resetting it. You are allowed to choose from the defaults of Never, one minute, five minutes, ten minutes, 15 minutes, 30 minutes, one hour, two hours, three hours, one day, two days, or enter your own time up to a maximum of 49 days and 17 hours. You also can set the action to take when a session limit is reached: either disconnect or end the session. You may allow reconnection from any client or only from the originating client.

Be careful when using these features, as they could be the source of a lot of user complaints. Even using what seems to be a reasonable idle session limit of one hour can sometimes mistakenly timeout. It seems especially prone to this when using custom database connectivity software; users perform a query that actually gets executed on a remote database server, and if the client doesn't provide any other keyboard or mouse input while waiting, the session can timeout waiting for the response from the database server to be returned to the client. On the other hand, limiting the active session time can be a very useful feature for Application Service Providers (ASPs) who need to monitor, and then disconnect, clients who are allocated a certain amount of prepaid time.

Figure 9.15 The Sessions tab.

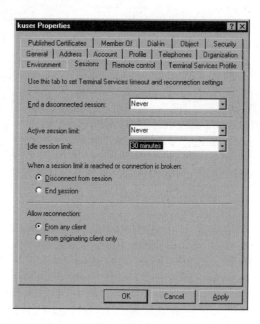

Using Citrix MetaFrame Utilities

Now let us discuss some of the Citrix MetaFrame utilities that are installed on top of the Windows 2000 Server, and how to utilize their various features.

Shadowing

The Shadowing (remote control) utility provides you with the ability to monitor and/or interact with a different user session. During a shadow session, the session being monitored is displayed in the shadower's session window. The monitored session can either be viewed only, or the shadower can interact with the monitored session, depending on the configuration. When placed in interactive mode, all keyboard and mouse strokes are passed to the monitored session.

Shadowing is one of the most powerful tools available on the MetaFrame server, and as is always the case with such tools, it has the potential for misuse. This should be taken into consideration when deciding whom to give shadowing permissions to. Microsoft Windows 2000 Terminal Services supports one-to-one shadowing (remote control) using the Remote Desktop Protocol 5 (RDP5). Like Microsoft, a Citrix MetaFrame server also allows for one-to-one shadowing using RDP from within the Citrix Server Administration Tool. Using the Independent Computing

Architecture (ICA) protocol, MetaFrame supports one-to-one, one-to-many, and many-to-one shadowing using the Shadow taskbar.

In previous versions, one could not establish shadow sessions from the console without installing the client and running a virtual session to itself to initiate the shadow session from. The MetaFrame taskbar now provides the ability to shadow user sessions from the console. The many-to-one shadow sessions provide for an excellent remote learning tool. Several students (or remote clients) can shadow one instructor who can teach from the comfort of his or her own office or training facility. Think of the savings in time and expenses that this could result in for companies that frequently fly clients or users across the country for software training.

WARNING

By default, a user being shadowed is prompted with a pop-up window telling them that \\server\user is requesting to control their session remotely and is given the option to allow or refuse the shadow session. This notification can be disabled in the connection profiles or in the individual user profile. Before disabling this notification, be sure that you have the authority and have obtained the necessary waivers from your users. Many companies now require a pop-up message at every initial server logon with some type of legal disclaimer and privacy waiver. This may also suffice for monitoring purposes, depending on the wording. Consult with your attorney before attempting to conduct any "covert" monitoring. Failure to do so could have serious legal ramifications.

There are two methods of establishing shadow sessions on Citrix MetaFrame. The first uses the ICA Shadow taskbar, and the second utilizes the Citrix Server Administration tool. The preferred method seems to be the first, using the Shadow taskbar, since it has the most features and the most flexibility.

Establishing a Shadow Session Using the Shadow Taskbar

Follow the steps in this section to establish a shadow session by using the Shadow taskbar.

1. Click on Start | Programs | MetaFrame Tools | Shadow Taskbar, or just click on the Shadow taskbar icon at the bottom of the MetaFrame toolbar.

2. This will start the Shadow taskbar. A new toolbar should appear at the top of your screen.

3. Click on the Shadow button and you will be presented with the Shadow Session option screen (Figure 9.16).

Figure 9.16 The Shadow taskbar and Shadow Session option screen.

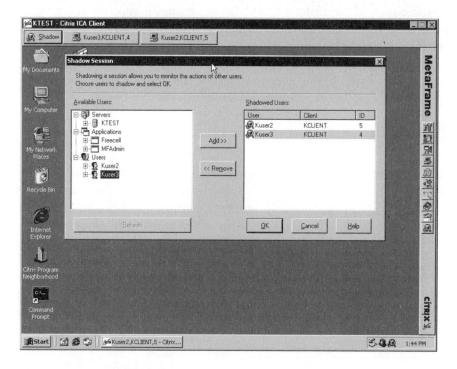

4. Expand the Users folder in the window on the left and highlight the user you wish to shadow. It may take a few seconds to enumerate the users and applications.

5. Click the Add button and repeat until all the users you wish to shadow appear in the right window.

6. Click the OK button to begin shadowing.

7. The user will be presented with a pop-up window, asking for permission to shadow them (this occurs by default; see previous Warning sidebar).

8. If the user accepts the shadow session or if notification has been disabled, you will now be able to view and/or interact with their session. You will also have a button added to the Shadow taskbar for each session you are monitoring. You can switch between sessions by clicking the respective button on the taskbar.

9. To log out of the shadow session, use the hotkey CTRL-* (default) or the hotkey you configured for the session. You may also right-click the Session button on the taskbar and click Stop Shadow.

Establishing a Shadow Session Using Citrix Server Administration

Now, let's establish a shadow session by using the Citrix Server Administration tool.

1. Click on Start | Programs | MetaFrame Tools | Citrix Server Administration, or just click the shortcut on the MetaFrame toolbar.

2. This will start the Citrix Server Administration tool in a new window (Figure 9.17). It may take a few seconds to enumerate the users and applications.

Figure 9.17 Citrix Server Administration.

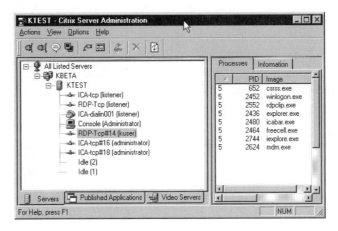

3. Right-click on the user you wish to shadow, then choose Shadow, or select the user you wish to monitor and choose Shadow from the Action pull-down menu.

4. The user will be presented with a pop-up window, asking for permission to shadow them (this occurs by default; see previous Warning sidebar).

5. If the user accepts the shadow session or if notification has been disabled, you will now be able to view and/or interact with their session.

6. To log out of the shadow session, use the hotkey CTRL -* (default) or the hotkey you configured for the session.

For IT Professionals

Expert Shadowing Rules

While shadowing is a great tool (and fun to play with), it does have its limitations. Here are some of the capabilities and limitations you will need to know in order to make the best use of the Shadow tool.

- The console session itself cannot be shadowed (a good thing).
- Sessions started using Citrix Server Administration are capable of only one-to-one sessions.
- Sessions can also be started and function the same using Terminal Services Manager (referred to as "remote control" instead of "shadow").
- You cannot shadow or enumerate RDP users with the Shadow taskbar, only ICA clients.
- Since the Shadow taskbar cannot enumerate RDP users, you cannot shadow RDP users from the console, nor can RDP support many-to-one or one-to-many sessions.
- If a user refuses the shadow session by answering NO or fails to respond YES to grant permission within approximately 30 seconds, the request will timeout, and in either case, return error message #7044 stating that "the request to control another session was denied."
- You may only start a shadow session from the same protocol, in other words, RDP to RDP, or ICA to ICA.
- You cannot shadow an ICA session from a RDP session, or vice versa.
- The shadowing session must be capable of an equal or greater video resolution than the session being monitored or the shadowing operation will fail.
- Be sure you have the hardware required for the task, as running multiple shadow sessions can use a large amount of server memory and system resources. Many companies that have a need for numerous shadow sessions usually dedicate one or more servers to the task. Load balancing can be extremely helpful in this situation.

Continued

■ Only administrators have the permissions to shadow other users by default. To grant other users shadow rights, create a special group, then assign that group shadow permissions in the Advanced Security tab of Connection Profiles. See the section titled "Specifying Shadow Permissions to a Connection Profile" for a detailed explanation.

Applying Group Policy

Group Policy is a feature used in Windows 2000 to enhance and control users' desktops and computers. Group Policy is enabled by the Windows 2000 Active Directory Service and can also be used with MetaFrame servers, installed as either domain controllers or member servers. The procedures for using Group Policies are the same on either platform, so any procedures we discuss in this section can be used in any configuration of the two.

Group Policy was designed and is used by administrators to help centralize administration of user desktop configurations, reduce user support requirements, and enhance the security of network systems. It does this by allowing the administrator or administrators to customize and control users' access to registry-based settings, security settings, software installation, and maintenance settings. They can automate many tasks using logon, logoff, startup and shutdown scripts, and operating system installation, and can perform Internet Explorer Maintenance.

User data files and folders can be redirected from the user's hard drive to network drives, where backups can be performed, or preconfigured desktop displays can be pushed to new users. All of these options are available with different levels of access and control being provided to different users and locations depending on the requirements. This flexibility allows for a developer to have complete (or near complete) access to their desktop and all kinds of applications, while restricting a data-entry operator to only the two or three applications they need to perform their job.

The features and controls provided by Group Policy are valuable to MetaFrame administrators because the server becomes the user's desktop machine when they are using a thin-client, Terminal Service Client, or ICA Client connection. This leaves the server vulnerable to inadvertent user damage. This is where Group Policy comes into play.

We will not go into a complete detailed discussion of all the finer aspects and programming issues of Group Policy in this chapter. That could again be an entire book in itself. We will try to focus on how to get started with Group Policies, how they can improve the user's experience with MetaFrame, and how they can benefit the MetaFrame administrator. From there you should be able to develop your own policies and apply them in a manner consistent with your environment.

Let's start off with some of the differences between Active Directory Group Policy and the old style NT 4.0 and Win9x System Policy editor. NT 4.0 allowed you to specify user and computer configurations that were stored in the registry. While some of the same types of things can be controlled, a look at Table 9.1 shows why the newer Group Policy method is the preferred method.

Table 9.1 System Policy and Group Policy Features

NT 4.0 System Policy Features	Active Directory (AD) Group Policy Features
NT 4.0 policies are applied to domains.	AD policies can be associated with sites, domains, and organizational units (OUs).
NT 4.0 policies can be controlled further by security group membership.	AD policies affect all users and computers in the site, domain, or OU where applied. They can also be controlled by security group membership.
Policies in NT 4.0 are not secure. A user can change policies with the registry editor (Regedit.EXE).	AD policies are secure. Only an administrator can change the settings. Updates can be pushed to clients on scheduled basis.
The settings are persistent (sometimes longer than intended). Settings persist until the policy setting is reversed, or until a user manually edits the registry. Often this is not the desired behavior.	AD policies are removed and rewritten whenever policy changes. They are removed when a policy no longer applies. This prevents a "burn" or a permanent change to the client machine registry.
NT 4.0 policies are limited to mandated desktop behavior based on the registry changes applied by the administrator.	AD policies can enhance the user's computing environment by allowing for more finely tuned desktop control.

For IT Professionals

Administrative Template (.ADM) files

Like NT 4.0, Windows 2000 uses Administrative Templates as part of its Group Policy structure. Some policies in NT 4.0, if mistakenly enabled, could require a visit to each desktop to restore or change back to the setting you want. Windows 2000 policies act like a filter applied over the registry, rather than a brute force overwrite like NT 4.0, and can easily be removed in seconds from your server configuration. Windows 2000 accomplishes this partly by implementing a new Administrative Template style. By default, three .ADM files are installed in the Group Policy console: System.ADM, Inetres.ADM, and Conf.ADM. Conf.ADM is not loaded by default and contains settings for Microsoft NetMeeting. Inetres.ADM contains settings for Internet Explorer. System.ADM contains settings for a variety of other features. This new style .ADM file still allows you to edit the template file and add to the existing 450 settings if you need to. However, any additional registry settings should be placed in \Software\Policies or \Software\Microsoft\Windows\CurrentVersion\Policies to avoid those unwanted persistent registry modifications. Also for this reason, you should *not* attempt to use any old NT 4.0-style .ADM files with Windows 2000. For more information about .ADM files, the Windows 2000 Resource Kit CD-ROM contains a searchable reference file, GP.CHM, which has many details about the Administrative Template settings.

Understanding Group Policy and Active Directory

Understanding how Group Policies function is a key factor in designing your Active Directory structure. I would strongly suggest that *before* you implement or upgrade an existing network infrastructure, you seek professional help either to assist in designing your Active Directory structure or by attending certified training programs in Active Directory. Small details in the way you design and implement Active Directory now could either save considerable time and effort in the future or be the source of a large overhaul project sooner than desired.

One of the most important design issues is group, group, and group-some more. Try to adjust your thinking and divide everything into groups.

The more ways and types of groups you can come up with, the more fine-grained control you will have. Now think of these groups as containers; containers are what Active Directory uses to store objects in.

There are two types of Group Policy objects, local and nonlocal. Every Windows 2000-based computer has only one local Group Policy object. In the section below, we will be discussing nonlocal Group Policies and how to configure them in a domain environment.

Group Policies can be applied (linked) to OU, Domain, and Site containers in Active Directory. They are applied in the following order:

1. Local

2. Site

3. Domain

4. Organizational Unit

The order in which policies are applied is important to remember because by default, policy applied *later* overwrites policy applied *earlier* if the setting was either Enabled or Disabled. Settings that are Not Configured are skipped and the setting applied earlier is allowed to persist. Organizational Unit profiles have the highest precedence and are applied beginning at the highest OU (in the Active Directory tree) containing the user or computer account, and ending with the one closest to the user or computer object. If multiple policies are applied at an OU level, they are applied in the order specified by the administrator.

A Group Policy object linked to a site applies to all domains at the site. A Group Policy object linked to a domain applies directly to all users and computers in the domain and by inheritance to all users and computers in any OUs below the domain. A Group Policy object linked to an OU applies directly to all users and computers in that OU and by inheritance to all users and computers in any OUs below that OU.

It is not possible to link a Group Policy object to a "generic" container. These are generally considered the *built-in* containers. If you look at the folders in the Active Directory window, the generic folder icons will look like a "plain" folder. The icon for an OU looks almost the same, but there is a small book on the folder. This means you cannot place a Group Policy directly on the built-in Users or Computers containers. They will, however, inherit a policy that is applied to the domain they are under.

TIP

Policy inheritance is a default behavior. There are, of course, ways to either force or prevent Group Policies from affecting certain groups of users or computers. The No Override and Enforce Policy Inheritance settings are powerful tools but excessive use can be confusing to administrators and should be avoided when possible. Sometimes, however, using these tools can be the most effective solution. As with any custom settings that may not be readily apparent to other administrators, be sure to document use of these tools and develop a policy or set a standard procedure for when they will be used.

Several of the settings available under the Security portion of the Group Policy will be ignored if linked at the OU level. To be effective, all of the settings under the Security section should be applied to the Domain section. This includes settings for password policy, audit policy, user rights, event log, and security options.

Computer policy processing is completed before the CTRL-ALT-DEL logon box is displayed. User policies are completed before the shell is active and available for the user to interact with. Windows 2000 Group Policies are processed every 90 minutes by default, so if a user changes something that is mandated by domain policy, it will be set back to the domain policy within the 90-minute time frame. This can be changed under Computer Configuration | Administrative Templates | System | Group Policy | Group Policy Refresh Interval for Computers. There is a time limit of 60 minutes for all of the client-side extensions to finish processing policy. A client-side extension that is not finished after 60 minutes will be stopped and the policy settings will not be processed. There is no policy setting to change the client timeout setting.

Creating a Custom MMC Console for Group Policy

In order for you to manage Group Policies, you will have to manually add the snap-in by creating a custom MMC Console. This is almost the same simple process that we covered earlier when creating a custom MMC console for Active Directory. To begin, click on the Start button and choose Run. Then, type **mmc** into the Open window. This will open a new, blank MMC console window. Next, from the Console pull-down menu, choose Add/Remove Snap-in. This will open an empty Add/Remove Snap-in window. Next, click the Add button, and the Add Standalone Snap-in window shown in Figure 9.18 will open and display the available standalone snap-ins.

Figure 9.18 Adding the Group Policy snap-in.

Choose Group Policy. Click OK and you can now choose the Local Computer policy object or you can click the Browse button to browse local domains for their policy and then pick from the available policies (Figure 9.19).

Figure 9.19 Browsing the domain policies.

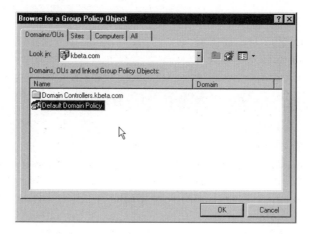

You can save this console using a meaningful name, and it will automatically be added to your Administrative Tools program listing. Click OK to open the Group Policy snap-in you just created and you can start configuring your user environment (Figure 9.20).

Figure 9.20 Group Policy snap-in.

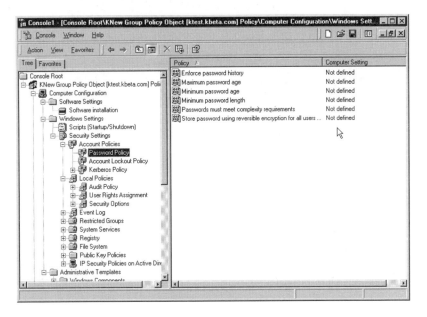

Notice that by default, all of the Computer settings are "Not defined." This means that when the policy is applied, they will be ignored. Simply double-click on an entry to modify and then link your policy to the container you wish to apply it to. The best way to learn Group Policies is by doing. Remember, it's a lot more forgiving than the old NT 4.0 System Policies. If a policy doesn't work the way you thought it would, or breaks something, simply remove it and no harm is done. Group Policy may seem difficult and like there is a lot to learn, but if you take it a little bit at a time, you will find that it will save you hours of workstation configuration time.

We discussed earlier how policies could be applied either locally or nonlocally. In the next example, we have added three snap-ins to our Group Policy MMC console. We will use the Local Computer Policy, the New Group Policy Object (created as a new policy object for the kbeta.com domain instead of using the Default Domain Policy), and the Active Directory Users and Computers snap-ins to demonstrate how inheritance works and how you can view the "effective" policy settings for a computer.

Looking in the right-hand window of Figure 9.21, we see three columns. The Policy column defines the policy for us. In this example, we are looking specifically at the Password Policy setting. The Local Setting displays the default policy settings for the local machine's password history (0), maximum age (0), minimum age (0), minimum password length (0), and complexity requirements (Disabled).

Figure 9.21 Local Group Policy settings.

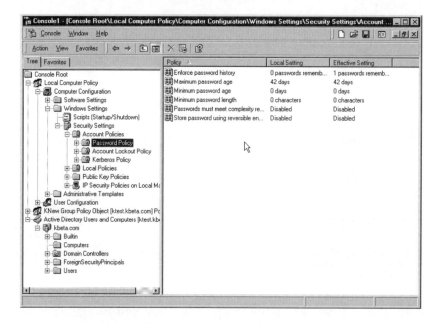

In the next example in Figure 9.22, we see what happens after we apply a policy to the domain with different settings for the Password Policy. The Local Settings remain the same, but the Effective Settings have now changed to the values we applied to the domain. In all cases (other than the exceptions noted above), domain policies will take precedence over local machine policies.

This allows administrators to have certain settings become mandatory throughout the domain. These same features can be applied to services, registry settings, file and folder permissions, and virtually every aspect of all the domain's servers and computers. Extreme care should be taken when disabling services to ensure that they are not required by other specialty servers or workstations, or that policy inheritance is blocked for those special requirements. This is where grouping and proper Active Directory design and forethought can really pay off for you.

Figure 9.22 Effective Group Policy settings.

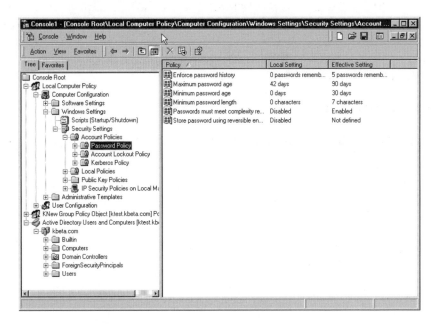

To get into more detail with policy settings, let's look at some of the user settings. In Figure 9.23, if we go to User Configuration | Administrative Templates | Windows Components | System, we have the option to Run Only Allowed Windows Applications. This is a recommended setting to help secure your system, especially if you have one group of clients connecting to your server from the Internet or from an "outside" corporate link.

Most "outside" clients will only need access to a few applications, and it would probably be an unnecessary security risk to give them "Full Desktop" access. To restrict them, you need only add the applications you want them to run and then apply this policy to their group container. Your corporate users will still enjoy the full desktop or whatever other applications you have granted them access to, while your server and data will be protected from would-be intruders. There are many more such restrictions, some of which you may want to apply to your corporate or "inside" users as well, such as removing the Run command, displaying a "Logoff" choice, or even disabling the ability to change their home page. Figure 9.24 shows a few more choices.

Figure 9.23 Restricting users to "Run Only Allowed Applications."

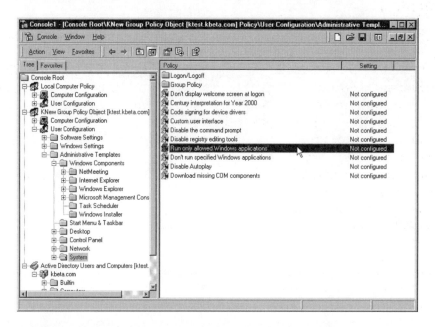

Figure 9.24 Additional user policy restrictions.

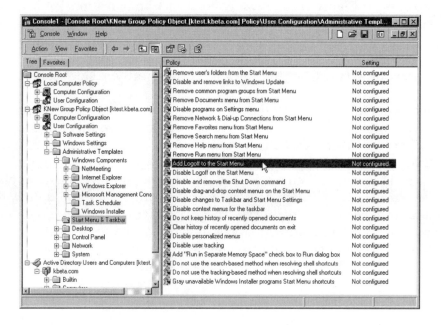

WARNING

While the Run Only Allowed Windows Applications is a good security setting to begin with, it does not provide ironclad security by itself. This setting only restricts users from running applications started from Windows Explorer. This does not prevent them from running processes that are started from other sources such as Task Manager. It also does not prevent them from running "non-allowed" applications if they are started from a command prompt. If you are using this setting, in most cases you should use the "Disable the Command Promp" setting also. You may even go so far as to also check the permissions of all sensitive .EXE files on the server and remove user permissions from the files themselves when deemed appropriate.

As the last example of user policies, we will show the location for the "Logon Warning." If you go to Windows Settings | Security Settings | Local Policies | Security Options, in the right-hand window (see Figure 9.25) you will see "Message text for users attempting to log on," and "Message title for users attempting to log on."

Figure 9.25 System logon warning text.

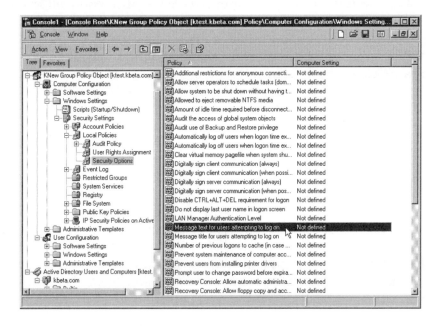

If you put text in these values, this will be displayed as a pop-up window to the user at logon. This is a great place for No Trespass, Security, and Privacy warnings. Once configured and enabled, every user must click OK on the pop-up window in acknowledgement of your warning to continue before being asked for their username and password. If worded correctly, this should meet most legal requirements for monitoring and notification of trespass to unauthorized users.

Connection Profiles and Session Configuration

Part of controlling the user's visual experience and restricting what he or she can do during a session is managed from within the Connection Configuration. Some of the more advanced features are also managed here. We discussed in another portion of the book how access to the MetaFrame server could be allowed or denied based on a connection protocol. Many MetaFrame administrators restrict normal users to only one protocol (usually TCP/IP, but it depends on your network topology) and reserve one or more connection types strictly for administrator connections. Obviously, if you are on a Novell-only network, you would have to provide user connections over IPX, but you could still reserve RDP connections for administrators only. I'm sure quite a few MetaFrame administrators still have a modem attached to their servers for emergency dial-in connections that they have restricted for use only to themselves. This is all done from within the Citrix Connection Configuration utility.

While many of the tools for a "plain" Windows Terminal Server and a MetaFrame server have been interchangeable, the Terminal Services Configuration tool for Windows 2000 and the Connection Configuration tool for MetaFrame have numerous differences and are not interchangeable. We will be discussing only the MetaFrame version of the tool here.

To begin, open the tool by clicking Start | Programs | MetaFrame Tools | Citrix Connection Configuration. This will open the main configuration window shown in Figure 9.26.

In the window shown in Figure 9.27, you will see the different connection types available to clients. To modify a client connection, we can double-click on the selected connection or select Edit from the Connection pull-down menu.

In the Edit Connection window, we have a blank for comments (such as "Users connection" or "Admins Only!"). We can also choose the network adapter on which we wish to allow connections of this type. This can be

Figure 9.26 Citrix Connection Configuration window.

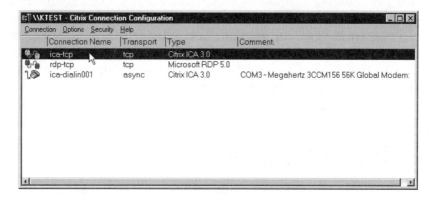

Figure 9.27 Editing connection properties.

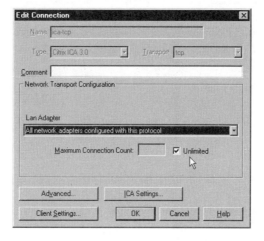

useful with multihomed computers—for instance, some users on an IPX-only network could connect to the MetaFrame server using IPX on one Network Interface Card (NIC), while other users could connect through a different NIC using TCP/IP only. Some system resources can be recovered by limiting the maximum connection count to the number of licenses you own; this could be a benefit especially on small servers that may be low on available resources to begin with. We will discuss the other buttons separately.

The Advanced button allows us to enable or disable logons to this connection type altogether, configure an autologon (a high security risk and not recommended in most environments). We also have the option of setting the timeout settings, initial program settings, shadowing, and reconnect options here, or allowing these to be inherited from the client/ user configuration settings. If specified here, these settings will override the client/users settings. A recommended performance enhancement is to disable wallpaper here; this can slow performance noticeably if complex wallpapers are used.

This is also where you must set the security requirements for your connection. This allows you to specify the encryption level for your connection. The default level is "Basic" encryption, as shown in Figure 9.28. This is considered weak by today's standards, as discussed in Chapter 6, and stronger encryption levels using the RC5 algorithm are available as an add-on with Citrix SecureICA. The SecureICA product provides 40-, 56-, or 128-bit RC5 encryption. If the server is configured to allow a minimum of 56-bit encryption, the client must connect with either a 56-bit or 128-bit SecureICA product or logon will fail. Full 56-bit and 128-bit RC5 encryption capabilities will be included as standard with the new Feature Release 1 (FR1) server update and version 6.00.910 of the client.

Figure 9.28 Advanced Connection Properties window.

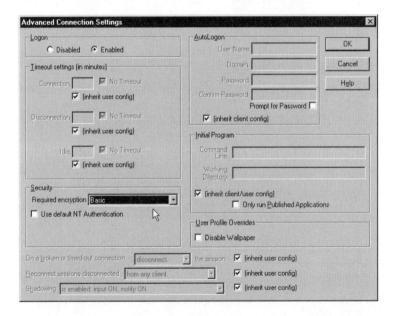

The ICA Settings button allows you to set the sound quality for ICA connections (Figure 9.29). Sound is not supported over RDP connections. There are three available settings.

Medium This is the default setting. All waveform data sent to the client is compressed to a maximum of 64 Kbps before being transmitted to the client. This may result in a slight decrease in sound quality played on the client machine, but will reduce the Central Processing Unit (CPU) utilization on the host machine. This setting is recommended for most LAN-based connections and some medium- to high-speed WAN connections.

High This setting plays all waveform data at its native data rate. Sounds at the highest quality level will require about 1.3 Mbps of bandwidth. This is pretty much equal to the amount of throughput achieved by most T1 connections. This is not recommended for use unless plenty of bandwidth is available and sound quality is of high importance. Don't think about using this on a WAN connection unless you have greater than T1 bandwidth on both ends, or are going to dedicate the T1 usage exclusively for this traffic. The adage, "Don't try this at home" certainly applies here, unless you keep it on your own network where it can be useful for bandwidth monitoring, load testing, and other purposes. This setting can also increase CPU utilization, not due to the sound processing itself, but due to the amount of network traffic being transmitted.

Low This is the recommended setting for modem and most low-bandwidth WAN connections. All waveform data sent to the client is compressed to a maximum of 16 Kbps before being transmitted to the client. This amount of compression results in a severe decrease of the sound quality played back on the client. The lower data rate allows for low-bandwidth connections. This also reduces CPU load on the host about the same amount as the medium setting due to the compression being used.

Figure 9.29 ICA sound settings.

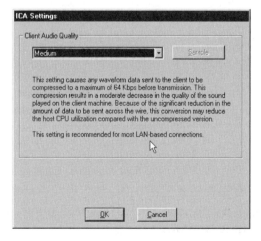

The Client Settings window shown in Figure 9.30 allows us to configure Client Mappings to Drives, Printers, Com Ports, LPT Ports, Clipboard, and Audio. These settings will override client settings (unless set to inherit user config). Log-on time can be reduced significantly by disabling mappings not being used, especially COM port mapping, and restricting the "Other Options" setting to only connect the client's main printer.

Figure 9.30 Client settings and mappings.

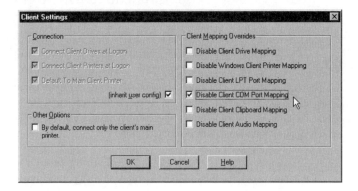

Specifying Shadow Permissions to a Connection Profile

By default, normal users do not have permissions to shadow other users. This is an advanced feature normally reserved for administrators only. Under some circumstances, however, you may find it necessary to grant shadow permissions to other users. This could be for temporary or long-term usage, such as with a distance learning program or corporate training over the WAN. Obviously, it would not be wise to give remote users—and probably not even your own users—full administrative rights over your server just so they can shadow. It may not be wise to leave these permissions on all the time, or long term, since you can't control whom they can shadow. If you do need this, special configurations and restrictions may have to be placed on the server or the domain. While it would be nice to have this added as a simple check box to the user property sheet, we can't have everything. The steps to grant shadow permissions are simple, but can be hard to locate and remember.

1. First of all, create a new group. We will call ours *shadow group*.

2. Next, add any users you wish to have shadow rights to the shadow group you just created.

3. Now all we have to do is assign them the permissions.

4. Since we are still in the Citrix Connection Configuration section, highlight the connection type you want to configure and select

Security from the Permissions pull-down menu from the main Connection Configuration Screen. You should see the ica-tcp Permissions window shown in Figure 9.31.

Figure 9.31 Assigning shadow users.

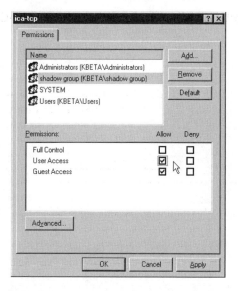

5. Click the Add button and add your "shadow group" from the user list. By default, it will be given Guest Access.

6. Check the box to grant User Access as well.

7. Click the Advanced button to bring up the advanced permissions window.

8. Highlight your shadow group and click on the View/Edit button as shown in Figure 9.32.

9. After clicking the View/Edit button, you will see a permission page with Query, Logon, Message, and Connect selected. Here is where you also want to select Shadow, as shown in Figure 9.33.

10. That's it! Click OK until you're back to the connection configuration screen and your new shadow group will be ready to start watching. Be sure to instruct the users on proper shadowing methods. You may also want to configure shadowing for view only if your application requirements allow it; this will keep the shadowers from inadvertently interacting with the monitored sessions.

Figure 9.32 Advanced user permissions.

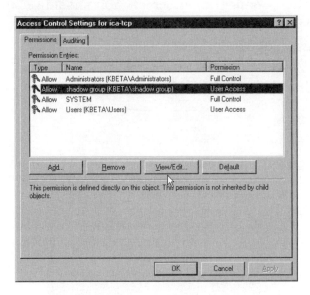

Figure 9.33 Granting the shadow permission.

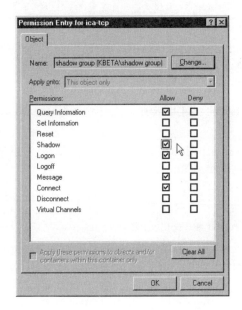

Summary

In this chapter, we have looked at many different ways the user experience can be customized and enhanced using Citrix MetaFrame. You can use Group Policies not just to save you configuration time, but also for providing different levels of permissions to different users. You can use shadowing to provide user assistance and distance learning.

Consider the network design, shown in Figure 9.34, where a company is able to use MetaFrame servers located in its public Demilitarized Zone (DMZ) to securely provide access to several external, DMZ, and even internal sensitive database servers, to users located on its internal corporate network, to dial-up users, and even to clients remotely on the Internet all from the same load-balanced MetaFrame Server Farm. By using Group Policies, remote, noncorporate Internet users can be restricted to connecting to the MetaFrame server and to only seeing one or two applications provided to them by the corporation. The MetaFrame servers could then connect them to Web pages or read-only copies of internal databases housed in the public DMZ. At the same time, a corporate user can log on to the same MetaFrame server and be provided with a full suite of applications, and even be granted access to the internal database systems securely.

Let's discuss in more detail exactly how this is done and how it meets today's security needs. For more details on this design, let's assume the Internet firewall is correctly configured, having all ports blocked from the Internet other than those needed for essential services into the Public DMZ. There is also a firewall in place restricting the dial-up users' access to the public DMZ and the private corporate network. As a "fail-proof" line of defense, they also have an additional firewall between the Public DMZ and their private internal network. There are Intrusion Detection Systems (IDSs) installed in both the public DMZ and the private internal network.

In a configuration like this, corporate workers can access the "extranet" MetaFrame DMZ servers and any other internal or external resources directly from their desktop machines. The private corporate network machines are inaccessible directly from the Internet and can only be accessed by passing through the MetaFrame server, which acts as an "Application Proxy." Corporate workers at home or traveling on the road could then access the network from the Internet, or from a direct analog/ISDN dial-up connection into the DMZ, and be presented with exactly the same desktop view, applications, and access to resources that he or she had from the desk at the office.

Figure 9.34 Secure extranet design with MetaFrame.

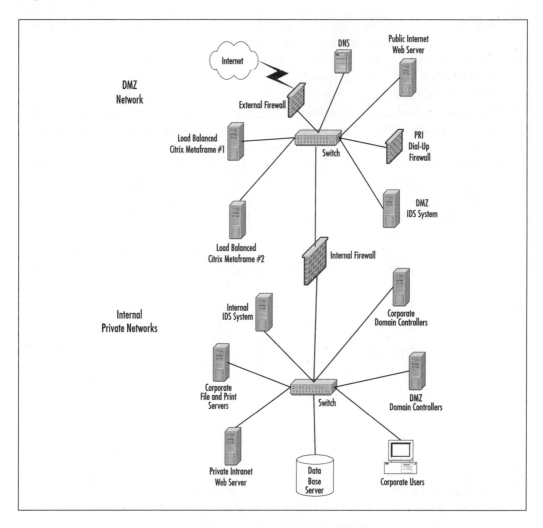

All this could be provided securely using the latest RC5 128-bit encryption. If they desired, they could even use "single–sign-on" so when the user logs in to the public DMZ MetaFrame server, he or she is authenticated by an "internal" protected domain controller. Users will not have to remember multiple passwords, and may appreciate having the number of them cut down substantially. Also, in this example, the company could provide secure access to highly sensitive intranet servers that are protected on the private network, and can be accessed (although inaccessible from the Internet directly) by their corporate users having the proper credentials and policies by passing through the MetaFrame servers.

FAQs

Q: I don't seem to have the Active Directory Users and Computers tool on my Programs list under Administrative Tools. How can I manage domain user accounts?

A: The machine you are on is not a domain controller. This choice would only be available in the Programs list of domain controllers. You may still manage Active Directory by either using RDP or ICA to run a remote session and use the tools on the Domain Controller, or you may create a custom MMC console to manage Active Directory from a member workstation or server (which requires admin privileges). See the section in this chapter on "Creating a Custom MMC Console."

Q: We want to use MetaFrame ICA shadowing for training, but normal users are unable to shadow—it only seems to work for administrators. Why?

A: Normal users must be assigned the rights to shadow. This is done in the Connection Profiles Advanced Security tab. Create a separate group called *shadow group* and assign it the rights to shadow. Then place the users you want to shadow in that group. Once permissions to the group are assigned, you can just drop users in and out of it to grant and deny shadow permissions.

Q: I tried to set the password policy for our Developers group to using complex passwords and seven characters, but it doesn't seem to work.

A: The password policy is located in the Security section of Group Policies. For the Security portion of the Group Policy to be effective, it must be linked to the domain. If it is linked to an OU, it will be ignored.

Q: I want to edit some Group Policies, but can't find the Group Policy Administration tool.

A: Group Policies must be edited using the MMC console, either as a stand-alone console, or from within the "properties" of an Active Directory container object. See the section in this chapter on "Creating a Custom MMC Console."

Q: We rolled out a new application and it seems to bring down our T1 whenever users connect to it.

A: Check the settings for client audio and make sure they are not set to High (1.3Mbps). Medium (64Kbps) or Low (16Kbps) settings should be used for most WAN connections.

Chapter 10

Configuring Terminal Sessions

Solutions in this chapter:

- Creating Sessions
- Configuring Sessions
- Applying Security across All Sessions

Introduction

In a thin-client environment, a virtual session is created when a workstation connects to the server. These sessions are configured to match the environment. The components of the session that can be configured to enhance the session's performance include:

- Protocols
- Availability
- Security and shadowing
- Disconnection and timeouts

The configuration of your Terminal Services sessions can prove to be quite a daunting task. As such, it may take you a while to come up with a configuration that is best suited for your environment. In some cases, the default configuration will suffice, but in others a large amount of planning and configuration may be necessary.

Security may be one of the most important configuration tasks you will face. Every environment requires some type of security policy. Your security policy will be based not only on how strict you want to be but also on the users that will access your system and on how they will be accessing the system.

Creating Sessions

Your client connections will determine what clients can connect and what manner they will use to connect. A default connection is created when you install Terminal Services. You can configure this connection and create new connections using the Terminal Services Configuration application.

Before we go through the process of creating a new connection, let's talk a little about Terminal Services user sessions. Before you implement your Terminal Services Server, you should come up with a plan for how many users will be accessing your server and what method they will use to attach. This information is what will guide you in creating your Terminal Services Connection and configuring user sessions.

First, make sure your hardware will be able to support the number of users you plan to have connected. A 500MHz Pentium III processor can handle about 40 user sessions, each user session will require a minimum of 20MB of RAM. This 20MB is what is required just to establish a session and log on. As the user begins to run applications, more memory will be needed. A typical user will require about 40MB of RAM to log on and run applications.

Next, you must make sure you have satisfied the necessary licensing requirements. You have two choices for licensing: per server and per seat. With per-server licensing, there is a limit on the number of simultaneous connections that can be made to your server. With per-seat licensing, every client that will ever connect to your server will have to have its own client access license. For all of your network clients, I suggest per-seat licensing. For all of your Internet clients, I suggest per-server licensing.

Next, you must decide what types of connections you want to create. Keep in mind that Windows 2000 Terminal Services does not support the variety of clients supported by Citrix MetaFrame. With Terminal Services, you are limited to TCP connections (using RDP) and modem (or dial-up) connections:

Now let's create a connection:

1. Right-click on connections in Terminal Services Configuration shown in Figure 10.1.

2. Select New. You will then be brought to the Terminal Services Welcome screen shown in Figure 10.2.

Figure 10.1 Terminal Services Configuration window.

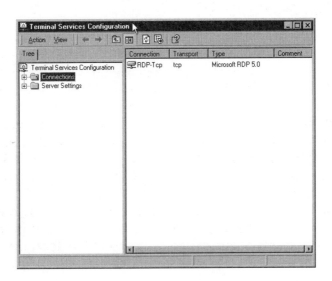

Figure 10.2 Terminal Services Welcome screen.

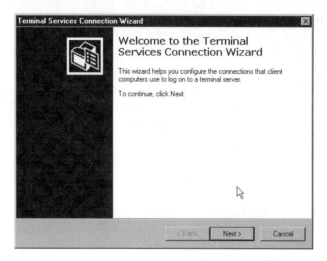

3. Next, you must select a connection type. The default available with Terminal Services is a Remote Desktop Protocol (RDP) 5.0 connection (Figure 10.3).

4. Now you are asked what encryption level you want applied to your connection (Figure 10.4).

Figure 10.3 Setting Terminal Services connection type.

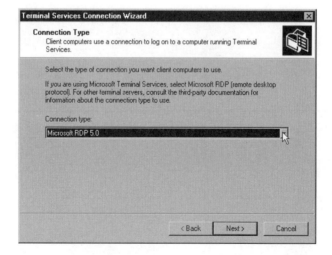

Figure 10.4 Terminal Services data encryption settings.

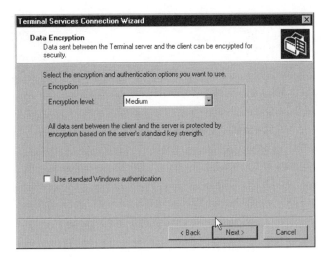

5. Following this, you are asked what Remote Control accessibility you want to install, as seen in Figure 10.5.

6. Next, you must specify a name for the connection and a transport type (Figure 10.6). The default transport type for Terminal Services is TCP.

Figure 10.5 Terminal Services remote control settings.

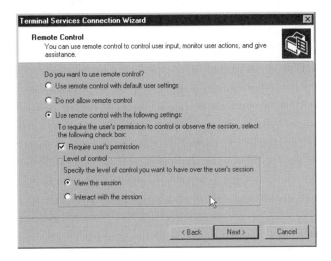

Figure 10.6 Terminal Services transport settings.

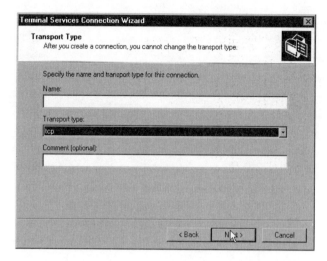

7. Your connection can be available to all network adapters, or only the adapters you specify, as seen in Figure 10.7.

8. The wizard will then let you know you have finished creating your connection (Figure 10.8).

Figure 10.7 Terminal Services network adapter settings.

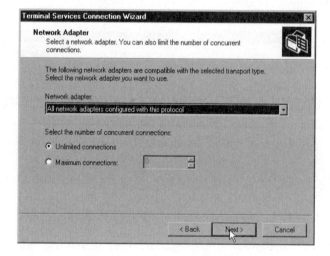

Figure 10.8 Completion of the Terminal Services connection.

NOTE

Each connection must have a unique connection type: either transport or adapter. If you attempt to create a duplicate connection without changing any of these parameters, you will receive an error similar to that shown in Figure 10.9. Many administrators think they can create two connections for the same logical connection and set different security or user parameters for each. This is not possible. If you only have one logical connection, you must set individual user or group parameters on that one connection in order to have different users run different settings.

Figure 10.9 Duplicate connection error.

Configuring Sessions

Once you have created your Terminal Services sessions, you can begin the configuration and customization of those sessions. Sessions can be configured on a per-server basis, a per-connection basis, per-group basis, or a per-user basis.

Configuration on a per-connection basis is performed using Terminal Services Configuration. Simply right-click on the connection you want to configure and select Properties. The first tab you will see is the General tab (Figure 10.10).

Figure 10.10 Connection Properties General tab.

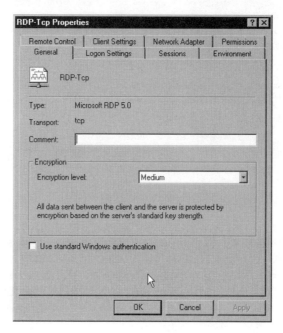

The General tab will give you the connection name, connection type, and the transport used for the connection. You can also enter a comment here, which should be something to help you better identify the connection. Your comment may provide a clue as to what users will connect to using the connection. If the connection is for users in your Miami office, then you may want to put something to that effect in the comment field.

The encryption level can also be set here, and the default is medium-level encryption. There are three levels of encryption that can be given to your connections: low, medium, and high. Low-level encryption is a one-way encryption, from the server to the client, that uses either a 40-bit or a 56-bit encryption key. Medium-level encryption is a two-way encryption that uses either a 40-bit or 56-bit encryption key. High-level encryption uses a 128-bit key.

You are also given the option of selecting whether or not to use standard Windows NT authentication for the connection. The type of Windows NT authentication used is determined by the environment your Terminal Services Server is running in. If your Terminal Services Server is running in an Active Directory environment, then directory authentication will be used. If your Terminal Services Server is running in a traditional Windows NT Domain model, then domain authentication will be used. If your Terminal Services Server is a stand-alone server, then users will only be authenticated against the local user database. If you have some third-party authentication software installed, you can elect to use that instead of using the Windows NT authentication.

The Sessions tab allows you to set session limits (Figure 10.11). You can limit how long a session can remain idle before it is logged off. This will keep your connections from being tied up by users who forget to log off. Automatically logging off idle users will allow the connection to be used by someone else. This is particularly important when using modem lines for dialing in, because only one person can be attached to a modem at a time. If you don't use a modem line, this may not be an issue. Disconnecting will also be beneficial if you are using per-server licensing, which limits concurrent user connections.

Figure 10.11 Connection Properties Sessions tab.

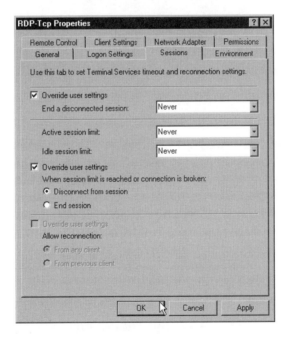

The way users may circumvent the idle timeout is by periodically moving the mouse so that the connection doesn't appear to be idle. This is why you can also set an active session limit. This will limit the amount of time a user can stay connected, whether idle or not. This will help to prevent users from monopolizing a connection.

WARNING

It is highly recommended that your Terminal Services Server not be a Directory Server or a Domain Controller. Not only can this cause performance issues, but installation and configuration issues as well. It may also represent a security risk.

The Session tab also allows you to configure what will happen when a user gets disconnected. You can either have the session end or leave the session running. Ending the session will prevent the server from being tied up by a user that disconnected without logging off. If you leave the session running, then users have the ability to reconnect to the same session at a later time. My advice is to end the sessions of regular users, but allow sessions started by administrators and company executives to stay running. Administrators are often running some process, inventory, or report that must run for an extended period of time. If the session is ended when the administrator disconnects, the administrator must leave his or her session open in order to run that report. If you allow the user to disconnect without ending the session, he or she can start the report, disconnect the session, and then return to the session once the report has finished.

NOTE

If you are not having trouble with sessions being unavailable or with lack of bandwidth, then there may not be a reason for you to set session limits. Remember, when you disconnect a user, that user must then re-establish his or her session. Some users may complain about being disconnected and having to reconnect. So, if it is not necessary, don't do it. The only thing you would accomplish by setting limits would be to make your job more difficult because of user complaints.

The Environment tab (Figure 10.12) is used to control two things. First, it will allow you to set what program will execute when the session starts. This allows you to configure a session to access only a certain published application. If no program is specified, then the session will begin with a basic Terminal Services desktop. The user can then execute any application he or she has rights to. The Environment tab can also be used to disable the user wallpaper on the client. Disabling wallpaper will help reduce bandwidth and the time needed for transmissions; thereby increasing the speed and responsiveness of the session. Remember, the more data that has to be transmitted during each session, the slower the session will be. The bitmaps often used for wallpaper can be quite large and will consume your bandwidth very quickly.

Figure 10.12 The Connection Properties Client Environment tab.

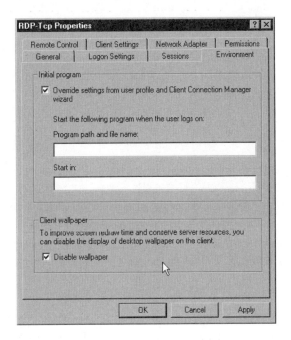

The Remote Control tab, shown in Figure 10.13, is used to configure shadowing. Shadowing allows a user with the correct permissions to remotely attach to another user's Terminal Services session. The "shadowing" user can then either view the actions of the "shadowed" user or remotely interact with the session. The level of control the shadowing user has can be configured under this tab. You can also configure whether or not shadowing will be allowed on this connection. Additionally, you can set whether the shadowing user can simply view the desktop or if he can remotely interact with the session.

One important thing to remember is that shadowing cannot be done to or from a console session. One way of getting around this is to open a client session on the console, using the client connection software. This will allow you to shadow a user session without having to go to a workstation. This is because the shadowing feature is built into the client software.

Figure 10.13 Connection Properties Remote Control configuration.

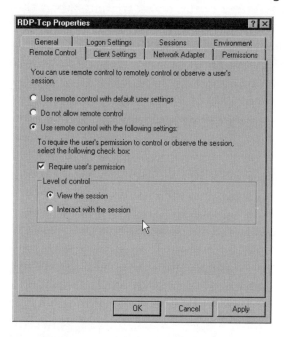

The Client Settings tab, shown in Figure 10.14, will allow you to determine how local clients' devices will be handled during the Terminal Services session. Unless you have added Citrix MetaFrame, some of the options here will be grayed out. This is because these features are unavailable without MetaFrame. The Client Settings tab is where you would go to allow the mapping of local printers. You can also select whether the client's main printer will be the user's default printer once he logs on to the Terminal Services Server. You can disable LPT port mapping and COM port mapping.

Disabling LPT mappings will prevent users from printing documents available on the Terminal Server that you do not want them to print. This could be confidential information or maybe copyrighted information. COM port mapping will allow you to use your local modems during your session. Disabling COM port mappings will also prevent users from redirecting classified information to a local COM port. You can also disable the Clipboard mapping here. Disabling the Clipboard mapping will help prevent users from saving files on the Terminal Server to local files.

You can also select to use user settings for these options. If this is chosen, each user or group of users can be given their own settings. This will help to customize the user environment. You may not want all users to have the same limitations on their sessions. The CIO of the company usually would not have the same limitations as regular users. Utilizing user settings instead of connection settings is a way of doing this.

Figure 10.14 Connection Properties Client Settings tab.

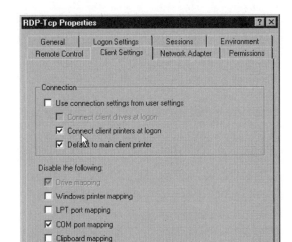

TIP

If you find that your clients are experiencing an unnecessarily long log-on time, you may want to consider disabling some of the client device mappings. One thing that I've found that causes problems is the COM port mapping. If your clients are connected to a modem server, they may experience extremely long delays while the COM ports are being mapped to the modem server.

The Network Adapter tab is used to configure what network adapters the connection is applied to (Figure 10.15). You can apply it to a particular adapter or all of the adapters in the systems. This is also where you would set how many users are allowed to attach to the connection. This can be used to prevent overuse of a particular connection, which would limit performance.

Adding a second network adapter can also be done for security purposes. Having two network adapters will allow you to separate your internal LAN from the Internet. If you add a second network adapter and disable IP forwarding or your Terminal Services Server, there will be no direct path from the Internet to your internal LAN. Adding a second network adapter is also useful if you use a private IP address range on your network. One of the network adapters in your server could be configured with a private address and one could have a public address that is accessible over the Internet.

Figure 10.15 The Connection Properties Network Adapter tab.

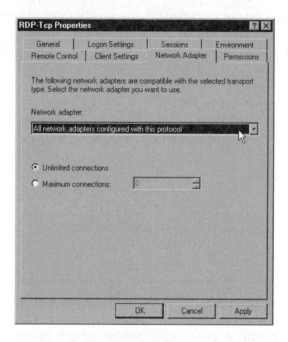

Applying Security Across All Sessions

A secure environment will prevent unwanted users from accessing your system. Security will also prevent valid users from accessing information or areas of the system they shouldn't. This will help prevent data loss and system corruption. There are several ways to secure your Terminal Services system, including using encryption, setting logon properties, configuring session permissions, and taking extra Internet-related security measures.

Encryption

One way to secure your Terminal Services sessions is by encrypting data before it is passed through the communications link. This will help prevent data from being intercepted and read by someone for whom it was not intended. You can install third-party encryption software if you wish, but we will cover the standard Terminal Services encryption here, which is standard RCA RC4 encryption. There are three levels of encryption that can be used with Windows 2000 Terminal Services: low, medium, and high.

When low-level encryption is used, there is only a one-way encryption. Only data sent from the client to the server is encrypted. This is done to protect things such as user names and passwords. The encryption algorithm can either be 40-bit or 56-bit. When a Windows 2000 client attempts to connect to the server, a 56-bit key is used for the encryption. When a client other than a Windows 2000 client tries to attach, a 40-bit encryption key is used.

Medium-level encryption is similar to low-level encryption, except for the fact that medium-level encryption is a two-way encryption. This means that data is encrypted during the session no matter who sends the data, the client or the server. Medium-level encryption also uses a 56-bit key when Windows 2000 clients try to attach and a 40-bit key when other clients try to attach.

High-level encryption is also a two-way encryption, where data traveling in both directions is encrypted. High-level encryption uses a 128-bit key for encryption.

WARNING

The 128-bit key used in high-level encryption is non-exportable. It can only be used in the United States and Canada. Federal regulations prohibit the use of this degree of encryption. If you have international clients that will be attaching to your server, you must use one of the lower levels of encryption. This rule applies to the encryption used with the Terminal Services clients or the MetaFrame clients.

The next step in configuring security is the securing of the actual session. Certain security measures can be taken to ensure that users who are allowed to connect to the server are not allowed to access areas that they are not supposed to. Applying security to your user sessions can either be a simple or a complex task. We will go through some of the various methods that can be used to secure your sessions. We will secure your sessions for standard user access and for Web access.

Logon Settings

The Logon Settings tab seen in Figure 10.16 allows you to decide what information will be required when a client logs on. You can choose to use client-provided log-on information, in which case, the client would provide a user name and password for logon. You can also specify the information that will be used for logon. This allows you to set up security based on a particular user, and then have everyone who logs on using this connection to log on as that user. You will then have more control over what rights each user who logs on will have. This, however, can also be very dangerous.

Figure 10.16 The Connection Properties Logon Settings screen.

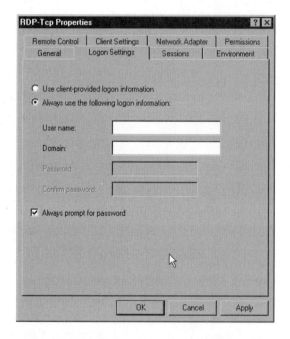

If you input all of the log-on information, a user trying to connect to your server won't have to know any log-on information and they will be connected. I suggest that the only time you input log-on information here is when users are connecting with Internet sessions (especially through a Web browser). If you do allow this, make sure you use some of the other methods listed here to lock down your server.

You can also require that a user input a password every time they log on, and this will help prevent unwanted users from accessing a connection. Requiring users to input a password is always a good idea, even if they are connecting over the Internet.

Specifying log-on information here is not a good idea if your users' passwords are set to periodically expire. If the password stored here is correct, the user will get an error message.

NOTE

Some companies' have written security policies regarding IT access while policies are implied. Before setting security parameters for items such as logons and passwords, you should consult your company's security policy.

Session Permissions

If you wanted to limit who has access to a particular connection, this would be set under the Connection Properties Permissions tab shown in Figure 10.17. You can control what users and groups can access your connection. You can also determine what rights they will have after they are connected.

There are three levels of access users can be configured for: guest access, user access, and full control. Guest access only allows the logon. User access allows the user to log on, run queries, and use messaging. Full control allows access to all system functions. By default only SYSTEM and the Administrators group have full control. I suggest leaving it this way.

Figure 10.17 Connection Properties Permissions tab.

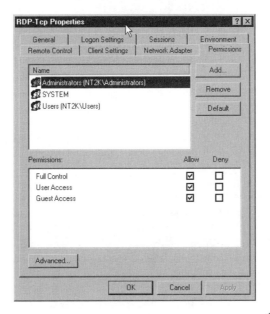

Special Internet Security Measures

Keep in mind that you will have to apply extra security measures to Terminal Servers accessible through the Internet, because any server accessible through the Internet is particularly vulnerable. The first step of security may be to institute a firewall, which can be used to secure open ports on your network. You can block all ports or protocols that will not be used for some specific purpose. You may want to consider a firewall that includes a DMZ, or demilitarized zone. A DMZ allows you to setup a portion of your network that is accessible from the Internet, while keeping the rest of your network totally shutdown to incoming Internet access.

If you have Terminal Services running on a Web Server, make sure that Web users only have access to the files and directories you want them to, especially FTP (File Transfer Protocols) users. The default accounts installed by Web servers can often provide a security risk. A hacker would already know the name of a valid account; all they would have left to do is find the password for the account. Depending on how complex your passwords are, this could be a very simple task. My suggestion is never use the default account for your Web services, or for any service, if at all possible.

For IT Professionals

Other Security Measures

Aside from Terminal Services' specific security measures, there are also basic Windows 2000 Security measures that you should have in place to protect your server. The first is account security. Make sure all user accounts have complex passwords. You should require passwords to be at least five characters, have one upper-case letter, and one number. You should also configure log-on time restrictions. If no one should be accessing your system after 9:00 PM, then disable logons after that time. Remember, nighttime is prime time for hackers. You should also make sure that user accounts that do not need access to Terminal Services have this option disabled in their account properties.

The next thing you should do is secure the file system. Many administrators tighten user security, but leave the file system wide open. You should limit access to the files and directories on your servers, especially to administrative executables. It is a good idea to make sure that only administrators have access to the executables for applications like Terminal Services Manager and Terminal Services Configuration. That way, there can be no "accidental" access of these applications.

Continued

Remember that a user does not have to log on to a Terminal Services session in order to access the file system and copy files. Everyone knows about the administrative shares created by Windows. A hacker simply has to attach to one, and he can copy anything he wants.

Group policies can also come in very handy when dealing with Terminal Services. Group policies can be used to deny or restrict access to objects in the directory tree. You can use a policy to outline what connectivity particular groups of users you have to your organizations Terminal Servers. When setting policies, I suggest totally locking down the policy and then giving access to only those resources or parameters you want.

Summary

Installing Terminal Services and creating your sessions is fairly straightforward. The hard part comes after the installation, because Terminal Services can require a substantial amount of configuration. Session configuration and security configuration are where your skills as an administrator will be used. You will have to decide on a Terminal Services configuration that will maximize the effectiveness of your organization. In your session configuration, you should try to maximize performance. In your security configuration, you should try to minimize risk. Particular attention must be paid to securing Internet accessible sessions, because they are slightly more vulnerable.

Each time a user session connects to your Terminal Services Server, additional resources are used. It is important that you plan ahead. You want to make sure that your server will be able to handle the user load that will attach to it. Power users who run resource intensive applications can require a considerable amount of resources above that required by normal users. It is important that you make provisions for these users.

You can use different session parameters to lessen the burden presented by each user. You can place limits on how long users stay connected during idle periods and non-idle periods. You can also limit what data or information is passed between the server and the clients during sessions. This will not only lessen the load on the server, but it can also increase session performance.

Security can be applied on a connection basis or a per-user basis. With security being the issue that is nowadays, you should be sure that you have taken the necessary precautions to secure your server and the rest of your environment. Users hacking into your Terminal Services Server may not only be able to gain access to your Terminal Server, but the rest of your environment as well.

FAQs

Q: I have two groups who perform administration on my Terminal Services Server. I want both groups to be able to shadow users for troubleshooting purposes. But, I only want one of these groups to be able to make changes to workstation configurations. What can I do?

A: Users can be given rights to simply view a session or to interact with a session. You simply apply the desired rights to each group.

Q: I want to use data encryption on my Terminal Services Server. I have clients who will be accessing the servers from South America. What is the maximum level of encryption I can use?

A: You can only use medium-level encryption. High-level encryption uses a 128-bit encryption key. 128-bit encryption is non-exportable and cannot be used outside of the United States and Canada

Q: What is the difference between low-level and medium-level encryption?

A: Low-level encryption is one-way, from client to server. Medium-level encryption is two-way.

Q: I have users who will only access my Terminal Services Servers on occasion. They will need minimal access, basically just log-on access. What level of user access can be given to these users? Are they the three levels of user access that can be set in Terminal Services?

A: These users can simply use the guest access to your server. There are three types of access that can be granted to your server. Users can have guest access, users access, or full control.

Q: I have a certain group of users who will only be running Microsoft Word from my Terminal Services Server. I want to set it up so that Word will automatically start when these users log on to the server. How do I do this? Where would I go to specify that users run Microsoft Word every time they log on to a particular connection?

A: The Connection Properties Environment tab allows you to specify an application that will be started on session start-up. Simply go to the Connection Properties Environment tab and specify the path to Microsoft Word.

Q: I find that users are often able to attach to my Terminal Services Servers without having to enter a password. I view this as a security issue. What can be done about it? I want to require that users always have to enter a password when they log on. Where would I do this?

A: Log-on settings under Connection Properties allows you to require users to input a password. This will require that users input a password any time they want to log on your Terminal Services Server.

Chapter 11

Installing and Publishing Applications

Solutions in this chapter:

- Selecting Compatible Applications
- Installing Applications on the Server
- Shadow Registry
- Application Compatibility Scripts
- Publishing Applications

Introduction

Two of the most important concepts to master in thin-client computing are installing and publishing applications. Installing applications involves selecting applications that are compatible with the environment, installing them on the server, testing, and if necessary, customizing the environment to make the application perform as desired. Publishing applications changes our traditional view of connecting to a specific server and running the applications it has installed, and moves us to an application-centric paradigm, in which we choose the application we want, and it is provided to us from whatever server it is available.

Published applications go hand-in-hand with Load Balancing, an add-on product from Citrix, that allows us to group a number of servers together into a Server Farm. Using Load Balancing, a client requests an application from the farm, the master browser determines which server capable of delivering that application is currently the least busy, and then connects the client to that server. This chapter will demonstrate how to install and publish applications in a load-balanced farm and how to manage those applications to achieve the best possible performance.

Deploying applications becomes a two-step process in some ways, although the process is completely centrally managed. First, the applications must be installed on the server. Second, the applications must be delivered to end users. When delivering applications to users, the way that a client connects—whether over a phone line or through the Internet—plays a role. Internet-delivered applications will require a different method of publishing than sending applications to Citrix MetaFrame clients.

Selecting Compatible Applications

When selecting applications for deployment, or selecting Terminal Services to deploy your application, there are some important guidelines to follow. The application should at the least be NT/Windows 2000 compatible. The application does not necessarily have to be compatible with the client platform—Windows applications can be delivered to Macintosh and UNIX clients, and with the use of MetaFrame for Solaris, UNIX applications can be delivered to Windows clients. Applications should be 32-bit if at all possible; 32-bit applications share memory space with each other, can multithread, and take better advantage of the native 32-bit environment offered by Windows 2000. DOS and 16-bit Windows applications all run in NTVDM (NT Virtual DOS Machine) and must go through the process known as *thunking*.

Microsoft has released the specifications for 32-bit Windows 2000 applications and provided suggestions for making them Terminal Services compliant:

- **File locking** Ensures that files are not locked during use, as this could prevent multiple instances of the application (or processes under the application, such as wizards) from running.

- **File permissions** Users may not have access to system files, and may not have the same permission levels as the administrator who installed the application.

- **File locations** Per-user data and configuration files should be stored separately to avoid collisions and manage permissions. In particular, applications should store temporary information on a per-user basis to avoid conflicts among users' information and preferences. You should do this by using the GetTempPath API rather than using a hard-coded path. Log onto the machine as an Aministrator and install the application.

These same guidelines also hold true for older 32-bit Windows applications.

16-bit Windows applications require thunking or WOW (Win16 on Win32), which is what Windows 2000 must do to translate the 16-bit instructions up to 32-bit, execute them, and then translate or "thunk" them back to 16-bit. This procedure takes time and about 20 percent more resources than a comparable 32-bit application; thus, the performance for a 16-bit Windows/DOS application suffers.

DOS applications can be the most troublesome type of application you deploy. DOS applications impose many limitations and can severely limit the performance of a Terminal Services server. Some DOS applications that directly attempt to write graphics characters to the video hardware are not only incompatible with Terminal Services, they are probably not compatible with Windows 2000 either. One of the most lamented limits of a DOS application is the screen size. DOS applications cannot run full-screen character mode on any client except the DOS MetaFrame client. One way around this is to use different fonts for the DOS session such as DOSfon (available from www.uwe-sieber.de/english.html). Some DOS applications overuse memory, and one instance can take up an entire gigabyte of RAM if not controlled, as in the DOS version of FoxPro. FoxPro can be controlled by adding the following line to the config.cp file:

```
MEMLIMIT=60,4096,8192
```

It is located in the FoxProXX directory, which sets memory limits to 60 percent—4MB to start, with a maximum of 8MB.

There are other DOS applications that require unique environmental variables set at runtime. This situation can easily be rectified by using a batch file to adjust the desired settings and then launching the application. Some DOS applications require a specific environment variable to be set to the username or a user-specific path. An example would be:

```
@echo off
set datapath=h:\%username%\appdata
start /B application.exe
```

This example would set the variable *datapath* to h:\jsmith\appdata and then the /B would start the application in the same window. The *datapath* variable is then made available to the application. This batch file can now be published in place of the original application executable. This approach also enables us to deliver the same application with different settings simply by copying the batch file and changing the necessary settings.

Installing Applications on the Server

A Terminal Services server is not much use without applications to deploy. While some Web developers find Notepad to be a mission-critical application, few others would. Installing applications on Windows 2000 with Terminal Services is a little different than installing on single-user platforms. Terminal Services must track all of the changes applications make to the registry, as well as common files it may place in the system directories, so that it may proliferate this information to each new user as they log on.

Installing an application on Terminal Services may be done in two ways, in User-Specific mode or User-Global mode. How the application is to be deployed, what its specific needs are, and its compatibility with a multiuser environment, will determine the mode in which the application is installed. Figure 11.1 depicts where files are copied in each mode.

User-Specific

In User-Specific mode, Terminal Services does not track the changes an application makes to the server and, as shown in Figure 11.1, all files are copied directly to the user's home drive Windows directory. Installing applications in User-Specific mode is no different than installing on a normal workstation. You have to log into the server as the user and perform the installation as normal. You may, however, need to temporarily assign to

Figure 11.1 User-Specific versus User-Global installation.

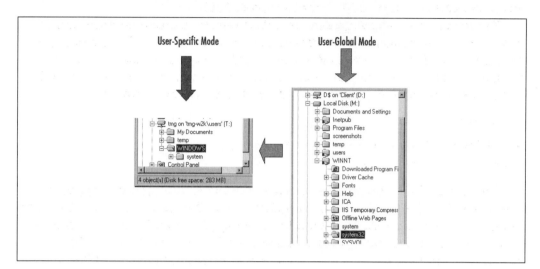

the user administrative or other rights on the server to be permitted to perform the install. These rights may vary and should be removed after the installation is complete. This mode only sets up the application to be used by the user that installs it. All registry changes, .INI files, and .DLL files are copied directly to the user's Windows and system directory on their home drive and will not be copied to new users as they log on. The application would have to be installed again for each user that wanted it.

Some applications may require this type of setup, but this means that as each new user is added to the system, the administrator would have to log on as that user and perform the installation. A User-Specific model would also require increased disk space, and upgrades would have to be done one user at a time. A User-Specific model also reduces your Return on Investment (ROI) due to increased disk space, administrative overhead, and upgradability.

User-Global

This is the recommended mode for installing all applications on Terminal Services. User-Global mode causes the system to copy all .INI and .DLL files to the system's Windows directory and shadow all registry changes to a special location called the *Shadow Registry*, which is discussed in depth later in this chapter. There are two ways to place the system into User-Global install mode. The first is by manually placing Terminal Services into Install Mode by opening a command prompt and typing:

```
change user /install
```

Leave this command prompt open and then browse to your application's setup program and perform the installation as normal. If the application does not require a reboot, then the system must be placed into Execute Mode by typing:

```
change user /execute
```

This will turn off tracking and let the system know that the installation of that application is complete. If the application requires a reboot then the system is automatically placed back into Execute Mode.

The second method is to use Add/Remove Programs from the Control Panel.

1. Open the Control Panel and double-click the Add/Remove Programs icon.

2. Choose the Add New Programs icon on the left and click the CD or floppy drive button and navigate to your application's setup routine.

3. By default this dialog only looks for Setup.exe and install.exe as indicated by the Files of Type box. If your application is a compressed package (like WinZip), change the Files of Type to "Programs" and it will list all .EXE's, .CMD's, .BAT's, etc.

4. Choose Next and your application will begin its setup routine.

5. Install your application as normal, and when complete, click Next and Finish to close the dialogs. This places the system back into Execute Mode.

TIP

Many applications ask for a Name and Company Name during setup. Enter a generic name or the company name twice as this will often be displayed each time the application is started. Putting your name here would surely serve your vanity; it would also guarantee that users would call *you* should they have problems with the application!

With the advent of the Microsoft Windows Installer, the way some Microsoft applications are installed on Terminal Services servers has changed. Microsoft now provides a device called *transforms* to modify the way an application is installed on Terminal Services. These *transforms* disable or modify some features of an application. For example, Microsoft Office 2000 can only be installed using a transform file. This disables the animated Office Assistants and changes all components to be installed to the hard drive or renders them not available. The "Installed on First Use" option is not acceptable in a Terminal Services environment because if a user attempts to use that feature, the system would prompt him to insert the Office CD and proceed to install the feature, thus circumventing the change control, so the transform removes the option. It also configures Office applications to display a text-based splash screen rather than the standard graphics-based splash screen. To use the transform you must install the Office 2000 Resource Kit, available for download from www.microsoft.com/office/ork/2000/download/ORKTools.exe, and install the Custom Installation Wizard and the Terminal Server Tools. This will make a program group called Microsoft Office Tools/Microsoft Office 2000 Resource Kit Tools. From this group, launch the Custom Installation Wizard:

1. Insert your Office 2000 CD.

2. Click Next to continue.

3. From the Open the MSI File screen, navigate to the data1.msi on your Office 2000 CD and click Next.

4. From the Open the MSI File screen, browse to the \Program Files\ ORKTools\ToolBox\Tools\Terminal Server Tools directory and select the termsrvr.mst transform file.

5. Click Next to apply the transform to the MSI.

6. From the Select MST File to Save Screen, specify a new file name for the custom transform you are about to create. Click Next.

7. In the Specify Default Path and Organization screen, provide the installation path for Office. The default will be *program files*, but I usually change this to n:\program files\Microsoft Office so as to not install it on the system partition. Provide the organization name to enter into the registration screen and click Next.

8. In the Remove Previous Versions Screen, choose which previous versions to remove. Unless you have a specific reason to leave legacy Office applications, just select Default Setup Behavior and click Next.

9. The Set Feature Installation States screen allows you to select or deselect the applications and options to install. I would recommend NEVER selecting Installed on First Use. This will prompt users for the Office 2000 CD and attempt to install more software on your server without your knowledge or consent. Click Next.

10. The next screen, Customize Default Application Settings, allows you to specify an ops file created with the Office Profile Wizard. If you have prepared this file, browse to the file's location and then click Next.

11. The Add Files to the Installation screen allows you to add files to be copied to the server during installation. This is useful for copying workgroup templates or other custom files to the Microsoft Office directory. Click Next.

12. The Add Registry Enteries screen is similar to the previous one, except it is used for registry settings. Add settings as needed and click Next.

13. The Add, Modify, or remove Shortcuts screen allows you to add or remove application shortcuts. I use this to prevent the Open Office Document and New Office Document from being added to the Start Menu. Click Next.

14. The Identify Additional Servers screen is not normally necessary for Terminal Services installations. This provides a network share point that users may use to install additional components of Office. Click Next.

15. The Add Installations and Run Programs screen allows you to identify other programs that you want Setup to run. After the Office installation is complete, Setup executes each command you specify in the order in which it appears in the box. Add any desired commands and click Next.

16. The Customize Outlook Installation Options screen allows you to customize the Outlook 2000 installation options. Change any desired options and click Next.

17. In the Customize IE5 Installation Options screen, specify how you want the installation of Internet Explorer 5 handled. Windows 2000 includes IE 5.0, so you would not need to install IE again unless your Office 2000 CD contains a later version. Click Next.

18. The Setup Properties screen allows you to add or modify various property settings used by Setup to control how Office is installed. Refer to the online help for a detailed description of how to use these settings. Click Next and then click Finish to save your settings.

19. Upon finishing the wizard, it provides you with a sample command line to run to install Office 2000:

```
setup.exe TRANSFORMS=M:\temp\TEST.MST /qn+
```

20. Exit the wizard and use the command line provided to install Office 2000 using the Add/Remove Programs icon in the Control Panel.

NOTE

For more information about the Office Profile Wizard, including a description of how to run the wizard and a list of the options it saves, see the "Office Profile Wizard Reference" in the Microsoft Office 2000 Resource Kit.

Testing the Applications

All applications should be thoroughly tested before deploying to clients. To do this, perform the following:

1. Create a normal user with the same permissions, home directory configuration, and log-in scripts that a production user would have.

2. Log in as this user, open the application, and perform each function that a user would do during the course of a day.

3. Functions such as opening, manipulating, printing and saving files, running reports, and any application-specific actions should be verified.

4. Ensure that real users test the application in all aspects, and that every function is scrutinized.

5. You should even check procedures that will not be used in order to establish their functionality for future reference.

6. If the application does not work for normal users, try logging on as an administrator and running the application. If this works then it is a permissions issue. Permissions problems can be discovered by using tools that monitor file and registry access, such as NT File Monitor and NT Registry Monitor both of which are available for free download from www.sysinternals.com.

TIP

If you are not familiar with how to use the application, get someone from the department or group that uses it and set them up to test it through MetaFrame. Have the person execute all the functions he or she would normally use and verify that they work as expected.

You may discover an application that has performance issues such as CPU over utilization or memory leaks, or that does not exit cleanly. Some applications allow a measure of control such as command-line parameters or environmental settings to help manage the application's use of resources. Creating Application Compatibility Scripts (covered later in this chapter) to set up environments at logon can control some applications. Citrix Resource Management Services can be configured to notify you if the CPU utilization exceeds a threshold you specify. The most common and accepted practice is a nightly reboot of the server to clear up any rogue processes or memory leaks that may occur. Use the Task Scheduler to schedule a batch file like that shown in Figure 11.2 to run every night to disable logons, clear the print spool directory, and reboot the server.

Figure 11.2 A batch file example.

```
@ECHO off
rem requires sleep.exe and shutdown.exe from the Windows 2000 Resource
Kit.
CHANGE LOGON /DISABLE
MSG * The Server will be automatically shutting down in 10 minutes.
Please save your work and log off.
SLEEP 300
MSG * The Server will be automatically shutting down in 5 minutes.
Please save your work and log off.
Rem Wait for 5 minutes
SLEEP 300
FOR /F "tokens=1,3,4 delims==" %%i IN ('quser') DO IF "%%k"=="active"
LOGOFF %%j
FOR /F "tokens=1,2,3 delims==" %%i IN ('quser') DO IF "%%k" == "disc"
RESET SESSION %j
NET STOP SPOOLER
DEL /Q /F %systemroot%\system32\spool\printers\
NET START SPOOLER
SHUTDOWN /L /R /T:1 /C
:end
```

TIP

See www.thethin.net for a Citrix/Terminal Services mailing list and searchable archives for information on other administrators' experiences with various applications.

It is a good idea to perform the following steps with the help of test users to ensure that everything is running efficiently:

1. With the users, develop a script that covers each task the user is to complete so as not to forget to run any reports or create print jobs, and have the application make any calls to outside applications such as Crystal Reports or Microsoft Excel.

2. Have the test users record the time it takes to complete each task or set of tasks and compare the times with the execution of the script on a normal workstation.

3. To ensure valid results, have the estimated maximum number of clients logged into the system and active.

4. During testing, use the Performance Monitor to analyze the application's use of processor and memory. Figure 11.3 shows the Performance Monitor and illustrates which counters are most useful in monitoring an application.

5. From the Terminal Services Session Performance object, select the counters for % Processor Time, Total Bytes and Working Set, then highlight all the ICA sessions that are executing the application.

6. Add these counters to the chart and have the test users begin their testing.

7. Add two more system counters to observe total system load; from the Memory Object add the Available Mbytes counter and from the Processor Object add % Processor Time.

8. Observe Performance Monitor as users log in, use the application, and log out, and watch the individual session's memory count and the two system counters.

9. When the % Processor Time approaches 60 percent, consider the processors at maximum.

Figure 11.3 Performance Monitor.

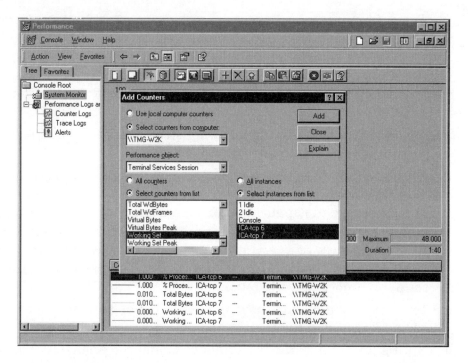

WARNING

Microsoft states that the processors are at maximum when at 80 percent, but when designing a fault-tolerant environment you may want to leave some extra space on all the servers to take on additional load in the event that one or more servers fail.

Consider the memory fully utilized when there is only 20–25 percent of the total left. If the memory utilization reaches 100 percent, then refer to the session total bytes and working set counters to determine which session is taking up more memory than expected. Contact the user of that session to determine what action caused the use of the excess memory. This excess usage may affect your memory requirements if the function is a common one.

For IT Professionals

Server Sizing

Two very important goals are: (1) For the application to work not only for a single user, but also for many users logged in simultaneously; and (2) to verify the server can perform adequately with the desired number of users logged on and using the application. Use a product such as WinBatch, from Wilson WindowWare (www.winbatch.com), to simulate many users running the application at once to detect any issues that multiuser computing may impose upon the application.

I had a situation where a consultant set up a server farm and was having problems with servers refusing connections. When the application testing was done, the servers were tested under a low user load with only IT staff performing the functions. Using Performance Monitor the sessions were observed to never exceed 12MB. All functions worked very well and the servers were estimated to support 40 users at 16MB per session plus 128 for the system. The servers were built out using Dual Pentium II 500 Mhz CPUs and 768MB of RAM. After the servers were placed into production, it was noted that at approximately 28–32 users, the servers began to refuse connections and reported an application load of 10,000. (Load values are discussed later in this chapter.) After some research, I discovered that the 16-bit PowerBuilder application did not release memory after it printed reports. After a couple of hours, several sessions were using 24–32MB of RAM, effectively doubling the session's footprint and utilizing all of the server's memory. With an estimated 3200 users scheduled to use the system, and the servers reduced to servicing only 30 each, it became very apparent we had underestimated the application. The only solution was now to add 128MB to each of 80 servers, but due to the initial RAM configuration, all the RAM slots were full, so some DIMMS would have to be replaced, adding another $40,000 to the project.

Shadow Registry

Most applications today add settings in the HKEY_CURRENT_USER registry location during installation. As discussed earlier, placing the system into install mode, either by command line or Add/Remove Programs, tells the system to track .INI and registry changes the application makes during installation. These tracked changes are stored or *shadowed* in HKEY_LOCAL_MACHINE\SOFTWARE\Microsoft\Windows NT\ CurrentVersion\Terminal Server\Install and the .INI files that are installed to the windows or windows\system directory are recorded in HKEY_LOCAL_MACHINE\SOFTWARE\Microsoft\Windows NT\ CurrentVersion\Terminal Server\Compatibility\IniFiles.

To understand the different drive letters and user directories explained in the following section, refer to these definitions:

- <HomeDrive> Is used to reference the drive letter specified on the profile tab of the Active Directory Users and Computers user object.

- <HomeShare> Is used to denote the UNC path that is assigned to the <HomeDrive>.

- <RootDrive> Is used to indicate the drive letter that is substituted to the <HomeDrive> and <HomeShare>.

- <HomeSpace> A general term used to signify the location where the user is to store personal files and settings; it usually consists in some manner of the other three terms defined here.

When a new user logs into the system, the system checks the user's windows and windows\system directories for the .INI files it has recorded in the ...\Compatibility\IniFiles key and copies those files that are newer or that don't exist from the server's system directories to the user's <HomeShare>. As illustrated in Figure 11.4, the system automatically creates in each user's <HomeShare> a \windows and \windows\system directory to store .INI, .DLL, and other files needed by applications. When newer .INI files exist in the system's \winnt directory, the old one is renamed with a .CTX extention and the new file is copied to the user's \windows directory.

When an application executes, it may attempt to access registry keys that do not exist in the user's HKEY_CURRENT_USER context. When this occurs, the system will check HKEY_LOCAL_MACHINE\SOFTWARE\ Microsoft\Windows NT\CurrentVersion\Terminal Server\Install, and if the requested key and subkeys exist, they will be copied to the correct location under HKEY_CURRENT_USER. If an application uses the API GetPrivateProfileString to access an .INI file that does not exist in the user's <HomeShare> \Windows directory, the system will look for the file in %systemroot%. If found, it is copied to the user's <HomeShare> \Windows directory.

Figure 11.4 User's home drive and Windows directories.

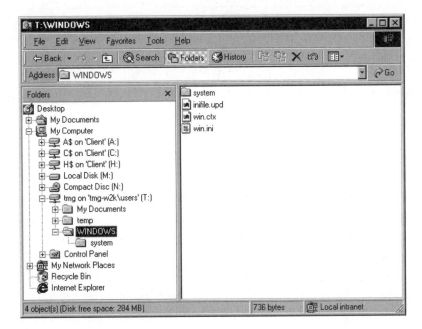

Application Compatibility Scripts

Application Compatibility Scripts (ACS) help us set up an environment for applications that were not written with multiuser computing in mind. Microsoft provides several prepared scripts when you install Terminal Services. These scripts provide needed modifications for the most common applications. They are listed in Table 11.1. Most of these scripts place a logon time script in the \Application Compatibility Scripts\logon directory and are called from the usrlogon.cmd script.

Table 11.1 Application Compatibility Scripts Included with Terminal Services

Script	Applications
cofc8ins.cmd	Corel WordPerfect Suite 8
coffice7.cmd	Corel Office 7
coffice8.cmd	Install script for the Corel WordPerfect Suite 8 for the Administrator
diskpr20.cmd	DiskKeeper 2.0
eudora4.cmd	Eudora Pro 4.0

Continued

Table 11.1 Continued

Script	Applications
msexcl97.cmd	Stand Alone Excel 97
msproj95.cmd	Microsoft Project 95 Multiuser Application Tuning
msproj98.cmd	Microsoft Project 98 Multiuser Application Tuning
mssna30.cmd	SNA Server 3.0
msvs6.cmd	Microsoft Visual Studio 6.0
msword97.cmd	Stand Alone Microsoft Word 97
netcom40.cmd	Netscape Communicator 4
netnav30.cmd	Netscape Navigator 3.x
odbc.cmd	ODBC – Always run this script, and place the system in Install mode before creating any data sources.
ofc43ins.cmd	MS Office 4.3 – Edit and run this script first.
office43.cmd	Microsoft Office 4.3
office95.cmd	Microsoft Office 95 – Be sure to read the instructions at the end.
office97.cmd	Microsoft Office 97
outlk98.cmd	Outlook 98
pchtree6.cmd	PeachTree Complete Accounting v6.0
pwrbldr6.cmd	PowerBuilder 6.0
sna40cli.cmd	SNA Client 4.0
sna40srv.cmd	SNA Server 4.0
ssuite9.cmd	Lotus SmartSuite 9
ssuite97.cmd	Lotus SmartSuite 97
visio5.cmd	Visio 5.0
winmsg.cmd	Windows Messaging

Figure 11.5 displays the contents of usrlogon.cmd. This script first calls SetPaths.cmd and sets the following paths to environment variables:

```
All Users:Startup              COMMON_STARTUP
All Users:Start Menu           COMMON_START_MENU
All Users:Start Menu\Programs  COMMON_PROGRAMS
Current User:Start Menu        USER_START_MENU
Current User:Startup           USER_STARTUP
```

Current User:Start Menu\Programs	USER_PROGRAMS
Current User:My Documents	MY_DOCUMENTS
Current User:Templates	TEMPLATES
Current User:Application Data	APP_DATA

These variables enable the other Application Compatibility Scripts to run without hard-coded system paths, and use any custom settings that may already be in place.

UsrLogon.cmd then checks for the existence of usrlogn1.cmd, which is created when an Application Compatibility Script is installed that does not require the <RootDrive>, and executes it if it does exist. Usrlogn1.cmd calls other scripts from the \winnt\Application Compatibility Scripts\logon directory. Usrlogon.cmd then checks to see if the <RootDrive> variable has been set and, if so, runs the **subst** command to connect the <RootDrive> to the user's %homedrive%%homepath%. UsrLogon.cmd then calls usrlogn2.cmd, which in turn calls other scripts that do require the <Rootdrive>.

Figure 11.5 USRLOGON.cmd.

```
@Echo Off


Call "%SystemRoot%\Application Compatibility Scripts\SetPaths.Cmd"
If "%_SETPATHS%" == "FAIL" Goto Done


Rem
Rem This is for those scripts that don't need the Rootdrive.
Rem


If Not Exist "%SystemRoot%\System32\Usrlogn1.cmd" Goto cont0
Cd /d "%SystemRoot%\Application Compatibility Scripts\Logon"
Call "%SystemRoot%\System32\Usrlogn1.cmd"


:cont0


Rem
Rem Determine the user's home directory drive letter.  If this isn't
Rem set, exit.
```

Continued

Figure 11.5 Continued.

```
Rem


Cd /d %SystemRoot%\"Application Compatibility Scripts"
Call RootDrv.Cmd
If "A%Rootdrive%A" == "AA" End.Cmd


Rem
Rem Map the User's Home Directory to a Drive Letter
Rem


Net Use %Rootdrive% /D >NUL: 2>&1
Subst %Rootdrive% "%HomeDrive%%HomePath%"
if ERRORLEVEL 1 goto SubstErr
goto AfterSubst
:SubstErr
Subst %Rootdrive% /d >NUL: 2>&1
Subst %Rootdrive% "%HomeDrive%%HomePath%"
:AfterSubst


Rem
Rem Invoke each Application Script.  Application Scripts are
automatically
Rem added to UsrLogn2.Cmd when the Installation script is run.
Rem


If Not Exist %SystemRoot%\System32\UsrLogn2.Cmd Goto Cont1


Cd Logon
Call %SystemRoot%\System32\UsrLogn2.Cmd


:Cont1


:Done
```

The ACS provides a routine known as <RootDrive>. This routine was developed to compensate for the NT 4.0 shortcoming of not being able to map the root directory of a drive letter beyond the share point—like Novell Net-ware's **MAP ROOT** command.

The <RootDrive> routine took the user's <HomeShare>, usually denoted as \\server\users\%username%, and used the **subst** command to "map" a drive to the user's <HomeShare>. Using only NT's facilities, a user's <HomeShare> was mapped to w:\jsmith. With that path, it was hard to configure applications to go to a path of W:\%username%; but with the <RootDrive> the system would take another drive letter, such as U:, and "subst" it to w:\jsmith making the root directory of "U:" the user's <HomeSpace>. It was then easy to configure applications to point their default, temp, and cache directories to U:\.

Windows 2000 now provides the capability to map the root of a drive to a directory below the share point; this is very effective if all users are con-figured correctly, but invariably a user will slip by without a home drive specified and the Application Compatibility Script's <RootDrive> facility will still provide a consistent environment for applications. As shown in Figure 11.6, drive H: is mapped only to the share point so that user "tmg" has to open H:\tmg to access his personal space. Drive T: is substituted to the T:\tmg so that all applications globally point to T:\ as the point of refer-ence. This provides each user separate user space that is referenced the same way in all sessions.

Figure 11.6 Subst command versus mapped-to-share point.

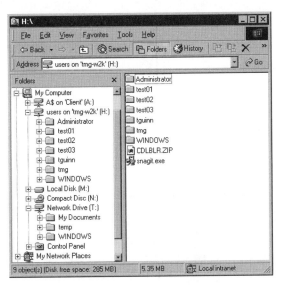

When you install many of the ACS's, you will be prompted for the Rootdrive letter to be specified by opening RootDrv2.cmd in Notepad as shown in Figure 11.7.

Figure 11.7 RootDrv2.cmd.

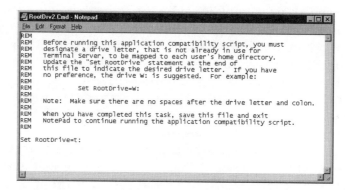

After entering the drive letter in the proper place, close Notepad and save the file, and the ACS will, continue its installation. You can fill in the same drive letter as your user's home drive, but if you do, be sure to comment out the subst lines in the usrlogon.cmd file in the \winnt\system32 directory. This does *require* each user to have a home drive and directory specified on the Profile tab of the user's account in the Active Directory Users & Computers console as shown in Figure 11.8.

If the home drive and directory are specified, the subst command (shown below) will fail and your setting in AD will remain. If the home drive and directory are not specified, it will still substitute the correct drive letter to the user's profile directory and application settings will be directed there.

```
rem Net Use %RootDrive% /D >NUL: 2>&1

Subst %RootDrive% "%HomeDrive%%HomePath%"

rem if ERRORLEVEL 1 goto SubstErr

rem goto AfterSubst

:SubstErr

rem Subst %RootDrive% /d >NUL: 2>&1

rem Subst %RootDrive% "%HomeDrive%%HomePath%"

:AfterSubst
```

You can easily make Application Compatibility Scripts of your own to help along other applications that aren't shown in Table 11.1. Simply determine the requirements of your application and write a script to provide for those requirements. Figure 11.9 is an illustration of a simple ACS I wrote for Attachmate's Extra Client. This application requires each

Figure 11.8 Terminal Services Profile tab.

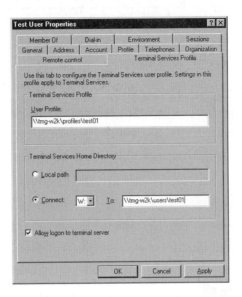

person to have a \extra\user directory to store such things as keyboard mappings. This script runs from the Usrlogn2.cmd, which is called from the usrlogon.cmd file. It looks at the user's Rootdrive and checks for the existence of the \extra\user directory and if not, creates the directory structure and then copies the initial files from the program's template user directory. Figure 11.10 uses a flowchart to map out the process of logging on to a Terminal Services server.

Figure 11.9 Application Compatibility Script for Attachmate's Extra Client.

```
Extra.bat

@echo off
if not exist %homedrive%%homepath%\extra\user\. goto mkdir
goto end

:mkdir
md %homedrive%%homepath%\extra
md %homedrive%%homepath%\extra\user
goto copyfiles

:copyfiles
```

Continued

Figure 11.9 Continued.

```
xcopy n:\extrawin\user %homedrive%%homepath%\extra\user /e >nul
goto end


:end
```

Figure 11.10 Terminal Services/Citrix MetaFrame logon process.

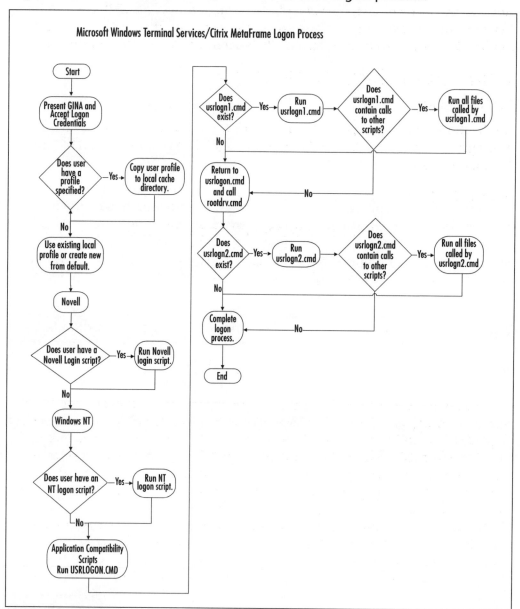

Publishing Applications

Publishing applications is a method used to define an application as a specific object for a user to access. This is the most important feature in MetaFrame and is the primary capability that allows us to move to an application-centric environment. These applications can then be distributed to users based on group membership, without regard to the server on which the application resides. With the addition of Citrix MetaFrame for Solaris, and the coming releases of MetaFrame for other platforms, published applications and Program Neighborhood provide the user a single application-portal to access applications from heterogeneous platforms.

Using Published Application Manager

Application publishing is configured from the Published Application Manager (Start | Programs | MetaFrame Tools | Published Application Manager) shown in Figure 11.11.

Figure 11.11 Published Application Manager.

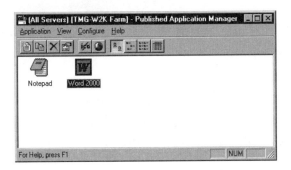

Published Application Manager has two views in which you may view application objects: Server and Scope. The Server option allows you to view applications published by a specific server or by all servers. Scope allows you to view published applications from an NT Domain perspective or a Citrix Server Farm perspective. For most implementations, the Server Farm and All Servers view will be used, and occasionally the Server Farm and Specific Server view may be used for troubleshooting.

Select these views from Published Application Manager's View menu and choose Select Scope or Select Server. The first time you open Published Application Manager from the Configure menu, choose Join Server Farm. This wizard will help you join an existing farm or create a new one. Once your server is in a farm, you can begin publishing applications. Let's start with Microsoft Word 2000:

1. From the Application menu, click New.

2. If prompted for a default server, select the server you are logged on to.

3. Provide an application name such as Word 2000.

4. Provide a detailed description if desired.

5. Choose Explicit as the application type.

6. Type or browse to the path of the executable for your application.

7. The working directory will be filled in automatically. Change it if you need to.

8. Select whether to maximize the application and if you want to hide the title bar. If the Hide application title bar checkbox is selected, the application's title bar is not displayed in addition to the ICA session title bar, thus eliminating the appearance of two title bars. Click Next.

9. The next screen presents several options. Select your options and click Next.

10. This screen allows you to place the icon for the application directly on the user's desktop or in a folder on the user's Start Menu. Click Next.

11. The next screen allows you to select Windows User Groups that may access the application. Click Next.

12. The next screen lists all the servers you have in your farm. If load balancing has been enabled, you may add additional servers that have the application installed to the Configured list. The Configured list tells MetaFrame what servers are capable of providing an application to users.

13. Click Next and then Finish to complete the wizard.

TIP

A best practice is to create a user group for each application and assign this group as the only group that may access the application. Assign users to the groups as needed and the application will show up in their Program Neighborhood client.

Multisession Applications

Applications such as 5250, 3270, and Telnet are capable of starting multiple sessions to their host from a single MetaFrame session. Bandwidth consumption from these applications is typically low, but if a large number of sessions are created it may interfere with the network traffic requirements of other applications. If this is a concern in your environment, you may want to consider installing additional network cards and placing them on separate subnets, where one interface is on the same subnet as the host machines, and the other interface is on another machine. By separating the interfaces and applying static routes, you can direct the ICA (Independent Computing Architecture) traffic through one interface and all host traffic out the other interface.

"Short and Drop"

Citrix Program Neighborhood allows users to create desktop shortcuts to their applications. This is done on a user-by-user basis and can be achieved by simply right-clicking on the icon and selecting Create Desktop Shortcut. This will create an icon on the user's desktop to that application which is specific to that user, and will maintain the log-on credentials and preferences of that user.

WARNING

These icons *cannot* be copied to other user's desktops; the user must create them or you must create them while logged in as the user.

Load Balancing

Since no server exists that can handle the thousands of connections that a large company may require, or offer the redundancy of a simple two-server implementation, Citrix offers an add-on product called Load Balancing Services. Load Balancing is an extremely powerful tool that enables us to combine the computing power of multiple servers into a single Server Farm.

This Server Farm and application-centric paradigm combine to create an excellent method of scaling computing power. By installing a single application on 80 servers that can service 40 users each, one icon in Program Neighborhood can be launched by 3200 users without regard to the server on which the application is running. This method also allows the upgrade of a single application to be done only 80 times instead of 3200, and Citrix Installation Management Services or scripts can often automate those 80 upgrades.

Load Balancing is based on performance data of each individual server, not just round-robin connections, and is calculated based on the following factors, also found in Figure 11.12:

- Pagefile Usage

- Swap Activity

- Processor Usage

- Memory Load

- Sessions

Figure 11.12 Load Balancing Administration.

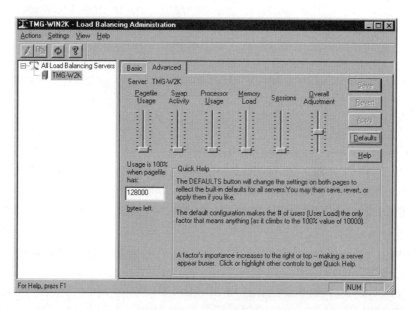

Load for each factor is computed on a 0–10,000 basis. Each factor contributes a percentage of the final load, which is also between 0 and 10,000. The computation is to multiply the ratio by the load for each factor. All of these intermediate results are added and the sum is divided by 100 (ratios being percentages). The ratios are always values between 0 and 100. Their values are computed from the relative importance. If you increase one importance slider, the associated ratio increments and the other ratios decrement.

Load Balancing determines which server to direct clients to by receiving a request from the client for a specific application over UDP port 1604. The ICA Master Browser determines from its resource list which servers are configured to provide that application. It then polls those servers for their load factors. It returns to the client the IP address of the server with the lowest load factor. Because the ICA Master Browser returns the server's address inside the data section of the UDP packet, it cannot be translated by a firewall. If the server is behind a firewall performing Network Address Translation (NAT), then the client must be configured to ask for the Alternate Address and each server must be informed of its Alternate Address.

TIP

The Pagefile Usage setting defaults to a very large number that is not in the best interest of load balancing. Always adjust this down to something more reasonable, such as half of the installed memory.

Creating an ICA File

ICA files are used in conjunction with Citrix Application Launching and Embedding (ALE) technology to define ICA connection information to the Netscape Plug-In, ActiveX, and Java Clients. An ICA file can provide an application in two ways, embedded or launched.

Embedded This method runs the application as a space inside the browser window and the application is run when the page is loaded.

Launched This method provides the user with a hyperlink on the Web page that opens the application in a new window.

Figure 11.13 shows a typical .ICA file and explains the various options.

Figure 11.13 The contents of an ICA file.

```
Use a simple text editor (such as Notepad) to create and modify ICA
  files.

A sample ICA file is shown below:


; Notepad.ICA - ICA file to access a Customer Database using Microsoft

Access
```

Continued

Figure 11.13 Continued.

```
;
; The [ApplicationServers] section contains the name of the
; connection or published application defined by the ICA file.
; The name below (Access) appears in the title bar of the client window.
;
[ApplicationServers]
Notepad=


; The section describes the attributes of the connection or
; published application defined in the [ApplicationServers] section above.
; The name in the square brackets must exactly match the name defined in
the
; [Application Servers] section above; in this example, Access.
;
[Notepad]
TransportDriver=TCP/IP
Address=192.168.100.13
WinStationDriver=ICA 3.0
Username=tmg
Domain=tmg-win2k
Password=010101010
InitialProgram=m:\winnt\system32\notepad.exe
WorkDirectory=m:\wtsrv\system32
UseAlternateAddress=0
;
KeyboardTimer=100
MouseTimer=50
;
; Use either ScreenPercent or DesiredHRES and DesiredVRES to specify
; the size of the client window.

; If both ScreenPercent and DesiredHRES and DesiredVRES are specified,
; only ScreenPercent is used. ScreenPercent is available only with
```

Continued

Figure 11.13 Continued.

```
; the Citrix Web Client.
ScreenPercent=75
DesiredHRES=640
DesiredVRES=480
DesiredColor=2


; The [WFClient] section describes the WinFrame Client.
;
[WFClient]


Version=2
```

The **[ApplicationServers**] section defines the remote application entry referred to by the ICA file. The [ApplicationServers] section contains the following fields:

```
[Application Server]
```

This is the section header. This field is required and must be entered exactly as shown.

```
EntryName=
```

Defines the name of the remote application entry. The name must be followed by an equal sign. This name is used in the title bar of the client window.

```
The [EntryName] Section
```

The **[EntryName]** section begins with the EntryName defined in the [ApplicationServers] section enclosed in square brackets, or [Access] in the above example. The [EntryName] section contains the following fields:

Continued

Figure 11.13 Continued.

```
TransportDriver=
```

The data transport type. Usually TCP/IP, but can also be IPX, SPX, or NetBIOS. This is a required field.

```
Address=
```

The address of the remote Citrix server. For TCP/IP connections, it can be the DNS name of a Citrix server, the IP address of a Citrix server, or the name of a published application, for example Database. For IPX, SPX, and NetBIOS connections, it can be the name of a Citrix server or the name of a published application. This is a required field.

```
WinStationDriver=ICA 3.0
```

Defines the presentation protocol as ICA 3.0. This is a required field.

```
Username=
```

Specifies the name of a user account to log on as. This is an optional field.

```
Domain=
```

Specifies the domain to log on. This is an optional field.

```
Password=
```

Specifies the password for the user account. This is an optional field. The password, if used, must be encrypted. To enter an encrypted password into the ICA file, use the Citrix ICA Client Remote Application Manager New Entry Wizard to create a remote application entry. When you are prompted for the username and password, enter the password that you want to use in the ICA file. Finish the New Entry wizard. Open the file

---

Continued

Figure 11.13 Continued.

APPSRV.INI in the Windows directory and locate the entry you just
created. Copy the password value and paste it into your ICA file.

ClearPassword=

Specifies the clear text (unencrypted) password for the user account.
This is an optional field. To use a clear text password, the Password
field must be set to a null value (for example: Password=).

InitialProgram=

Specifies the path of the application on the Citrix server to be
automatically launched when the connection is made. Include any command
line options. This is an optional field. If no initial program is
specified, Program Manager is launched. If the name of a published
application is specified in the Address field, the name of the published
application must appear here prefixed with a pound sign (#), for example
#Database. The published application name must be entered exactly as it
is in the Address field.

WorkDirectory=

Specifies the working directory used for the application.

ScreenPercent=

Specifies the horizontal and vertical pixel resolution as a percentage
of the client desktop size. If the ScreenPercent field is present, the
DesiredHRES and DesiredVRES fields are ignored.

DesiredHRES=

Continued

Figure 11.13 Continued.

Specifies the horizontal window size in pixels. If the ScreenPercent
field is present, the DesiredHRES and DesiredVRES fields are ignored.

DesiredVRES=

Specifies the vertical window size in pixels. If the ScreenPercent field
is present, the DesiredHRES and DesiredVRES fields are ignored.

DesiredColor=1 | 2

DesiredColor sets the color palette depth. Use 1 for 16-color and 2 for
256-color. The default is 2 (256-color).

UseAlternateAddress=0 | 1

This is an optional field, only used to support accessing a Citrix
server across a firewall. Firewalls use IP address translation to
convert public (Internet) IP addresses into private (Intranet) IP
addresses. Public IP addresses are called "external" addresses because
they are external to the firewall, while private IP addresses are called
"internal" addresses.

When an ICA client is configured for TCP/IP server location, it sends a
directed UDP datagram to the server location IP address using TCP/IP
port 1604. For communication to be successful between an ICA client and
a Citrix server with an intervening firewall, the firewall must be
configured so it will pass UDP port 1604 packets. Server location is
configured in Remote Application Manager by selecting Settings from the
Options menu.

If a fixed server location address is specified, the ICA client contacts
that server to determine the address of the ICA master browser. When
the ICA client connects by server or published application name, the
ICA master browser returns the address of the desired server or
published application.

Continued

Figure 11.13 Continued.

If UseAlternateAddress=1 is specified, the client will request the IP
address of the Citrix server's alternate address. UseAlternateAddress
can only be used for TCP/IP connections. You must specify the IP
address of the Citrix server that is configured for server location by
including the statement TcpBrowserAddress=ipaddress in the [WFClient]
section of the ICA file, where ipaddress is the IP address of the Citrix
server; for example, 123.321.234.23. You must also use the ALTADDR
command on the Citrix server with IP address ipaddress that is accessed
by the ICA file.

See the "Load Balancing and Application Publishing Across a Firewall"
topic in the WinFrame Readme for more information about alternate
addresses and the ALTADDR command.

KeyboardTimer=value

Specifies a time interval, in milliseconds, during which keyboard input
is collected before being sent to the Citrix server. The default value
of 100 milliseconds is optimized for WANs; in a Dial-In or LAN
environment; reducing this value may give better responsiveness. Using
too low a value in a LAN environment may cause a large number of small
packets to be generated, which may affect network performance.

MouseTimer=value

Specifies a time interval, in milliseconds, during which mouse input
will be collected before being sent to the Citrix server. The default
value of 100 milliseconds is optimized for WANs; in a Dial-In or LAN
environment, reducing this value may give better responsiveness. Using
too low a value in a LAN environment may cause a large number of small
packets to be generated, which may affect network performance.

The [WFClient] Section

Version=2

Continued

Figure 11.13 Continued.

Specifies the version of the client software. Do not change this value.
This is a required field.

TcpBrowserAddress=ipaddress

Specifies the IP address of a Citrix server used for server location.
This field is required if UseAlternateAddress=1 is specified in the
[EntryName] section.

***FOR BITMAP CACHING TO WORK WITH THE WEB CLIENT:

In the section WFClient add the following lines:

PersistentCacheEnabled=On
PersistentCacheSize=42935633
PersistentCacheMinBitmap=8192
PersistentCachePath=C:\WINNT\Profiles\amitb\Application
Data\ICAClient\Cache

In the section for the application add the following line:

PersistentCacheEnabled=On

Now bitmap caching will work. For switching off, you can switch off
PersistentCacheEnabled in the application setting. Please note that if
setting under application name and WFClient differ then setting under
application name will take precedence. PersistentCachePath should be
suitably changed to correspond with the actual user and the directory
where he wants to put the cache files. PersistentCacheSize and
PersistentCacheMinBitmap may also be changed according to the
requirement.

To create an ICA file, perform the following steps:

1. Open Published Application Manager by going to Start/Programs/MetaFrame Tools and selecting Published Application Manager.

2. Highlight the application you want to create the ICA file for and select Write ICA File from the application menu.

3. Choose "A lot! Please explain everything" and click Next.

4. Fill in the screen size for the application. You can specify the size in pixels or a percentage of the screen size. I usually use 90 percent of screen size to help users get a screen that is proportionate to their screen, but still discernable from their local desktop. You will also specify the color depth here. Opinions vary as to whether higher color depth affects performance, but as a rule, if the application does not *need* more than 16 colors, don't provide it.

5. The next dialog asks for your encryption level. MetaFrame SecureICA option pack offers several levels of encryption above what ICA inherently provides. Without the extra option pack, Basic is the only level available.

6. Next you will be asked for the name for the ICA file. If you click the Browse button and select the location, MetaFrame will fill in the filename for you.

7. Next, the wizard will ask if you would like an HTML template file created as well. Answer Yes and click Next.

8. Choose embedded or launched. The next steps will vary depending upon this choice. Launched will skip to Step 11.

9. Choose Netscape Plug-In/ActiveX control or Java Client.

10. Specify the size of the window.

11. Choose whether you want a verbose page. The verbose page will contain many comments and instructions on how to further modify the page to suit your needs, where as the nonverbose page will contain no more than the link or control.

12. Enter the filename or click Browse and indicate where to save your new HTML file.

Figure 11.14 shows the HTML file created by the wizard.

Figure 11.14 Example HTML file.

```
<!DOCTYPE HTML PUBLIC "-//IETF//DTD HTML//EN">
<html>
<head>
<meta http-equiv="Content-Type" content="text/html; charset=iso-8859-1">
<meta name="METAMARKER" content="null">
<title>Demo Application Page</title>


<script language="VBScript">
<!—
option explicit
dim majorver
dim ua
dim ie3
dim ie4
dim aol
dim minorver4
dim update
dim winplat
dim nav
dim intButton
set nav = navigator
ua = "Mozilla/2.0 (compatible; MSIE 3.02; Windows NT)"
minorver4 = ""


if len(ua) >=1 then 'nav object is supported
    winplat = mid(ua,instr(ua,"Windows") + 8, 2)
    majorver = mid(ua,instr(ua,"MSIE") + 5, 1)
    ie3 = majorver = 3 and (winplat = "NT" or winplat = "95" or
winplat = "32")
    ie4 = majorver = 4 and (winplat = "NT" or winplat = "95" or
winplat = "32")
    update = instr(ua,"Update a")
```

Continued

Figure 11.14 Continued.

```
      aol = instr(ua,"AOL")


      if ie4 then minorver4 = mid(ua,instr(ua,"MSIE") + 7, 3)
end if
—>
</script>


</head>


<body>
<p>
<FONT color=#ffffff>


<!— DIRECT.EXE EMBED —>


<script language="JavaScript">
<!—
// YOU SHOULD ONLY NEED TO CHANGE THE VARIABLES BELOW.
//
// icaFile: location of the .ICA file for both the OBJECT and EMBED.
   var icaFile = "po.ICA";
// width and height: pixel-size of the embedded application.
   var width = 800;
   var height = 600;
// start attribute: if Auto, application fires up upon pageload.
If Manual, application waits to be clicked by user.
   var start = "Auto";
// border attribute: On/Off, to specify border around application
window.
   var border = "On";
// Want vertical/horizontal space around the app? Set these just like
for the <IMG> tag.
   var hspace = 2;
```

Continued

Figure 11.14 Continued.

```
    var vspace = 2;
// Where is the ActiveX CAB file located? It's probably best to leave
this set to Citrix:
    var cabLoc =
"http://www.citrix.com/bin/cab/wfica.cab#Version=4,2,274,317";
// Where is the Plugins Reference page located? It's probably best to
leave this set to Citrix:
    var plugRefLoc = "http://www.citrix.com/demoroom/plugin.htm";
// END OF CHANGES. DO NOT CHANGE THE VARIABLES BELOW.
//


// The following is the ActiveX tag:
    var activeXHTML = '<CENTER><OBJECT classid="clsid:238f6f83-b8b4-
11cf-
8771-00a024541ee3" data="' + icaFile + '" CODEBASE="' + cabLoc + '"
width='
 + width + ' height=' + height + ' hspace=' + hspace + ' vspace=' +
vspace
 + '> <param name="Start" value="' + start + '"><param name="Border"
value="' + border + '"></OBJECT></CENTER>';


// And the Plugin tag:
    var plugInHTML = '<CENTER><EMBED SRC="' + icaFile + '"
pluginspage="' +
plugRefLoc + '" width=' + width + ' height=' + height + ' start=' +
start +
 ' border=' + border + ' hspace=' + hspace + ' vspace=' + vspace +
'></CENTER>';


var userAgent = navigator.userAgent;
if (userAgent.indexOf("Mozilla") != -1) {
if (userAgent.indexOf("MSIE") != -1) {
if (userAgent.indexOf("Windows 3") > 0)
```

Continued

Figure 11.14 Continued.

```
{ document.write(plugInHTML); }

else

{ document.write(activeXHTML); }

}

else

{ if (userAgent.indexOf("Win16") > 0) { document.write(plugInHTML); }

else { document.write(plugInHTML); }

}

}

//-->

</script>

<noscript>

<a href="po.ICA">

Your browser does not support JavaScript! You'll have to click here to

launch the application.

</a>

</noscript>

</FONT>

</body>

</html>
```

These files can then be placed into a Web server's directory and will *probably* work if the Web server and the MetaFrame server are on the same subnet, the files are placed in the same subnet, and the client can access the Internet. The default file points to www.citrix.com for the client files for ActiveX, Netscape Plug-In, and Java. If your clients do not have Internet access you must modify the HTML file to point to a public area on your Web server and place the Web client files in that location. The ActiveX client and Netscape Plug-In must be made available to the client to be downloaded at runtime. The ActiveX client and Netscape Plug-In are available from the \winnt\system32\clients\icaclients\ICAWeb directory on the MetaFrame server. Copy these files to a publicly accessible folder on the Web server. As shown in Figure 11.14, you can see that the HTML file is initially set to acquire the client files directly from the Citrix Web site, unless the clients do not have Internet access. If this is the case, modify the HTML code as outlined under the following sections.

Netscape

For Netscape, modify the following:

```
var plugRefLoc =
```

Modify this line to reflect the location of the Netscape Plug-In files. This can be done easily by using Notepad (or your favorite HTML editor) to create another HTML page such as:

```
<html>
<a href="wfplug32.exe">Click here to download the
Netscape Plug-in for 32-bit Windows</a>
<a href="wfplug16.exe">Click here to download the
Netscape Plug-in for 16bit Windows</a>
<html>
```

And setting the plugRefLoc to the URL of the previous file.

Internet Explorer

For Internet Explorer, the line is as follows.

```
var cabLoc =
```

Modify this line to reflect the path to the ActiveX .cab file such as:

```
http://webserver/download/disks/disk1/ActiveX/wfica.cab#Version=
4,2,274,317
```

Summary

Citrix MetaFrame and Windows 2000 Terminal Services provide a very robust environment for deploying applications. We have taken a look at how to select compatible applications, from 32-bit Windows applications to legacy DOS applications.

We covered how applications must be installed on a Terminal Services server and why. Terminal Services must track all the changes an application makes to the environment to provide a stable system for your users. The installation modes User-Specific and User-Global, help us tell the system when to track application installations.

The shadow registry and shadow file system store the information tracked during installations. The system uses this repository to provide required registry entries and files to users, as they need it.

For applications that are not necessarily multiuser-friendly we covered Application Compatibility Scripts. Application Compatibility Scripts allow us to provide unique settings and constructs for applications at runtime. This facility enables us to configure a great many settings as a user starts a session, and they are easily developed for new applications.

Publishing applications enables us to move beyond our traditional paradigm of client-to-server connections and move to an application-centric archetype of client-application connections. By defining an application as an object, we allow our administrators to define a user's experience by application permissions rather than file permissions. With this capability we can improve our quality of service without increasing our personnel, and by implementing thin-client devices we eliminate the obsolescence of user desktop PCs. This also enables us to make individual applications available through corporate intranets or even the Internet using ALE.

Your applications and their overall compatibility and performance will determine your users' acceptance of this technology. Always listen to your users for feedback during your test stage, and remember that your users' opinions will ultimately determine your success.

FAQs

Q: When I open the properties of a published application, the settings are all grayed out. What's wrong?

A: This happens when you have not correctly selected a scope.

Q: One of the servers in my load-balanced farm has stopped accepting connections; it has 40 licenses and only 25 users logged on. What's wrong?

A: The server may be fully utilized in one area or another. From a command prompt run "query server /app" and if the server in question has a load of 10,000 then one or more performance items may be at maximum usage.

Q: My application needs command-line variables passed to it at runtime; how can I do this?

A: Create a batch file that sets the environment variables and passes the necessary information to your application, and then publish the batch file.

Q: My users use Thin Client Terminals to access a published Program Neighborhood, but need access to the Printers folder. How can I allow them access to this folder without a full desktop opening?

A: Make a copy of explorer.exe named explorer2.exe and place it in your "M:\program files" directory. Make a folder on the root of your system drive and name it "Printers.{2227A280-3AEA-1069-A2DE-08002B30309D}. Now publish a new application called Printers Folder and put "m:\program files\explorer2.exe /n,/root,m:\Printers.{2227A280-3AEA-1069-A2DE-08002B30309D}" as the path. This will place an icon called Printers Folder in Program Neighborhood. Users can now have access to the Printers folder without starting Explorer and starting a full desktop.

Chapter 12

Utilizing the Internet

Solutions in this chapter:

- **Providing Business Applications over the Internet**

- **Overview of Connecting to Sessions over the Internet**

- **Configuring the Server to Provide Applications through a Web Page**

- **Infrastructure Impacts**

Introduction

For most organizations, the Internet represents the future of their business. However, the trend is not limited to e-commerce where businesses sell products to customers over the Internet. Businesses can more fully utilize their technology potential by easily extending services to remote offices and a field sales force through an intranet, and between vendor and client businesses (Business-to-Business). Sharing applications is an effective way of reducing internal IT costs and an exciting way of adding value to Business-to-Business (B2B) relationships. Client-server technology delivered over the Internet can be the quickest way to enhance business value.

Internally, a company can reduce licensing and maintenance costs by standardizing common applications and providing upgrades over an internal network. In B2B relationships, this reduces the need for each enterprise to purchase software applications so that they can exchange compatible files for stocking, shipping, and accounting information, or to use cumbersome processes to convert this information between applications. Additionally, the ability to deliver applications over the Internet eliminates the need to invest in hardware and software to provide for dial-up networking to remote offices and between companies exchanging data.

Citrix MetaFrame is a solution that provides all these advantages and gives the opportunity to further reduce maintenance, telecommunications, upgrade, and system administration costs. It also has a flexible interface that gives the enterprise the ability to adapt application delivery to suit users who have different comfort levels with technology. Applications can be presented so that it appears to the user that they are running the applications on their own machines or, alternatively, applications can run inside a Web browser that makes it clear that they are running remotely. With the recent NFuse release, users can view a cleaner interface.

This chapter explores these ideas further, showing how to configure Citrix MetaFrame for Web access and exploring the potential impacts that the installation of Citrix MetaFrame may have on existing environments.

Phoenix Manufacturing Case Study

As you progress through our discussion of Citrix MetaFrame delivery over the Internet, you can observe the processes that the hypothetical company Phoenix Manufacturing followed in their implementation.

Phoenix produces a wide variety of products and is very reliant on market research, supply, production, warehousing, and distribution planning to ensure that their perishable line of products meets market demands. If they do not accurately forecast demand, they run the double risk of having to scrap spoiled varieties that cannot be sold and sending customers to competitors because Phoenix cannot meet their demand for other varieties. Effective B2B collaboration is necessary for the company's continued success.

Over the past year, Phoenix North America has installed Citrix MetaFrame at their east coast facility, with clients at this and their Rocky Mountain facility. Although the installation has gone well, they have moved cautiously and have not implemented the remote features of MetaFrame application publication. Remote users, both internal and external, still use a 1-800 dial-up connection to log on the company's domain server, and then need to log on the application server for the resources they want to use. The connection is slow because significant parts of most applications reside on the users' computers and significant parts reside on the server, fat-client style. It is Phoenix's goal to nearly eliminate the cost of 1-800 access, save data-entry time by streamlining the application access process, and drastically reduce the need for field support while improving access to the data needed for production and distribution planning.

Phoenix's challenge is to facilitate the use of data on the various platforms and operating environments that exist across the company. Old, medium, and new technologies exist side by side; in fact, and almost every major operating system is in use in North America because this company, like most others, has tried to keep up with technological advances and has left no stone unturned in its successful effort to be competitive. Figure 12.1 shows Phoenix's connected community.

Figure 12.1 Phoenix's connected community.

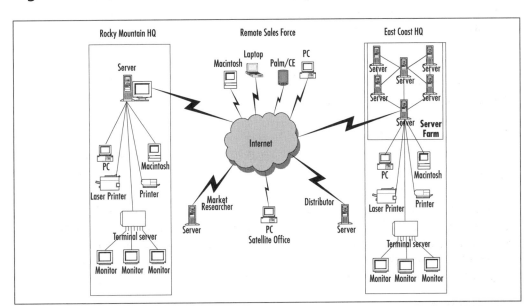

Providing Business Applications over the Internet

For some time we have witnessed the power of the Internet to enhance businesses. Many successful attempts have been made to tap this power and optimize business potential. Companies wish to move in this direction for many reasons, not the least of which is reducing the Total Cost of Ownership (TCO). TCO has been one of the major driving forces in technological spending since its introduction to the corporate environment. The introduction of Citrix MetaFrame brings TCO down significantly by extending the useful life of existing technical infrastructure.

The Total Cost of Ownership Advantage

There are several measurable hard costs that reduce TCO immediately. Eliminating the need for a high-end server and support staff on location at each branch office is perhaps the most obvious cost benefit. As with internal intranet operations, eliminating the need to physically configure each person's computer separately drastically reduces the staff hour cost of installing applications to users' machines, such as those in field offices and remote sales staff. The applications are installed on a central server and served up to users in true thin-client fashion. In other words, only a Web browser is run on the user's machine with all of the applications running on the server; only screen shots are passed between the two without interactive processing. Since the applications are installed on a central server, releasing upgrades and patches also becomes a much shorter and simpler task, eliminating the need to touch every machine. A cost savings closely related to this is seen in extending the useful life of existing wide area networking (WAN) and telecom resources by reducing Internet traffic and freeing up bandwidth. This allows normal company and e-commerce growth to continue without additional infrastructure purchases.

Equipment costs are also reduced because upgrading computers to accommodate applications becomes unnecessary. Local processing power is no longer a consideration because all processing takes place on the server. User machines only need the capacity to run the Citrix required minimum browser efficiently with Internet connections fast enough for user needs. See Table 12.1 for a comprehensive list of compatible browsers. Even where replacement equipment is desirable or needed due to breakage or failure, the cost of thin-client equipment such as "Win Terms" is about one third the cost of standard new full capability computer equipment, further reducing TCO. Connecting B2B users who wish to share applications, as described earlier, is easy because the businesses do not need to be concerned about hardware or communication equipment compatibility, nor about software compatibility beyond the required browser.

Table 12.1 Supported Browser/Platform Combinations

Operating System	Browsers Supported
Windows 3.1	Internet Explorer 4.1 Netscape Navigator 4.08
Windows NT	Internet Explorer 4.0 Internet Explorer 5.0 Netscape Navigator 4.01 Netscape Communicator 4.61
Windows 95/98	Internet Explorer 4.0 Internet Explorer 5.0 Netscape Navigator 4.01 Netscape Communicator 4.61
UNIX	Netscape Navigator 4.01
Linux	Netscape Navigator 4.01 Netscape Communicator 4.61
Mac	Netscape Navigator 4.01 Netscape Communicator 4.61

Examples of soft costs that are reduced by the Citrix thin-client solution include the satisfaction and increased productivity of remote users who no longer have to wait for someone to upgrade their applications, nor do without equipment that needs to be sent in for upgrades. With Citrix, as soon as the upgrade is made on the server, all users are using the new version. Another advantage is that use of applications over a thin-client connection gives users the perception of faster connections. With only screen shots being transferred across the Internet and all processing taking place on the server, traffic to and from the Internet is greatly reduced, giving users truly better performance. A centralized server environment also provides an enterprise greater control over the application environment by making it impossible for users to damage applications by inadvertently deleting critical files such as .DLLs or by installing unstable personal applications.

As a result of implementing Citrix MetaFrame technology, Phoenix Manufacturing anticipates cutting this year's Information Technology (IT) budget by over ten percent by avoiding new desktop equipment purchases and upgrades to their telecommunications infrastructure. They also antici- pate that the following year's projections can be reduced by as much as 20 percent while maintaining a technological edge.

Whether used in conjunction with an intranet or a virtual private network (VPN), the ability to allow users in remote offices access to software located in a centralized site offers many cost-saving and performance-enhancing opportunities. Businesses providing applications from high-end servers within large Server Farms will provide better performance to end users than is currently possible using desktop computing or less powerful servers at remote locations. Keep in mind that this sort of deployment scheme can be taken even further. By outsourcing the entire IT operation to an Application Service Provider (ASP) and third-party support, the company can reduce or eliminate the need for an Information Technology department. This is particularly true for small- and medium-size companies. Companies no longer need to buy expensive hardware for individual employees. The same work can be accomplished through the use of Internet-ready devices connecting to an ASP's services. This application has great potential for cost savings.

Business-to-Business Arrangements

B2B arrangements are typically considered to realize a reduction in costs by collapsing processes that are duplicated between two companies. For example, in a Supply Chain Management method, a peanut butter manufacturer has to perform accounts receivable invoicing when selling peanut butter to a grocery distributor. The distributor must execute a similar function in accounts payable. While somewhat reciprocal, these accounting processes nearly duplicate the time and effort involved. To reduce costs in a supply chain, the manufacturer might simply provide its accounting application over the Internet to the distributor—or at least the account reporting data. Another example might be in Customer Relationship Management (CRM): the distributor may provide access to its CRM application through the Internet so that the manufacturer can better serve the distributor's clients.

Phoenix Manufacturing has found that they could conduct Tactical Account Planning (TAP) functions by giving their third-party distributors direct access to Enterprise Resource Planning (ERP) data using a Citrix MetaFrame ERP bolt-on application. This eliminated Phoenix's need to extract, convert, and deliver what they felt was appropriate data to the distributors. This translated into time savings and, with the distributors being able to access original data files, they were able to better understand the bigger picture of product availability through Phoenix's production and warehouse planning data.

Providing applications across the Internet can solve several problems for companies using technology. Investment capital can be maximized when introducing new products. For example, upon completion of a new application, a software company would like to make it available for future potential clients to view. This would previously have required tying up capital in the creation and distribution of demo CDs. If this company instead provides the demo over the Internet using preexisting Web servers, they save investment capital and distribution time in the process while being able to enhance the product in real time based on user feedback. Utilization of this technology to provide application demonstrations can also increase the ease with which kiosks are installed. No longer is computing power required for a kiosk.

While deploying software across the Internet, a company need only provide machines that can act as clients for their software distribution server that is safely located anywhere offsite. With proper bandwidth management and security, this technology can even be used in point-of-sale devices. Servers can be run from a central location, allowing the hardware required in these devices to be drastically reduced. Load balancing can be conducted at the server end with technicians present to ensure proper operation.

Overview of Connecting to Sessions over the Internet

The delivery mechanism that Citrix MetaFrame has provided enables the connection of all types of platforms over the Internet as well as within a local area network (LAN). This includes machines designed to operate under Windows, UNIX, Windows Terminal Server, and Macintosh platforms. Any computer system that can run a Citrix compatible browser using Internet protocols can access applications over the Internet through MetaFrame.

Using MetaFrame Client and VPN

When using Citrix in a VPN, many factors must be considered in order to provide proper performance. While Citrix is designed to run over low-bandwidth links, heavy use of single application installations on the servers by end users in a branch office may overwhelm the VPN or any other type of connection. For this reason, implementing a Server Farm should be considered with member servers present on remote networks. This allows for single administration of a Server Farm while providing greater connection speeds to clients when a Server Farm member is local. In Figure 12.2, Phoenix's single Server Farm, which is centrally administered, provides the same Independent Computing Architecture (ICA) connections to different networks.

Figure 12.2 Phoenix's single Server Farm spanning multiple remote networks.

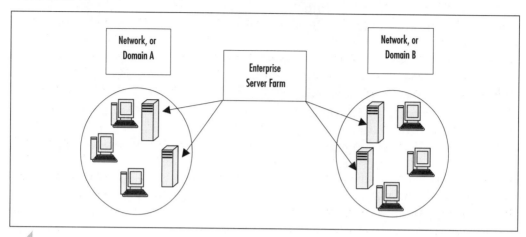

NOTE

Keep in mind that a VPN connection may very well be able to support the ICA traffic of an entire remote network. This can be accomplished by allowing only ICA traffic to cross the VPN link. Internet browsing that requires graphics processing and other bandwidth intensive uses can be processed at a central location with a faster connection. This will give ICA clients a greater sense of speed. It will seem as though they can browse the Internet at 1.54 Mbps when they only have a 56 Kbps connection to the Internet because the ICA session resides on a server with access to a T1 line.

If VPN connections are capable of sustaining all the Citrix traffic of remote networks, ICA Gateways should be implemented first to ensure proper conversions of data for browser communications and conversions to accommodate networking protocols. ICA Gateways contain lists that allow Citrix clients and servers to contact other Citrix Servers on different networks with different protocols. This setup is required for proper Citrix operation across VPN or WAN connections, as browser lists are determined via broadcasts. This ensures complete conversions rather that just supporting one browser or protocol within another.

Server Farms

Historically, client-server installations have been built around the single installation of each application on a server with all clients accessing the appropriate server. Over time, it has been recognized that some applications attract many users while others have only a few. Also, the usage of different applications fluctuates during the course of a month. While Microsoft Word may see fairly steady use, applications such as Microsoft Excel, and those for accounts payable and accounts receivable, experience higher usage toward the end of each month, quarter, and fiscal year and, possibly, at the middle of the month, depending on billing cycles. Planning and forecasting packages are typically used more heavily toward the beginning of each year, quarter, and month and presentation software use may fluctuate with sales and marketing programs and project reporting cycles. In a Server Farm, several servers are dedicated to running enterprise applications and all applications are installed on each of the servers. Load balancing is used to distribute the user workload and processing demand across all of the servers in the farm.

Phoenix Manufacturing noticed these variations in server usage because some server capacities would be overwhelmed at times and be underutilized at other times. As hardware costs have come down and application licensing has adjusted to the advances in client-server technology, it has become practical for them to build a Server Farm. They established it at their East coast facility where all remote processing is managed. This provides Phoenix with continuous 24-hour, seven-days-a-week operation as the workload of failing servers is transparently distributed to the rest of the farm while repairs are made. It also allows for planned maintenance activities to take place without user disruption.

Using a Web Browser

One required component in application publishing to the Internet is a Web server. When providing an application in this manner, the Web server will house both the HTML file that links to the application and the .ICA file that contains information about the application server. Microsoft's Internet Information Server (IIS) that acts as the Web server can run on a MetaFrame server with the applications; however, Citrix does not recommended this.

Both the Web server and the application server must be available to each client that is trying to reach them; that is, group and individual permissions must be set up for appropriate access to each server. When new applications are installed, application access can be assigned by group and individual during installation. The flow of access to applications in the Citrix Server Farm through NFuse is illustrated in Figure 12.3.

Figure 12.3 The NFuse/Citrix application access flow.

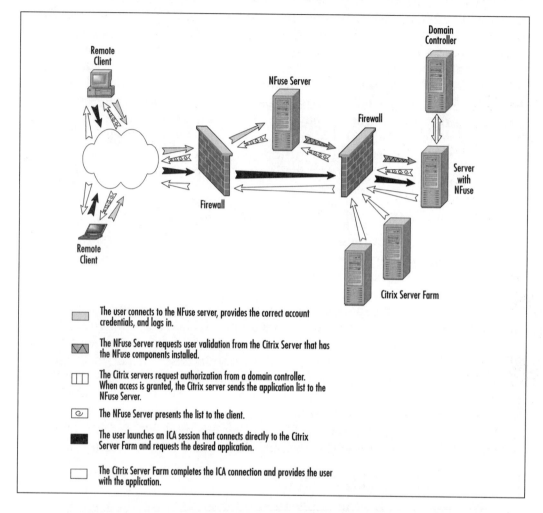

With the NFuse application portal technology installed on Citrix MetaFrame, an application can be provided over the Internet through a process known as Application Launching and Embedding (ALE). The ALE process executes a program on a MetaFrame server when the proper hypertext link is selected. There are two methods that utilize the application, *application launching* and *application embedding*. Both are initiated from a Web browser window displaying the Citrix MetaFrame client interface. Through the use of Application Launching, an application appears in its own window on the client desktop separately from the Web browser window from which the hyperlink to it is clicked. Application Embedding displays an application within a browser window in the HTML environment.

Applications can be set up to run in the browser as soon as the Web server is accessed; a company's unique Web page can give link access to approved applications; or a new desktop can be displayed to give the user access to a range of applications. Both of these processes can be used over the Internet or on an intranet with equal ease.

NOTE

When using the Application Launching method, the file WFICA32.EXE is required to be installed on the client machine. This method has been known to confuse some users who believe the application is actually running on their machine. If this is a concern, try using Application Embedding. Seeing an application running within a Web page does not leave much room for questions as to where the application is running.

For IT Professionals

ICA Clients for ALE

Since NFuse extends the capabilities of ALE, users have the option to deliver applications that can be launched from a Web page or embedded within the Web page. Citrix ICA Java Client and Citrix ICA Windows Web Clients (ActiveX and Netscape plug-in) support embedded applications. ICA Clients that support launched applications include:

- Citrix ICA Windows Web Clients (ActiveX and Netscape plug-in)
- Citrix ICA Win32 Client
- Citrix ICA Win16 Client
- Citrix ICA Java Client
- Citrix ICA Unix Client
- Citrix ICA Macintosh Client

When an application is published through Citrix MetaFrame for use in the ALE process, two files are created. One is the HTML Web page file that links to the application and the other is the ICA file that establishes the correct type of connection. This Web page contains the formatting required to run the ICA file and to establish the correct type of connection. The ICA file, on the other hand, is plain text and contains only information about the ICA connection that is being created.

The final component in this process is the Web client. Citrix MetaFrame can use three clients:

- A Netscape plug-in Client
- A Microsoft ActiveX Client
- A Java Client

The Netscape plug-in client, which works only with Netscape, requires manual installation before an application can be run.

The Microsoft ActiveX Client is distributed by diskette, though the diskette is not needed, as the ActiveX Client is usually automatically downloaded from a corporate server or Internet server when it is run for the first time. It works with Microsoft's Internet Explorer, but it can also be used independently of Explorer.

The Java Client requires by far the most administrative overhead. However, if installed properly, it can provide an application that can operate on almost any Web-capable machine.

The Java Web Client that comes with Citrix MetaFrame operates in two different modes. The first mode, *application mode*, requires less administrative overhead and more end-user knowledge. When using the Java Web Client in application mode, the Java Web Client resides on the client machine that has an active Java Virtual Machine (JVM) version 1.1 or higher. This method of using Java allows the end user to initiate ICA connections from a command prompt and specify parameters to be used in the session. The session that is created in this mode is run from a window on a desktop and does not require a Web browser that supports Java.

The other mode that a Java connection creates is *applet mode*. This mode requires more administrative overhead, but puts less of a burden on end users and gives the administrator more control. When running in applet mode, the Java Web Client must be installed on the Web server where sessions are created. These Java ICA sessions will be initiated by the end user with a Java-compatible Web browser. When a session is created, the Java ICA Client is downloaded from the Web server and associated with ICA files. The client then uses the ICA files to create an ICA session with the Citrix Server. When using the Java Web Client in applet mode, the end user must have a Web browser that supports JVM 1.1 or higher.

Configuring the Server to Provide Applications from a Web Page

There are two methods of providing Citrix services to Internet users. One is the original Citrix-provided Web access and the other is the new portal technology called NFuse, which was released early in 2000 by Citrix. The NFuse service extends the original Citrix installation by providing seamless integration with Web delivery of newly published applications. It also provides a cleaner presentation of user-group specific applications. Whereas the ICA client permits all users to see all published applications regardless of group security and access restrictions, NFuse limits the view to just the applications that the user has access to. Using the original method involves taking additional steps. These include creating files and modifying the Web page in order to present each application that is to be published to the Internet. Once NFuse has been installed, the publication of any new application involves only designating user access with the application installation. No other steps need to be performed.

TIP

Citrix ICA Clients are available for download at http://download.citrix.com. Citrix has partnered with a large number of companies that are licensed to redistribute the ICA clients with their products. These include manufacturers of terminals, handheld and custom devices, wireless devices, and operating systems.

Once installed, clients can be updated through the client-server connection. An administrator places the latest ICA Client versions in the client update database on the MetaFrame server. As ICA Clients connect to the server, they will recognize that they are older than the version in the update database. As a result, the ICA Client will prompt the user to accept the update.

ICA Clients are offered at no cost to the end user. Citrix works in advance with OEMs and device makers to ensure ICA Clients are of the highest quality and are well supported.

When moving to the Internet, security is a major consideration that cannot be overemphasized. The firewall is the primary means of control between the Internet and the enterprise. Additional measures can be used such as a Demilitarized Zone (DMZ) and portal technologies. To protect against eavesdropping between external connection points, encryption such as Secure Socket Layer (SSL) and Citrix Secure ICA are the best security measures. Security issues are described in the next section. Another feature of NFuse is that the communication does not rely on User Datagram Protocol (UDP) information being broadcast to the Web browser.

Configuring the Original Installation

When publishing applications to Internet users, the primary configuration is already complete by virtue of the initial installation. What needs to be done on the server is to access the Published Application Manager and create the .ICA and .HTM files. The files must be saved together in the folder that the Published Application Internet link points to. If the page that is presenting the published application is to have a company approved appearance, the page will need to be modified to include the new application link. On the other hand, if the created .HTM template is to be used, it will require modification.

1. Log on to the Citrix server and launch the Published Application Manager tool.

2. Right-click on the desired published application and select Write ICA File from the drop-down list as shown in Figure 12.4.

3. Select the amount of assistance required by selecting the desired choice and then select Next.

Figure 12.4 Creating the ICA file.

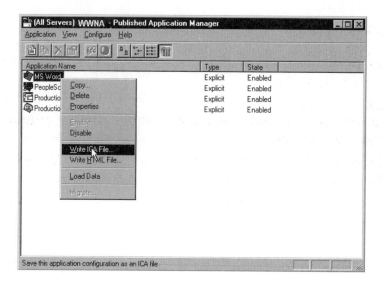

4. Select the application's display attributes that will be viewed on the client. This can be done as pixels or as a percent of the browser window. Phoenix chose to specify the window as a percentage. This size is for the window in the Web browser, not necessarily for the application. This setting designates the size defined in the .ICA file, or it can display maximized in the embedded window. Choose the numbers of colors to be made available and select Next as shown in Figure 12.5.

Figure 12.5 Specifying application window size and available colors.

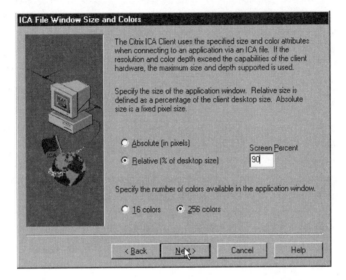

5. Select the Basic encryption level to be used when accessing this application as shown in Figure 12.6. Please note that in order to utilize the other encryption settings, the Citrix Secure ICA Services must be installed.

6. Enter the name and location of where the ICA file is to be stored. This file is to be stored in a public share and will be hyperlinked from the Web site.

7. Select whether or not to create an associated HTML template for the application. If not, select No and then select Finish.

8. If creation of a template file is desired, select Yes and then select Next.

Figure 12.6 Encryption settings.

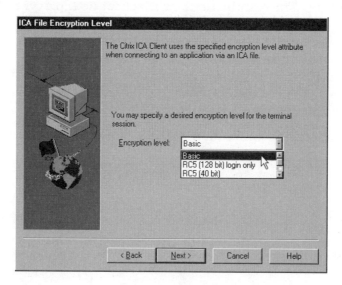

Determining How the Application Is Displayed

The next step will determine how the application is to be displayed on the client PC. Selecting either choice requires separate follow-up option selections. Therefore, each selection path will be outlined separately.

By selecting Launched, the application will be displayed in a separate window, outside of the browser, while selecting Embedded displays the application in the Web browser. It was Phoenix's decision to launch the application in a separate window set to 90 percent of the client display size. This allowed for a screen that automatically displays in a size taking up a larger amount of desktop "real estate" for any client, as opposed to a locked size defined by pixels that would be the same on all clients regardless of the size of the local client's display. To begin:

1. Select Launched for the desired application appearance and then select Next.

2. Select Verbose if comments in the HTML code are desired. These comments will describe the parameters for the Web-client components.

3. Enter the name and location of where the .HTM template file is to be stored. This must be stored in the same public share as the ICA file. A warning will indicate the significance of editing the HTML file, as shown in Figure 12.7.

4. Select OK to complete the .ICA and .HTM file creation.

Figure 12.7 HTML file editing.

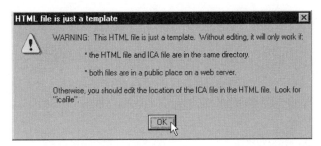

Perform the following series of steps for embedded applications and windows.

1. Select Embedded for the desired application appearance and then select Next.

2. Select the desired ICA Web client type and then select Next. The choice for Java Client will require more manual administrative coding. See Figure 12.8.

Figure 12.8 ICA Web client selection.

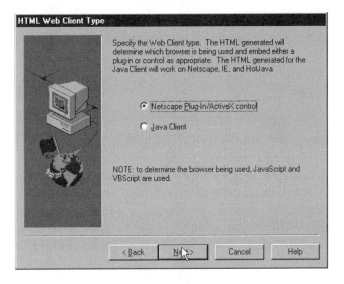

3. Specify the width and height of the application window as shown in Figure 12.9. This size is for the window in the Web browser, not necessarily for the application and will either display as the size defined in the .ICA file, or will display maximized in the embedded window. Keep in mind that the client may not be able to display large browser windows above 800×600.

Figure 12.9 Embedded window size setting.

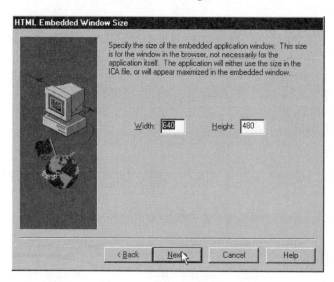

4. Select Verbose if comments in the HTML code are desired. These comments will describe the parameters for the Web-client components.

5. Enter the name and location of where the .HTM template file is to be stored. This must be stored in the same public share as the .ICA file. A warning will indicate the significance of editing the HTML file, as indicated in Figure 12.7.

NFuse

NFuse is an application portal technology. It allows organizations to integrate and publish interactive applications into any standard Web browser. NFuse includes both a Citrix Server component and a Web server component, as well as a Citrix ICA client component to deliver applications in thin-client fashion through Web browsers.

NFuse combines the browser integration capabilities of Citrix's Application Launching and Embedding (ALE) technology with the management and dynamics of Citrix Program Neighborhood. It provides Citrix users with the ability to easily deploy and manage personalized application content via the Internet and enables enterprises or Application Service Providers (ASPs) to provide customized environments to meet specific user or organization needs.

The key features of NFuse include:

- A Web interface to Program Neighborhood for simplified application access

- Dynamically customizable user interface creation from a single "template" Web script

- Central control of application deployment through server-side scripting and .ICA files

- Configurable application name to IP address resolution, which enhances security by eliminating use of the UDP-based ICA Browser

- COM-compliant Java objects accessible from Web server scripts such as Java Server Pages and Microsoft's Active Server Pages

- Simplified script writing with proprietary HTML extensions

- The Web Site Wizard that helps create complete NFuse-enabled Web sites

NFuse is compatible with most popular Web site development tools such as HotMetal, Microsoft FrontPage, Cold Fusion, and Macromedia's DreamWeaver. NFuse pages can also be enhanced using other COM and Java compliant tools. However, Java support is not required in the chosen Web browser. NFuse requires an ICA client on the access device, but it generates HTML pages dynamically.

A Java Virtual Machine (JVM) is not needed to view pages generated by Citrix NFuse Web sites. However, if you decide to deploy the ICA Java Client to access published applications, the Web browser must have a JVM compatible with the ICA Java Client.

TIP

Citrix has made NFuse available to its customers at no cost as a download from its Web site. You can access NFuse on the Citrix Download Page at http://download.citrix.com. Complete product documentation is also available.

Configuring the NFuse Components

To configure a NFuse Web deployment, two setups are required. The NFuse service must be installed on one of the Citrix servers in the farm that houses the applications being served, and the NFuse extensions must be installed on the Web server that will present the applications. Once these components have been installed and configured, the published applications on the farm will be automatically displayed on a per user/group basis in the application list after they have logged into the NFuse site and have been authenticated. The access attributes assigned to the applications in the Citrix Published Application Manager determine what applications will be displayed to which users/groups. In essence, once this configuration is in place, the administrator only needs to publish applications on the farm in order for them to appear for the users/groups that the application is targeted for. No other action is required in regards to either the NFuse services or the Web server extensions.

For IT Professionals

NFuse and Program Neighborhood

NFuse and Program Neighborhood both provide the ability to manage application access and deployment. However, NFuse provides some powerful capabilities to manage creation and deployment of personalized Web content. It also enables user-specific applications to be delivered to all Citrix ICA client platforms via a Web browser.

NFuse uses a Web server component to communicate with the Program Neighborhood Service on the Citrix Server, whereas Program Neighborhood uses a Win32 application running on a user's computer to communicate with the Program Neighborhood Service on the Citrix Server. The Web server component of NFuse displays the applications a user can access as HTML pages in their Web browser.

The NFuse Web Site Wizard can be used outside the NFuse environment. It can be installed on any PC because it creates a fully working set of HTML pages that allows users to log on and start applications. If you are familiar with Web site development, including Active Server Pages, Java Server Pages, or the Citrix Tokens included with NFuse, you can either create NFuse pages from scratch or further customize the ones generated by the wizard.

Installing the NFuse Services on the Citrix Server Farm

The NFuse services need only be installed on one server in the farm. However, it may be desirable to install it on all the servers in the farm for backup redundancy. This will ensure that, if a server is down or has been removed from the farm for service, there will be no interruption to the serving of the applications to the Web clients. It should be noted here that during the installation, the setup will inquire as to what port the farm should listen to for request from the Web server. The default is 80, but any port that is user-definable and is not in use by any other service can be used. To identify an open port on the network, the command is as follows:

```
netstat -a
```

This command displays all connections and listening ports. Please ensure that the port number selected is remembered since it will also be used later on for the Web server extensions installation. To begin the procedure:

1. Log onto the Citrix server.
2. Invoke the NFuse services installation file program, NFuseForMF.EXE.
3. Click Next on the Welcome screen.
4. Click Accept on the License Agreement screen.
5. Select the Citrix NFuse Services and Web Site Wizard and click Next. If you do not select Citrix NFuse Services, only the Web Site Wizard will be installed. If you do not select Web Site Wizard, you will have to create your Web pages on the Web server manually or from a machine where the Web Site Wizard is installed. It creates Web site templates for future use. The wizard can be installed on any machine to allow remote creation of Web sites. As this was Phoenix's initial installation of NFuse, both the services and the Web Site Wizard were selected for installation, as shown in Figure 12.10.
6. Select the desired destination folder for the Web Site Wizard.
7. Determine and enter the default program folder destination and click Next.
8. Enter the TCP port on which the NFuse Services Citrix Server should listen for requests from the NFuse Web server (the default is 80) and click Next. If an alternate port number is used, a notification message will remind you that any Citrix NFuse Web servers that will communicate with the service must be configured to make requests to the port number that was defined, as indicated in Figure 12.11.
9. Confirm the listed setup information and click Next.
10. When the dialog box confirms that the installation has completed, click Finish.

Figure 12.10 Citrix NFuse component selection.

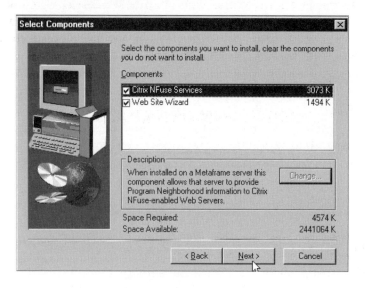

Figure 12.11 Citrix NFuse alternate port warning.

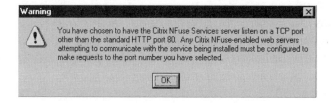

Installing the NFuse Web Server Extensions

Installation of the Web server components is minimal. However, caution must be taken because this installation will shut down Internet services on the Web server during setup. Any Web services running will be interrupted. It is best to plan this installation when the target Web server can be taken out of service or when usage is expected to be at its lowest and all users have been notified of the potential impact on their work. To install the Web server extensions, perform the following steps:

1. Log onto the Web server.

2. Invoke the NFuse Web server extension installation file, NfuseWebExt.EXE.

3. Click Next at the Welcome screen.

4. A question dialog asks if you want to stop Internet information services as shown in Figure 12.12. If you choose Yes, it will prevent this machine from serving Web pages during the installation and will automatically restart the services at its conclusion. If you choose No, the installation will discontinue.

Figure 12.12 IIS suspension.

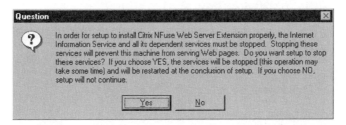

5. Click on Accept at the License Agreement screen.

6. Select the desired destination folder for the NFuse Web Server Extensions and click Next. In most cases, the default path is chosen.

7. As shown in Figure 12.13, choose a setup type and click Next. Choosing NFuse Objects installs all operational components. Choosing Example Files provides some guidelines to follow for Web site development. Since this was Phoenix's initial installation, the former was selected so that all of the components could be installed.

Figure 12.13 Citrix NFuse Web extensions setup type selection.

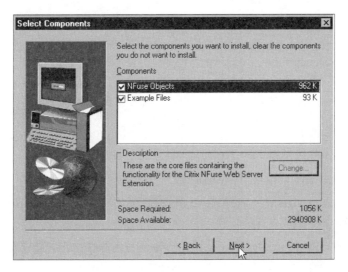

8. Enter the name of the Citrix Server where the NFuse Services were installed.

9. Enter the port chosen during the NFuse Services installation and click Next. If a port other than the default 80 has been chosen, a warning dialog appears similar to that in the NFuse Services installation as shown in Figure 12.14.

Figure 12.14 Citrix NFuse alternate port warning.

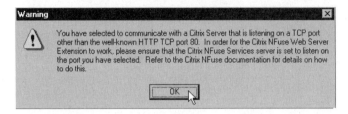

10. Configure the root Uniform Resource Locator (URL). The root URL is the directory in the physical file system on the Web server that the root URL maps to. The default path, \inetpub\wwwroot, can be accepted but you may browse to another location. The correct location of this URL should be verified on the Web server.

11. At the Setup Confirmation Screen, verify that all entries are correct and click Finish. Otherwise, click Back to make changes to the appropriate screens.

Using the Web Site Wizard to Set Up an Initial Site

The Web Site Wizard can be used to create an initial site as an example, but the site created consists of essentially generic pages. The administrator may wish to use a Web editor such as Microsoft Front Page to apply elements that give the site a corporate look. The example pages generated are compatible with most WYSIWYG (What You See Is What You Get) Web editors. You can walk through the Web Site Wizard by performing the following steps:

1. Log on a PC where the Web Site Wizard has been installed.

2. Launch the Web Site Wizard.

3. Click Next on the Welcome screen.

4. Click Accept on the License Agreement screen.

5. Select the MetaFrame in your farm running the NFuse services. If you have multiple MetaFrame servers and farms, you can override

the server and port number defined during the Web server installation. Because Phoenix has only one Server Farm with NFuse services installed on one server, they accept the default as shown in Figure 12.15 and click Next.

Figure 12.15 Server selection.

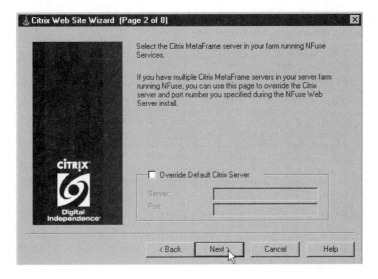

6. Select the Web site scheme that will define the look and feel of the Web pages you will be creating and click Next.

7. Select a layout model for your Web pages that is compatible with your Web server and click Next as shown in Figure 12.16. The choices are for Microsoft Internet Information Server, Netscape Server, and Apache Server (UNIX-based). For each of these there are two layout models—*Tag Based* and *Scripting Based*. Tag Based provides a template using standard HTML tagging. Scripting Based uses Active Server Page (for IIS) or Java (Netscape or Apache) script code. The advantage of Tag Based is that it is simple to implement. Scripting gives Web pages greater functionality.

8. The Netscape and Apache Tag Based selection takes you to additional screens that have additional parameters to be set up:

   a. Enter the URL Mapping for Servlet, which is the virtual path to the NFuse servlet.

   b. Enter the path and URL to the directory on the Web server where the Web pages will be published

   c. The next screen comes back to "Select how published applications will be viewed" as described in Step 9.

Figure 12.16 Layout model selection.

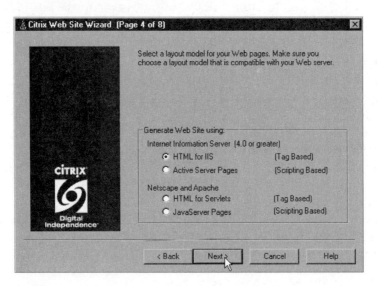

9. The HTML for IIS, Active Server Pages, and Java Server Pages selections continue with, "Select how published applications will be viewed," whether they will be launched in a separate window or embedded in a Web page. If launching in a separate window is desired, an option for seamless is available to make applications appear to be running on the client machine. If applications are to be run embedded in a Web page, the Web client type (ActiveX for Internet Explorer [IE], Netscape plug-in, or Java applet) must be chosen. If Java applet is chosen, your browser must be Java enabled and, if using IE, it must not be set at high security. The embedded selection gives a warning that a Web page can take advantage of an ICA client copied into the created directory. This allows the server to determine which browser the client is using and installs the appropriate ICA Web client in the client's browser.

10. Select the appearance of links that will populate the client Web for launching published applications. The choices are as follows:

   a. **Show Icon** This will show the icon defined at application installation if it differs from the default application icon.

   b. **Show Name** This will show the name defined at application installation if it differs from the default application name.

   c. **Show Details** This gives an application description if one was entered for the application.

   d. **Show Folders** This gives a tree view of available applications.

   e. **Allow user to view application settings** This puts a button on the Web page that goes to a settings page when clicked.

11. Determine the type of login page to be generated and click Next as shown in Figure 12.17. Allow Explicit Logins requires the user to login with the User ID and password established by the network administrator. Allow Guest Logins allows anyone who has access to the network to select Log In as Guest on the Login screen, which provides an anonymous user ID and password hidden from the client that gives limited access to applications as defined by the network administrator. Both can be selected to allow both privileged users and guests to login. The additional option for Explicit, Force Domain, gives a two-box login that hides the domain from the display, but presents a slight security risk, as the domain is then listed in the source code of the Web page.

Figure 12.17 Determining the login page type.

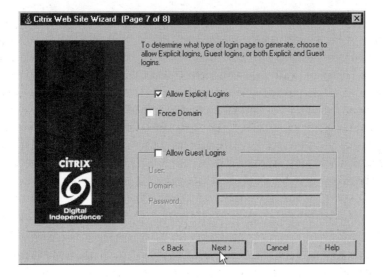

12. At the Setup Confirmation Screen, verify that all entries are correct and click Finish. Otherwise, click Back to make changes to the appropriate screens.

Web Access Screen Examples

The following are example displays of the login, launched, and embedded access screens for the Citrix published Web applications for the original setup using both .ICA files and NFuse.

Figure 12.18 shows an example of a published desktop embedded in the Web browser, utilizing the original .ICA file method of Web access.

Figure 12.18 Embedded application utilizing the ICA method.

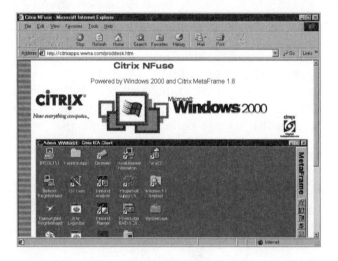

Figure 12.19 shows the three-box login that is generated for the explicit type of login that does not force the domain for the NFuse portal access.

Figure 12.19 NFuse portal.

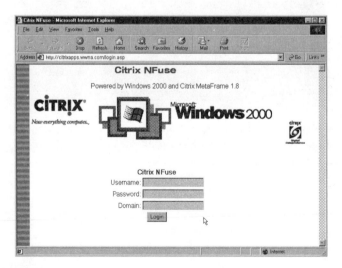

Figure 12.20 shows an example of how the "launched" application list provided by the NFuse portal looks. Show Icons, Show Names, and Allow users to view application settings were selected in this case.

Figure 12.20 Launched application list.

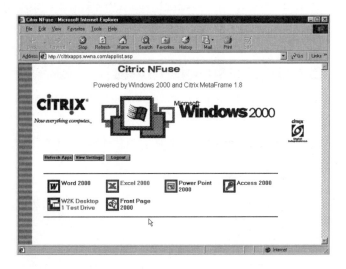

Figure 12.21 shows an example of how the "embedded" application list provided by the NFuse portal looks with an embedded application running.

Figure 12.21 NFuse embedded application.

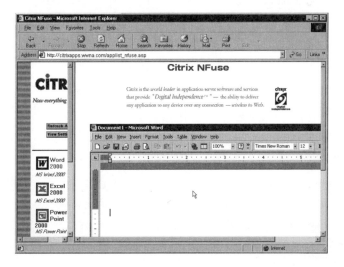

Infrastructure Impacts

When moving your Citrix MetaFrame functionality out to the Internet, you may notice a variety of infrastructure impacts and opportunities to improve the ways that hardware and telecommunications work for you. Most impacts are positive in terms of reduced need for hard upgrades, reduced bandwidth usage, and Server Farm utilization. The one impact that must be clearly understood is firewall setup.

Firewall Setup Considerations

Below is a checklist for making connections using an .ICA file. Ensure that all of the following are set at the firewall.

1. A valid external IP address(es) has been mapped to the Citrix server(s) inside the firewall.
2. Port 1494 for TCP/IP is opened.
3. Port 1025 and above (the high ports) are opened for TCP and UDP outbound.

On the Citrix Server(s) run the ALTADDR utility. Each Citrix Server that is mapped from the firewall must map the corresponding address *to* the firewall. This is done from the command line and must be done from each Citrix server that is mapped to an alternate address. For example:

```
ALTADDR /SET InternalIPAddress ExternalIPAddress
```

Given that the internal IP address of a Citrix server is 10.3.2.1 and the firewall has mapped an External IP address of 208.140.11.10, from that Citrix server you would specify at a command line:

```
ALTADDR /SET 10.3.2.1 208.140.11.10
```

You will also need to change the Template.ICA file on the Web server with the following:

```
Address=[Nfuse_ipv4_AddressAlternate]
```

The Connection Sequence is performed as follows:

1. Your client Web browser connects to the IIS server at port 80, where it asks for username and password if needed.
2. The NFuse extensions on the IIS Server connect to the NFuse Service on the Citrix Server using port 81 (by default 80, but you can specify anything).
3. The Citrix Server (Farm) returns from the master ICA browser all information about the applications for that specific user.

4. The IIS Server pastes this application information into a template .ICA file, thereby creating links in the Web interface of the client to an array of .ICA files. Check the template .ICA file to see what is actually put in it.

5. By clicking on an icon in the Web browser, the client downloads the corresponding .ICA file and starts the local ICA Client.

6. The ICA Client uses the given information to open a connection to the Citrix Server serving up that particular application using the default port-number (1494) or the one explicitly given in the ICA template file.

If the Citrix Server is protected by a firewall, you will need to open port 1494 for this to work by default. For excellent white papers about this, you can go to www.citrix.com/cdn and become a Citrix Developer Network (CDN) member.

You can assign a port number for communications between your Web server and your MetaFrame Server (for example, 81, 82, 83, and so on), but ICA uses port 1494 and UDP port 1604 for communications between the ICA client and the Citrix Server. (UDP is not needed when using NFuse.)

To see if the firewall is correctly set up, use the standard client and connect to the server creating an entry with the external IP address instead of the server name. If you can connect, the ports and the firewall are configured correctly. When using a Web browser to gain access using NFuse, the connection information is processed on the server rather than the client, therefore eliminating the UDP broadcasting.

When a user connects to an NFuse page you have to configure that service to use port 80 to talk with the NFuse HTTP service and that then passes the client application list to the client. When the client clicks on the application, an .ICA file is created on the fly. This .ICA file contains the IP address of the least busy server and no name resolution is needed, thus there is no need to use 1604. Once the user gets the .ICA file, the Web server has done its job and is no longer needed to make a connection.

If you have changed the ICA port on the server using the ICAport command, the Template.ICA file will need to be modified by adding the line:

```
ICAPortNumber=whatever port number you selected
```

TCP Port 1494 must be open inbound and the high ports (1025 and above) opened outbound for TCP.

As shown, the NFuse Web components can be configured to resolve application names to IP addresses, eliminating the need for the ICA Client to use the UDP-based ICA Browser. Additionally, Citrix's Secure ICA product can provide additional security by way of encryption of ICA sessions.

Summary

The technology presented by the Citrix's MetaFrame approach to application delivery opens tremendous possibilities for companies large and small and creates new enterprises. Application Service Providers (ASPs) are springing up across the landscape providing affordable access to high-powered applications such as Enterprise Resource Planning (ERP) solutions, Manufacturing Resource Planning (MRP) solutions, large-scale database engines, and integrated customer service applications. With the ease of delivery that MetaFrame offers, companies can outsource their entire server operations to remote providers of raised floor capacity. These advances bring competitive advantages of scale to small and medium size businesses that were previously too costly and out of reach.

The creation of the World Wide Web and the refinement of Web browsers have streamlined the flow of information throughout the business world. Citrix MetaFrame has taken this innovation and simplified it even further. They have collaborated with browser developers to make connecting through Internet sessions simple and reliable. Platforms of all types are able to use common applications without major modification or reconfiguration. Where a Web browser can be run, the client piece for Citrix can be downloaded if it is not already included with the browser and updates can be made to be transparent to users. With the release of NFuse, client-side administration has become almost nonexistent so that connecting through the Internet to the company is as easy as browsing for your favorite Web sites.

Even server configuration has been made simple through the clear installation assistance that comes with MetaFrame. Besides the normal security concerns that come with working on the Internet, administration of user access to applications and the Web site look and feel become the most important considerations. With the original configuration, new application setup adds elements to an .HTM file to provide user access. NFuse simplifies even this by making these changes automatically, leaving the administrator to ensure adequate application management and access permissions.

The most significant area of concern is with IT infrastructure. Establishing Server Farms can be costly where server support is currently minimal. However, in most existing companies, a series of servers have already been installed and what needs to be done is to redistribute applications for load balancing. The other consideration is security and the challenges to it from exposure to the Internet. As we have seen, the first line of defense is careful setup of the firewall. Other steps that can be taken are the use of virtual private networking (VPN), Secure Socket Layer (SSL) technology, and encryption, which are not specific to MetaFrame communication. New innovations that are MetaFrame specific are releases of Secure ICA and ICA encryption.

Phoenix Manufacturing found that implementing the full capability of Citrix MetaFrame greatly improved their information throughput from their market research vendor to Tactical Account Planning (TAP) distribution promotions. It shortened the time it took to receive market data, improving supply chain management and production planning which in turn improved packaging and warehouse planning. This resulted in more reliable distribution and delivery of their perishable products. Rather than dealing with miscommunication and painful lags in reliable information, Phoenix and their partners were able to rely on technology to make business more efficient and competitive.

Many companies across this country and around the world are finding exciting opportunities for using thin-client delivery systems. With the increasing favorable cost and availability of communications bandwidth growing and the lowered capacity requirements that the Citrix MetaFrame technology brings, we are finally realizing the productivity dividends that the computer age has long promised.

FAQs

Q: Should I implement Citrix Feature Release 1?

A: Feature Release 1 (FR1) was released in September 2000 and was built to run with NFuse version 1.5 which came out at the same time. The material in this chapter is based on NFuse version 1.0.47. FR1 will not work with version 1.0.47 or earlier while Version 1.5 includes the functionality of 1.0.47 but has more configuration settings including the ICA Secure Socket Layer, also a new feature. Few companies have implemented nor plan to implement these new versions in the near future. FR1 will only give you benefit if you have migrated to version 1.5 of NFuse.

Here is a listing of other useful FAQ sites you can access online:

General Citrix FAQs: www.citrix.com/support/
Click on the FAQ tab.

MetaFrame FAQs: www.asiweb.com/metaframe/faq.asp

FAQs for the Citrix/SAP joint project:
http://press.citrix.com/library/doc/Citrix_SAP_joint_mySAP.doc

FAQs for Solaris/Unix MetaFrame: http://onefish.earthweb.com/faq.html

FAQs for NFuse 1.5 and Feature Release 1:
www.citrix.com/products/library/pdf/NFuse-FAQ.pdf

Chapter 13

Optimizing, Monitoring, and Troubleshooting Windows 2000 and Terminal Services

Solutions in this chapter:

- Optimizing your Resources

- Monitoring Server Performance

- Troubleshooting

Introduction

Once a server is up and running, it is up to the administrator to manage the environment for optimal application performance and to monitor the server and its terminal sessions.

Administrators need to identify performance bottlenecks and trouble-shoot them. As changes are made to the server and to the environment, the administrator will need to optimize the server on an ongoing basis.

When applications are provided with the ability to map drives and print to locally connected printers, a third level of complexity enters into the thin-client configuration. Users require a savvy administrator to trouble-shoot these applications and their outputs of data and printing.

Optimizing Your Resources

Windows 2000 and Terminal Services are not automatically tuned to the optimal settings for a multiuser environment. Windows 2000 requires us to tune its memory usage and application behavior to make the most of our resources. These "tweaks" range from installation methodology to registry changes to application options. This chapter will cover some of the most important changes that you can make to increase performance and maxi-mize your Return on Investment (ROI).

Handling Changes in the Environment

Change control is of paramount importance in a Citrix environment. You must implement a very strict process with documented policies and procedures regarding how changes may be made. Remove Domain Administrators from the local administrators group and add only the indi-vidual domain user accounts of the fewest possible number of designated Terminal Services administrators. Large companies, especially with a large number of administrators, must limit administrative access to the Terminal Services servers.

When implementing a change-control doctrine, it is wise to create a board of administrators familiar with Citrix to provide a system of checks and balances. Depending on your organization, this could be two to 20 people or more made up of other IT staffers and administrators. Many problems can be solved more quickly if discussed with other administra-tors, even if they are not familiar with Citrix and multiuser servers.

WARNING

While a board of administrators is important to keep changes controlled and effective, it does have the potential to impede the growth and serviceability of your farm. I worked with a company recently that needed to apply several service packs and make some registry modifications. The issues they were having were specifically listed in the service pack's list of corrected issues, but implementing the list of recommended changes would take six months to make it through change control. They had to set up a lab and test each modification individually and get it approved. While change control is effective if used correctly, do not let it get to the point that the change control procedures themselves are hindering the effectiveness of your business.

An effective change control procedure should do each of the following:

- Provide a mechanism for testing changes in a lab environment before deployment to production.

- Allow for formal approval of changes after the systems are in production.

- Provide revision control and backup/restore procedures during the initial development stage.

- Allow changes to the farm to be proposed and evaluated, for performance and availability impact to be assessed, and for approval or rejection in a controlled manner.

- Allow all parties materially affected by proposed changes to the server farm to assess the impact of the changes.

- Facilitate changes to platform development during the initial stages of configuration.

- Provide documentation of the development of your server farm, including all proposed changes.

When making changes to a Citrix Server Farm, the impact of taking a server offline is usually large, affecting a large number of users. If the change causes the server to stop functioning, it is important to have procedures in place to restore the server to production quickly. There are two basic methods to achieve this goal: tape backup or imaging. Refer to Figure 13.1 for an illustration of a change control flowchart.

Figure 13.1 Change control flowchart.

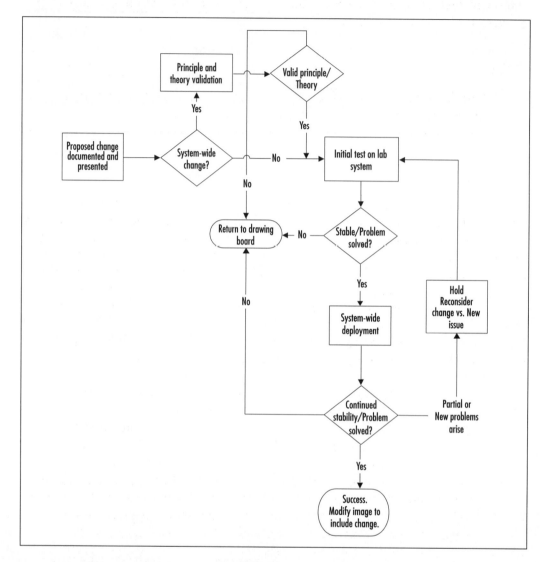

Tape Backup

Tape backup is the older and slower method, but it is sometimes more acceptable depending on your environment. Tape backup also allows you to perform the backup while the server is still online. Be aware that you must have the software and/or licenses to allow the backup of open files.

When first setting up your farm and tape backup solution, do a backup and then replace the drive with a blank one and test the restore procedure. Some backup software packages have problems with remapped drive letters and others take several hours to restore only a few Gigabytes of data. Time the restore and make sure that the server can be brought back up in a reasonable amount of time.

> **NOTE**
>
> When backing up your server to tape, be sure to select the options to include the registry and system files.

Imaging

Using imaging software such as Norton Ghost (www.symantec.com) or Drive Image Pro (www.powerquest.com) is a more recent method of backing up a server and restoring it or creating new servers using the same image. You can use drive imaging to produce a *gold* build (an image that you are satisfied with and which has the quality that you would like to duplicate) of one server and then deploy it to other servers to minimize the differences from one server to the next. This method does have a drawback in that the server must be offline to create the image. Ideally, it is best to have a spare server that can be taken down and imaged; then, your changes can be applied and tested. If the changes are determined to be unacceptable, then that server can simply be re-imaged.

As discussed in Chapter 11, you may select one server to build the ideal build and then image the rest of the server farm to match. Once approved, the image can be recreated from that same "master image server" and the image re-applied to the rest of the farm. This ensures that all the servers are always running the same service packs, hotfixes, registry modifications, and so on. If at any time, even after a full-scale farm re-image, the new changes are determined to be detrimental to the farm, it can be re-imaged one version back in a relatively short amount of time. Most images for an average server of about 2GB of data take about 20 minutes to apply, and if you use multicasting, all your servers can be re-imaged concurrently.

Increased Users

A wise person once told me you should do the correct sizing for today's users, multiply it by the growth percentage of the company—and finally, double it, and add four. In a perfect world, this formula would last you for about 12 months after implementation. However, we all know it will go more like: Do the correct sizing for today's users, multiply by 90 percent, subtract six, and hope for the best. Here are some methods to help you cope with your growing pains.

For IT Professionals

Not Enough Communication

I performed a large implementation for a manufacturer in which I installed several MetaFrame servers to provide Microsoft Office 97 applications to a customer service center. The goal was to reduce the number of problems that the individual users could cause on their own machines. We set the client up with Windows NT Workstation 4.0, locked down the desktop, and assigned read-only mandatory profiles. We set Program Neighborhood to provide shortcuts to the Office applications on the desktop and placed Outlook 98 in the Startup group. Outlook then started at logon and established the Independent Computing Architecture (ICA) protocol connection, enabling other applications to launch more quickly. Because of the mandatory profiles, we used KiXtart (an advanced login script processor available free from www.kixtart.org) to determine the important variables to account for in setting up the Outlook profile at logon. We used one logon script for the entire company and used logic operators to determine what actions were performed based on NT group membership. We had added a section to run our Outlook profile configuration routine based on user group and computer name. Another administrator added a section to the script that caused our section to be skipped over.

The next morning when everyone logged on again, no one could access Outlook. After several hours of troubleshooting why the profile was not getting created, we discovered the command causing our section to be skipped. The administrator that made the change had no idea that his change impacted our project, but from the end users' and our client's point of view, it was our fault and reflected poorly on our implementation. This illustrates why you should have some kind of change control mechanism in place to ensure that when a change is made, it is reviewed, approved, and documented so that if problems arise, the cause can be quickly pinpointed and corrected.

One of the easiest ways to facilitate resizing is to create a standard platform and make sure all your servers are the same exact hardware. This will allow you to build one server, do your testing, and then use an imaging product to apply this "gold" build on the rest of your servers. Now, adding more users is as easy as installing another server and applying the image. Using a "gold" image and storing *no* user data on the MetaFrame servers also allows us to use only one hard drive. If the hard drive fails, replace it and re-image the server. This "gold" image will also help us do other tasks as well.

If a standard platform and imaging are not options, then there are other methods to handle more users. Windows 2000 scales very well in a multiprocessor environment, depending on the applications involved. I have had success with larger servers with four or more central processing units (CPUs) when using 32-bit multithreaded applications, but unless you have the need for a few of these powerhouses, I would go with a larger number of dual-processor machines to spread the load and provide another level of redundancy.

If you follow the CPU utilization numbers outlined in Chapter 11, you should have some room to increase the number of users on each server until CPU utilization moves from 60 percent to 80 percent. If your servers are already running at 80 percent or above, I recommend that you do not increase the number of users unless you install new CPUs on your existing servers or increase the total number of servers, the latter being my preference. If after examining your CPU situation, you determine that adding users is safe, examine your memory usage. RAM is usually easy to install and a relatively inexpensive way to increase your server's capacity.

To better illustrate this, take a company called Eastgate Merchandise. Eastgate has boutiques all across the United States. They have decided that they will use a 1-800 number to take orders from across the country, so they set up regional call centers to take orders. The orders are all entered into a central database and transmitted to the store closest to the customer. The data center is in Boise, Idaho and there are call centers in Philadelphia, Dallas, Phoenix, and Sacramento with 250 operators at each location. All the call centers access the order entry program from a Citrix session to the data center in Boise. Eastgate now wants to open a new call center to service the booming towns in Alaska.

The Alaska call center will consist of 100 operators. The data center consists of a database server and 20 Pentium III 667MHz servers with 1GB of RAM and one 9GB hard drive. The servers run at a full load of 50 users each and average about 65 percent CPU utilization and max out at around

700MB of RAM. If Eastgate adds the 100 new users to the servers, it will place five more users on each server. This should not raise the overall CPU/RAM utilization above 80 percent and the servers should perform just fine. However, if one or more servers fail it would cause 55–110 users to be spread across the farm and bring utilization above 80 percent for one or more other servers and cause poor performance. The best practice here would be to install two more servers to support the 100 new users. This would keep the farm as a whole at about 60 percent utilization, so that when a server does fail the remaining servers can easily support the increased load.

New Applications

The *only* way to implement new applications is to thoroughly test the application in the production environment. New applications can't be installed on a *live* server in your production environment, but if you don't use a machine with the same configuration as your production server with the same drivers, drive letters, and other applications installed, it just can't be considered a valid test.

This is where the "gold" image comes into play again. If you maintain an image of your current production servers, use it on another server of the same model as a production server. This machine can be smaller (i.e., it does not need a gig of RAM and dual PIII-750s). It can have 128–256MB RAM and dual PII-450s, as long as the Hardware Abstraction Layer (HAL) and Small Computer System Interface (SCSI) drivers are the same. Apply your image to this machine and install your new application and run your tests. Make sure to run your existing applications at the same time as the new application to ensure compatibility.

New applications should be thoroughly tested in the same manner as your initial load testing. Use a program like WinRunner by Mercury Interactive (www.mercuryinteractive.com) or WinBatch by Wilson WindowWare (www.winbatch.com). These programs allow you to write scripts to test the application in an automated fashion, and emulate one to 1000+ simultaneous users. Use them to write scripts that test every aspect of the applications, including printing reports, screen shots, and so on, as well as saving and e-mailing files in other versions. If the application includes its own security, you may have to manually test that it does indeed restrict a lesser user from accessing restricted information if a greater user is logged on at the same time.

Internet Configuration Changes

As your Internet connections, applications, and uses change, so might your Terminal Services configuration. Citrix ICA is vulnerable to variable performance due to other applications traversing congested wide area network (WAN) links. Configuring routers and switches to prioritize ICA traffic or using packet-shaping technologies from Packeteer or Net Reality can improve your ICA performance and reliability up to tenfold.

Table 13.1 lists the default ports used by ICA and Remote Desktop Protocol (RDP). Depending upon your company policy, the ICA User Datagram Protocol (UDP) port may not be allowed due to the security concerns over UDP's connectionless nature. Citrix has addressed this issue with Feature Release 1 and Service Pack 2.

Table 13.1 TCP/IP Ports Used by Terminal Services and MetaFrame

Protocol	Port	TCP/UDP
ICA connection	1494	TCP
ICA browsing	1604	UDP
ICA XML	Default 80 but easily changed	TCP
RDP	3389	TCP

When you establish an ICA connection, it can proceed in one of two ways:

- If you are connecting directly to an individual server and not a published application, the client sends a Transmission Control Protocol (TCP) packet from its Internet Protocol (IP) address to the server's IP address with a destination port of 1494 and a source port of something between 1024 and 65535. The server will then respond to the client on the source port and begin the connection.

- If you are connecting to a published application, the process is a little different. The client sends a UDP packet to the Master ICA Browser on UDP port 1604 to ask what server can service the application it is requesting. The ICA Browser then responds with the server that is capable of servicing that application; if load balancing is being used, it will return the least busy server.

If users call and report difficulty connecting to your server, ascertain exactly what symptoms are being displayed. Published applications are dependent on the UDP port for browsing, so ask the user to try connecting directly to a server. If the user can do a direct connect, then you should investigate:

- Ensure the security group has not closed or otherwise restricted the ICA UDP traffic from crossing the firewall.

- If the firewall is performing address translation, verify that the user's client is configured to use the alternate address.

- Verify that the server has been configured to provide its alternate (public) address using the **altaddr.exe** command.

Performance Tuning

As I stated before, Terminal Services are not necessarily ready for "out-of-the-box" production. There are several settings in Terminal Services that can be tweaked to enhance performance. These settings range from the simplicity of turning off the blink of the cursor to reduce transmitted screen updates, to the complexity of changing the TCP/IP buffer size to optimize WAN/Internet performance. I will list some of my favorite tweaks to improve Terminal Services performance.

WARNING

Please note that before editing the Windows 2000 registry, you should have a backup of the registry available to use if you need to restore it. Some of the lines in this section have been wrapped for readability.

Solid Cursor Setting the cursor to solid is especially effective in low-bandwidth situations. A blinking cursor sends a few bytes of data every time it blinks, so disabling the blinks saves precious bandwidth.

```
"HKEY_USERS/.default/Control Panel/Desktop"
Change: CursorBlinkRate Reg_SZ value to -1
```

Start Menu Refresh Rate: Q216445 You can set the menu refresh rate to a faster time to receive a quicker response time on the menus.

```
"HKEY_USERS\DEFAULT\Control Panel\Desktop"
Add Value: MenuShowDelay REG_DWORD: 10
```

Disable Paging Executive: Q184419 To decrease (improve) response time, disable paging the executive files to keep all kernel code and driver in memory. This will move the kernel and drivers into memory. Microsoft recommends that the server have plenty of memory before attempting this setting (1GB or more).

```
"HKEY_LOCAL_MACHINE\System\CurrentControlSet\Control\Session Manager\
Memory Management"
```
```
Value DisablePagingExecutive set to 1
```

Change IOPageLockLimit: Q102985 Limit on the number of bytes that can be locked for Input/Output (I/O) operations.

```
"HKEY_LOCAL_MACHINE\System\CurrentControlSet\Control\Session Manager\
Memory Management"
```
```
Change value: Default is 0, Installed MB of RAM * 128.
```

Convert the number to Hexadecimal; for example, 1GB of RAM is 1024MB * 128 = 131072. Enter this as the decimal value.

Set L2 Cache for Processors with **256KB and up: Q183063** If second-level cache is larger than 256KB, such as a CPU with a 1024KB cache, add this registry setting to allow Windows 2000 to be able to access over 256KB on the second-level cache. Be careful with this setting, it could slow your server down.

```
"HKEY_LOCAL_MACHINE\System\CurrentControlSet\Session Manager\
Memory Management"
```
```
Add Value: SecondLevelDataCache REG_DWORD: 1024 (decimal)
```

Disable Dr. Watson: Q188296 Dr. Watson is a useful tool when needed, but end users usually should not see errors reported on it when running a session.

```
"HKEY_LOCAL_MACHINE\Software\Microsoft\Windows NT\CurrentVersion\
AeDebug\Auto"
```

A 0 will display a message box when Dr. Watson is running. A 1 (default) tells the Debugger to start on Boot. To keep Dr. Watson from running, delete the AeDebug subkey. To get Dr. Watson back, type **drwtsn32 -i** at the command prompt.

Please refer to Appendix A, "Secrets," for more ways to improve Terminal Services performance.

Monitoring

A key to ensuring a successful implementation is continual monitoring of the performance of your servers. You must track and prevent bottlenecks when possible and respond to them when they do occur. There are many tools available to assist you in maintaining a Citrix Server Farm.

Session Utilities

The Citrix Server Administration tool launched from the MetaFrame Tools group (or Start/Run/mfadmin) is the tool you will use most for watching user activities on your servers. Figure 13.2 depicts Citrix Server Administration with the server selected in the left pane and the Session tab selected in the right pane. This view allows you to see:

- Which users are connected
- The session identifier (ID)
- Whether they are using ICA or RDP
- The client name
- How long they have been idle
- What time they logged on

Figure 13.2 Citrix Server Administration Sessions view.

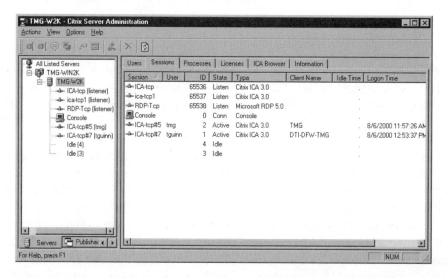

Figure 13.3 shows the ICA Browser tab where you define the server's role in the ICA Browser network. For installations large enough for a Master ICA Browser, you would configure the Master ICA Browser to "Always attempt to become the Master ICA Browser." and then one or two other Machines as "No Preference." The remaining servers would be set to "Do not attempt to become the Master ICA Browser." When load balancing, adjust the "Master ICA Browser Refresh Interval" down to about 60 seconds. This setting controls how often this server updates the Master ICA Browser with its status. The "Master ICA Browser Update Delay" controls how long this server waits after a client connects or disconnects to update the Master ICA Browser.

Figure 13.3 Citrix Server Administration ICA Browser information.

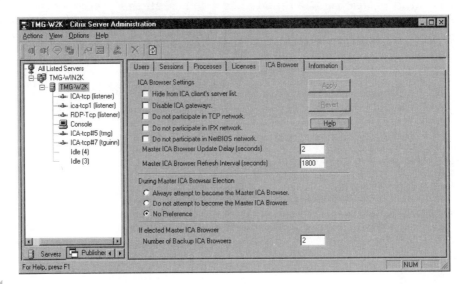

TIP

An ICA Master Browser can solve many browsing issues that administrators have struggled with over the last couple of years. If the ICA Master Browser runs on a server that also provides applications to users, the user load can interfere with the performance of the ICA Browser service, thus causing it to stop responding or crash. In installations of five or more Citrix servers, I recommend using a lesser machine such as a single processor with 128–256MB of RAM to be used as an ICA Master Browser. This machine will be loaded with Windows 2000 Terminal Services and Citrix MetaFrame.

To minimize the licensing costs of the server, you can use the five-user MetaFrame for Terminals license. This license is about one-fifth the cost of a full enterprise license and will provide the services you need. It will only allow ICA connections from Windows-based terminals (WBT) such as Wyse Winterm, but you won't need that functionality. (To connect from your desktop you can use the RDP protocol.) This server will publish no applications and serve no users at all. Configure it using the Citrix Server Administration tool to "Always attempt to become the master ICA browser," then pick one or two of your other servers and configure them to "No Preference." The remainder of your servers should be set to "Do not attempt to become the master ICA browser." Now when configuring your clients, set all of them to point to the Master ICA Browser's IP address.

In Figure 13.4, if you select a user from the left pane and choose the Processes tab on the right, you will see a list of all the processes running for that user with their associated Process IDs (PID).

Figure 13.4 Citrix Server Administration Processes tab.

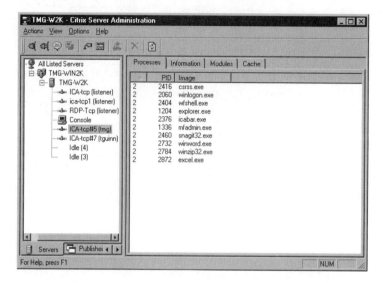

As shown in Figure 13.5, the User Information tab shows many details about the user session. These details include:

- The name of the user who is logged on to the session on the server
- The name of the client computer
- The version of the software installed on the client computer
- The directory in which the client is installed
- The product ID of the client
- The hardware ID of the client
- The address of the client, if applicable
- Server and client buffers
- Client color depth and resolution
- The name of the modem, if applicable
- The encryption level, if applicable
- The license used by the client

Figure 13.5 Citrix Server Administration User Information tab.

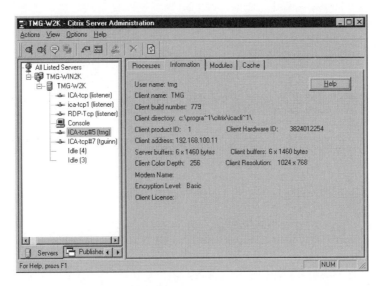

You can use this information when a client calls in and reports a problem to ensure that the client is connecting with the correct settings. This will allow you to check his or her client version, the winstation name (to ensure it is unique), the color depth, and probably the most useful—the IP of the client. The Process tab will also allow you to see if the client is running programs other than the ones he or she says are running. I use the process list to monitor what applications a user is running and compare that to performance monitor data for that session. This can provide some correlation to CPU or memory issues.

At the bottom of the Citrix Server Administration tool is a tab labeled Published Applications, shown in Figure 13.6. This view allows you to monitor your farm from an application point of view. Choosing the farm in the left pane will show you all the applications published from that farm. Selecting the individual applications will show you the servers that provide them and the details about the application's location and working directory. Most important, it will show you the application's load level for the various protocols. These numbers should always remain 0–9998. If the number exceeds these values, refer to Table 13.2 for an explanation of the load-balancing load levels.

Figure 13.6 Citrix Server Administration Published Applications tab.

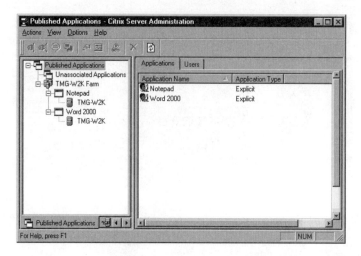

Table 13.2 Load-Balancing Load Levels

Load Value	Function
9999	There is no load-balancing license installed.
0 to 9998	This is a "normal" load level.
10000!	The application is disabled for this Citrix server.
10000	Either the server or the application load is at 100 percent.
10001	The server is out of licenses.
10002	One of the following has occurred: No port listeners are available; logons have been disabled on the server; the server is out of swap space; the application is disabled; or it is an anonymous application and no anonymous user logons are left.

Shadowing Sessions

The shadowing sessions tool is probably the best help-desk tool ever conceived. When users call with application problems, a help desk technician can shadow the user's session and *watch* exactly what the user is doing. They can then guide the user, or take control of the machine and show the user how to perform an action or change a setting.

Shadowing has options that should be configured before your deployment. By default, the ICA connection is set to inherit user settings, and user settings are by default set to allow *shadowing*, *interactive*, and *notify*. Interactive means that the person doing the shadowing can also control the mouse and keyboard. Notify specifies that the user is presented with the dialog shown in Figure 13.7 and can accept or refuse the shadow connection. If notify is disabled, the user will have no way of knowing when they are being shadowed except that the screen tends to flicker when the shadowing begins.

Figure 13.7 Remote Control request dialog.

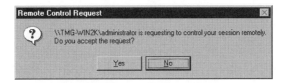

Shadowing can be accomplished by logging into a session yourself and then launching the Shadow taskbar. This will open the dialog shown in Figure 13.8, where you can pick the users to shadow. After clicking OK, a taskbar will be displayed (as shown in Figure 13.9), which has buttons corresponding to the sessions you selected. You can conveniently switch between sessions using these buttons.

Figure 13.8 Shadow Session taskbar setup.

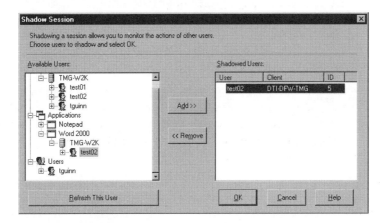

Figure 13.9 Shadow Session taskbar.

Shadowing is a powerful tool that can potentially be abused; it is important to set security on the ability to shadow. By default, the system and the local administrators groups are granted shadowing capabilities. As mentioned before, by removing the Domain Admins group from the local administrators group, you can limit access to shadowing as well. I would create a local group called *Shadowing*, and grant that group shadowing permissions and then add individual domain users to the group. If you use a domain group and add it to the local group, then other administrators could just add themselves to the domain group. This does involve some administrative burden, but in large organizations where there are many users with administrative rights, it is the only way to prevent unauthorized users from adding themselves to the shadowing group.

To change the permissions on shadowing, open the Citrix Connection Configuration from the MetaFrame Tools group. Select the ICA-tcp connection item and from the Security menu select permissions. Click the Advanced button to display the access control settings. From this dialog you can configure which groups/users have the ability to shadow. Select a group and click the View/Edit button to see the individual permissions settings. To enable shadowing for any user or group, check the Allow Remote Control check box.

I have used shadowing to help out my office administrator while I was on the road. By dialing into the office network, I could start up a session and then shadow her. This way, I could walk her through most any task that she had questions about. There is just no comparison between seeing the user's screen and having the user describe what they are seeing. Please refer to Figures 13.10, 13.11 and 13.12 to follow the steps to enable remote control and shadow a user.

Figure 13.10 Advanced Connection Settings dialog.

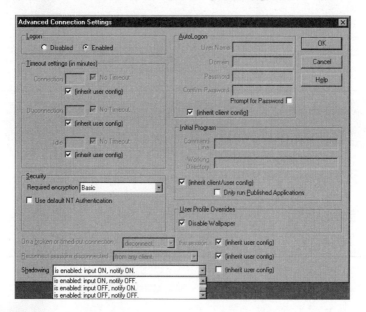

Figure 13.11 Remote control properties.

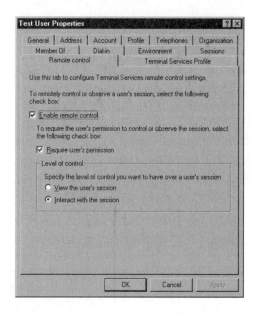

Figure 13.12 Connection permissions for remote control.

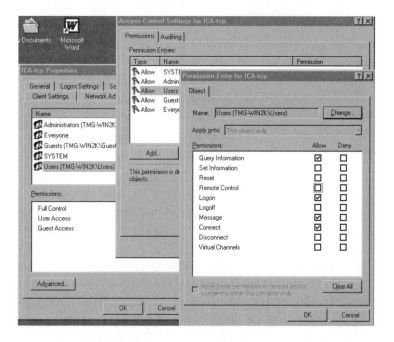

Troubleshooting

Invariably issues will arise when you have 15–100 users all logging in to one server. Covering every type of issue that *might* arise would take a book larger than your desk could support, but thanks to computers' ever-expanding hard drives and the Internet, there are some excellent resources that can help. Here are a few of my favorites:

- **www.thethin.net** Web site and mailing list maintained by Jim Kenzig; my first stop for help.

- **www.thinplanet.com** Great site with forums, news, resume banks, and job listings.

- **http://support.microsoft.com/search** Microsoft's Knowledge Base

- **http://ctxex10.citrix.com/tcxpert.nsf** Citrix's Knowledge Base

- **http://ctxex10.citrix.com/icaforum.nsf** Citrix discussion forum

- **www.brainbuzz.com/apt/t.asp?au=SOAPUI7&at=SOAT1** Thin-Client Discussion forum on BrainBuzz

Aside from application issues and user error, some of the most common problems you will encounter are:

- Establishing drive mappings

- Connectivity issues

- Users downloading files (viruses)

- Printing

Establishing Drive Mapping

Drive mappings in Terminal Services have additional considerations. When setting up Terminal Services and MetaFrame, MetaFrame will ask if you would like to remap the server drive letters. This feature is included to help users when connecting to the server and mapping the local drives of their client. If you remap the server drive letters, they will become, for example, M:, N:, and O:. When a client connects, Citrix can map the C: drive on their client to the letter C: inside the server session. See Table 13.3 for an illustration of this.

If you are installing MetaFrame and you choose to remap the drives, and if after the reboot the drives are still C:, D:, and so on, check to see if you have any software RAID such as mirroring set up. MetaFrame can't remap the drive letters if the system drive is mirrored. Break the mirror, delete the partition from the other drive and re-install MetaFrame. After MetaFrame is installed, re-establish your mirror.

Table 13.3 Client Drive Mappings

Client drive	Server drive	Session drive
C:		C: is mapped to Client C:
D:		D: is mapped to Client D:
E:		E: is mapped to Client E:
	M:	M: is server M:
	N:	N: is server N:
	O:	O: is server O:

Resolving Connectivity Issues

Terminal Services and MetaFrame are used extensively to provide remote access to applications to users connecting over slow data links. These links, especially when they involve the Internet, can be very unreliable when trying to maintain an ICA session. Timeouts, latency, and dropped connections can cause disconnected sessions and/or slow response. While the ideal solution is of course *more bandwidth*, this is usually not an option, so we must once again tweak the OS to provide better reliability to users. Slow response time can be corrected mainly by administration. You can tweak such things as:

- Low-color graphics
- No or text-based splash screens
- Turning off blinking cursors
- Not publishing the whole desktop
- Using packet-shaping technology (Quality of Service)

For disconnected sessions, we can tune some of the TCP/IP stack to be more forgiving of lost or slow packets. Try these registry edits to optimize your server:

Increase TCP/IP Buffer Size: Q177266 Increase the TCP/IP buffer size to enhance performance. Change the TCP/IP buffer size from 4356 to 14596.

```
"HKEY_LOCAL_MACHINE\System\CurrentContolSet\Services\LanmanServer\
Parameters"
```

```
Add Value: SizReqBuf REG_DWORD:
```

This parameter has a range of 512 to 65536. The decimal value of 14596 is a better choice.

Solid Cursor Setting the cursor to solid is especially effective in low-bandwidth situations. A blinking cursor sends a few bytes of data every time it blinks, so disabling the blinks saves precious bandwidth. After setting this to –1, the cursor at the console may appear to blink extremely fast. This is normal; it will be solid to the client.

```
"HKEY_USERS/.default/Control Panel/Desktop"
Change: CursorBlinkRate Reg_SZ value to -1
```

With the introduction of Feature Release 1, Citrix now allows you to use more than 256 colors in your connections. These added color levels are great and have been requested for several years, however, they do bring with them a price—more bandwidth. At the time of this writing I have not seen an extensive study of the increase in bandwidth when using the 16- and 32-bit settings, but when I dial up with my modem and get a 26.4 Kbps connection from my hotel, the 16-bit setting *is* slower and I very quickly turn my setting down to 256. However, when using my Digital Subscriber Line (DSL) connection at home or a local area network (LAN) connection, the high-color settings are very usable and look very good.

The following two figures show where color depth can be controlled.

1. Figure 13.13 shows the server setting in Published Application Manager. This is only effective for published applications and can't be set server-wide.

2. Figure 13.14 shows the client setting where the user can either take the server setting or override the server and choose their own setting.

Depending on the application, you can also increase your performance by disabling or replacing any splash screens the application may display upon startup. These splash screens are usually large bitmaps and may take several seconds to transfer. The Office 2000 Resource Kit replaces the graphic splash screens for all the Office products when you apply the Terminal Services transform file. Contact the manufacturer of your software package to find out if the splash screen can be disabled or replaced. Another type of bitmap to disable is wallpaper. Use the Group policy editor to disable wallpaper for Terminal Services users logging in to Citrix.

Figure 13.13 Color selection from Published Application Manager.

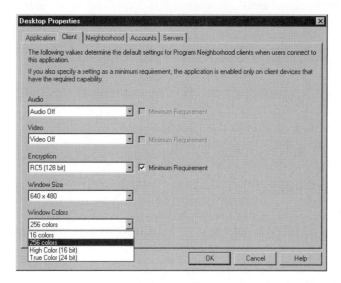

Figure 13.14 Color selection on the Program Neighborhood application set properties.

Publishing individual applications can also speed up performance and make security simpler. See Chapter 11, Installing and Publishing Applications, on how to publish applications instead of the entire desktop. You can also implement a QoS device to prioritize ICA and RDP traffic such as PacketShaper from Packeteer (www.packeteer.com), WiseWAN from NetReality (www.net-reality.com), and QoSWORKS from Sitara (www.sitaranetworks.com). These devices can prioritize, limit, cache, and guarantee various bandwidth levels for specific protocols, and in some cases the individual published application within an ICA stream.

Preventing Users from Downloading Files

Allowing users to browse the Internet through a thin-client session can potentially introduce rogue programs or even viruses into the farm if users are allowed to download files from the Internet. To disable the downloading of files with Internet Explorer, follow these easy steps:

1. From a command prompt, type **change user /install**.

2. Open Internet Explorer and go to the Tools menu and then select Security.

3. For the selected zone, click the custom level button and scroll down to the Downloads section.

4. Disable file and/or font downloads (depending on your concern).

5. Near the top of this list you can also disable various types of ActiveX and Java downloads as well.

6. Click OK and close the browser.

7. From the command prompt type **change user /execute**.

This disables downloads for everyone on the server. To disable it for a group of users it can also be configured via Group Policy as demonstrated in the following steps:

1. Open the Active Directory Users and Computers applet.

2. Create a new Organizational Unit (OU) and call it *Citrix Servers*.

3. Move all your Citrix servers into this OU.

4. Right-click on the OU and choose Properties.

5. Click the Group Policy tab.

6. Click New to add an object and name it *Normal Users* as shown in Figure 13.15.

7. Highlight the new object and click Edit. This will show the Group Policy displayed in Figure 13.16.

Figure 13.15 Group policy dialog in Active Directory Users and Computers.

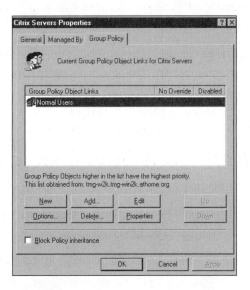

Figure 13.16 Group Policy settings.

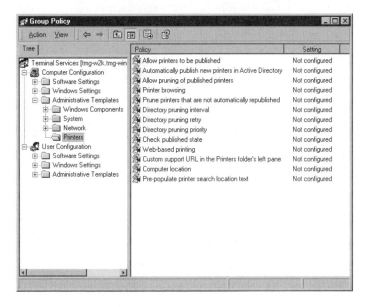

8. Expand the User Configuration object down to Windows Settings/Internet Explorer.

9. Select the Security Key, and in the right-hand pane, double-click the Security Zones and Content Ratings value.

10. In the Security Zones area, choose Import the current security zones settings.

11. Click the Modify Settings button.

12. Select the Internet object in the zone list as shown in Figure 3.17

13. Click the custom level button and scroll down to the Downloads section.

14. From here you can enable or disable file and font downloads.

15. Click OK and close all the dialog boxes and the Users and Computers applet.

Figure 13.17 Security settings for Internet Explorer in Group Policy.

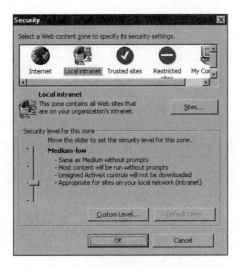

Printing

I am sure that you have discovered in your Personal Computer (PC) administration duties that printing is the source of a majority of your help desk calls. Between drivers, print servers, queues, and connectivity, printing takes up a lot of your non-Terminal Services/Citrix time, and so it is in the Terminal Services/Citrix world. If you are just using Terminal Services, then your printing is limited to classic Windows printing. Mapping a printer and either putting the setting in a logon script or saving it in the user's profile is the solution here and works well when you maintain control of these printers and their queues and drivers. When using Citrix however, MetaFrame enables you to automatically map printers to your client computers' printers. Herein lies the problem; you sometimes have little or no control over what printers your end users have connected to their PCs. The following sections explain what you can do to keep this under control.

How Printing Works

Printing in MetaFrame works just like it does in normal Windows 2000, except for some minor changes. When users print to network printers on the local LAN, Terminal Services spools the job to the Print Server and prints the job as normal. If the user prints to a printer connected to the workstation's parallel or Universal Serial Bus (USB) port, MetaFrame spools the print job through the ICA client to the local port.

Depending on your connection to the server and the size of your print jobs, printing can take several minutes to start. When you begin a print job, the information is passed to the print spooler and converted into a file in a language the printer understands. In some cases this file can be larger than the original. This file is then transferred to the client PC's print spooler. This is a standard file transfer and is subject to the line speed of your connection. If your client is connected via a LAN, then the printing process is usually quick and the user sees little difference from normal printing. If the client is on a dial-up or slow WAN connection, however, the transfer can take significantly longer to complete and thus the print job takes a long time to start.

Resolving Printing Problems

Most of the problems with printing in MetaFrame stem from the various printer drivers and the user's perception of speed. MetaFrame provides a mechanism to help reduce the myriad of drivers loaded on the server by using a printer driver *substitution* file. This file is called wtsuprn.INF. On a fresh system this file exists in the form of wtsuprn.TXT. Once modified, it is renamed to wtsuprn.INF. An example of a printer substitution file is included with the product. This file will allow you to "remap" most of your printer drivers to a few known, good drivers.

For example, almost all Hewlett Packard (HP) printers will emulate an HP LaserJet 4 and most HP DeskJet Printers will emulate an HP DeskJet 660C. These two drivers are included with Terminal Services and are the safest and most stable. While Terminal Services does include many of the newest printer drivers, I still set up my wtsuprn.INF file to substitute the LaserJet 4 and DeskJet 660C for most every other printer. This makes it easy to add a new client printer by simply entering a new line item with that client's print driver name and setting equal to one of my installed and tested drivers. For Hewlett Packard's official word on Terminal Services and HP printers see www.hp.com/cposupport/printers/support_doc/bpl07374.html#P561_26653.

This is the sequence MetaFrame checks for client printer/driver association when employing wtsuprn.INF.

1. <client name>#<printer name> in wtsuprn.inf

2. <printer name> in wtsuprn.inf

3. <client name>#<printer name> in wtsprnt.inf

4. <printer name> in wtsprnt.inf

5. <client name>#<client printer driver name> in wtsuprn.inf

6. <client printer driver name> in wtsuprn.inf

7. <client name>#<client printer driver name> in wtsprnt.inf

8. <client printer driver name> in wtsprnt.inf

9. <client printer driver name> in HKEY_LOCAL_MACHINE\SYSTEM\ CurrentControlSet\Control\Print\Environments\Windows NT x86\ Drivers\Version-2

10. <client printer driver name> in ntprint.inf

If a match is found, the new name is substituted for the driver name when the printer creation is attempted.

TIP

Avoid installing the HP Printing System. HP now has "corporate" drivers for most of their printers that only include the drivers and not all the extras.

Summary

In this chapter we have covered how to minimize the problems you may have, and then discussed the procedures for how to solve the problems that you do encounter.

By minimizing and controlling the number and quality of the changes in your environment, you will also reduce the issues that arise from haphazard or unauthorized changes. Establish and use a change control methodology and verify that you can recover from a change gone bad. Whether you use tape backups or imaging software, use it, test it, and be confident in it.

Using a standard build or a "golden" image, make sure all your servers are the same. This will minimize the confusion that can arise when a user has a problem and reports it but has no idea to which server they were connected. Using this "golden image" process is the best way I've found to easily scale the environment and recover from a disaster.

New applications should be tested in a semiproduction environment to prove their interoperability with the existing production applications. These new applications should be tested using the same methodology that your initial applications were tested with. Make sure that every facet from running reports, printing, and file access works as expected.

Make sure your group communicates with the security/WAN/Internet group to guarantee the configuration stability and reliability of your links to your end users. It only takes one small change to close down access through a firewall or a hasty router change to bring your network connectivity down.

Terminal Services servers are not the best they can be without a lot of help from the administrators. Tune the server to perform at its best in your situation. Research settings and read the Microsoft Knowledge Base. Once a week I go to their support site and read "What's New" for the last 7–14 days. I also utilize discussion groups and mailing lists on the Internet because I think the best source of information is your peers.

Use the server's built-in utilities to monitor your server to make certain your tweaks are indeed helping the performance of your servers. Monitor your users and see what they are running and then use Performance Monitor to measure the resource utilization in their sessions. I was once watching a session and saw the memory use spike to over 32MB. When I called the user to find out what he was doing in the application that would cause this, I found out our application used several MB of RAM that it did not release when it ran reports. In this situation you could then shadow the user to watch exactly what was done to cause the anomaly.

Consider your users' requirements versus his or her expectations when evaluating connectivity concerns. Do not provide high-color or sound in a very low-bandwidth setting. Adjust the TCP/IP timeouts when dealing with satellites or very latent connections. Use group policies to secure the server to users' curiosities and download habits.

Plan for a successful printing deployment from the beginning and test as much as possible. Make sure the users are aware of both the capabilities and the limitations of printing with Terminal Services/MetaFrame. Be very careful with the print drivers and use the substitution file wtsuprn.INF to reduce the amount of drivers that you must maintain on the server.

Your deployment will encounter its share of issues, but if you prepare both yourself and your end users, the issues can usually be solved quickly and efficiently. Make use of all your resources such as mailing lists, discussion boards, knowledge bases, and support contracts.

FAQs

Q: How do I disable Active Desktop on a Windows 2000 Terminal Services Server?

A: Launch Terminal Services Configuration from under Administrative Tools on the Start menu. Then click on the Server Settings folder and double-click the Active Desktop option and disable it.

Q: What are some good sources for technical information on Terminal Services?

A: An excellent resource for information on Terminal Services is www.thethin.net which maintains a mailing list of over 2000 users. Everyone answers questions and helps the group, and the site's owner Jim Kenzig maintains a very informative FAQ and utilities section.

Q: I want to make certain that our company's owner can never be shadowed when he is using the MetaFrame server; what can I do to protect his sessions?

A: From the Active Directory Users and Computers applet, edit the user and from the Remote Control tab, uncheck the Enable Remote Control check box. Also, ensure the ICA and RDP connection properties in the Connection Configuration are set to inherit user settings.

Q: I tried to print to my client printer, and nothing came out. What went wrong?

A: Check to see first that the printer is indeed online and the client can print to the printer. Verify that the correct driver is installed and available on the server and that it matches the driver name on the client. Also, how long did you wait? Some print jobs can be quite large and take several minutes to download to the client print queue before they begin to print. Check the print queue on the server and on the client to see if it spooling at all. Lastly, stop and restart the spooler service on the server.

Q: I printed a page and got 50 pages with codes on top. How do I fix that?

A: This is usually caused by an incorrect printer driver. If you are using the wtsuprn.INF file to substitute a driver for your printer, you may need to try another driver. If not, this could be caused by a corrupt printer driver. Reinstall the driver on the Terminal Services server.

Chapter 14

Managing Citrix MetaFrame 1.8 for Windows 2000 Fast Track

Solutions in this chapter:

- **Understanding Mid-Tier Architecture**

- **Connecting Client Types**

- **Designing and Deploying Terminal Services and MetaFrame**

- **Managing Your Systems**

- **The Value of a Thin-Client System**

- **The Future of Windows and MetaFrame**

Introduction

Today businesses are faced with the challenge of a global economy. Users expect applications to be reliable and have a consistent interface regardless of what platform a client is running on. This demand for cross-platform applications and platform independence has arisen from the universality of HTML and the expansion of the Internet. The Internet has proven to be the great equalizer with its concept of universally accessible data.

Applications are not the same as HTML pages. They are written to work on specific operating systems to provide specific functions. When a business wants to share out those applications the same way that an HTML page is shared universally, there arrives the dilemma—they can't do it. Unless they use Windows 2000 Terminal Services with Citrix MetaFrame.

Welcome to independent computing!

Understanding Mid-Tier Architecture

Citrix developed the concept of a mid-tier architecture for application sharing. Mid-tier architecture combines the strengths of the mainframe computing architecture and the distributed computing architecture.

The mainframe was the first type of computer. As you can see in Figure 14.1, the mainframe model supports remote terminals. Traditionally called dumb terminals because they contained no independent processing capabilities, mainframe terminals today are actually considered "smart" because of their built-in screen display instruction sets. Terminals rely on the central mainframe for all processing requirements and are used only for input/output. The terminals are simply a screen and a keyboard. As the user enters information through keystrokes, that data is sent to the mainframe which processes the data and sends the graphics back to the terminal screen. The advantages to using terminals are the cost savings and the ease of maintaining them. This is a single-tier architecture, with all processing occurring at a single level on the network.

When personal computers (PCs) became popular, they were rapidly implemented in businesses. It didn't take long for someone to try connecting them together so that they could share data and printers. This evolved into the distributed computing architecture. Each node on the network was intelligent and handled its own tasks—passing data between nodes only after it has been processed. Applications began to be written to take advantage of the distributed processing power of PC networks. These networks were called client/server since some of the processing occurred on the client and the remainder occurred on the server. Distributed computing is a two-tier architecture (Figure 14.2).

Figure 14.1 Mainframe computing architecture.

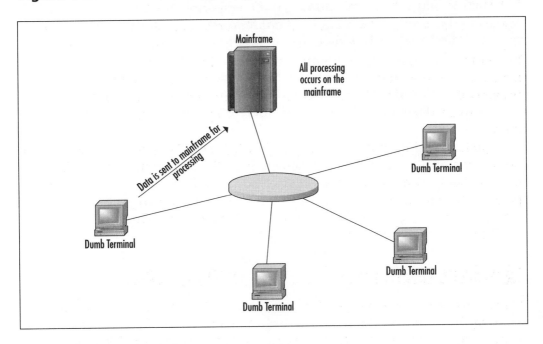

Figure 14.2 Distributed computing architecture.

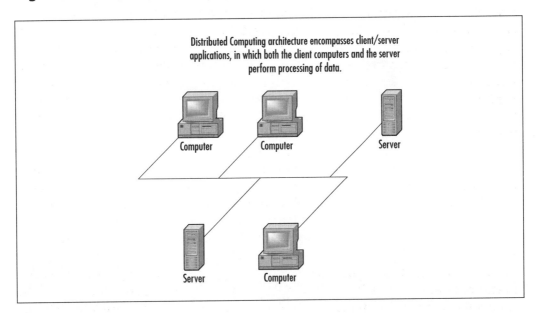

Citrix MetaFrame running on top of Windows 2000 Terminal Services exemplifies thin-client computing. Thin clients are those that have full access to data, yet consume a minimal amount of bandwidth, hence the term *thin*. In the distributed computing architecture, the clients are considered *fat* because they consume as much bandwidth as is necessary to process data—sometimes downloading or uploading large chunks of data in order to perform their functions. Thin-client computing is a mid-tier architecture because it involves three tiers of computing devices in which the MetaFrame server is in the middle (Figure 14.3).

Figure 14.3 Thin-client architecture—the mid-tier.

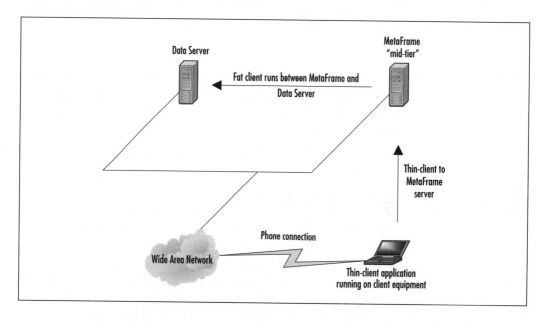

Remote Node and Remote Control

Citrix MetaFrame on Windows 2000 Terminal Services brings about another fusion of technology models, combining the features and strengths of each product. Utilizing MetaFrame on Windows 2000, you can combine remote node services, remote control services, as well as provide either service separately. The difference between remote node and remote control is this:

- Remote Node provides a network connection over a telephone line, Integrated Services Digital Network (ISDN) line, Digital Subscriber Line (DSL) link, or Virtual Private Network (VPN) connection, making the user's PC appear to be connected locally to that network. All services, such as file and print services, function the same way as they do when the user is directly connected.

- ■ Remote Control provides a graphical terminal emulation of a network node over a telephone line, ISDN line, DSL, VPN, or any other network connection. The user is faced with a secondary desktop and must use that secondary desktop in order to access file and print services.

With Citrix, the user can connect to Remote Access Services (RAS) and access the network as a node. On top of that, the user can run a remote control session from a Citrix MetaFrame server. In addition, a Windows 2000 server (with or without Citrix) can have the RAS service installed locally and manage that as a separate remote node service, although this is not recommended for large Citrix implementations. Citrix can also provide direct dial-up remote control sessions through the Citrix session management.

NOTE

To learn more about RAS, see Chapter 2, "Routing and Remote Access Services for Windows 2000."

Connecting Client Types

The essential difference between running a Windows 2000 Terminal Services server and using it in conjunction with Citrix MetaFrame is how the client application functions. Knowing how to connect the client types is the key to utilizing the functionality of both technologies. There are two supported protocols that drive the manner in which people can connect: The Remote Desktop Protocol (RDP) and Independent Computing Architecture (ICA).

Remote Desktop Protocol (RDP)

The Remote Desktop Protocol is the transport method for the keyboard strokes and mouse clicks to travel to Windows 2000 Terminal Services as well as for the resulting graphical user interface to travel back to the terminal where the session is being run. RDP was available in version 4.0 on Windows NT 4.0, Terminal Server Edition. On Windows 2000, RDP has been enhanced to version 5.0, which provides the same basic service at a higher performance level.

Supported Operating Systems

There are four clients that use the RDP 5.0 protocol:

- Client for Windows for Workgroups 3.11 using 32-bit TCP/IP
- Client for Windows CE
- Client for 32-bit Windows operating systems, including Windows 95, Windows 98, Windows NT, and Windows 2000
- Terminal Services Advanced Client (TSAC) for Internet

Supported Protocols

RDP runs only on TCP/IP, and does not support any other protocols. So while it can use native Internet protocol, it cannot execute across a network that does not have IP running across all links. For example, if you have a network segment that runs IPX and no IP whatsoever, and this network segment sits between the segment where Windows 2000 Terminal Services resides and the segment where the terminal emulation session has been initiated, then the session will not boot up because RDP cannot traverse the network on top of TCP/IP with that segment not running TCP/IP in between. This is illustrated in Figure 14.4.

Figure 14.4 RDP will work solely on TCP/IP segments.

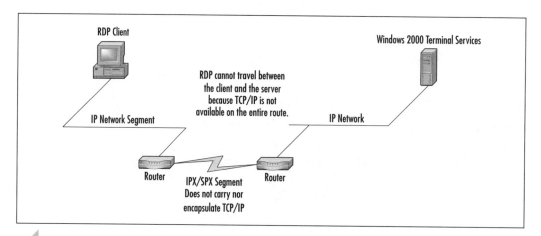

NOTE

For more information about the RDP client, see Chapter 5, "Deploying Terminal Services Clients."

The Independent Computing Architecture

The Independent Computing Architecture protocol is the transport vehicle for Citrix MetaFrame clients. This protocol optimizes the client access to applications by using compressed draw commands to update the graphical user interface (GUI), only updating those graphics that have changed rather than the entire GUI. Keyboard strokes and mouse clicks are also compressed.

Supported Operating Systems

ICA supports multiple operating systems. Table 14.1 lists all of the ICA clients available for Citrix MetaFrame. Some Internet browsers, including recent versions of Internet Explorer and Netscape, support ICA natively. All of the clients listed in the following table are available on the Internet at www.download.citrix.com.

Table 14.1 ICA Clients

Client Name	Operating Systems Supported
Win16	Windows 3.1 Windows 3.11 Windows for Workgroups 3.11
Win32	Windows 95 Windows 98 Windows NT 3.5*x* Windows NT 4.0 Windows 2000
Macintosh	Apple Macintosh
Windows CE	Windows CE palm devices—all releases
EPOC32	EPOC 32 Release 1.0
UNIX	CompaqTru64 Digital UNIX HP/UX IBM AIX Linux SCO SGI Solaris for X86 (Intel) machines Sun Solaris Sparc SunOS
DOS32	DOS clients supporting 32-bit networking

Continued

Table 14.1 Continued

Client Name	Operating Systems Supported
DOS16	16-bit DOS clients
Java	Internet browsers supporting Java
Application Launching & Embedding (ALE)	16-bit plug-ins for 16-bit Windows-based browsers 32-bit plug-ins for older Netscape and IE browsers ActiveX Java Applet

Supported Protocols

A concept unique to Citrix MetaFrame is the product's vision of "any client, any application, any network, anywhere." As you can tell by the extensive list of supported clients, Citrix MetaFrame is very close to supporting "any client." It is also capable of supporting most networks. The ICA client can be run across standard telephone lines, ISDN, DSL, and even legacy X.25 networks. ICA supports all manner of WAN links including leased lines of any speed from fractional T1 to the high end of optical capacity—OC48 and above. ICA clients can even function over broadband frame relay, Asynchronous Transport Mode (ATM) networks, and wireless connections.

What drives this functionality is that the ICA client runs on top of multiple types of protocols, including:

- TCP/IP
- IPX
- SPX
- NetBIOS
- Direct Asynchronous connections

The Direct Asynchronous connection is not the same as a RAS connection. Instead, the Direct Asynchronous connection is created with a complete ICA protocol stack, without the need for an underlying IP, IPX, SPX, or NetBIOS protocol. You can only get a Direct Asynchronous connection on Citrix MetaFrame, because it is not supported by stand-alone Windows 2000 Terminal Services.

NOTE

You can read more about Citrix ICA clients in Chapter 6, "Citrix MetaFrame Clients."

Licensing

The licensing requirements for a Windows 2000 server do not include licensing for Terminal Services. When you specify your licensing requirements, you should make certain you have enough Terminal Services Access licenses for the total number of concurrent users running RDP clients that you will have at peak usage times.

Likewise, when you license Citrix MetaFrame services, you need enough Citrix licenses for the total number of concurrent users running ICA clients at peak usage times. Citrix offers licensing in packs of five or ten licenses.

Application Load Balancing

One of the main reasons for using Windows 2000 Terminal Services with Citrix MetaFrame is to enable applications and network resources to be shared among all clients. With Windows 2000 Terminal Services alone, your only choice is to scale a server up in size to accommodate growth in the number of clients. Scaling up in size means that you would add more processors, more RAM, and more hard drive space. With Citrix MetaFrame, however, you can install application load balancing.

Citrix's application load balancing feature enables multiple servers to provide an application to a client based on the server that is the least busy. As a result, servers share a fairly equivalent number of concurrent sessions and users receive a higher average performance.

For example, Acme Co. has two Citrix MetaFrame servers each providing an application called APP1, and each server has 20 user licenses available, as shown in Figure 14.5. Given 21 users, *without* application load balancing, 19 users could be attached to SVR1 with two users attached to SVR2 because the user selected the server from which to run APP1. *With* application load balancing, the users connect to APP1 and the application load balancing system, through its algorithm, decides which server is the least busy and divvies up the sessions between both SVR1 and SVR2. That way, the sessions are more equitably distributed between them. With application load balancing, 11 users can be attached to SVR1 with ten attached to SVR2.

Figure 14.5 Acme Co.'s network.

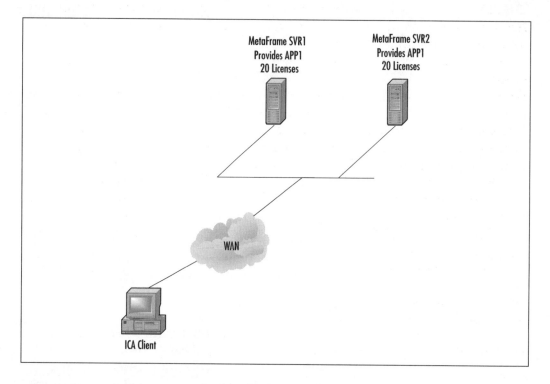

Designing and Deploying Terminal Services MetaFrame

Performance is the key to success for thin-client projects. Users will be the litmus test of whether the applications perform at a level that meets their needs for efficient productivity. If the application cannot perform well, or at all, then users will consider the entire project a failure. The only way to ensure viable performance is through a solid design along with a deployment plan that includes validation testing.

Design

Designing Windows 2000 Terminal Services and Citrix MetaFrame begins with sizing the servers. This is a matter of determining the number of users who will be utilizing sessions simultaneously, as well as what types of applications they will be using. Once you know that, you can test out how many users you can run per processor, how much RAM each user will need, and how much hard drive space is required.

With the various Windows 2000 Server versions capable of supporting up to 32 symmetrical multiprocessors on a single machine, you can scale up considerably. With Intel's Physical Address Extensions (PAE) running on a server, you can scale beyond 4GB of RAM. With hardware Redundant Array of Independent Disks (RAID), you can support extremely large amounts of disk space.

Application load balancing provides increased scaleability to your design. You can add more servers, rather than limit yourself to a single large server. When you create a design that uses multiple servers, you gain in performance, redundancy, and failover. However, when you choose to increase the performance capabilities of a server, you gain in lower cost of ownership because of reduced administrative overhead. These are important factors you should consider when designing your systems.

The placement of the servers on your network will determine your bandwidth utilization, which impacts your entire network's performance as well as the user's application experience. Whenever you place a server on the network, try to place it close to the data servers it pulls data from. The best performance will be on the same network segment. Since you have a thin client, there is less concern for the thin client using too much bandwidth than there is of the Citrix MetaFrame server using too much bandwidth between itself and the data servers. Proper server placement is demonstrated in Figure 14.6.

Figure 14.6 Design servers close to data.

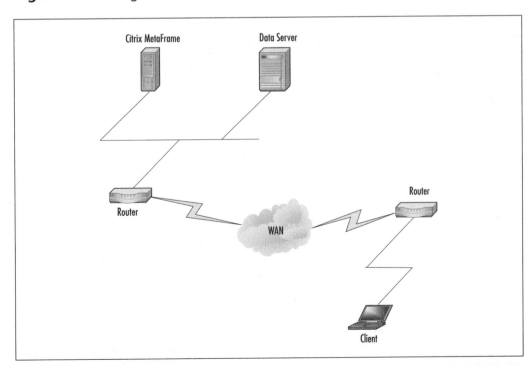

NOTE

Chapter 3, "Designing Terminal Services for Windows 2000" and Chapter 4, "Designing Citrix MetaFrame," discuss designing thin-client systems in detail.

Deploying MetaFrame

You can go about deploying a Citrix MetaFrame server in a lot of different ways. Some administrators install the server and configure it with little planning, and sometimes that works well for them. However, most people don't experience total success with the "throw-the-CD-in-and-hope-for-the-best" method. A solid deployment plan is usually a key to consistent success.

Your plan should have a planning phase, in which you:

1. Envision the results.
2. Document your business requirements.
3. Gather your resources.
4. Get budget approval.
5. Put your team together.

You then move to the next phase in the process, where you:

1. Size your server hardware.
2. Determine the need for application load balancing.
3. Decide whether to increase the servers' hardware capabilities or increase the number of servers as necessary.
4. Place the servers on the network.
5. Design your client access methods.
6. Determine remote access usage.

Then you have the opportunity to test all your theories in the next phase when you:

1. Build a lab.
2. Build one or more test servers.
3. Install your applications.

4. Configure users.

5. Build one or more client workstations.

6. Configure the client access method.

7. Troubleshoot all systems to make certain everything works the way you want it to.

8. Adjust the network as necessary.

Finally, you reach the deployment phase, in which you:

1. Select a group to be the pilot.

2. Roll out the pilot server or servers and clients.

3. Determine whether everything worked, and if it didn't, return to the lab.

4. If everything worked, you roll out the rest of the network.

NOTE

Chapter 5, "Deploying Terminal Service Clients," and Chapter 6, "Citrix MetaFrame Clients," discuss installation and deployment in detail.

Configuration

There are many different ways to configure Windows 2000 Terminal Services and Citrix MetaFrame. This flexibility allows the thin client to meet a variety of business requirements. Things that you should consider when you configure your servers are:

Shadowing (called remote control by Microsoft) Shadowing is a tool that allows help desks and technology support groups to assist users from remote locations. For example, if you configure shadowing, when a user has a problem the help desk administrator can take control of the user's session and *show* the user how to solve the problem.

Security and Profile Management Using remote client administration, administrators can create profiles to manage the session and its security settings.

Session Management The administrator can view the sessions running and monitor the activity and processes without actually watching the user's GUI. This is different from shadowing.

Group Policies With the Active Directory, an administrator can manage the way that thin-client servers act. This can range from security to GUI configuration. Some of the options are shown in Figure 14.7.

Figure 14.7 Group Policy configuration options.

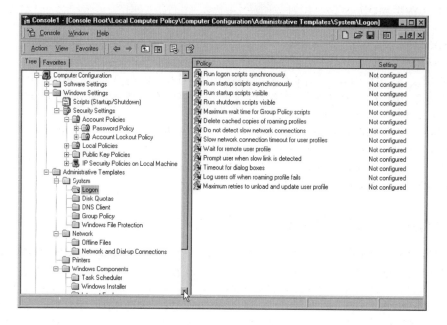

TIP

Much more about configuration appears in Chapters 8, "Installing Citrix MetaFrame," Chapter 9, "Configuring the User Experience," and Chapter 10, "Terminal Session Configuration."

Utilizing the Internet

Businesses are increasingly using the Internet to provide services to their employees, vendors, and clients. Some businesses develop entirely new applications, or new interfaces to applications, that run in an Internet Web browser. Other businesses prefer to use an existing application and deploy it over the Internet.

The solution to this second problem is found in Windows 2000 Terminal Services and in Citrix MetaFrame. Both Windows 2000 Terminal Services and Citrix MetaFrame can provide applications through an Internet browser. Microsoft released their Terminal Services Advanced Client in the summer of 2000. Citrix MetaFrame has a method of publishing applications on the Internet through .ICA files and through the NFuse product, which is available for free at www.download.citrix.com.

Naturally, security is a major issue when you allow an application to be shared with the public over public lines. If only certain people should have access to an application, the placement of the Citrix MetaFrame server should be on a demilitarized zone (DMZ) and access should be granted only to those users. In addition, you can remove file and print shares from the server so that it is only providing an application. If applicable, you can limit the user's access to just the application you are providing. For security or other reasons, you can disable the ability to copy from the GUI, print from the application, and map drives.

Managing Your Systems

It is not unusual for a company to initially buy a single Windows 2000 Terminal Services server or a Citrix MetaFrame server and then expand to two or more servers. Citrix MetaFrame, with the multiple client and multiple protocol support, can help bring applications to users regardless of the type of workstation they are using. Once administrators and managers realize how they can apply a MetaFrame box to their current problems, they tend to buy more servers to support more users.

Regardless of the number of servers, they must still be managed. Fundamental management of any server includes:

- Change control management
- Monitoring
- Troubleshooting

Change control will avoid some problems by minimizing the number of changes that are made in the environment. Change control management should include a written policy regarding who is authorized to make changes to the environment. After that, you should make certain to use the security mechanisms within Windows 2000, such as delegation of authority in the Active Directory, to ensure that authority is granted properly.

Other preventative measures include creating a standard image for the MetaFrame servers to avoid the confusion that can arise from non-standard configurations. Applications should always be tested in a testing environment before placement in the production environment. Finally, you should have an emergency tape backup system and disaster recovery plan.

Windows 2000 includes Performance Monitor (referred to as "PerfMon") to help monitor services and processes running on the server. In addition to monitoring the server's performance, an administrator will want to monitor the sessions that are running using the Terminal Services and MetaFrame utilities.

The Value of a Thin-Client System

Before you decide to install a thin-client system, you will probably want to determine what value the system will bring to your network. One of the things that Citrix MetaFrame can do is extend the life of hardware. This is valuable benefit since the costs of upgrading many individual PCs can be avoided by simply installing one or more servers.

For example, Acme Co. has 100 Macintoshes on the network. The company has decided to use a 32-bit Windows application for accounting and requires that every employee must have that application on his or her desktop. Acme Co. has determined that the costs for replacing the Macintosh computers with 32-bit Windows systems will be $3000 per unit, with the unit cost breakdown shown in Table 14.2. The total cost of replacing the systems will be $300,000.

Table 14.2 Unit Cost for Each Acme Replacement Computer

Item	Cost
Pentium III PC with 128MB RAM	$2000
Operating system license	$200
Network access license	$35
Replacement application licenses	$765
Total	$3000

However, Acme examines the cost of implementing a Citrix MetaFrame solution to deliver the new accounting application to the Apple Macintosh equipment still existing on the network. The cost of the hardware for the servers and the operating system licenses for Windows 2000 and Citrix MetaFrame totals only $60,000.

The value of using Citrix avoids nearly a quarter of a million dollars in hardware and licensing costs, but that is not the only value to consider.

When Acme Co. implements Citrix, they avoid the need to train 100 people on a new operating system. The only new item is the accounting application that every employee must be trained on anyway.

After implementing Citrix, Acme Co. realizes a reduction in the need for deskside support calls for the 100 Macintosh users of the accounting application. Had Acme Co. used the accounting application directly installed on users' PCs, they would have required deskside support for 100 percent of their help desk calls. Compare this to Citrix MetaFrame where it's likely that 80 percent of the help desk calls could be solved before deskside support is required. The support costs for a typical PC user are $100 for the new application. By contrast, the Macintosh user's support costs are $20. This results in a cost savings of $8000.

The Future of Windows and MetaFrame

What does the future hold for thin-client systems? The latest industry buzz has been over Application Service Providers (ASPs). ASPs provide applications, typically for a subscription license, and host all the supporting infrastructure on their own network. Some businesses may look to this as an alternative to reduce their support and maintenance costs. Both Microsoft and Citrix have plans to develop products and services to provide for this growing market.

Microsoft Windows 2000

"Whistler" is the code name of the successor to Windows 2000, due out by the end of 2001, and "BlackComb" is the code name to the successor to Whistler, due out by the end of 2003. The Windows 2000 product set was originally built for the business consumer. Microsoft is building the future version of these operating systems with some of the features that home consumers are most interested in. Even so, both Whistler and BlackComb will include Active Directory improvements as well. Eventually, the Active Directory will likely be capable of providing metadirectory services, connecting multiple directory services—such as Novell Directory Services (NDS) or the user access lists in applications—into a central system.

Citrix MetaFrame

Citrix consistently adds features and functions to its products. As Microsoft has upgraded its operating system, Citrix has followed suit with an upgraded product to complement Microsoft's feature enhancements. Citrix's products add functionality that is specific to certain types of application usage.

- VideoFrame provides on-demand streaming audio and video applications published on a central server, using ICA.

- Citrix Extranet 2.0 is a VPN software product, which focuses on providing applications securely over the Internet.

- Citrix Load Balancing Services, Installation Management Services, and Resource Management Services are products that reduce administrative overhead and enhance application performance.

- SecureICA encrypts transmissions over the ICA protocol.

- Citrix UNIX Integration services can connect Citrix MetaFrame services to X11 desktops.

- NFuse enables a different method of publishing interactive applications to a Web browser. NFuse is an application that can assist ASPs in deploying applications to subscribers.

Since Citrix and Microsoft are always planning and developing new products and enhancements to their existing products, the future looks bright indeed.

FAQs

Q: We use a Remote Access Server that is *not* Windows 2000. Clients are able to map drives to Windows 2000 and print files over PPP connections with TCP/IP. Can we use this RAS server with Citrix MetaFrame?

A: Yes. As long as you can run one of the protocols—TCP/IP, IPX, SPX, or NetBIOS—then you should be able to run the ICA client to a Citrix MetaFrame server.

Q: When we design our Active Directory, we also want to place our Terminal Servers into the network. Should we add Terminal Services to our domain controllers?

A: No...and possibly yes. If you want to add Terminal Services in order to share out applications, you should only install it on member servers to ensure that there is little overhead and the application performs well. However, Windows 2000 offers you an Administrative Mode with two free licenses that you can install on a domain controller and then manage it remotely—and for those benefits, you definitely would want to install Administrative Mode on a domain controller.

Secrets

Solutions in this Appendix:

- **Investigating Appsrv.INI Parameters**
- **Improving Terminal Services Performance**

Appsrv.INI Parameters

The appsrv.INI file contains the user settings which define application servers and other preferences. Build 4.20.715 and later of the client contain information regarding only Custom ICA connections. For any earlier versions (any platform), this file contains information for all entries in the Remote Application Manager.

There are three main sections, WFClient, Application Servers, and Connection. They will be found inside square brackets within the file, as follows: [WFClient], [Application Servers], [Connection]. WFClient contains general settings that apply to all ICA connections configured from the client. Application Servers contains the enumeration of entries for connection to servers or published applications. For Connection, every entry that is configured will have a section dedicated to it that specifies all of its own specific parameters. In other words, a published application of Wordpad will have its own section [Wordpad].

NOTE

On Windows 2000 client machines, many settings in the appsrv.INI have been moved to a different file. Connections and setting preferences are now stored on a per-user basis similar to the way Internet Explorer remembers each user's settings. When a user makes new connections, a copy of the appsrv.INI, wfclient.INI, and pn.INI are copied to a Citrix subdirectory under his or her personal home directory (by default C:\Documents and Settings\username.domainname\Application Data\ICAClient). The settings in these files would take precedence over the generic client settings.

Here is a sample appsrv.INI file. Note that the numbers in front of each line are added for reference purposes only.

1. [WFClient]
2. Version=2
3. LogFile=C:\Program Files\Citrix\ICA Client\wfclient.log
4. LogFileWin16=wfcwin.log
5. LogFileWin32=C:\Program Files\Citrix\ICA Client\wfcwin32.log
6. LogAppend=Off
7. LogConnect=On

8. LogErrors=On

9. LogTransmit=Off

10. LogReceive=Off

11. LogKeyboard=Off

12. Hotkey1Char=F1

13. Hotkey1Shift=Shift

14. Hotkey2Char=F3

15. Hotkey2Shift=Shift

16. Hotkey3Char=F2

17. Hotkey3Shift=Shift

18. Hotkey4Char=F1

19. Hotkey4Shift=Ctrl

20. Hotkey5Char=F2

21. Hotkey5Shift=Ctrl

22. Hotkey6Char=F2

23. Hotkey6Shift=Alt

24. Hotkey7Char=plus

25. Hotkey7Shift=Alt

26. Hotkey8Char=minus

27. Hotkey8Shift=Alt

28. Hotkey9Char=F3

29. HotKey9Shift=Ctrl

30. DisableSound=Off

31. DisableCtrlAltDel=On

32. MouseTimer=0

33. KeyboardTimer=0

34. ColorMismatchPrompt_Have16_Want256=On

35. ColorMismatchPrompt_Have64K_Want256=On

36. ColorMismatchPrompt_Have16M_Want256=On

37. DosConnectTTY=On

38. ConnectTTY=Off

39. ConnectTTYDelay=1000

40. TcpBrowserAddress=

41. IpxBrowserAddress=

42. NetBiosBrowserAddress=

43. BrowserRetry=3

44. BrowserTimeout=1000

45. LanaNumber=0

46. ScriptDriver=SCRIPT.DDL

47. ScriptDriverWin16=SCRIPTW.DLL

48. ScriptDriverWin32=SCRIPTN.DLL

49. ScriptFile=

50. PersistentCacheEnabled=Off

51. PersistentCacheSizc=64424508

52. PersistentCacheMinBitmap=8192

53. PersistentCachePath=C:\Program Files\Citrix\ICA Client\Cache

54. UpdatesAllowed=On

55. COMAllowed=On

56. CPMAllowed=On

57. VSLAllowed=On

58. CDMAllowed=On

59. MaximumCompression=Off

60.

61. [Smartcard]

62. ;==

63. ;== When SmartcardRequired=yes, connecting to a remote

64. ;   application will require a smartcard provided that no other

65. ;   remote applications are currently executing.N.B. When enabled

66. ;   with the 32-bit DOS client this also prevents the use of insecure

67. ;   command line options including /iniappsrv.

68. ;== Omitted entry defaults to 'Off'.

69. ;==

70. SmartcardRequired=no

71. ;==

72. ;== Setting a bypass switch to yes tells the system to get its User

73. ;   information from the commandline or appsrv.ini file instead of the

74. ;   smartcard.

75. ;== Omitted entries default to 'No'.

76. ;==

77. BypassSmartcardDomain=no

78. BypassSmartcardUsername=no

79. BypassSmartcardPassword=no

80. ;==

81. ;== Supported Smartcards

82. ;== MPCOS   - cards by Gemplus

83. ;== TB-1000   - cards by Microcard

84. ;———

85. ;== Supported values for CardReader key

86. ;== GCR410   - Gemplus GCR410 Smartcard reader

87. ;==

88. CardReader=GCR410

89. ReaderPort=COM2

90. Timeout=1000   ; given in milliseconds

91. [Common Default Information]

92. ProgramGroup=Citrix ICA Client

Line 1 shows the beginning of the [WFClient] section.

Line 2 shows the version number

Lines 3–5 specifies the log file locations.

Line 3 specifies the log file location used by the 16 bit DOS client.

Line 4 specifies the log file location used by the Win16-bit client.

Line 5 specifies the log file location used by the Win32-bit client. You can change the log file location and name to suit your individual preference, or leave the defaults. Log data could instead be sent to standard out or standard error by specifying **stdout** or **stderr** instead of a file name.

Lines 6–11 specify the logging options. The command and default option is highlighted.

Line 6, **LogAppend=Off** The event log can either be overwritten by new events, or new events can be appended to an existing log file to maintain a history. Specify On to append and save history; Specify Off to overwrite old events and create a new log.

Line 7, **LogConnect=On** Logs an event when the ICA Client connects or disconnects from a Citrix server. If it's changed to On, it will log an event whenever the Client connects or disconnects; if turned Off, it will not log connection events.

Line 8, **LogErrors=On** Logs ICA Client errors. If On, it logs an event whenever an error is encountered by the Citrix Client. If off, errors will be ignored.

Line 9, **LogTransmit=Off** Intended primarily for technical support. When it is switched On, this logs an event for each packet of information sent from the Citrix Client to the Citrix Server.

Line 10, **LogReceive=Off** Intended primarily for technical support. When switched On, it logs an event for each packet of information received by the Citrix Client from the Citrix Server.

Line 11, **LogKeyboard=Off** Intended primarily for technical support. When it is switched On, it logs an event whenever you press a key on the keyboard or move the mouse.

Lines 12–29 control the "HotKeys" settings. Be careful when changing these entries manually, as the placement in reference to the GUI HotKeys settings is not intuitive. There are two settings for each Hotkey, a "char" value, and a "shift" value. If compared to the columns in the HotKeys GUI, observe that the *char* settings for Hotkey 1 Char=F1 is in the *Right* column of the GUI and the *shift* settings for Hotkey 1 Shift=Shift is in the *Left* column of the GUI.

Lines 12–13 correspond to the **Task List** hotkey. This displays the Windows Task List for the local Windows desktop on the client machine. You can also use CTRL-ESC to display the task list if you are not using SHIFT-F1 as an ICA Client hotkey.

Lines 14–15 correspond to the **Close Remote Application** hotkey. This disconnects from the Citrix Server and exits the ICA Client. Depending on how the application is configured, this either leaves the application running in a disconnected state or exits the application.

Lines 16–17 correspond to the **Toggle Title Bar** hotkey. This causes the ICA Client to either display or hide its Windows title bar.

Lines 18–19 correspond to the **CTRL-ALT-DEL** hotkey. This sends a CTRL-ALT-DEL to the server and displays the Windows Security Login dialog box.

Lines 20–21 correspond to the **CTRL-ESC** hotkey. This sends a standard CTRL-ESC to the server. When sent to a Winframe server, the remote task list appears. When sent to a MetaFrame server, the remote start menu appears.

Lines 22–23 correspond to the **ALT-ESC** hotkey. This is used to cycle the focus through the minimized and maximized windows of programs that are running in the ICA session.

Lines 24–25 correspond to the **ALT-TAB** hotkey. This opens a pop-up window that displays the programs running in the ICA session and lets you cycle through them. The selected program then receives the keyboard and mouse focus.

Lines 26–27 correspond to the **ALT-BACKTAB** hotkey. This does the same as the ALT-TAB, but cycles through the programs in the opposite direction.

Lines 28–29 correspond to the **CTRL-SHIFT-ESC** hotkey. This is not used on Winframe servers. On MetaFrame servers, it displays the Windows NT Task Manager.

Line 30, **DisableSound=Off** This enables sound on any client computer having a Sound Blaster 16-compatible sound card installed. Published applications and desktops may play sounds on the client machine when set to Off. To remove sound capabilities, set this to On. The sound settings may be further customized for High, Medium, and Low quality settings using the GUI.

Line 31, **DisableCtrlAltDel=On** This disables use of CTRL-ALT-DEL within the ICA session to prevent users from shutting down the server.

Line 32–33, **MouseTimer=0** and **KeyboardTimer=0** This value specifies in milliseconds how often to send mouse and keyboard updates to the server. Leaving this at 0 (unchecked in the GUI) makes the session more responsive to keyboard and mouse movements. Checking this in the GUI changes the MouseTimer=100 and the KeyboardTimer=50; this improves performance if you dial into RAS and then use a network to connect by reducing the number of packets sent from the client to the server.

Lines 34–36, **ColorMismatchPrompt...** were required with the older Remote Application Manager clients. The Program Neighborhood User Interface ignores these settings. This was to provide greater compatibility in the earlier, more problematic days of Windows video driver development. Most of today's video drivers do not have problems with the 256 or greater color displays and are able to match colors closely without using this feature.

Lines 37–39, **DosConnectTTY=On**, **ConnectTTY=Off**, **ConnectTTYDelay=1000** These settings allow you to use TTY emulation to get through a dial-up network device, such as some security devices and X.25 PADS that require ASCII authentication before forwarding the connection to the Citrix server.

Lines 40–42, **TcpBrowserAddress=**, **IpxBrowserAddress=**, **NetBios BrowserAddress=** These settings let you specify the browser address for their respective protocols to search for published applications.

Line 43, **BrowserRetry=3** This setting lets you choose the number of times a client will resubmit a master browser request that has timed out.

Line 44, **BrowserTimeout=1000** This is the number of milliseconds a client waits for a response after making a request to the master browser. Users with high latency connections may need to increase this setting to successfully browse the list of published applications before timing out.

Line 45, **LanaNumber=0** This is the Lana of the network card protocol. This is used to tell NetBIOS which protocol to bind to. You can have NetBIOS over NetBEUI, IPX, or TCP. Changing this number toggles from one to another. The default setting is 0 for NetBEUI.

Lines 46–49, **ScriptDriver=* ScriptFile=** This is what the ICA client uses to process scripts. It's normally used for dial-up connections forwarded through PBXs, and so on. You can specify the path and filename to a script file that will process commands needed for special authentication requirements.

Line 50, **PersistentCacheEnabled=Off** Turn this to On (or check the box in the GUI) to store bitmaps and other commonly used graphics files in a cache on the client's local hard drive. Turning this on can improve performance on low-bandwidth connections. Leaving it off can save drive space on LAN or high-speed connections.

Line 51, **PersistentCacheSize=64424508** This selects the amount of disk space (in bytes) to use for the bitmap caching.

Line 52, **PersistentCacheMinBitmap=8192** This selects the smallest size bitmap (in bytes) that will be saved in the local client disk cache.

Line 53, **PersistentCachePath=C:\Program Files\Citrix\ICA Client\ Cache** This specifies the location of the local client bitmap cache. If the directory does not exist, it will be created.

Line 54, **UpdatesAllowed=On** This allows the client to accept automatic software updates pushed from the server. When set to Off, it prevents automatic updates from occurring.

Line 55, **COMAllowed=On** This allows the client to perform COM port mapping.

Line 56, **CPMAllowed=On** This allows the client to map local printers.

Line 57, **VSLAllowed=On** This automatically loads the appropriate VSL component prior to loading the main client code. The VSL component provides support for the Microsoft and Novell TCP stacks.

Line 58, **CDMAllowed=On** This allows the client to map local drives.

Line 59, **MaximumCompression=Off** This setting is set to On if the box for "Use data compression" is checked in the GUI. If you have a low-bandwidth connection, enabling data compression could improve performance by reducing the amount of data to be transferred. If you are connecting over a LAN or high-bandwidth connection, turning this on could actually reduce performance due to the extra processor and memory resources required to compress and uncompress the data.

Lines 60–92 show SmartCard reader data. Most of this should be automatically configured as you install the smartcard support. If you need further assistance, contact Citrix Technical Support.

Improving Terminal Services Performance

As mentioned in Chapter 13, here are some additional ways to improve your Terminal Services performance.

Enable AutoEnd Tasks: Q191805 This parameter tells any task that will not respond to the shutdown notice to end. This will help in timely logoffs where a program seems to hang and the user's session does not end as quickly as it should.

```
"HKEY_USER\.DEFAULT\Control Panel\Desktop"
Add Value: AutoEndTasks REG_SZ: 1


And: WaitToKillAppTimeout REG_SZ: 20000
```

The default of 20,000 milliseconds (20 seconds) can be increased. If the user process does not end by this time, AutoEndsTasks is executed.

Disable Background Grammer Checking in Microsoft Word Background grammar checking has a significant negative impact on scalability, and can reduce the number of users supported by 50 percent. To disable it for everyone:

1. Open a command prompt and type **change user/install**.
2. Minimize the command window and open Microsoft Word.
3. Go to Tools | Options | Spelling & Grammar.
4. Clear the check box for "Check grammer as you type."
5. Close the dialog box and close Word.
6. Go back to the command window and type **change user/execute**.

All *new* users will now receive this setting; existing users will have to be changed manually.

Index

E

EAP. *See* Extensible Authentication Protocol

E-business structure, 507

Electronic mail (E-mail) messages, 8

E-mail. *See* Electronic mail

Embedded method, 409

Encapsulation. *See* Generic routing encapsulation

Encryption, 122, 243, 244, 264, 374–375. *See also* 128-bit encryption; Data; High-level encryption; Low-level encryption; Remote Desktop Protocol; Rivest Shamir Adleman; SecureICA; Terminal Services; XOR encryption
  algorithm. *See* RC4 encryption algorithm
  key. *See* 40-bit encryption; 56-bit encryption
  level, 472
  levels, 40, 352
  setting, 27

Encryption/decryption process, 99

Encryptoin settings, 439

End user license agreement (EULA), 133

End users, 285–286, 315

End-to-end secure communications, 100

End-to-end security, 99

End-user knowledge, 436

ENIAC. *See* Electronic Numeral Integrator and Calculator

Enterprise license server, 181

Enterprise Resource Planning (ERP), 430

Entry-level servers, 64

Environment. *See* Citrix; Lab environment

EPOC, 209

ERP. *See* Enterprise Resource Planning

Error correcting memory, 109

Ethernet, 5. *See also* 10-Megabit Ethernet; 100-Megabit Ethernet; Gigabit Ethernet
  LAN, 172

EULA. *See* End user license agreement

Event Logging, 92

Excel, 278

Execute mode, 388

Expert shadowing rules, 338–339

Extensible Authentication Protocol (EAP), 79

External IP addresses, 454

External network connection, 76

F

Failover capabilities, 159

Fast Ethernet LAN. *See* 100Mb Fast Ethernet LAN

FAT. *See* File Allocation Table

Fat clients, 18, 46

Fat-client solution, 57

Fault tolerance, 65, 149, 151

Fault tolerant environment, 394

Fault-tolerant solutions, 9

FC-AL. *See* Fibre Channel Arbitrated Loop

FCC. *See* Federal Communications Commission

Feature Release 1 (FR1), 308–309, 352, 480

Federal Communications Commission (FCC) regulations, 70

Feedback. *See* Users

Fibre channel, 65–66, 151. *See also* Connection-oriented fibre channel

Fibre Channel Arbitrated Loop (FC-AL), 151

File Allocation Table (FAT), 149
  FAT32, 149
  partitions, 272

Files
  downloading. *See* Users
  e-mailing, 466
  locations, 385
  locking, 385
  permission, 385
  redundancy, 67
  server, 161. *See also* Central file server
  system, 149–150

Firewalls, 116
  administrators, 52
  setup considerations, 454–455
  usage. *See* Address translation

Fixed Internet Protocol, 88

Flex, 69

Floppy disks, creation. *See* DOS ICA client; Windows 32-bit client

The Global Knowledge Advantage

Global Knowledge has a global delivery system for its products and services. The company has 28 subsidiaries, and offers its programs through a total of 60+ locations. No other vendor can provide consistent services across a geographic area this large. Global Knowledge is the largest independent information technology education provider, offering programs on a variety of platforms. This enables our multi-platform and multi-national customers to obtain all of their programs from a single vendor. The company has developed the unique CompetusTM Framework software tool and methodology which can quickly reconfigure courseware to the proficiency level of a student on an interactive basis. Combined with self-paced and on-line programs, this technology can reduce the time required for training by prescribing content in only the deficient skills areas. The company has fully automated every aspect of the education process, from registration and follow-up, to "just-in-time" production of courseware. Global Knowledge through its Enterprise Services Consultancy, can customize programs and products to suit the needs of an individual customer.

Global Knowledge Classroom Education Programs

The backbone of our delivery options is classroom-based education. Our modern, well-equipped facilities staffed with the finest instructors offer programs in a wide variety of information technology topics, many of which lead to professional certifications.

Custom Learning Solutions

This delivery option has been created for companies and governments that value customized learning solutions. For them, our consultancy-based approach of developing targeted education solutions is most effective at helping them meet specific objectives.

Self-Paced and Multimedia Products

This delivery option offers self-paced program titles in interactive CD-ROM, videotape and audio tape programs. In addition, we offer custom development of interactive multimedia courseware to customers and partners. Call us at 1-888-427-4228.

Electronic Delivery of Training

Our network-based training service delivers efficient competency-based, interactive training via the World Wide Web and organizational intranets. This leading-edge delivery option provides a custom learning path and "just-in-time" training for maximum convenience to students.

Global Knowledge Courses Available

Microsoft
- Windows 2000 Deployment Strategies
- Introduction to Directory Services
- Windows 2000 Client Administration
- Windows 2000 Server
- Windows 2000 Update
- MCSE Bootcamp
- Microsoft Networking Essentials
- Windows NT 4.0 Workstation
- Windows NT 4.0 Server
- Windows NT Troubleshooting
- Windows NT 4.0 Security
- Windows 2000 Security
- Introduction to Microsoft Web Tools

Management Skills
- Project Management for IT Professionals
- Microsoft Project Workshop
- Management Skills for IT Professionals

Network Fundamentals
- Understanding Computer Networks
- Telecommunications Fundamentals I
- Telecommunications Fundamentals II
- Understanding Networking Fundamentals
- Upgrading and Repairing PCs
- DOS/Windows A+ Preparation
- Network Cabling Systems

WAN Networking and Telephony
- Building Broadband Networks
- Frame Relay Internetworking
- Converging Voice and Data Networks
- Introduction to Voice Over IP
- Understanding Digital Subscriber Line (xDSL)

Internetworking
- ATM Essentials
- ATM Internetworking
- ATM Troubleshooting
- Understanding Networking Protocols
- Internetworking Routers and Switches
- Network Troubleshooting
- Internetworking with TCP/IP
- Troubleshooting TCP/IP Networks
- Network Management
- Network Security Administration
- Virtual Private Networks
- Storage Area Networks
- Cisco OSPF Design and Configuration
- Cisco Border Gateway Protocol (BGP) Configuration

Web Site Management and Development
- Advanced Web Site Design
- Introduction to XML
- Building a Web Site
- Introduction to JavaScript
- Web Development Fundamentals
- Introduction to Web Databases

PERL, UNIX, and Linux
- PERL Scripting
- PERL with CGI for the Web
- UNIX Level I
- UNIX Level II
- Introduction to Linux for New Users
- Linux Installation, Configuration, and Maintenance

Authorized Vendor Training
Red Hat
- Introduction to Red Hat Linux
- Red Hat Linux Systems Administration
- Red Hat Linux Network and Security Administration
- RHCE Rapid Track Certification

Cisco Systems
- Interconnecting Cisco Network Devices
- Advanced Cisco Router Configuration
- Installation and Maintenance of Cisco Routers
- Cisco Internetwork Troubleshooting
- Designing Cisco Networks
- Cisco Internetwork Design
- Configuring Cisco Catalyst Switches
- Cisco Campus ATM Solutions
- Cisco Voice Over Frame Relay, ATM, and IP
- Configuring for Selsius IP Phones
- Building Cisco Remote Access Networks
- Managing Cisco Network Security
- Cisco Enterprise Management Solutions

Nortel Networks
- Nortel Networks Accelerated Router Configuration
- Nortel Networks Advanced IP Routing
- Nortel Networks WAN Protocols
- Nortel Networks Frame Switching
- Nortel Networks Accelar 1000
- Comprehensive Configuration
- Nortel Networks Centillion Switching
- Network Management with Optivity for Windows

Oracle Training
- Introduction to Oracle8 and PL/SQL
- Oracle8 Database Administration

Custom Corporate Network Training

Train on Cutting Edge Technology

We can bring the best in skill-based training to your facility to create a real-world hands-on training experience. Global Knowledge has invested millions of dollars in network hardware and software to train our students on the same equipment they will work with on the job. Our relationships with vendors allow us to incorporate the latest equipment and platforms into your on-site labs.

Maximize Your Training Budget

Global Knowledge provides experienced instructors, comprehensive course materials, and all the networking equipment needed to deliver high quality training. You provide the students; we provide the knowledge.

Avoid Travel Expenses

On-site courses allow you to schedule technical training at your convenience, saving time, expense, and the opportunity cost of travel away from the workplace.

Discuss Confidential Topics

Private on-site training permits the open discussion of sensitive issues such as security, access, and network design. We can work with your existing network's proprietary files while demonstrating the latest technologies.

Customize Course Content

Global Knowledge can tailor your courses to include the technologies and the topics which have the greatest impact on your business. We can complement your internal training efforts or provide a total solution to your training needs.

Corporate Pass

The Corporate Pass Discount Program rewards our best network training customers with preferred pricing on public courses, discounts on multimedia training packages, and an array of career planning services.

Global Knowledge Training Lifecycle

Supporting the Dynamic and Specialized Training Requirements of Information Technology Professionals

- Define Profile
- Assess Skills
- Design Training
- Deliver Training
- Test Knowledge
- Update Profile
- Use New Skills

Global Knowledge

Global Knowledge programs are developed and presented by industry professionals with "real-world" experience. Designed to help professionals meet today's interconnectivity and interoperability challenges, most of our programs feature hands-on labs that incorporate state-of-the-art communication components and equipment.

ON-SITE TEAM TRAINING

Bring Global Knowledge's powerful training programs to your company. At Global Knowledge, we will custom design courses to meet your specific network requirements. Call (919)-461-8686 for more information.

YOUR GUARANTEE

Global Knowledge believes its courses offer the best possible training in this field. If during the first day you are not satisfied and wish to withdraw from the course, simply notify the instructor, return all course materials and receive a 100% refund.

REGISTRATION INFORMATION

In the US:
call: (888) 762–4442
fax: (919) 469–7070
visit our website:
www.globalknowledge.com

SYNGRESS SOLUTIONS...